THE
PASSION OF PEACE

THE PASSION OF PEACE

Ciaran McKeown

Ciaran McKeown

for Brendan & Lucy
— so lovely to meet you
both.
Ciara

**THE
BLACKSTAFF
PRESS**

The author is grateful for permission to quote from the
following works:
'Non-Violence in an Aggressive World' by A. J. Muste in
Peace Movements in America, ed. Charles Chatfield. Excerpt
reprinted by permission of Schocken Books, New York.
'Neither an elegy nor a manifesto' in The Selected John
Hewitt. Reprinted by permission of John Hewitt and The
Blackstaff Press.
War and Peace by Leo Tolstoy, trans. Rosemary Edmonds.
Excerpt reprinted by permission of Penguin Books Ltd.
Excerpt from 'Whatever you say, say nothing' from (in world
excluding USA) North by Seamus Heaney, reprinted by
permission of Faber and Faber Publishers; (in USA) Poems
1965-1975 by Seamus Heaney, © 1975, 1980 by Seamus
Heaney, reprinted by permission of Farrar, Straus and
Giroux, Inc.

The author also wishes to express his gratitude for the
comprehensive work done on the index by Oula Jones (née
McCaughan).

First published in 1984 by
The Blackstaff Press
3 Galway Park, Dundonald, Belfast BT16 0AN

Printed in Northern Ireland by
The Universities Press Limited

British Library Cataloguing in Publication Data
McKeown, Ciaran
The Passion of Peace
1. Peace People
I. Title
327.1'72'09416   DA990.U4

0 85640 325 3

When the typical reformer or revolutionist proclaims the new order, he goes on to urge men to organise, agitate, get out the vote, fight . . . A world of peace will not be achieved by men who in their own souls are torn with strife and eagerness to assert themselves. In the degree that the anti-war or pacifist movement is composed of individuals who have not themselves, to use Aldous Huxley's phrase, achieved detachment, who have not undergone an inner revolution, it too will experience the same failure to achieve self-discipline, integrity, true fellowship among its own members which has afflicted other movements for social change.

Abraham J. Muste

The careful words of my injunction
are unrhetorical, as neutral
and unaligned as any I know:
they propose no more than thoughtful response;
they do not pound with drum-beats
of patriotism, loyalty, martyrdom.

John Hewitt

Preface

It will be obvious from this book that I have lived a somewhat tumultuous life and one that has involved many people, both supportive and adversitive. Not only would it be impossible to name all who should be mentioned if this were primarily a work of record, but quite a few would be grateful to remain anonymous; and I have thought it prudent not to identify others.

A similar difficulty afflicts me in expressing public appreciation of those who have been intimately involved with me through the period so subjectively described, including the recent—at times traumatic—experience of writing the book itself. In the latter regard, I am especially grateful to my friend John Boyd, the distinguished Irish dramatist, for his patient war of attrition on my literary carelessness; and to Colm and Angeline Kelly for their comments and encouragement.

I might have been broken by some of the experiences recounted herein, had it not been for the exceptional friendship with which I have been blessed. And here I would single out Gerry O'Reilly: when I was a chronically unemployable, controversial public figure in the small cauldron of Northern Ireland, Gerry allowed me little time to wallow in the self-pity of failure, or to deceive myself over who was responsible for my predicament, and taught me his own craft of typesetting with the latest high technology. But he taught me more than the means of an independent living with my hands: under his mastership, this apprentice finally learned how to work, after half a lifetime of living on ideas. Something of the virtues of patience, humility and reliability of the craftsman have penetrated the arrogance of the intellect, and may even have provided an authentic perspective for the dreamer.

Since I have chosen an autobiographical approach to a quarter of a century in Northern Ireland, I have no difficulty in deciding to whom this book is dedicated. The family in which I grew up, and its present extensions, and the family which I have fathered, are all part of the experience which has produced this account. Like many a parent, I see more clearly with the passing years, the ceaseless care with which my own parents nurtured their six children; I have felt the influence of a deeply spiritual mother and the strength of a dedicated father steadying me during some very unstable times, long after I left home. Should I ever fulfil something of what I have promised, it may be accounted for by that intimate attention in childhood from exceptional parents.

And through the most difficult years of all, my wife, Marianne— who has also at times had to father and mother me—has continued that love with which my life has been so gratuitously blessed. With such love, the passion for peace must become irresistible.

Ciaran McKeown, 1984

From
Innocence to Violence

In January 1982 a young girl looked with wistful eyes at me, and said, "You're very lucky, I was only born in 1964." We had been talking, in the company of Northern Ireland's senior dramatist, John Boyd, about 'The Sixties'; and not for the last time, I was taken with the 'nostalgia' for the Sixties, among teenagers of the Eighties.

"Ah, the *Thirties*! That was *my* time," said John Boyd, a pant of satisfaction indicating that he had spent the decade well. Twenties, Thirties, Forties, Fifties, Sixties, Seventies, Eighties—each decade, each era, seems to have a distinctive atmosphere, and for those who were young in any of them, that aura made it *their* time. Oscar Wilde's dictum that 'youth is wasted on the young' may amuse us more as we get older: but it would be a sad old person indeed who could not easily recall a time when the world seemed entirely fresh, full of endlessly new possibilities. To stay young, to identify with the young of any age, each of us must have had a time that was *our* time. And nobody else's time could ever have been so exciting.

It is hard to separate that feeling of the 'special time' of one's own youth, from one's perception of the wider history of the period. 'The Sixties' was a time of great excitement—and trauma—for me; yet I remain convinced that it was also a significant decade for the whole human race. It was, after all, the time in which the 'global village' was born, in concept, in phrase and in the technological reality of satellite television, of men circling the earth, and going to the moon. We had not yet found general agreement on how to resolve conflict without force, but in the age of total self-destruction weaponry, fear of their *own* strength had begun to restrain the appetites of the powerful. Crises in Berlin and Cuba did *not* cause World War Three.

There was a tangible sense that a totally new epoch had dawned for mankind. Danger and opportunity are not new: but danger and opportunity of a scope that could transform or destroy the earth itself, and every living thing on it—surely this must mean the birth of a new age, or the end of everything.

My story, set largely in Northern Ireland, with its roots deep in old orthodoxies and antagonisms, is the story of a Sixties person who opted early, and with zestful hope, for the new, golden age. Much of what followed was the old, stupid tragedy, redeemed occasionally by flashes of vision, and always by the everyday courage of ordinary people. The story reveals terrible wastage of life and of hope, even moments when despair would have been logical; and pessimism is indeed the proper response to the continuing tragedy and intransigence in Northern Ireland, and to the wider phenomena of the arms race, the blood trade in arms, and the increasing starvation in a time of incredibly productive food technology.

But it is also a story of survival, personal survival, the survival of a community, and the survival of hope itself. Only hope could justify the telling of so much that is hateful, and I am grateful to have survived, and to be full of hope. I was particularly lucky to have got time in the early Sixties to work out my beliefs and values before things fell apart in Northern Ireland: my survival owes much to knowing how to hope. I have therefore tried to describe how I arrived at my views, and difficult though it may be for one person to follow another through the process of self-questioning, I hope that readers will 'survive' this egocentricity.

Young people, like young plants bursting from the earth, are, I believe, entitled to be egocentric, bumping thoughtlessly into others as they try to find their way, and their place; and behaviour that is unpleasant in the old, is at least acceptable from the young.

Thirties people, Sixties people, Eighties people—all of us living at this time, are, I hope, the young generation of a new civilisation that must survive without recourse to available arms. In moving from the old ways to the new, we will inevitably repeat many of the old mistakes, wasting much of our own and others' lives. It is because this story of much tragedy is also a story of the survival of hope, that it has been written: for I, like any teenager today, am wistful—not for the Sixties or any other past decade, but for the Nineties and the next millennium, for that special time when the world is always young and innocent.

The year 1960 signalled the end of the Second World War as reference point and background shadow for my generation. Phrases like 'pre-war prices' gave way to terms like 'inflation'. The making and breaking of families and fortunes, the lot of both winners and losers in any war, were fading dramas. No new system of values or social order, to replace that staggered by the First World War and shattered by the Second, was coming into focus: we were poised instead for the onset of The Permissive Society, after a period of 'You never had it so good'. A new generation, not sapped by war, began to question its inheritance.

The War had divided the world into East and West. We in the West saw ourselves as the Goodies who would see to it that the Baddies—

the Russians behind the Iron Curtain—did not destroy the freedom assured by the defeat of Hitler's Baddies. The Russians were now cast as the most evil people on earth, all Godless Communists, torturing within their own country, and forever plotting to take over the rest of the world. Stalin's successor, Nikita Krushchev—Malenkov did not get time to be hated, and Bulganin appeared as Krushchev's foil— was now World Enemy Number One; and lest anyone be deceived by his cheery peasant wit, we were reminded that he was The Ukrainian Butcher. But all was well, for General Dwight D. Eisenhower, who had won The War even more than had Winston Churchill, was in charge of the Free World; and every year, on his birthday, Churchill, now hailed as The Greatest Living Englishman, was wheeled to the window of his Hyde Park home, so that people could cheer and remember that we had won The War. The world was safe for democracy.

I was born of Belfast parents, in Derry, or Londonderry, in Northern Ireland, in 1943; and at Christmas 1949 we came to live in Belfast. So I was about seven or eight when I learned that the big untidy gaps in central Belfast were bomb sites, places flattened by Hitler's Luftwaffe during the Blitz. The Germans had strafed Belfast's main street, Royal Avenue, and machine-gun bullet marks were still visible on the Central Library. The idea of planes coming all the way from Germany to shoot and bomb in this now-safe city put The War, in my child's mind, well back into human history, to a crazy time prior to normal daily safety. It could never happen again: grown-ups wouldn't let it . . . .

Of course, wars went on happening: the Korean War, Suez, Cyprus, Hungary, Kenya, Aden, Indo-China, to mention a few; but these wars were not The War, and they did not impinge unduly. I do recall being moved to tears by a report from the BBC's Ivor Jones in Budapest, when Russian tanks crushed human bones 'like egg-shells'. That image was stronger than another of the time, the 'Molotov Cocktail'. If only I could have gone to speak to Mr. Krushchev, I was sure I could have persuaded him not to crush people like egg-shells. I was thirteen.

Such dramas were still part of the grown-ups' world, something hanging over from The War: with time, they would grow out of it, surely. In my world of football and bikes and boxing, the most memorable developments were when one neighbour got a television, then another acquired a second-hand car: hitherto, only the rich— publicans, bookies, and doctors—had their own four-wheelers. The worst tragedy, for us, was the Manchester United plane crash at Munich: for weeks, we would dash down in the morning to hear of the condition of those not killed immediately, unable to take it in when Duncan Edwards finally died.

Other young heroes would take the place of the Busby Babes, and our world would continue, while the Big World went on being run in obscure places and ways, by men who seemed to be from another century—as indeed they were.

My children look at me strangely, as if I too am from another century, when I explain to them that we did not have a television until I was fourteen. They struggle to appreciate my excited recollection of actually being able to watch the English Cup Final, live, in black and white. Suddenly too, around that time, the Russians launched a 'sputnik', which sounded both comical and sinister compared with Western references to 'artificial earth satellites'.

The first space traveller, the Russian Yuri Gagarin, seemed a nice man, in spite of being an evil Godless Communist. Western leaders congratulated the Russians on their achievement, in spite of hating them. The world, if still quite safe, began to look a little different. The Russians, who were supposed to be backward, were setting the pace, while the Americans kept blowing rockets up in full view at Cape Canaveral: as the comedian Bob Hope explained it, "Their Germans are better than our Germans!"

It was onto this changing world stage of television and spacemen and cars for ordinary people, that John Fitzgerald Kennedy strode in January 1961. With his thrilling rhetoric and youthful charisma, he appealed immediately to a "new generation, born in this century". We were going to "begin again the quest for peace". The freshness was emphasised by contrast with the foregoing 'Goodies-Baddies' slanging match across the world, and he was heard "in the huts and villages" around the globe. He brought, above all, hope, and spoke to and for our generation more than any politician then alive: and live statesmen at that time included De Gaulle, Adenauer, Nehru, Krushchev, and more domestically, Churchill, Macmillan and de Valera.

Good Pope John XXIII, known in Northern Ireland as 'the Protestant Pope', was ensconced in the Vatican, after the seemingly endless reign of Pius XII, who, for us, was a remote, ascetic figure. Innocent of the theological and ecumenical consequences of John's initiatives, we simply warmed to the sight of this roly-poly man, slipping out of his ecclesiastical prison to visit prisoners in the jails of Rome.

In Northern Ireland, the IRA (Irish Republican Army) had launched an old-style guerilla campaign against police and army barracks. It aroused no support, staggering on fitfully for six years, before the use of Special Powers in both Belfast and Dublin combined with public apathy to persuade the Republicans that theirs was a lost cause—in 1962.

In Britain, Ban-The-Bomb rallies aroused considerable support without having the slightest effect on the threat of living under the nuclear shadow. Macmillan's slogan, 'You never had it so good', still fitted a mood of optimism for people who had won The War, lost an empire, retained a constitutional monarchy and looked forward to ever rising standards of living and of democratic participation.

Part of that apparently imminent utopia was the rapid expansion of free education to include university level, for anyone with the requisite ability. This formal equality of opportunity seemed a natural step in the evolution towards the egalitarian society. Few realised that the investment in their development was very much that—an investment—to produce the skills demanded by the emerging techno-logical society. Reports indicating the need to 'produce' thousands of physicists, chemists, engineers, teachers, and so on, coincided happily with the rhetoric of reformers to cause a bulge in university and polytechnic building programmes, sometimes financed by defence departments. There was little corresponding examination of the value of this sudden expansion in training, for actual lives to be lived.

It was also the age of 'youth', a pop-star culture, a whole area of the economy based on youth as consumer. It became fashionable for young people to dress and speak outrageously, as if that had never happened before, and to talk openly about such taboo subjects as sex, again as if it were an entirely new phenomenon. Widespread availability of contraceptives was, of course, relatively new: the Pill had arrived, and the term 'sexual liberation' was heard. People were going to be 'free' as never before: free to have free education, free health, free love. Yeah, yeah, yeah, yeah . . . . The Beatles burst upon the scene, seeming for a time to have created 'The Sixties'. Certainly, they shattered my prejudices about pop music, and I remain a fan.

I am probably fairly typical of a percentage of the population which saw itself university-bound, and took for granted much that amazed our parents. I caused my parents considerable anxiety by fooling around at university, when it seemed to them that God-given talents and state-given opportunities imposed the duty to acquire a first-class degree and a doctorate. Such visible success would confirm the family's self-perceived progression from nineteenth-century famine and eviction in different parts of Ireland, through working-class Belfast to middle-class suburbia for our parents, and the limitless beyond for us. The fact that my parents had instilled idealism into their children compromised the more secular ambition: but it would be some time before either side of the generation gap would appreciate this.

Undergraduate messing-about was a startling change for me. After leaving school, I had spent eight months as a novice monk in the Dominican Order, following in the footsteps of my older brother and sister. I would later accept that there was a dash of escapism in my presumed 'vocation' to the religious life. I had had little difficulty in acquiring A-levels in mathematics, physics and chemistry, but I did not relish the prospect of doing examinations for years merely to become the property of some amorphous corporation. But, at the time, with childish simple-mindedness and a complete lack of child-like humility (ever a problem!), I thought I was devoting my life to 'know, love and serve God', as the Penny Catechism put it. I thoroughly enjoyed—and still value—most of those eight months of monastic experience. But towards the end of that period, I began to suffer distressing symptoms of claustrophobia, sleeplessness and nausea, which collectively, and within a few weeks, told me, my novice-master and local doctors that this was not to be my vocation. It was my first taste of failure, my nervous exhaustion being at least partly induced by intense efforts to know the meaning of life, and of truth with a capital 'T'.

The university was a different universe altogether. Science under-graduates had a loaded timetable, with almost every available hour taken up with lectures or practical work. But myself and a like-minded pal used to take ourselves down among the coffee-drinking arts and law students, to discuss the Great Issues of the Day. Instead of acquiring exam-worthy information on the consequences of the theories of such as Einstein and Heisenberg, we would raise such concepts as Relativity and Uncertainty with our fellows in other faculties, to see if comparable ways of thinking might apply to their worlds. We would question law students on the values and principles upon which their laws of conduct were based: and would be taken aback to find that law students, in most cases, seemed not to care about the philosophy of law, and to regard it as an obscurantist necessity on the way to a successful career at the Bar. My friend and I may have been somewhat ahead of our time, but we were severely behind with our work and spent that first undergraduate summer repeating failed exams—while the aforementioned lawyers and company were swanning around Europe or the United States.

Having escaped once into a monastery to get away from the demanding study of science, so now I escaped into the Arts Faculty where the mathematics, which I had passed, were equally applicable, and where I would have time to join the coffee-table chat that made the place *feel* like a university.

Chatting was all I did, for long enough. I was not at first among those luminaries who would rise to speak in the debating societies, an action which filled me with apprehension, and therefore with admiration for the apprentice politicians and barristers on stage. Study remained low on the agenda, well behind football, table tennis, chess and pipe-smoking. Nor was I unduly concerned with how the utopia which we conjured daily over coffee was to be accomplished. I had to contend with more captivating questions: as a past-pupil of a boys-only grammar school run by the Irish Christian Brothers, I never really came to terms with sitting in a library with the aroma of feminine scent wafting about. The rustle of skirts was an invincible distraction to concentration.

Yet I did enough to be accepted as an honours philosophy student in a department which was the ultimate escape for someone with my strong aversion to the discipline of study. Lectures were few and far between, and no-one seemed to care if one ever turned up. I must have been at times the most idle student in the Queen's University of Belfast, getting up from coffee as friends scurried off to lectures or the library, to wander up to the smoking-room for a game of chess, or for a walk around the quad if the weather was pleasant. I was saved from either expulsion or becoming a dissolute by two gifts which have been alternately blessings and burdens to me—an active mind, and an acute memory.

Indeed, it was in this ideal arrangement for the lazy that my mental activity increased greatly. Just when I had finally escaped even the basic discipline of checking into lectures, I found I could no longer dodge a number of questions that had been floating round my head for years. I had no doubt that I could resolve them, for my arrogance was as marked as my indiscipline—if a thing could be understood, I could undertand it. With nothing better to do, and with just a tinge of urgency that three easy-going years as a philosophy undergraduate might be the last chance I would get before having to earn a living of some sort, I decided to pursue the basic questions resolutely in my own mind. I did not propose to study what others might think—library-squatting would have been too much like work for the young gentleman, and would have interfered with his smoking habits.

My existence had not been entirely forgotten by the head of the department, the kindly Dr Theodore Crowley. While I was usually out of his sight, I must not have been out of his mind, for he called me in in the early summer of 1963, and made a flattering proposal: I was to produce, for publication, the definitive English version of St. Augustine's *Contra Academicos*.

Dr. Crowley was also an international bridge player, and a

Kerryman, and I strongly suspect that he knew exactly what he was doing in handing me this charge. He said that the Latin and French versions were satisfactory but that all English translations to date were inadequate. Clearly, the bright young translator would have to spend a lot of time, during the summer vacation, trapped at his desk between two dictionaries and a blank page. As well as the flattery implied, this arrangement suited me, for I could work at home at whatever hours I liked, and the *Contra Academicos* was concerned with the very topics which interested me.

For several years, I had been irritated by loose ends in my mind. Fascinating though subatomic and astronomical physics can be, there is an obvious limit to their purpose and their interest: even if we knew how the most minute transactions of matter and energy took place, even if we could calculate back to how our universe began, this kind of information tells us nothing about why matter, energy, the universe or we are here at all, and nothing about the very fact that we are conscious beings. I grew up listening to public utterances about the wonderments of modern science, but it seemed to me that at most science could only scrape the surface of what there is to be known. I wanted to know why we were here, how we could even question our own existence, what was it that happened inside us when we said we *knew* something, how could beings like us, geared to speculate on the infinite, be pinned inside the finite space of our mortal bodies, what did we mean when we uttered the sound 'God', what did words like 'value' signify; and so on—the questions that most people ask themselves briefly at some time, and that philosophers have been asking always.

Even within science, I had become less interested in the sheer accumulation of information—partly out of work-shyness—and more in the process by which new theories emerge. For instance, I was more curious to know how Einstein thought of Relativity, than about Relativity itself. The 'Uncertainty Principle' of Heisenberg struck me as amusing in its very name, which was like a contradiction in terms; it is a lovely principle—that the precise location and momentum of a particle cannot be observed since the act of observation moves the particle—and I believe that a similar principle should be stated for journalists who imagine that they record events accurately. Not only is it *always* impossible to give a precise rendering of what has already transpired, but the way in which events are recorded and reported may change the course of events. The observer is never some 'objective', disconnected person, however dispassionate in judgement.

Uncertainty also has its place in philosophy. The way in which the same problems, in different forms, emerged in philosophy over

the centuries, persuaded me that each individual and each genera
must ask the same questions all over again, and that there could ne ...
be a time when humanity as a whole could accept, without
questioning, a dominant philosophy: question and uncertainty are
necessary aspects of freedom. This conviction made the idea that men
should fight wars with the motivation or excuse of any 'ism' all the
more horrifying: and the twentieth century, with its mass murder in
the name of Nazism, Marxism, capitalism and nationalism, has
provided all the evidence the human race needs *for all time* that no-
one can have the 'certainty' to justify killing in the name of any
freedom.

Augustine in his *Contra Academicos* was concerned with whether
we could know 'Truth', and how, and I started quite vigorously to
the task of the translation. Not only was Theodore Crowley forcing
me to revise my rusty French and limited Latin, but the exercise of
trying to find just the right English word was a very effective way of
forcing a lazy thinker into some kind of discipline.

'God' gave me most trouble: not in translation, but in meaning.
Clearly, even assuming God's existence, here was a word that we used,
which must refer to a being beyond the limits of language to describe;
worse, unlike other words, which related to some kind of image or
thought, 'God' was unimaginable and unthinkable, and should
therefore be quite unspeakable. One might legitimately whisper about
what one has seen through a glass darkly; or remain silent if the word
God did not refer directly to a real being.

All of this was very uncomfortable stuff for a young Catholic from
an orthodox family. I did not want casually to throw the baby out
with the bathwater, but neither could I honestly use words
meaninglessly.

Like Pirsig with his motorbike, I was getting 'stuck' with the
problem of God. I couldn't simply leave God to the one side, and
proceed with words like 'knowledge', 'value', 'cognition', 'truth',
'justice', or 'infinity': the answer to the God question would transform
all the other answers, one way or the other. I poked at my own
consciousness of my self, as the likely area for an answer, since God,
if God existed, must be a self-conscious being.

I tried systematically to remove all images and distractions from
my mind, in order to hold such non-imaged concepts as 'value' steadily
before me. But 'God' could not be 'held': the moment one began to
try definitions, such limits evaporated. God, to be God, had to be
limitless, therefore non-definable—therefore the word was either
useless or quite unlike any other word we used, referring like a weak
signal to something it could not begin to describe.

For weeks, while my brothers and friends were away for the vacation, I kept at this with relentless concentration. I took long solitary walks along the nearby river Lagan, staring for I do not know how long at the rippling water, considering its movement, its existence, its impressions to my senses, my imagination: its connection, not so much to everything that exists, but to my own processes of observation and thought. Trees also had their magnificent reality subjected to this desiccation of their objective existence.

Such unrelieved activity should have been enough to drive me nuts. But what really threatened to unhinge me was the action of trying to observe the process of falling asleep! Attempting to catch the moment when conscious control of the imagination ceases, is not a way to fall asleep, or to solve any metaphysical puzzle. I do not recommend it! But it was precisely at such a moment that I experienced a terrifying insight. I suddenly 'saw', rather than reasoned towards, the 'person' of God: that a limitless, yet powerful self-consciousness with *intrinsic* existence, beyond verbal description or the power of the mind to hold by itself, was the unutterable truth above and beneath and pervading everything: the problem of words remained— for it is impossible to communicate the idea compellingly that existence is *necessary* to the very *idea* of God. Unlike humble mystics who might be rendered blissful by such an experience, or trained yogis who could take it in their stride, I was almost paralysed with fear. This dread was quickly followed by nausea, a feeling of weightlessness—I was not exactly lifting off the bed, but I could not feel myself lying solidly on it either!—and then a more obvious shaking fright. I was too afraid to turn back to the initial subject of the 'dread', and at the same time, I had a deep sense that to 'pray' would have been to cheat on a true experience: if I was going to 'face' God, it would have to be squarely.

This traumatic experience settled the 'God' problem, in principle at least; although in practice I ran away from the implications of this insight, the existence of God, for me, was not a matter of 'faith' but of knowledge.

Although I attended lectures occasionally and submitted a few essays, my connection with the philosophy department was desultory from that autumn until I was generously awarded a third class honours degree and invited to do a doctorate. From 1963, my concern was to discover how the values and vision which I felt I had grasped, might work in my own life and in the lives of all. Combining with a childhood opposition to the public execution of Caryl Chessman in Death Row, San Quentin (and a deep doubt about the infallibility of an orthodoxy which could *ever* justify murder by capital punishment) my personal and world view was then—and ever since—theistic nonviolence.

I began to notice what was going on around me just a little more. I found myself uneasy with the sloppy thought delivered with the passion of certitude in the Students' Union. There were nationalists with a small 'n', unionists with a small 'u', liberals with a small 'l', the uncertainty of these appellations by no means the scientific thing of physics; then there were various socialists, none of them with a small 's', all of them the 'true' socialists, most of them echoing an abandoned faith in the 'true' church. Nevertheless, the general level of debate was high, concerned with human rights, poverty, disarmament, and the end of all forms of discrimination. But it was at the coffee table level, as the November student council elections approached, that I was amazed to discover that the same high-minded speakers of the debating societies were preoccupied with the Protestant/Catholic breakdown in votes. It was pointed out to me, with all the patience of parents instructing a child, that those who controlled the Council, and therefore student money, were almost all Protestant, while the powerless debating societies were the arena for Catholic dominance.

This was the beginning of the era of the 'student revolution', an ephemeral phenomenon which threw up such names as Danny the Red, Rudi Dutschke and Tariq Ali, and slightly later, would help alter the course of American involvement in South East Asia. The rhetoric of that period was already audible in Queen's University debating societies: and some of the themes that would be articulated in the Civil Rights Movement of the later Sixties had begun to be aired.

It has been said that the 'student revolution' was a contagion carried by television and paperbacks, a movement played up by the media and resented by those who had to work for a living. Students in one place saw students in another engaging in public demonstration and riot, in venues as far apart as Tokyo, Berlin, Paris and the United States: according to the media legend, this was a copycat syndrome. It would be impossible to say how much validity there is in this view, but there is no doubt that students everywhere were seen domestically as having been influenced by persons or events half a world away, and, insult of insults, were being entirely derivative, like children imitating each other in the school yard.

Even more sinister, it seemed, these impressionable young people, even from good family backgrounds, were easy meat for the insidious teachings of Marx, Marcuse and Mao Tse Tung.

By the end of the Sixties, I had had more experience of both 'student politics' and the 'student revolution' than anyone I know anywhere in the world: and I may therefore say with a little authority that the above impressions were only partially valid. What was much more true, in my opinion, is that the first efforts of the television age to come to terms with the emerging 'global village' meant that those events which made good spectacle, easily and articulately televised, were carried around the world. And students were, for a while, easy 'copy', in journalists' terms. They were also 'youth' in the age of the Beatles. They were also the generation which would have to create a new vision and order to replace that shattered by the Second World War. The importance of the 'student revolution' was thus inflated beyond its actual relevance in most cases; and I think the French students were first to realise that their activity was another 'product', a spectacle, to be consumed by the television industry.

The 'copycat' effect was also accelerated by the simple fact that domestic perceptions everywhere on issues of justice and liberation in a supposedly post-imperial age, were bound to be similar. The opposition to armed establishments everywhere was a result of a widespread simultaneous appreciation of the lunacy of any further war in a nuclear age, as well as a dawning realisation that the Great Victories of the two World Wars were dubious accomplishments and possibly disasters in the light of history. As the Americans gradually became more murderous in Vietnam, for instance, there was a feeling that the Nazis had been beaten, but that Nazism had won.

There was also, I think, an element of unconscious revolt against the investment in students to make them useful units in a technological society. In some cases, this was quite explicit; and in the Baader Meinhof motivation in Germany, there was a tone of deep resentment that was at odds with that movement's proclaimed concern for the Third World in its vulnerability to Western exploitation. There was often a greater sense of frustration that the economic miracle at home was so much materialist ash, rather than a life-reverencing compassion for the starving.

But in Belfast, in late 1963, while tuned in to the same wavelengths as students elsewhere, leaders of student opinion were sitting around discussing the Protestant/Catholic numbers game. I couldn't quite believe it until I went along to the Student Council on the night of its Executive elections and watched the two-to-one breakdown in voting, exacting reflecting the population breakdown both inside and outside the University.

It might be thought that even someone with my solitary preoccupations of the previous years would have to have been pretty dumb not to have realised that this was inevitable: and certainly reactions to my questioning of this revelation ranged from peevish to patronising. But the fact is that my background was rather unusual in Northern Ireland terms. My Catholic parents had settled for the first ten years of their married life in the largely Protestant area of

Derry's Waterside. We children (six of us) were not particularly aware of that: indeed, I was surprised again, thirty years later, to hear the media describe the Waterside as a 'strongly Loyalist' area. When we moved to Belfast, the new, post-war houses at Cavehill, where we lived, were divided equally, one half of the street for natives (mainly Protestant), the other half for engineers and designers from England (plus a few from Scotland and Wales), brought over after the War to staff the embryonic aircraft and missile factory of Short Brothers and Harland.

So while I went to a Catholic school in Belfast, my childhood friends were a mixture of Irish (Protestant and Catholic) and English, Scots and Welsh (often of no religious persuasion whatsoever).

In the twelve years before I went to Queen's, I can recall only about three examples of sectarianism. Shortly after we came to Belfast, a neighbour's children used to throw stones at us McKeowns, shouting 'Fenians' at us. Our parents told us to take no notice, vaguely explaining that these neighbours came from an area where that kind of behaviour was not uncommon. It transpired that the neighbour was from the Loyalist Shankill Road area, and had been shipwrecked during the War: his erratic behaviour was put down to 'war nerves'. I remember an Englishman ticking him off for being rude to my mother, and his surprise that the Englishman did not appreciate that she was a 'Fenian'. He was even more surprised when the local Englishmen not only did not put out the Union Jack on the Twelfth of July Orange Day (high point of the five-month annual season of celebration of Protestantism), but regarded it as a rather strange and unBritish thing to do! Gradually, local Orangemen ceased the practice, and took themselves off to the Twelfth parades with their sashes and bowlers well wrapped up. I must add that the neighbours on either side of us were also from the Shankill area, and better neighbours could hardly have been imagined. The offending neighbour also changed to the point where he offered me a lift on his motorcycle: with some trepidation (the beginning of bigotry?), I accepted.

I recall also being pulled from my bike on the Shankill Road, on the way from school. A boy no bigger than myself, presumably detecting a 'Fáinne' (a silver lapel ring indicating willingness and ability to speak Irish), yelled "Fenian Pig", grabbed my handlebars and spat in my face. I hopped off to chase him, but was confronted by older youths who told me in emphatic terms to clear off if I didn't want 'done'.

On another occasion, I was cycling to the Ligoniel library, a distance of about three miles from home, when a gang of youths, all a few years older than me, got round the bike, and wanted to know, very threateningly, if I was a Catholic or a Protestant. I told them it was none of their business, that a person's religion was their own business. They were not about to debate, and observed in nasty tones that I thought I was a funny boy. Finally, I said I was a Catholic (it being a sin to deny one's faith!) and waited to see if I was to be added to those who have 'died for their faith'. Their reaction, however, was one of puzzlement. "How do we know you are?" and "Prove it", were the responses. It was obvious that they were Catholics and also that they were somewhat disappointed that I was too, and that they were thus cheated of a reason for frightening the life out of me, or worse. I mentioned the school I went to and the one my father taught in. "What's yer name?" I was asked. "Wee Sammy's his da!" one of them said, and they walked away.

I cannot recall any political discussions as such, at home. To the extent that there was any tangible political attitude coming across, it was that 'politics' were faintly corrupt, and that decent people simply got on with their own lives, loved God and neighbour, and if they had the talent and opportunity, developed a civilised interest in the arts. Towards this latter end, my parents, out of a meagre enough income, provided the opportunity for each of their six children to have private piano tuition.

I think that we absorbed from our parents a concern for truth and justice, without any specific relation to the immediate political community, almost an abstract ideal: and past pupils of my father consistently remember him as 'tough but just'.

So in Queen's University in 1963 and later, I could identify strongly with the passionate concern of Catholic students about human rights: but I simply could not automatically regard Protestant students as political enemies.

Nor could I get steamed up to regard the English as intrinsically corrupt, the nationalistic teaching of Irish history notwithstanding: or for that matter, the real history of brutal and devious British imperialism notwithstanding.

All the old sores of Ireland seemed to me like the Second World War, part of a stupid and savage history, which we had absolutely no reason to get worked up over, or to repeat, not in these enlightened days of free education, free health, free love . . . six years before the guns came out in earnest.

Naïveté and unusual background notwithstanding, I still refused to accept this Protestant/Catholic approach to student politics: that is, I accepted totally that it was a fact, but I refused to accept that it should continue, or that it was impossible to change it. I was finally goaded into action by John Duffy, then President of the Literary and

Scientific Society, later the organising secretary of the Social
Democratic and Labour Party, who told me sharply, "It's all very well
for you to criticise, Ciaran—but you don't actually take any part, you
don't take any responsibility."

"You're right, John. I will get stuck in—and I'll prove my point,"
I replied, with that humility which so many have found endearing.

The point to be proven was that the Protestant/Catholic nature
of student politics would continue as long as *both* sides continued it:
I had been arguing that the Catholics, however valid the cry of
gerrymandering, discrimination and so on, defined *themselves* as a
minority as long as their politicians organised on a Catholic basis only.
I also believed that most Protestants and Catholics wanted out of this
mutual trap. Certainly, most students could not care less about it, and
there were signs of change in the public politic.

In 1963, Captain (now Lord) Terence O'Neill had succeeded Lord
Brookeborough (Northern Ireland's Prime Minister for twenty-two
years) and the era of 'a Protestant Parliament for a Protestant People'
seemed destined to end. O'Neill, an Old Etonian type, wanted a
liberal-progressive image for Northern Ireland, and his presentation
was in tune with the vogueish international ecumenism, so much
identified with the late Pope John XXIII; on the other hand, he warned
Protestants that more than half the children of school-going age were
Catholics.

O'Neillism had already indicated its generosity of approach when
the Lord Mayor of Belfast, Sir William Jenkins, had ordered the Union
Jack to be flown at half-mast in mourning for Pope John. And Jenkins
resisted the challenge from another emerging force, Ian Paisley, who
protested vociferously at this action.

It was enough to shake the foundations of traditional Unionism,
that Terence O'Neill should greet a Mother Superior as School
Principal and that Sir William Jenkins should observe civilised
protocol. That is by no means the same thing as to say that almost
all traditional Unionists were incurable bigots: far from it, for most
Unionist people were quietly in favour of quiet change towards a more
progressive society. What was not always appreciated was that the
100 per cent control of government, immutable so long as 65 per cent
of the population uniformly voted Unionist, was a foundation of
Unionist power which demanded the equally immutable definition of
the Catholic/Nationalist 35 per cent as a permanent minority of
second class citizens. *This is the fundamental issue in relation to
parliamentary democracy in Northern Ireland.*

The Government of Northern Ireland from 1920 onwards had all the forms and trappings of parliamentary democracy: but one in three of the citizens was born into the certainty of permanent exclusion from full citizen's rights. This condition could either be benign or malignant, largely at the whim of Unionist leadership. It could be oppressive and contemptuous, as often under Brookeborough, or it could be generous and well-intentioned as under O'Neill: but it would be the same fundamental condition, and the Catholics could either accept it meekly or violently, and both benign and malign responses were forthcoming from the Catholics as well.

It is not the partition of Ireland, *per se*, which is at the root of Northern Ireland's conflict: it is the internal flaw which inhibits the emergence of a universal consensus, freely expressed at the ballot-box by citizens who know that they have equal universal suffrage. When 35 per cent know that their vote can never have any effect on government, their vote is not equal universal suffrage, however free they are to vote for their own representatives. A 'United Ireland', moreover, in conventional terms, would merely change the dimensions of this consensus problem: 25 per cent of the population, being Unionists, would be in the same position in an all-Ireland as the 35 per cent of Nationalists within Northern Ireland.

The foregoing is merely a statement of the problem in the abstract, and at voting level. The living reality has been complicated almost beyond grasp by the involvement of the sense of identity and the religious persuasions of the two distinct groups: one, which had total power and continual fear of losing it, the other, with no power and never ceasing to seek it. It was inevitable that over two generations this difference would be emphasised and protected, even as the citizens otherwise sought a decent *modus vivendi*. The ability to survive in this unhealthy structure depended greatly on the most repressive law of all: 'whatever you say, say nothing', a remarkable social principle in a society as loquacious as Ireland's. This pervasive law was the title of a poem by Seamus Heaney, and the following words from it give a sense of what it meant:

> Smoke-signals are loud-mouthed compared with us:
> Manoeuvrings to find out name and school,
> Subtle discrimination by addresses
> With hardly an exception to the rule
>
> That Norman, Ken and Sydney signalled Prod
> And Seamus (call me Sean) was sure-fire Pape.
> O Land of password, handgrip, wink and nod,
> Of open minds, as open as a trap,

Where tongues lie coiled, as under flames lie wicks,
Where half of us, as in a wooden horse
Were cabin'd and confined like wily Greeks,
Besieged within the siege, whispering Morse.

But 1963 was a special year, a year when the forward-looking impulses of Pope John and President Kennedy were at their height with the deaths of both. In the year of the Beatles, we were living in the most modern of all 'modern times', and O'Neill and his advisors were going to make Northern Ireland 'with it'. Brookeborough was gone, the IRA was moribund, and the off-stage roars of Ian Paisley seemed like a last cry from the disappearing backwoods.

O'Neillism wafted into the university, and was espoused by such as Edmund Curran, then Chairman of the Unionist and Conservative Club (later defeated by another student contemporary, Austin Currie, for a seat in the Northern Ireland Parliament at Stormont, and now Deputy Editor of the *Belfast Telegraph*, Northern Ireland's largest circulation newspaper). Hitherto, the debating societies had been dominated by Catholics, not least because Protestant students found much of Unionism intellectually indefensible, such as the control by gerrymandering of the predominantly Nationalist city of Derry. O'Neillism could be defended and O'Neillite Unionists began to appear more visibly. The 'in-phrases' of the time were 'the need for dialogue' and 'good community relations'.

It was in this context that I plunged into student politics, and set out to de-sectarianise their basis. It was said then, and often since, that I did not understand the 'realities', namely that Unionists are Unionists and Nationalists are Nationalists and that they'll never change. I have to say with all the force at my command, that it is precisely because I did understand, and was even shocked into appreciation of those realities, that I have been moved ever since to appeal to another reality as the basis for all politics: namely, the humanity, individual and collective, that is far more valuable and essential than any datum of historical or cultural inheritance.

Ironically, the charge of naïve idealism changed quickly to one of Machiavellianism as I began to succeed at a rate that surprised me, and as the strategy for this change became obvious. I gathered together a group of independently minded people, believing more or less the same thing. We accepted that there could be forty unchangeable Unionists and forty similar Nationalists (whatever the size of the 'u' or the 'n'!) out of the 120 members of the student council: therefore we wanted to ensure that forty genuinely independent people be persuaded to stand for the Council, and campaign vigorously to get elected, so that the two-to-one line-up in the elections would be completely obfuscated, and the chance of being elected on merit increased. The traditionalists on both sides were rather bemused at our support among the wider student body to whom we appealed directly, and there were charges of 'stacking the council'. The phrase 'McKeown's mafia' began to be heard; the more elegant phrase coined by Brendan Meegan, 'group of like-minded people', was much more accurate, for no one was required to proclaim or renounce their political tendencies. This also led to the idea that we had either 'no politics' or 'no principles'. My personal success in getting votes was attributed by 'in' student politicians to my being an 'unprincipled' vote-getter: 'unprincipled' here referred to my practice of bombarding the place with leaflets and appearing everywhere possible around election time, a barnstorming style that struck the traditionalists as unseemly. But personal vote-getting was important, though less so than encouraging others to stand—and encouraging them in turn to overcome their embarrassment and go out and ask for support. Paradoxically, I believe that the fact that I was initially so shy and nervous of this myself, drew people in to help who might otherwise have left the field to the assured platform speakers hitherto dominating the scene. The best 'political mechanic' around, for instance, was the aforementioned Brendan Meegan, who, for such a retiring, unassuming figure, had an uncanny grasp of who was where and with what support in the various faculties. The 'idealists' became very good pragmatic politicians, which seemed to some like cheating: idealists were supposed to be losers, and we were not playing by that rule.

For reasons which I hope may become obvious, these efforts had an experimental importance beyond the mere political capering of students in a regional university. By attempting to create, through conventional political techniques, a dominant middle ground owing nothing to any sectarian or ideological interest, we would be causing the automatic end of 'Protestant ascendancy'—with Protestant support. We would also be causing Catholics to take responsibility instead of indulging forever in the expression of self-pity at their secondary position: this would require as much effort as for the Protestants to change, for it was all too easy for Catholic students to acquire an outstanding reputation for oratory based on polemics and the passions of injustice and frustration, rather than for justice and participation.

The assault on the Student Council was one line of the strategy: the other was an effort to involve Protestants from the Unionist tradition in the public debates. The most significant forum for this was the New Ireland Society, of which I was elected secretary and then

President. The Society had as its aim 'to bring together all those interested in the social, economic, cultural and political development of Ireland, and the eventual reunification of Ireland'. This latter clause inhibited the participation of Unionists: Ed Curran told me that if it were removed, he could join, and that he spoke for many. I announced in my campaign for the presidency of the Society that I would move the deletion of 'eventual reunification of Ireland', at the Annual General Meeting—which was also the election meeting. The 'in' opinion was that the 'green' (Nationalist) vote would sink me on this issue, especially when some of the former leaders of the Society returned to oppose the change. But on the night, only seven votes were cast against, and nearly 250 for; I was elected easily, and quite a few Unionists, including Ed Curran, began to participate in the debates.

By this time, spring 1965, the politics of 'dialogue and good community relations' were at their height. My predecessor, the enlightened Conor Bradley, had instituted a 'New Ireland Community Relations Award', and it was my privilege to present the first such award to Belfast's Lord Mayor, Sir William Jenkins, at the Society's Annual Dinner. Protocol suggested that the function should include a toast to The Queen, and to the dismay of the greener members, I insisted on doing this, the more so because of the Lord Mayor's presence, and the Award. Apart from two, who later became Nationalist politicians, the Society's members rose for the toast.

That autumn, the 'group of like-minded people', now a mixture of Protestant, Catholic, Unionist, Nationalist, Liberal and Labour, was ready to take on the Student Council Executive elections, hitherto so grotesquely characterised by the two-to-one sectarian vote pattern. We ran a 'ticket', American-style, a 'slate' of candidates for the major positions. Our man for President, David Crawford, an ex-public-school boy, was beaten by a few votes, I was beaten by one vote for the position of Secretary, but several of our colleagues were elected, and the varying pattern of voting ensured the victory of our basic purpose: the two-to-one Protestant-Catholic pattern of generations had been shattered. Almost as consolation, I was proposed and elected by a large margin for the more minor position of Societies Secretary on the Executive.

The reality or otherwise of the change in student power was to be tested quickly and sharply. A move began from the National Union of Students of England, Wales and Northern Ireland (NUS) to prevent any college union from being a member of two 'national unions': this was clearly directed at Northern Ireland Colleges which were also members of the Union of Students in Ireland (USI). The NUS had been dominated by Queen's Belfast Student Presidents, Bill Savage and

Geoff Martin (later the EEC representative in Belfast), and the move was seen in Belfast and Dublin as a Unionist effort to partition the Irish union. Geoff's younger brother, Robin, was President of the Queen's Student Council, which proceeded to 'suspend' its membership of USI, pending consideration of full withdrawal. In addition to the backwards political aspects of this, many students were uneasy that they might no longer be able to avail themselves of the excellent student travel arrangements made by USI with Aer Lingus, a service rapidly becoming big business in the million-pound turnover category.

In January 1966, during this 'suspension', fellow Executive member Bob Carson and I were sent as 'fraternal observers' rather than as delegates from Queen's to the USI Annual Congress in Cork, with clear instructions not to speak or vote as delegates, which we did not do. But Gordon Colleary, then President of USI, introduced me as an after-dinner speaker on the last evening, as 'President of the New Ireland Society in Queen's'. I said nothing controversial and was received most warmly. But this action was made the subject of a successful 'no-confidence' motion at the subsequent Executive meeting, and my resignation was demanded. I refused to resign until the matter was discussed by the full Student Council. Had the Council been the old Protestant-Catholic arrangement, I would have been thrown out forthwith. But while it had a Protestant majority, *this was no longer a sectarian majority*. There was a sizeable middle vote, which not only thought the Student Executive should not be playing 'border politics', but also sensed that this was a move to beat McKeown on the inside, since he was likely to win at the ballot-box.

The debate on the night might have been a nasty affair, poisoning the whole purpose of removing sectarianism, had it not been for Cyril Toman. Cyril, a warm-hearted littérateur who sometimes strove to appear as a revolutionary, reduced the matter to comedy by comparing it with great wit to divorce proceedings. In relief, the Council threw the issue out, and this outcome preserved my friendship with those behind the 'partition' move, which also fizzled out. The 'good community relations' dynamic emerged more strongly than before, and the 'green' vote which had observed my New Ireland performance somewhat sourly, now adopted me more enthusiastically as a champion!

The 'doings' of student politicians in those days attracted outside and media attention, which was flattering beyond our relevance. But this further encouraged our direct involvement in public issues, and following the initiatives of such as Dr. Conn and Mrs. Patricia

McCluskey of Dungannon in starting campaigns directed at Westminster for democracy and social justice in Ulster, I set up study
groups in Queen's on various issues of social justice and the economy.
We were determined to change our society by intelligent, informed,
constitutional means, eschewing the violence and the sloganising of
the past. Our student efforts had an intrinsic validity, but we were
also conscious of them as training, and fondly imagined that a whole
generation of well-equipped, non-sectarian politicians would emerge
to fulfil what Terence O'Neill was timidly beginning. This was three
years before guns took over.

Guns did come out briefly and murderously in June 1966, when
a Catholic barman named Peter Ward was shot dead by Loyalist
extremists, an event shocking in its isolation. O'Neill, referring to "this
evil thing in our midst", banned the Ulster Volunteer Force, a
Protestant paramilitary force believed to have been responsible for
this, and another killing at the time, of a man named John Scullion.
For a moment, the demogoguery of Ian Paisley seemed sinister rather
than buffoonish, when one of the those convicted, Hugh Arnold
'Dandy' McClean, stated in court, "I wish I'd never heard of that man
Paisley, or decided to follow him."

Another of those convicted was Andrew Augustus 'Gusty' Spence,
at the time of writing still serving in Long Kesh (Her Majesty's Prison
The Maze) the sentence which the judge said should be not less than
twenty years. I am happy to call Gusty a friend. He is a former British
soldier who served in Aden and Cyprus, who told me during a prison
visit that he had done things as duty in uniform far worse than that
for which he had been convicted in Belfast. He began reading history
in jail, and the poetry of Siegfried Sassoon, studies which altered his
perspective not only on the First World War (which, because of the
slaughter of the Ulster Division at the Somme, and its contemp-
oraneity with resistance to all-Ireland Home Rule, holds a special place
in Loyalist mythology), but on the aspirations of Irish nationalists. It
also changed his views on the desirability of summoning young men
to arms on traditional slogans, and as 'commander' of the Special
Category prisoners in his compound in Long Kesh, he has had a
remarkable transforming effect on young men coming in on convictions
of sectarian murder, attempted murder or associated activity. He has
more than 'repaid his debt to society', and while it is almost too late,
I hope that he will be released before the end of the twenty years, and
that his release might mark the beginning of the politics of forgiveness,
just as the crime for which he was convicted marked, in a sense, the
beginning of the politics of murder in my generation.

Among students, Ian Paisley remained an object of disbelief, and a gift for satire. But on the streets, he was now more than a source of excitement for middle aged ladies thrilled by the lurid sexuality and biblical bellicosity of his style. Already, in October, 1964, he had threatened to lead a crowd of Loyalists to remove an Irish Tricolour from the election headquarters of the General Election Republican candidate in West Belfast, Liam McMillen, unless the Royal Ulster Constabulary (RUC) were ordered, under the Flags and Emblems Act, to remove it. The then Minister of Home Affairs, Brian McConnell, ordered its removal, and a riot followed.

In the summer of 1966, continuing his protests against ecumenism, Paisley led a crowd to the headquarters of the Presbyterian Church in central Belfast, during the attendance at the annual Assembly of the Governor, Lord Erskine, and Lady Erskine. Lady Erskine was deeply upset by the disorder caused, and the Erskines left their post soon afterwards. Incidentally, Paisley had led his march via Cromac Square in the Catholic Markets area, and that had also produced a riot. He was bound over to keep the peace, but refused to pay the fine imposed, and went to jail. The local papers, which had hitherto tended to ignore his various anti-ecumenical activities, now had no choice but to give him banner headlines in those otherwise hopeful days of 'dialogue and good community relations'.

But while his belligerence, and his campaign of 'O'Neill Must Go' —intensified after O'Neill invited the Southern Irish Premier, An Taoiseach Seán Lemass, to Stormont, to promote good relations between the two parts of Ireland—increased his media visibility, Paisley still seemed too much of a throwback ever to be taken seriously. Most Protestants, even if they felt he had a point, were embarrassed by his antics, notably his protests against leading visiting clergy. And a cartoon of the time, of Paisley skulking behind a pillar in the Vatican, scrawling the legendary Belfast graffito, 'No Pope Here' seemed to sum up a consensus that he was, by and large, a less than serious phenomenon. Certainly, few in the middle Sixties seriously imagined that his mixture of seventeenth century religious intolerance and nineteenth century loyalism could so divide Protestant opinion that he could, within six years, cause the removal of three Unionist leaders and the wreckage of that Unionist unity on which Northern Ireland's constitutional permanence depended. Even if a proportion of Protestants could be affected by his oratory, it seemed reasonable to assume that they would appreciate where their own best interests lay.

Paisley's activities combined with the efforts of such as the McCluskeys to attract attention to Northern Ireland, causing it to be dubbed 'John Bull's political slum' by the *Sunday Times*. This augured the end of the era of Westminster's convention of 'non-interference in the internal affairs of Northern Ireland', although it would be another three years before London would be forced to act directly. At the time, the media tended to present Terence O'Neill as a brave, lone, enlightened figure trying to lead Unionism into the twentieth century, in spite of Paisleyism. This focus on O'Neill was extremely counter-productive. His English upper-crust manner grated more on middle-class Unionists, especially his political colleagues, than it ever did on Catholics, who vaguely expected top Unionists to sound English. His Cabinet members and others of close rank naturally resented the implication that they were all incurable backwoodsmen while O'Neill was the only 'white man' around. And the landed aristocracy, from whom O'Neill sprang, made little effort to conceal their contempt for the recently rich Unionist bourgeoisie, referring in particular to the brightest of the latter, Brian Faulkner, as 'the shirtmaker'. O'Neill sealed this resentment by inviting Lemass to Stormont without even consulting his Cabinet—they were not to be trusted with statesman-ship. It was inevitable that some of them would be only too glad to play the Paisleyite card to up-end him: and Paisley and his advisers had the cunning to widen this division.

Just as there were many Paisleyites who felt that there *must not* be change, so there were many Catholics who felt that there *would not* be change. The scepticism of the latter seemed to be confirmed when O'Neill, after three years of gesture politics, defended a decision to locate near Coleraine a new university for Northern Ireland, rather than in the obvious site, the city of Derry. The decision, in 1966, produced the first big, concerted wave of Catholic protest, well in advance of the Civil Rights movement. This protest also blooded a young schoolmaster, John Hume, now a Member of the European Parliament, and leader of the Social Democratic and Labour Party (SDLP), representing most of Northern Ireland's Catholics.

1966 also saw my own involvement in politics other than among students. I was chairman of a group of 'National Democrats', a ginger group associated with, but not quite part of, the National Democratic Party (NDP). This party had been formed with the purpose of providing a conventional structure through which the 'new politics' of research and argument, rather than slogan and aspiration, would approach the ballot-box. Its leaders included erstwhile student leader John Duffy, and Gerry Quigley, leader of Ireland's largest and mainly Catholic teachers' union. The first clear focus for its efforts was the West Belfast seat in the March 1966 General Election, target for a number of emerging politicians, among them Gerry Fitt, the colourful Stormont politician then representing the Docks area.

The NDP saw Gerry Fitt as merely a more able version of the one-man bands whom minority politics tended to throw up. He had used the labels 'Irish Labour', 'Dock Irish Labour', and 'Republican Labour', but it was obvious that these meant 'Gerry Fitt Labour'. Far from trying to recruit him, the National Democrats saw his brilliant lonerism as a block to the development of organised Catholic minority politics in Belfast, of a kind that might also attract what was usually called 'moderate Protestant opinion'.

The NDP's candidate, Joseph Lavery, was by far the earliest into the ring, and our student group went canvassing in the Beechmount area of West Belfast. The political innocents of a few years earlier were seasoned canvassers of student votes, and, as we joked at the time, 'people are easier to canvass than students': they gave their answers without the prolonged smart-chat of student politics. At house after house, we got the same answer: Mr. Lavery was a good man, but he'd lose to the sitting Unionist; the only man who could win was Gerry Fitt if he stood, and he'd lose if Lavery stayed in. West Belfast has a strong betting tradition in both its Catholic and Protestant ghettos, on cards, dogs, horses, boxers—and politicians: and it was crystal clear when our canvassing group compared notes before returning to party headquarters, that the smart money would be on Gerry Fitt if he got a clear run at the sitting Unionist.

We came in from the cold night and were offered tea in the smoke-filled room. The party leaders had been discussing a statement for release to the papers. The 'young canvassers' were called on to report. The conclusion of my report was profoundly unpopular: we should pull out in favour of Gerry Fitt, urge him to stand, support him, and be part of the resultant victory.

There followed a brief, shocked silence. Then Gerry Quigley seized on my remark that "the name of the game in elections is winning", to give us an impassioned lecture on the seriousness of the NDP's purpose, and that it was "no game".

It was clear that he was widely supported in the smoke-filled room, and the meeting moved uneasily back to considering the statement in favour of Lavery's candidacy. We left.

Some weeks later, after public exchanges in the media between supporters of Fitt and of the NDP, the NDP retired from the contest, which Gerry Fitt went on to win. He held the seat, arguably one of the hottest in Europe, until 1983, when he lost it to Gerry Adams of Provisional Sinn Fein. (Shortly after this, Gerry Fitt became Lord Fitt of Bell's Hill, thus fulfilling my jocose prediction to him ten years earlier in the Stormont bar—when he appeared to be impatient to get back to the realpolitik of Westminster—that he would end up as 'Lord Fitt of Dock'. His elevation has not been universally popular in

Northern Ireland, perhaps least so in West Belfast: this is partly due to local resentment of the extravagant descriptions of him in Fleet Street and Westminster as the bravest politician in Ireland; partly to local resentment of anything English; and partly to some native meanness of mind. Gerry Fitt, over a quarter of a century of service to constituents, earned some recognition and reward, which Ireland was not able or willing to give him; and his wife, Anne, always a Lady, had equally earned recognition for her unsung, unpaid, and always willing constituency work for the thousands who sought the Fitts' help regardless of political differences. I share some of the local contempt for the Fleet Street 'puff-job' on Lord Fitt, as well as for some of Gerry's own Anglophilic postures of recent years: but when the scales are weighed for his generation's politicians, he will emerge as having made a considerable contribution both to 'politics' and even more so to people.)

Before this excursion into electoral politics in 1966, I had already been approached by some senior members of the NDP, and asked to stand for its chairmanship, a flattering response, no doubt, to my unusual poll success in the university. But apart from realising that a student blow-in, however presentable a spokesman, would be deeply resented by a wide section of those who had worked to develop the party, I was far from being convinced that even forming the NDP was a bright idea. On the one hand, John Duffy's challenging words continued to echo, and I appreciated that if there was a problem in the political sewers, whoever tried to correct it was going to smell somewhat. I think I would have been prepared to stomach the smell of party political compromise at that time. But my deeper unease was the sense that the very existence of the NDP merely confirmed the Catholic minority as a permanent minority, however attractively organised. The same dilemma would emerge when men for whom I had a high regard, John Hume and Austin Currie, would later move to form the Social Democratic and Labour Party (SDLP) with Gerry Fitt as leader.

In 1966, I also had personal reasons for avoiding the pull into party politics. I still had to finish my degree, and I wanted to complete the de-sectarianising process among students. To this end, I was considering running for President of the Students' Representative Council, but beginning to dither as my period as an undergraduate came to an end. Not only was I about to get a poor degree, but I was becoming unhappy with the results of all our politicking. Younger students with no idea of how much sensitive work had gone into the 'quiet revolution', espoused an unpleasant, if fashionable, militancy. 'Nationalism with a small "n"' was becoming mere 'anti-Unionism', heavily laced with the rhetoric of paperback Marxism. The formation of a small university group of Paisleyites signalled an inevitable reaction, should those who saw themselves as my supporters or successors stray beyond the carefully developed consensus for a decent equality, which was our aim.

Socially, some of my friends were moving away from the early Beatles exuberance into drugs and pseudo-mysticism, just as some seemed to feel that my political activities were distancing us. The doctorate which I was being encouraged to do by both Dr. Crowley and Dr. Cahal Daly (now the Roman Catholic bishop in Belfast, and widely noted for theological and philosophical scholarship, ecumenism and opposition to violence) was quite an attractive proposition after such a long period of running around smoky, boozy meetings, canvassing, planning, and speaking. I began to appreciate how easily in practice, politicians can lose touch with their original ideals, and to realise that I had lost something of the joy in pursuit of knowledge.

I had disappointed my parents who saw little point in my political capers if it led to general failure on my part. And, for good measure, a girl who captivated me even from a distance, had repulsed my suggestion of a barbecue date with a blunt, "Look, Ciaran, leave it, my mother is dying of cancer." (This formidable refusal was not the end of the matter; Marianne McVeigh and I were married two years later, and we're still here, after sixteen years, with seven children.)

But in the summer of 1966, my life was at a crossroads, having traded an academic career for political activity which, despite its 'success', involved so many stupid wrangles and manoeuvres, with both fellow students and 'grown-up' politicians.

I took myself off to England to package peas for money and a fairly wild round of student summer parties; and returned home to run slap into the old Stormont bigotry. I had applied for a post-graduate scholarship, had been refused, appealed, and was summoned to Dundonald to the Ministry of Education headquarters. There, two of the most senior civil servants, one of whom I would later meet in quite different circumstances, interrogated me on my 'politics', and in particular, on my prominent association with the New Ireland Society.

I was stunned by this, and not a little intimidated, for they were fairly formidable, and held my immediate future in their hands. But when they virtually asked me for an assurance that I would not involve myself in student politics if I were to get a scholarship, I refused, and said that I would have to follow my conscience, which could not be bought by a scholarship. I felt hurt and angry, when I emerged from their imposing sanctum into the everyday traffic of

Belfast. I felt degraded rather than flattered by this attention, for I had been consistently vigorous in opposing such blanket views as that all Unionism, and therefore all Unionists, were corrupt: yet it seemed as if an extensive political intelligence network was operating and interfering even in such peripheral matters as student politics!

Not surprisingly, I decided firmly to run for President of the Students' Council. I won by a handful of votes: the 'impossible' of a few years earlier had been accomplished by the 'group of like-minded people' which included O'Neillite Unionist, Labour, Liberal, and Nationalist supporters, as well as a core uncommitted to any party or ideology.

It was deeply satisfying to prove that something which the laws of sectarianism deemed impossible, could be done. But I was restrained from sharing the sense of triumph which erupted among some who had supported me, especially among the newcomers. Some of the latter, apart from being ignorant of the long effort that had been made, declaimed themselves as 'socialists' and berated me for having 'no politics' beyond an 'obscurantist pacifism'. They were actually at one with my adversaries in seeing me primarily as a Machiavellian political mechanic and would seek me out more for discussion of tactics than of issues—they had all the answers for the latter. Rather than relishing the position towards which I had been moving for so long, I began to be nauseated at the prospect of being stuck with student politicking as a full-time official for a whole year.

In those days of little visible violence, I did not realise that my nonviolent convictions were a world away from the tactic-based opposition to violence of not a few of my friends. I could see the value of both individual and co-operative enterprise, and appreciated the welfare state's aim of providing a decent minimum in health, education and shelter. I could not for the life of me see how any intelligent person could be exclusively 'socialist' or 'capitalist', and found myself being described as 'right-wing' on some issues and 'left-wing' on others, without ever understanding how this instant spectrum-labelling process was operated.

In cultural terms, I regarded both Unionism and Nationalism as much the same thing, anachronisms in an age of interdependence, when with greater liberation from the restrictive aspects of tribalism, the diverse arts of all might be appreciated. I was a 'republican' only in the universal sense of regarding every citizen as equal in rights, and a democrat in the same sense, seeing democracy as *demos-kratis*— the strength of all the people. So I was not Unionist, nor Nationalist, nor Republican, nor Loyalist, nor Liberal, nor Socialist, nor Capitalist, nor Communist, nor Trotskyite; nor was I noticeably orthodox either—so I was up to my eyes in student and other politics, but did not belong in any group, not even in 'McKeown's mafia'!

My disenchantment seemed to match the decline in the liberating impulses of the early Sixties. In the United States, Lyndon Johnson was out of his time and out of his depth with the fabricated war in Vietnam. In Britain, Harold Wilson was proving to be little more than a political acrobat, balancing the lobbies and going nowhere in particular with a lot of glib clichés. In France, the towering figure of De Gaulle was becoming vulnerable. Germany's economic miracle was not producing happiness as promised. In Northern Ireland, O'Neill was still secure, but had yet to try anything other than gesture politics, and had stepped backwards with the ill-fated second university decision.

It was a relief to become involved once more in public politics, early in 1967, this time without any trace of a party tag. The NDP were extending their operation in Belfast, where some had rationalised their humiliation at the hands of Gerry Fitt by allowing that Fitt would be a useful mouthpiece at Westminster, while they would control the ground politics in the city. It became clear months before the local government elections that Gerry Fitt's Republican Labour and the NDP would cut each other's throats, when, in the shorthand of the day, donkeys with Union Jacks on their backs would be returned en masse for the Unionist Party.

This issue was important. Local government was a much greater source of Catholic grievance than central government, because injustice in the allocation of houses and municipal jobs were carried out at that level, whereas central government had to conform to approximation or even parity with Westminster legislation. Local government elections still had property-qualified voting rights, which naturally favoured the Unionists; and to put their advantage beyond reach, the Unionists had 'gerrymandered' the boundaries—that is, the boundaries were so drawn as to give relatively more seats to quite heavily populated Catholic/Nationalist areas.

It therefore made plain political sense not to increase the Unionist advantage in Belfast's City Hall by dividing and negating the minority vote. So I intervened to set up a pact between Gerry Fitt's organisation and the NDP. I met Gerry Fitt first, along with Senator Paddy Wilson, his most faithful lieutenant.

(Paddy, with whom I became very friendly, was murdered in 1973, his body hacked by more than fifty stab wounds in one of the more gruesome sectarian murders of that year. I later still became involved with associates of the loyalist terror gang responsible for his death: it is a curiously Northern Irish twist that I was indirectly helping one of their number to get a fresh start, after a jail term, in the later Seventies, when he was picked up for Paddy's murder, and is now, regrettably, serving a life sentence. I know that some of Paddy's friends will baulk at the word 'regrettably': yet I think that Paddy would not have, for he was a most forgiving man. I felt closer to him on the subject of nonviolence than to any other politician, with the possible exception of Paddy O'Hanlon, another prominent SDLP politician. The police had been warning leading Catholic politicians that they were targets for sectarian assassins, and most, including Gerry Fitt, had acquired licensed guns for their protection. Two nights before he was murdered, Paddy and I discussed this personal gun issue, in McGlade's Bar, a downtown pub frequented by journalists and politicians, and from which Paddy went on his last journey alive forty-eight hours later. We were both agreed that we would not have a personal weapon, on principle: we were of one mind that the peace and justice which we sought had to be obtained politically and nonviolently, or 'the game wasn't worth the candle'.)

In 1967, Paddy was an obvious candidate and certain winner on Gerry Fitt's Republican Labour ticket to the City Hall. Yet when I outlined the possible deal with the NDP, whereby each group would agree to keep out of certain constituencies, Paddy was immediately ready to sacrifice his spot.

Gerry, despite his contempt for the ponderous political ability of the NDP—a contempt he expressed with hilarious irreverence—was open to the idea. He knew that the NDP leaders were aware of his ridicule the length and breadth of West and much of North Belfast: one of Gerry's political weapons has always been the brutally humorous caricature of his opponents. He wanted to be sure that they would respond genuinely to such a proposal before going any further. Although he pictured them sitting around a big table, saying to each other, "Think of a big word to impress the people in the Pound Loney—no, that's not big enough, give us a longer one!", he was politician enough never to underestimate the opposition, and was forever wary of traps, even from the most unlikely source. Paddy Wilson, who would have laid down his life for Gerry Fitt, would have done so in the conscious knowledge that Gerry would walk over him for a winning vote: it was, curiously, this winner quality in Gerry that the gentle Paddy respected most in the formidable one-man political machine.

The NDP were similarly wary when I approached them. But it was agreed that we should meet in the South Antrim home of that most genial man, and NDP stalwart, Paddy Rowan. The Rowans laid on hospitality fit for the King of West Belfast, and Gerry responded with a performance that would have aroused the envy of the most celebrated court jester. He kept the company in stitches with anecdote after anecdote on how his lone presence had discomfited the safely ensconced Unionists at Westminster.

Something of the pre-violence flavour of the politics of the time may be gauged from one such story. Gerry, being a full-time politician, was immediately exasperated at Westminster by the comparative idleness of the part-time Unionists, who nevertheless had access and influence, and looked down their noses at him. Gerry did not need a course in political science to know that when nothing else is available, use satire—it came naturally. One of the influentially connected Unionists was Sir Knox Cunningham. Like his fellows, Sir Knox was quite the Tory chap in London, but at home, he protected his already rock-safe seat by turning out with the Orangemen to march in full regalia in the July 12 procession. In 1966, a large photograph of the domestic Sir Knox, beating a big drum for the delight of the faithful, appeared in a Belfast newspaper.

Like a prankish schoolboy, Gerry Fitt had dozens of copies made of this photograph, which he substituted for menu cards in the Members Dining Rooms and Bars at Westminster, pinned on noticeboards and even stuck up in the toilets, taking care to distribute a few among the lobby correspondents. Gerry's description of the Unionists running about Westminster in a panic trying to remove this threat to their image of imperial respectability in the Mother of Parliaments, conjured up a most merry pantomime. Long before we got down to discussing the local government deal, his humour had created a camaraderie of common cause. The basis of the deal was quickly enough agreed, and was then to be subjected to approval by Gerry's party (which the NDP scarcely believed existed) and the NDP's party Executive.

Gerry's machine was actually more of a 'party', as it turned out, than the NDP Executive. Both groups met separately a few nights after the initial meeting. Marianne and I attended Gerry Fitt's meeting with his faithful workers and it was fascinating to hear the realpolitik among these genuine ward politicians, who were prepared to sacrifice a great deal of time, money and effort to get their men in, had a punter's sense of who the winners and losers might be, and were far more wary of the ambitious than of the cerebral among the NDP. They were also a little dubious, lest Gerry's ringcraft be compromised by too close an association with 'a bunch of green teachers', as they characterised the NDP. Moreover, these men had no pretensions about appealing to 'moderate Protestant opinion'—but they were genuinely concerned about the ordinary Catholic and Protestant working-class people, and felt that Gerry as a 'socialist' would do more for the Protestants than their own Unionist representatives.

Gerry Fitt in this company was impressive, less egotistical, more persuasive than was his usual overwhelming style, taking time to hear and argue the angles raised. They were close to giving their backing when a namesake of mine, a teacher who was also a part-time journalist, came into the meeting, and announced that the NDP were having difficulty: he explained that the NDP's lone Stormont MP, John Brennan, who was also their lone symbol of working-class identification, was holding out against having one of Gerry's men stand in a ward in his constituency. The meeting broke up with the understanding that all bets were off if Brennan was still holding back the next day.

The pact collapsed. Gerry's crowd won hands down, in comparison to the NDP, with the Unionists winning more seats than they should have. Among those returned to the City Hall were Paddy Wilson, and also Paddy Kennedy, who went on to win John Brennan's seat after all. Three short, briefly hopeful, finally violent years later, Kennedy was to the fore in demanding the resignation of the Southern Taoiseach, Jack Lynch, after the latter had sacked two of his Ministers, Charles Haughey and Neil Blaney, on suspicion of involvement in gun-running.

The NDP had been given another lesson about the realities of street-to-street, ballot-box politics, and the importance of 'personality' in presenting policy and representing people. But Gerry Fitt had also learned, and made friends in a new and larger constituency: this would later be important in the formation of the SDLP, which subsumed both Republican Labour and the NDP, in 1970.

Whether the emergence of a strongly organised and united minority politic in 1967 would have held back 'the Troubles' by both bulwarking O'Neill and extracting reforms at a decent pace from him, is a recurring speculation of dubious value.

Student politics brought me into contact with both governmental and ecclesiastical politics in that year. The first incident arose out of a Westminster proposal in the winter of 1966-7. The Wilson government surprised its socialist base in the universities by suggesting a much higher differential fee for overseas students. Except in cases of real hardship, overseas students were to pay the 'economic' fee of about £250 per year, instead of the £70 for everybody else. The targets for this move were obviously those scions of African, Asian and Indian families who could drive around in sports cars while enjoying a cheap and thoroughly British education. But the move suggested possible discrimination against poor Third World students struggling to prepare themselves for vital work in their homelands, an image which gave the fashionable militancy a perfect focus for expression, and a 'nationwide student strike' was called for.

My first reaction when called upon to organise a 'student strike' was incredulity. I mean, what is a 'student strike'?

We quickly established that while some of the overseas students were well off, a few even very rich indeed, most were in modest circumstances, and some had difficulty in surviving. There were some on scholarships, on an understanding that they would return to poorer circumstances; not all seemed determined to fulfil this duty, once qualified. The evidence was enough to persuade us that we should oppose the differential fee system, and the research also had the side-effect of increasing mutual awareness of the overseas group, which helped alleviate the loneliness some felt, as well as bringing some cultural diversity to a parochial university.

But rather than stomach the embarrassment of a 'student strike', I proposed a 'Day of Voluntary Labour' in the community, to draw attention to the issue. The more militant dismissed this sourly as a typical McKeown stunt, and a refusal to 'face up to the issues'. But it proved very popular with both students and public: it had Rag Day energy without the excesses, as students visited hospitals to play music, decorated in homes of pensioners recommended by the welfare agencies, and painted in institutional homes, within the limits of a day's teamwork, which some later extended. The thousands who took part were generally a friendly and enlivening presence wherever they went, explaining without any great propaganda intensity that they were also opposing the differential fees rise.

The local media were flooded with 'good news' stories. We evoked a benign response from the Stormont Minister of Education, Capt. W. E. Long, and a public invitation to discuss the issue with him at his Ministerial office. Goodwill was created at a time when 'student' was becoming a dirty word associated with drugs, higher taxes and everything that might be going wrong with the world. After our discussion with the Minister, he announced that whatever Westminster might do, he had decided unilaterally against imposing the differential in Northern Ireland. The point had been won, while in Britain they were still trying to work out whether the patchy 'strike' had been the first blow of a new militancy—or an embarrassing farce.

Later in 1967, the internal rumblings in the O'Neill Cabinet made a bizarre manifestation when the youngish, ambitious Home Affairs Minister, William Craig, announced the banning of 'Republican

Clubs'. This invocation of the hated Special Powers Act, an Act publicly envied by the South African premier, Henrik Verwoerd, came slap in the middle of the O'Neill rhetoric of a new deal for Catholics. A politic other than Unionist versus Republican was obviously afoot, for the latter's militancy was not only dormant but disarmed. (The IRA had reportedly sold its arms to the Free Wales Army which had promptly lost them to the British Special Branch.)

The general assumption was that Craig was trying to ride the Paisleyite undercurrent in Unionist politics, to discredit O'Neill and those policies seen by Paisley as 'appeasement of Ulster's enemies', that is, of those Ulster citizens who were Catholics/Nationalists.

Among students, the banning was received with light-hearted incredulity. It was widely known among ordinary people that there was no 'IRA scare' in the offing, a fact borne out by the dry, factual description of the network of Republican Clubs by W. D. Flackes, the BBC's Northern Ireland political correspondent. Billy Flackes never acquired the suave, pseudo-authoritative manner of much less informed broadcasters, but there can be no-one else who had such detailed knowledge of everybody and everything that had the remotest political relevance in Northern Ireland at that time: and when he depicted the ramshackle and largely social nature of the then 'Republican Clubs', the joke was public. In any normal society, that would have been the end of the matter.

But this was Northern Ireland.

With infectious hilarity, a bunch of students, some of them apolitical, some even from Unionist backgrounds, formed 'The Republican Club of the Queen's University of Belfast', and applied for the formal recognition which would entitle them to use the university's name. A few were certainly serious about the affair; but the general feeling was that Craig was involved in some obscure and irrelevant internal politic which was fair game for satire. The issue put me in the odd position as a 'political' Catholic President of a Council which was approached to promulgate the club's recognition.

Far from ignoring the move, Craig got up within the privilege of Stormont and named a number of students as members of a new republican and socialist conspiracy. This naming of names absolutely thrilled those named, and given our knowledge then, to say nothing of the subsequent career of some of those named, emphasised the farcical nature of the affair. But I found, when I went to check the parliamentary record, that farce had become absurdity: for Craig's order made it illegal for any club or association, however lawful or constitutional in character, to call itself 'republican'. He was trying to ban the very word republican.

Here was a rock-solid government, under no external threat, moving to close all possible gaps in an all-out extermination of a non-existent conspiracy; and in doing so, was prepared to invoke the Special Powers Act, and make an Order which broke the bonds of the English language. If I presided over the recognition of the club, I would be breaking the law of the land! The joke suddenly began to turn nasty when Ed Curran, Chairman of the Tory Club, announced his opposition to recognition of the new club. If a heated debate were to develop, much of what we had been trying to do would be wrecked; if I pushed ahead with the perfectly reasonable request for recognition, I would be seen as 'subversive', and if I did not, I would be accepting the Order's absurdity.

I decided that Bill Craig could not make such an absurd Order, and based my decision on the attempt to ban the legitimate use of the word 'republican', hoping at the same time that this approach would dissolve any confrontation on the issue.

But Ed Curran would have none of this: and it is a measure both of how quiet the times were, and of how strange a place is Northern Ireland, that our student conflict over the matter justified a television confrontation between the two of us on the BBC's teatime current affairs programme. In the light of my present experience, I might have avoided any TV debate on it; but in those innocent days, we imagined that a well-delivered argument on the Box would win the day. It has taken me a long time to realise that the average viewer sees and hears what he or she wants to see or hear, and that one's appearance counts as much, if not more than, one's integrity. All my rational attention to the wording of the Order, and to Bill Craig's powerlessness to alter the Queen's English, could not prevent one section of the population from seeing me as 'Republican'; and of course, Ed was naturally happy enough to be seen as a Unionist. I began to be aware of this from the reaction of some of the university stewarding and catering staff, a stiffening in their friendliness that suggested that if a government minister said it, he must know what he was talking about—and 'what is a decent fellow like you doing defending the Republicans?'

As worrying as Ed Curran's espousal of the Craig line was the increasingly petulant militancy in support of the club: Craig's Order was in real danger of creating militant republicanism within the university!

I approached the University Vice-Chancellor, Dr. Arthur Vick, with whom I had always had a civilised relationship, and suggested to him that the matter be considered by the University's lawyers, both in the Faculty and in the Legal Advisory Committee. I also pointed out the potentially divisive nature of the Minister's Order, and asked if the University might be able to bring some influence to bear on the matter. It was understood between us that the Students Representative Council would proceed with recognition, which would then go automatically to the Academic Council for ratification or otherwise— at which point, the issue would disappear into the hands of lawyers. I was hoping that the lawyers would consider the issues involved at the greatest possible length.

I then took the unusual step of leaving the President's chair to propose the club's recognition, arguing that abstract issues of academic freedom were involved, as well as immediate concern for the improved climate within student politics, which could be damaged by any old-fashioned polemics on the issue. The recognition was passed overwhelmingly, and the issue did indeed disappear into the University for months.

Then, in late November, shortly after I had left office, and while I was in the United States representing British and Irish students in a 'Conference on the Atlantic Community' at Georgetown University, Washington, the University announced that it could not ratify the club's recognition. Its reason was that as a public body, in receipt of government funds, it could not act in a manner contrary to a Government Order. A sour 'I told you so' anger roused the militants, who organised a protest march on Craig's Belfast home. I felt that this was playing into his hands, but I was three thousand miles away and preoccupied with meeting such as the late Senator Robert Kennedy. Had I been at home, I think the University authorities and lawyers would have been the target for my enquiries: I would have liked to hear them justify publicly, on grounds other than the extensive bribe of public funding, the decision to support such an absurd Order.

Militant republicanism did indeed take root thereafter in the university, and eventually the dynamics of the foregoing years were badly damaged.

Between these two points in the Craig affair, I had an indirect conflict with the Roman Catholic bishop in Belfast, Dr. William Philbin, on the issue of support for voluntary schools, which in Northern Ireland terms, means mainly the Catholic schools. This issue of separate schooling is a hardy perennial among Northern Ireland's multiple problems. A fair proportion of Catholics would favour school integration, but even more strongly oppose the use of the issue by Unionists as the scapegoat for our divisions.

I knew from experience that many of the 'progressives' on the 'Nationalist with a small "n"' side, while favouring integration in the abstract, were not going to raise the issue, not only to avoid trouble with Church authorities, but on the much more secular grounds that

...ot an easy issue: the division of children from an early age is clearly a damaging experience; yet parents also have the conscientious right and duty to determine their children's education. Nor is it any solution to propose a 'value-free' education, to use a phrase of the time, or to settle for the lowest common denominator of a totally secular education. While I am personally in favour of integration, I think it has to be achieved with full consideration of private rights, and of the actual quality of the education proposed: but above all, my feeling was that such an issue of conscience, involving children, should be discussed, among the Christians involved, in tones worthy of the highest Christian standards of charity.

The issue intruded jaggedly when Terence O'Neill's government finally made a solid offer to increase financial support for Catholic schools, which had hitherto received a 65 per cent grant towards both current and capital expenditure. Under the new deal, Catholic schools would receive 100 per cent support for current expenditure and 80 per cent for capital expenditure—provided that the six-person school boards included two public representatives to provide for public accountability. This amounted to substantially increased support and continuing majority control for the Church.

It was attacked immediately by Dr. Philbin as a sectarian plot to take over the Catholic schools.

There was a heated debate on the matter at Queen's. I observed, without mentioning names, that it was rather unChristian to characterise an offer as a plot, before there had been time to consider it fully. The 'student leader calls Bishop unChristian' storyline caused embarrassment to my sister, a Dominican nun teaching in a Convent high school next door to the Bishop's residence.

My father, headmaster of the then largest Catholic secondary school in Belfast, did not comment to me one way or the other on the matter. (When I got in a tangle with the Church over an article I had written on much the same issue, eight years later, and was ordered out of my father's school on prizegiving night by a leading cleric, Canon Pádraig Murphy, who said that I was 'persona non grata in any Catholic institution', my father sought an apology from the Bishop for the cleric's rudeness, and on being rebuffed, after further suggestions that he should restrain my 'anti-Catholic' views, he resigned after forty years' faithful service to Catholic education.)

Some weeks after the outburst by Dr. Philbin, the Catholic bishops met under the leadership of the quiet and thoughtful Cardinal

Conway, and accepted the O'Neill government's offer. (Sixteen years later, Dr. Philbin's successor, Dr. Cahal Daly, praised the efforts and support of the old Unionist administration, in relation to Catholic schools and hospitals. It is sixteen years late, with a war in between, but it is genuine, and we may once more hope that generosity of tone might begin to characterise the dialogue of opinion-shapers on this issue.)

My term of office as student president over, I enrolled to begin a doctoral thesis on 'leadership and values'. But enrolling was about as far as it went. Almost immediately, I flew to the United States to represent British and Irish students at that Washington conference, and on a subsequent three-week tour of the US. My first serious acquaintance with the United States was with the FBI. I had travelled out two days early to visit my prospective brother-in-law, Tony McVeigh, in Philadelphia. I thoroughly enjoyed the side-trip, and duly arrived at the Key Motel in Washington in time for the conference—to find large gentlemen expressing loud relief at my arrival, followed by angry queries, "Where in hell have you been, another hour and we'd have been dragging the East River in New York, you checked through immigration two days ago?"

These protective fellows were not ordinary cops, and they explained to me very heavily that I was in the care of the US. government during my stay, and that I should therefore understand that nothing was to happen to me, and that I must not wander off on my own. I'm afraid I disobeyed them somewhat, and later wandered around Harlem on my own, to the consternation of the tour guides. It was by no means the last time in this pacifist's life that I have felt obliged to slip away from the armed custody of foreign hosts.

The FBI took its protection racket seriously: a few weeks later, similar gentlemen visited my brother-in-law's apartment building in Philadelphia to inquire if a bearded Irishman had been seen thereabouts a few weeks earlier.

The conference itself was no more and no less pointless than such affairs generally are, the real benefit being in the private meetings with American students, professors and government officials. The Vietnam war was the big issue of the time, and a State Department official told us candidly, "The United States is in Vietnam to protect her own interests": this was the coolest, most bald explanation we got for the American involvement. American students were in a conscientious swither over the war, feeling guilty, but not wishing to appear unpatriotic while fellow Americans were in the front line. The presence of ten European student leaders was a novel opportunity to clarify their views. The Europeans (from France, Spain, Germany, Holland, Norway, plus myself) were opposed to the war, apart from the two Germans, who were surprisingly unrepresentative of German student opinion at that period. I found myself as the neutral, native-speaking English spokesman of the group, balancing the self-righteous expressions by the Europeans about American imperialism in Asia with reminders of the long history of European imperialism, and the spread of the European war disease throughout the world. Paddy the Irishman was therefore quite popular, except perhaps with the Germans.

These two Germans, one of whom had been leader of the Munich Conservative Students Association, were real misfits among us, and their disposition caused quite a scene when we met Senator Robert Kennedy.

Bobby Kennedy was in the middle of his agitated Hamlet phase. The Senator for New York was even bigger in charismatic attraction than his murdered brother, and electrifyingly so to the young. We met him in mid-November, before Eugene McCarthy won the New Hampshire primary election—a victory which began the slide in Lyndon Johnson's prospects for another term, precipitated Kennedy's fatal entry into the race, and ultimately ensured the return of Richard Nixon.

Bobby Kennedy was markedly different in manner from any of the politicians and officials we had met. My first two impressions of him were of shyness and physical dynamism. For all the 'ah, you're ah welcome ah' kind of diffidence, he vibrated the energy that the American power machine must demand. Quite small, shirt-sleeved, tie-loosened, he gave the impression at forty-one years of age against our average early twenties, that he could have come round the table of his surprisingly small office and scattered the ten of us. I had the sense that it would be the most exhilarating adventure to run with him, but that that very attribute must invite intense and jealous hatred: he was the kind of man who would, sooner or later, have unconsciously invited his own assassination.

Almost immediately, the legendary ruthlessness came powering through the shyness, when the Germans opened the questions. The first began: "West Germany is now the third most powerful industrial nation in the world, surely she has the right to have a nuclear weapon of her own?"

Kennedy: "Well, I'm opposed to the spread of the atom, and besides, I think that would be bad for Germany's diplomatic relations with her neighbours, especially the Soviet Union." This reply was given in a dangerously quiet tone, a hint of menace in every rasped word, and I was gathering myself to intervene with a less abrasive query, when the German returned to the attack:

"But she is the third most powerful industrial nation in the world, surely she has the *right* to have a nuclear weapon of her own?"

Kennedy was chilling: "Well, as I said, I'm opposed to the spread of the atom, and I think it would be bad for Germany's relations with her neighbours, especially the Soviet Union: and besides, I think that's the price you've got to pay for what you've done to humanity!"—this last burst with a side glance at a large, old-fashioned representation of eldest brother Joe, in pilot's gear, on an office wall.

I was stunned speechless by Kennedy's bluntness, and by the simplemindedness of the implication of Germany's sole guilt in the 'great' European-based world wars. Again, before I could divert the conversation, the second German came in over the top: "The United States says she is pledged to the freedom of Berlin, yet in 1962 when the Russians build this wall, the Americans do nothing about this wall—why is this so?"

Kennedy: "What did Willy Brandt, Mayor of Berlin, say at the time?"

"But you are pledged to the freedom of Berlin, yet when the Russians build this wall, you do nothing!"

Kennedy: "What did the Bonn Government say at the time?"

"And President Kennedy, he comes to Berlin, and he says, 'Ich bin ein Berliner', yet he does nothing about this wall?"

Kennedy: "At the time, Willy Brandt said, 'Do nothing'; at the time, the Bonn Government said, 'Do nothing'. Get your facts straight!"

We had been hoping for about ten minutes with Kennedy, and already this unpleasant exchange had bitten deeply into our time: so I cut in and said, "Senator, I hear you are planning to come to Ireland in the spring," at which Kennedy flashed the famous toothy grin.

"Ah, you're Irish?"

"Ah, you guessed. Every time the Kennedys come to Ireland, they come to the South, President Kennedy, Jacqueline, your mother, your brother, but never to the North, and there are many people in Northern Ireland who responded to the Kennedy inspiration, and I think we could assure you of a big welcome."

Kennedy: "Do you think that might damage North-South relations?"

I remember the two of us smiling as that question hung in the air for a moment, for I was quite surprised that he would immediately ask that; when I answered, "I think that would be hard to do," he laughed at the in-Irish ambivalence, and then said that he would try to come.

Cuba was discussed and Kennedy was notably gentle on this topic. Then, when it was clear that our time limit had gone by the board, I asked him if he did not consider it his moral duty to run for President, since it was clear that President Johnson was incapable of ending either the Vietnam war, or the deeper East-West conflict, and since there was no-one with sufficient credibility on the Republican horizon?

For the only time in the thirty-five minutes that we spent in that office, Bobby Kennedy agonised out loud with a series of 'ahs' and 'ers' for over thirty seconds before saying, "I think you'll have to accept that I know what you're saying, and I know what you're asking, but at this time it would look like Bobby Kennedy against Johnson, and that would be bad for the party and bad for the country, but I know what you are saying and I think you'll have to accept at the present time that it would look like Bobby Kennedy attacking Johnson." This tortuous reply did not conceal contempt in the 'Johnson' references. One of the others then asked if he might run in 1972, and again the atmosphere in the room changed when he replied:

"I can't tell you where I'll be in five years' time. Five years ago, I was Attorney-General of the United States. Today I am Senator for New York. Five years is too long a time, we might not be alive then."

For all the brusque toughness, the dynamo behind the desk was tangibly mortal. We filed out and round some corridors in the Senate building to where Senator Edward Kennedy, like a large barrister, was firmly questioning a witness in a committee hearing on housing. The accent, the unmistakable Kennedy voice was there, but little of the phenomenon we had just met, came through.

I was deeply saddened by Bobby Kennedy's death six months later, a more personal feeling than that caused by President Kennedy's assassination. It was more like the sadness for a small boy whose enthusiasm took him into a great adventure from which he did not emerge. No great intellectual, impatient, as ruthless as he was compassionate, Bobby Kennedy struck me at heart as having a small boy's vulnerability and innocence. When Robert McNamara said the West had lost its most compassionate leader, and Jimmy Hoffa described him as "still playing cops and robbers", perhaps both were correct.

The rest of that trip was a useful familiarisation with urban, small town and mid-west America, then Chicago, Boston and New York: for me, a formative experience and an inkling of the size and diversity, not only of the United States, but of the whole human family.

Soon after my return home, and rather to my surprise, I moved to Dublin to work as full-time Deputy President of USI. The Southern

Minister for Education, Donogh O'Malley, had recently comm.
Southern government to free second-level education, in a remark.
piece of in-Cabinet one-upmanship. O'Malley had proclaimed his
intention as the government's intention, and such a popular initiative
could not then be squashed!

For all that the Proclamation of the Irish Republic announced that
the children of the nation would be cherished equally, the grim fact
was—and substantially remains—that only the rich or comfortably
well-off could afford to put their children through school and college.
Even secondary school was beyond the reach of most after the age of
about fifteen.

O'Malley's move was rightly celebrated as revolutionary, in its
context. But for us in Northern Ireland, where free third-level education
had been an available reality for the bright for a generation, and for
all with the minimal academic ability from 1961, the big fuss merely
emphasised how backward the South was in such areas, and how much
effort would be needed to achieve parity with the North.

So we had tended, in our renewed involvement with USI, to focus
on this, and while the Britain-funded Northern students were rather
resented at times for this insistence, their well-developed political drive
was welcomed in a sphere of student politics that still had the stale
odour of gentlemen's smoking rooms about it.

1968 was *the* year of student militancy: in May students had a
genuine role in the 'revolution' that weakened De Gaulle in France; they
were visible, vocal and brave in Dubcek's Czechoslovakia; in Germany,
the Baader-Meinhof impulse was alive. In Northern Ireland, to which
I was a weekly commuter, the determined thoughtfulness of the
foregoing years was giving way to increasingly dogmatic militancy.
In Southern Ireland, there was plenty of strident stuff about a 'thirty-
two-county socialist republic', but little corresponding willingness to
sacrifice anything to open up the educational enclaves to the masses
who were forever being liberated verbally.

My two years with USI (I went on to be elected President in 1969)
were not notably happy or productive, although my predecessor,
Howard Kinlay, and I did achieve formal recognition by the
government, made substantial by some government funds for the
union; and we saw two small moves towards increased access to third-
level education—one a bank loan scheme, the other a limited, means-
tested governmental grants scheme. With a southern General Election
in 1969, we tried to extract election-time promises on the issue, even
deciding to put up 'issue' candidates in the hope of embarrassing a
Minister into an O'Malley-type promise. There was some enthusiasm
for the idea; however, all but myself had exams to do, and could neither

stand nor canvass. We ended up with the strange spectacle of myself, a bearded student Northerner, with an uneasily suspect civil rights aura, standing in Dublin's largest working-class constituency, supported in the door-to-door canvass for free education in the South, by a bunch of Northerners who came down, exams or no exams—and who included at least one man, for whose Worshipful Grand Master relations in the Orange Order, such an exercise was like a Muslim campaigning at Jerusalem's Wailing Wall for Jewish rights.

For a while, our sheer energy and visibility caused a ripple, and it looked as if we might pick up enough of a protest or dormant republican vote to sway the last seat in a multi-seat, proportional representation contest: but in the last few days, we began to hear consistently the question, 'was it true that I was a communist?', and previously well-disposed locals backed off with strange looks. I learned a lot, but we had little effect. The irony of the 'communist' smear was that while my activity might have been regarded as radical by some, at home in Queen's I found myself struggling to restrain the wilder catch-cries and being labelled 'reactionary' or 'moderate' (i.e. 'wet') for my trouble.

The stage was being set for a disastrous phase of so-called 'nonviolent' civil rights activity, for which the necessary preparations had not been made. I had put in years of effort, had accompanied Gerry Fitt on the first 'civil rights tour' with four Westminster MPs the previous year, yet here I was, at twenty-five years of age, being regarded by sloganising twenty-year-olds, well manipulated by others of my own age, as almost an 'old fogey!'

Marianne completed her finals in June 1968, we married in September, set up home in Dublin in the first week in October, and came home to Belfast on that October 5 weekend to a city agog with the news that bloody riots had erupted in Derry at a civil rights march. Prominent Members of Parliament had been batonned, including the redoubtable Gerry Fitt (who sported his pate plaster on television for weeks afterwards), and Eddie McAteer, leader of the established Nationalists, shortly to be ousted by emerging John Hume.

It would be another year before out-and-out gun battles on the streets: but the Sixties as an era of hope was dead, though we could not accept that at first.

From
Violence into Chaos

In the world outside our little student world, the situation also seemed to be one of disintegration: Martin Luther King was shot dead in April, Bobby Kennedy in June; in May came the strange events in France which the media presented as a 'revolution', flattering the contemporary militancy, and suggesting that 'The System' was about to be destroyed, with no indication of what might follow. In August, the Russians rolled into Prague and crushed the Dubcek liberalisation process in Czechoslovakia. In October riots broke out in Derry; in November the Americans elected Richard Nixon President. Tragedy on a terrible scale loomed in Biafra and Bangladesh.

In Northern Ireland, Ian Paisley was being taken more and more seriously, and was showing a formidable talent for commanding media coverage. The would-be reformer O'Neill, under increasing pressure, began to have votes of confidence in himself passed, and thus suffered from a law of diminishing returns culminating in his resignation in April 1969. A number of explosions, attributed automatically by the media and the Unionists to the defunct IRA, were much later proved to be the work of anti-O'Neill Paisleyites; but in the short term, they had the designed effect of 'proving' that there was still an armed republican threat, which demanded repressive measures, and certainly not reform.

Civil rights agitation moved from the patient process of lobby and publicism to street militancy. Austin Currie squatted in a house to draw attention to a blatant piece of discrimination by which a nineteen-year-old single girl was given a house while a large family on a waiting list remained homeless. Mrs. McCluskey had organised housing marches. Students formed the Joint Student Action Committee for Civil Rights.

Under our noses, a process of incoherent disintegration was happening, similar to that described by Leo Tolstoy in his epic, *War and Peace*:

> In 1789 fermentation starts in Paris: it develops and spreads and finds expression in a movement of peoples from west to east. Several times this movement is directed towards the east and comes into collision with a counter-movement from the

east westwards. In the year 1812, it reaches its extreme limit —Moscow—and then, with remarkable symmetry, the counter-movement follows from east to west, attracting to it, as the original movement had done, the peoples of Middle Europe. The counter-movement reaches the departure point in the west of the first movement—Paris—and subsides.

During this period of twenty years an immense number of fields are left untilled; houses are burned; trade changes its orientation; millions grow poor, grow rich, move from place to place; and millions of Christian men professing the law of love for their neighbour murder one another.

War and Peace, from The Epilogue

The period October 1968—January 1969 was the last moment in the history of Northern Ireland when restraint might have prevailed, reform been won, and sectarian passions kept dormant. After that, there was little anyone could do until those passions had expended themselves, or proved their murderous unreason.

By the autumn of 1968, the 'fermentation' process was bubbling insistently. Things were getting ready to 'blow'. That atmosphere of irrationality must be appreciated even as the factors which any historian or constitutionalist might note are taken into account: systematic injustice had created a disposition to revolt as soon as revolt was felt to be possible; self-reinforcing prejudice would not only regard justice as appeasement, but would sense its encouragement to revolt.

Under the British Welfare State, more and more Catholics felt able to demand justice, and, in particular, the free education system had created a generation of articulate Catholics who would see themselves as nothing less than first-class citizens, and would never be treated otherwise without protest.

It is also true that the efforts of such as Dr. Conn and Mrs. McCluskey, of Gerry Fitt, and negatively by Ian Paisley, meant that the stink from Northern Ireland was reaching the nostrils of Westminster and of the London and world media.

The most significant factor in October 1968 was uncertainty: everyone knew that things could not go on as before; but what would happen, no-one could lay down precisely. This uncertainty aroused great fear among Protestants that their presumed millennium of Stormont solidity, secured by whatever the government of the day might impose under the Special Powers Act, under the protection of Westminster Statute—and the convention of Westminster blind eyes —was suddenly vulnerable: and as some of them saw it, all because of a bunch of hairy students! Many more tended to blame O'Neill for being weak or stupid, or even, as Paisley alleged, a traitor.

Many Catholics rejoiced in the uncertainty: anything was better than the certainty of second-class citizenship, especially since an actual improvement in conditions had enabled more and more to sit up and *notice* that they were second-class citizens. Most Catholics were, however, cautious enough in their expression of hope, for they knew, by reason or instinct, that change must come in a restrained and intelligent manner, or it could precipitate sectarian violence, if not outright civil war: and such disorder would provide the Unionists with both excuse and post-facto justification for repression.

The disarmed IRA, credited by O'Neill's Home Affairs Minister William Craig, and of course, by Ian Paisley, with the rise in civil rights agitation, was actually puzzled by what was going on: under the influence of a Dublin-based academic Roy Johnston, their militant tradition had emphasised the socialist impulse always inherent in Ireland's sporadic risings against imperialism, and now overlaid it somewhat clumsily with an ill-digested Marxism.

The Marxist rhetoric, besides leaving them vulnerable to alienation and even ostracisation from the overwhelmingly Roman Catholic, anti-Communist orthodoxy, came awkwardly and unconvincingly from the mouths of Belfast's working-class Republican activists. Nevertheless, they were able to establish some common cause with Protestant working-class interests, in resisting the high-rise redevelopments which would mean the destruction of the old street communities inhabited by Catholic and Protestant alike. Far more effective than any Marxist noise was the summary by the legendary Loyalist representative, the Paisleyite Johnny McQuade, who put the matter in one sentence: "When the people of Belfast say house, they mean something with a front door and a back door!"

Slum clearance was the main concern of Belfast's working class at that time, not the old Orange-Green affair, which had seemed, Paisleyism notwithstanding, to have been declining in the preceding few years. So the disarmed IRA was in the somewhat bemused position of watching civil rights agitation emerge from the very community which they had failed to excite by their physical force campaign from 1956-62—the Catholic middle class, concerned more with equality of citizenship and opportunity, than with such specific issues as the high-rise flats.

Some interpreted the uncertainty as the dawn of the long-awaited 'revolution'. One such was Michael Farrell, a prominent student speaker in the earlier years of the Sixties, who returned from a two-year post-graduate course in Strathclyde's political science department, just as the 'fermentation' was visibly bubbling. Ironically, his professor at Strathclyde was Richard Rose, author of *Governing Without Consensus*, one of the few really valuable books about Northern Ireland in particular, and about consensus to regimes in general.

Farrell, a man of considerable intelligence and presence as an orator, was then chairman of a Belfast group known as the 'Young Socialists'. Between students and other youths, their number in our debates amounted to about 70-100, so that they were constantly outvotable in meetings that were attended by as many as 800.

Farrell's speeches were often exciting: he spoke of uniting the Protestant and Catholic working class in a great struggle against the interests of capitalism and imperialism. On the vexed question of confrontation with the police, he would urge that police be regarded as 'brother workers', who should be fraternally persuaded to let us through—a whimsical image, to say the least! For a few at least among the eventual marchers, the idea was to get very close indeed to the police, and, if necessary, to provoke them into action which would then 'prove' that the police were the 'pigs' that the propaganda already asserted they were, while those who directed such 'pigs' were worse again.

Throughout this period, I argued, much more boringly, that if we marched in areas, or in a manner, which stirred the sleeping bigotry, we would cause people to takes sides at an early stage, confirm them in bigotry and violence, and possibly even let loose a sectarian civil war in which the killers and victims would be the same Protestant and Catholic working class whom we wished to unite. As far as the police were concerned, if we went right up to the lines, instead of sitting down and taking whatever might come, I suggested that that would allow the whole effort to be depicted as a derivative 'student riot'.

Farrell would dismiss my warnings of a sectarian shooting war as 'faint-hearted nonsense': the curious feature of these clashes was that, while Farrell was increasingly cast as the exciting revolutionary leader, and I as 'moderate' (a label I despised), Farrell received thunderous applause, yet my proposals received overwhelming support when it came to voting.

On three separate occasions that autumn, the Young Socialists proposed marching from Belfast to Derry, trying to echo Mao's Long March. On each occasion, it was opposed on the same grounds that it would release sectarian feeling, and that such a march should only occur when the political groundwork of canvassing support along the route had been done in advance, if that were even possible. And on each occasion, after heated debates and tumultuous applause and standing ovations for the more fiery speeches, the proposal to march was rejected by the same overwhelming vote.

I noted throughout this period that John Hume, and his then close colleague Ivan Cooper, leading the civil rights effort in Derry, were adopting a similarly tough, yet restrained approach: and John Hume was emerging rapidly as a significant figure on the landscape, much more determined and polished than the diffident schoolteacher of a few years earlier.

At one point, Farrell's Young Socialists, frustrated by the controlled pace being imposed upon the 'revolution' by the 'moderates', got up to walk out after yet another defeat. As I got up to discourage them from the walk-out, one wise friend said, "Let them go, Ciaran, they're more trouble than the Unionists!" I felt they might eventually come around to the nonviolent approach, but more pressingly, I was afraid they might engage in disastrous unilateral action. I appealed to them to stay, that we were all working for one man, one vote, and that we would abide by any majority decision, providing it did not run counter to nonviolence, and that their commitment was a vital part of the effort. They hesitated, then stayed. I will never know whether it would have been better if they had left then: all that was achieved was a matter of several weeks' delay before they did take unilateral action.

It was an exciting time, and not without its levity. I half seriously suggested at one point that we should name ourselves 'CRAIG' — 'Civil Rights Action Infiltrated Group', satirising Craig's parliamentary allegation of conspiracy the previous year, and making possible posters such as 'CRAIG demands one man, one vote' which he might have found hard to repudiate!

The name 'People's Democracy' which quickly attached to the student marchers was little more than a joke between myself and a local printer: at the end of one long meeting, which had been full of talk of 'mass democracy', five civil rights demands were agreed, which would be put on posters. The printer grabbed me at the back of the hall, and said that he couldn't get all the demands as well as 'Joint Student Action Committee for Civil Rights' onto one poster. We tossed various labels and initials between us, rejecting 'mass democracy' because of its vague Roman Catholic resonance. Finally he said, "Why not just 'People's Democracy'?" Without any reference to the 'mass democratic' meeting then breaking up, I said, "OK, go ahead, People's Democracy". There was no subsequent objection at any of the meetings, which actually had an anarchic structure, held together more by the excitement of the time, than by any constitutional cement. Eventually, 'People's Democracy' became a small splinter group under Michael Farrell's leadership, although all of us who were involved in the original impulse have suffered something of the Trotskyite taint of association through the name. As the noted *Irish Times* writer, John Healy, often observes, "Stick around long enough in Ireland, and the joke turns serious."

Incidentally, it was during this period that Bernadette Devlin popped up out of nowhere. At the end of each debate on a proposed demonstration, the chairman for the evening would call for a volunteer to go to the local police station at Donegall Pass, to sign the appropriate legal notice of intention to march. On one such occasion, again following a defeat for the Young Socialists, one or two of my friends were about to go forward when I suggested that they let one of Farrell's people do it, to encourage their participation. I discovered afterwards that an attitude of 'let the moderates sign for their own bloody march' was being adopted by Farrell's supporters. The result was a quite unusual silence, as no-one volunteered, whereas the chairman would usually have had to pick from several volunteers. Suddenly, to general relief, a small, mini-skirted figure stood up, and declared in tones of utterly unnecessary defiance, "If there's not a man in this hall with the guts to sign it, I will." Amid great applause and whistling, the mini-skirted figure made itself visible, and the British tabloids soon had a focus other than Paisley in Northern Ireland. Bernadette Devlin had arrived, and in that moment demonstrated the instincts of timing and unnecessary polemics which have been a feature of her style.

I have always had mixed feelings about Bernadette. I do not regard her as the passionate worker for social change that her speeches suggest. But I like her personally, and have regard for her instinctive political talents. She will not, I know, agree with my view that to cast oneself always as the underdog, is indicative of a serf mentality, which, in her case, I feel, made her contribution over several years much more negative than it need have been. I would still hope that her cheerful good nature, her talent and experience, might yet make a positive contribution, especially now that she has succeeded in overcoming so many pressures—not least a near-fatal assassination attempt by loyalists.

Besides producing 'personalities', the mood of emotional uncertainty reduced the element of personal responsibility, an aspect which made me most uneasy, even when we were apparently successful. One incident demonstrated this vividly. As usual, I had been arguing that in the event of our being attacked by anyone— police, passers-by, Paisleyites—we should ignore it, absorb it, if necessary sit on the street with our backs to it, and take whatever was coming. As usual, this line was being supported with a kind of restless respect from a group otherwise enjoying the mass-consciousness of involvement in a quasi-revolutionary situation: they enjoyed Farrell's idea that we should go right up to "our police comrades", but didn't support it. (In these debates, the Young Socialists referred to everybody as 'comrade', while the rest of us adopted the usage 'citizen chairman, citizens . . .', etc: the sound of gunfire was still a long way off.)

The uneasy feeling between the disparate groups found an outlet when a speaker suggested that only those on the march should decide the tactics, not those debating it the night before. Caught unawares, we let the idea go, as much because further debate might land us with an impatient decision to go through police lines if necessary: in the hysteria of the time, some felt that anybody who had not actually been batonned by the police was not a full-blooded member of the struggling masses!

But I was very worried about the chaos which might result, and, next morning, with no concern for 'mass democracy', I had printed at my own expense, thousand of leaflets with notes on what to do if attacked by anybody. I got various 'citizens' to distribute these to the actual marchers, and tried to ensure that the front lines of the march were well manned by citizens rather than comrades. The demonstration remained disciplined. This assumption of personal responsibility was both respected and unpopular: understandably, marchers wanted it both ways—they wanted intelligent, nonviolent tactics, but they also wanted revolutionary excitement. Intelligent, nonviolent tactics unfortunately demanded restraint, which ran counter to the appetite for excitement.

This ambivalence was there from an early stage. On our first attempt to march to the City Hall, we had scarcely gone a hundred yards when I was approached by a senior police officer who informed me that Paisley had a crowd out in Shaftesbury Square to confront our march. I pointed out that we had a perfect right to march, that we had served notice, declared the route, and that Paisley was mounting an instant counter-demonstration. The officer agreed but said he had a duty to prevent public disorder, and asked if we would re-route. I asked what if we did not: he said he would have to insist in the interests of public order. I noted to him again that we were within the law, but that we would, in the interests of peace, re-route, and we then proceeded by a much longer route which would bring us to the back of the City Hall. The marchers were in high enough spirits, it was a mild autumnal day, and we proceeded cheerfully by the new route, with civil rights songs breaking out now and again.

Word filtered back through the ranks about the Paisley counter-demo and the police 'advice', and a regular chant of 'one man, one vote' gave way to '*Sieg Heil*, RUC, SS, RUC'. There was an ugliness of tone in this chant, an edge of mob hatred which chilled me, and has given me an aversion to crowds that has never really left me, even in the midst of cheering, emotionally positive crowds—for it showed how individual humanity can be swamped in the presence of any form of mass hysteria.

It was also acutely embarrassing for Marianne and myself, for we were having an amicable conversation with a young policeman as we walked along, to the sound of 'SS, RUC'!

We continued in good enough order to Linenhall Street behind the City Hall. It was when we were about a hundred yards from the Hall that police treachery met us full in the face. Paisley had angrily rushed his frustrated crowd to the front of the City Hall—by the route we should have taken—and the police, rather than confront the Paisleyites blocking our legitimate purpose, had lined up several deep at the back of the City Hall. They suddenly moved against us, reaching for their batons. We turned the front line instantly and sat down. The police stopped in their tracks. I regret to record that some police expressions had been of gleeful anticipation. The entire march sat down, and an afternoon of stalemate began. A senior officer appeared almost immediately. With cameras around, he could not allow his men to be seen beating obviously nonviolent students off the street, especially after giving Paisley a clear run, and after the furore over the batonning of defenceless people, including parliamentarians, in Derry.

This time, I replied to police requests to disperse by pointing to the fact that we had acted completely lawfully, and had bent over backwards to accommodate the police in the problem created by Ian Paisley, but that we were not moving. It was a most curious spectacle for Belfast, and no-one could be quite sure how it would end. People came out of offices and shops to stare and talk among themselves. The marchers, having made themselves as comfortable as possible, were remarkably quiet, apart from the occasional snatch of song: they seemed to be discussing among themselves as they might have done on any afternoon in the Students Union coffee bar, except that they were sitting in the street and there was no coffee.

Occasionally, passers-by handed out chocolate or crisps; sometimes it was abuse or a half-hearted attempt to slap or provoke at the edge of the crowd. But mainly the event was characterised by cheerful curiosity. After about an hour and a half, however, there were signs that something had better be done to ensure a peaceful and honourable outcome. It would be dark early, the rush-hour traffic would be on, and there were rumours that the shipyard men were coming up to hack us off the street if the police would not, and that dockers were coming armed with hooks to protect us from police and shipyard men alike. I could not be sure how accurate this information was, although the police took it seriously enough—I was in no frame of mind to trust anything the police said in the situation. (Years later, a man who became prominent in the Provisional IRA told me that he and his mates, dockers all, were on their way up, with hooks concealed for battle.)

I had been walking up and down the line occasionally to check on how everybody felt, and on one of these little strolls, met Jimmy Kelly, one of Ireland's leading political commentators over forty years. Jimmy suggested that we should get a Cabinet minister down to hear our case, and then we could disperse. It was the best suggestion coming forward, and arrangements were made in an office in Linenhall Street to get through to Stormont Castle. I was told that no minister was available, because it was Wednesday afternoon, a difficult day. I argued that it was unlikely that the patient students would move unless a Cabinet minister was forthcoming. Shortly afterwards there was another call from Stormont. By this time, Michael Farrell, who had not been on the march, had arrived from his teaching job at Belfast Technical College, along with a few supporters: they were at the front of the march and were beginning to harangue the police.

From Stormont came the offer of two of the most senior civil servants, the permanent secretary at Home Affairs and the Cabinet Secretary, to come to the Students Union to receive our civil rights demands formally on behalf of the government. I undertook to put this to the students. When I returned to the street, it looked to me as if indiscipline had entered into the no-man's-land of a few yards between the march and the police. I went up and down the line explaining the offer, and said that I would be setting off back to the university, and that if they wished, they could follow. We set off, and virtually the entire march followed, leaving Michael Farrell, who had acquired our transhailer, making a speech at the police while the demonstrators disappeared behind him.

My sense of an afternoon's disciplined and successful nonviolent demonstration was not as deeply or as widely shared, even among those who agreed with the tactics, as I would have liked—I suppose being batonned would have felt more like victory! When debate resumed, there was a fair amount of 'next time, we'll not re-route', and 'next time, we'll go whether Paisley is there or not'. I have to confess that I gave in momentarily to this feeling, and used the expression, "if we're blocked again, we'll sit there till hell freezes over". Partly, I suppose I was trying to confirm the nonviolent tactic; but I was also angrily determined not to be conned by the police reacting to other pressures.

The hysterical applause which greeted this pledge disturbed me deeply, and I resolved never to inflame a crowd like that again: it was degrading and embarrassing.

When the two civil servants arrived, they were shown into a private office, and I was sent for: it was quite a surprise to find that one of them was Mr. (later Sir) Harold Black, one of the two civil servants who had been proposing to withhold my scholarship two years earlier on the grounds of my political activism! In that earlier interview, I had found him the more pleasant of the two, and it was the same now—he cheerfully accepted my apology that debate was continuing on the formulation of the demands, and that there might be some delay. The other man was very ratty, much aggrieved at being sent as a message- boy to a bunch of students: I said we would be as quick as possible, that I appreciated their coming, and that it was a much better situation than blood on the streets. Back in the debating hall, I had an angry exchange with that evening's chairman(now a successful solicitor) who responded to my request that we should not delay the public servants unduly, with "Let them wait!" I retorted that justice and good manners were entirely compatible, and that our confrontation was with their political masters, and that we should not make whipping boys of public servants.

There is always the danger that good manners may be mistaken for weakness; but a cause that involves truth and justice can really only be expressed with dignity.

The last few months of 1968 followed the tone and pattern outlined above. On occasions when I was in Dublin, the so-called 'moderate' line, effectively articulated by such as Nick Ross and Brendan Keenan (respectively well-known broadcasters with BBC and RTE today), continued to obtain majority support.

In early December, the recalcitrant Home Affairs Minister, William Craig, responding to the increasing pressure from Westminster on the O'Neill government, made a speech suggesting resistance to any attempt by the London government to reduce the powers of Stormont. He had already embarrassed the hapless O'Neill by describing Nationalism as 'a poison' in the community, and with the suggestion that democracy was impossible in a Roman Catholic country. His 'UDI' (Unilateral Declaration of Independence) speech, as it became known, was too much for O'Neill, as well as sounding too much like Ian Smith in Rhodesia, to London ears, and Craig was sacked. O'Neill had earlier sacked Harry West, his Agriculture Minister, for what he considered inappropriate ministerial conduct over a land deal; he was generally resented by his colleagues over his one-man-band style of reform; now with the sacking of Craig, the internal Cabinet resentment began to symbolize substantial alienation in the community at large.

On December 9, O'Neill made a desperate 'Ulster is at the Crossroads' speech, appealing both for the maintenance of public order, and for reform to proceed. For a moment, his tactic appeared to succeed. He received messages of support from around the Unionist associations, and in the media. The student element of the civil rights movement voted to have a 'moratorium' on all civil rights agitation until January 25, 1969, at which point we would review what real progress O'Neill was proposing.

Farrell's Young Socialists were deeply disappointed that the revolution was being postponed for at least seven weeks. They tried once more to get support for a Belfast-Derry march, and were overwhelmingly defeated, for the last time, in mid-December.

Then, while students were at home for Christmas, Farrell and a small group of supporters filed notice of intention to march. I heard it on the Boxing Day news, with a report that Captain William Long, Acting Home Affairs Minister after the Craig sacking, was meeting with officials to consider whether to ban the 'proposed People's Democracy march from Belfast to Derry'. I recall vividly the sense of frustration and of foreboding, that such a long period of effort and restraint was about to be set aside, that the cause which so many had so faithfully and honourably supported was about to be severely retarded, and a murderous phase of sectarianism let loose. It was all the more galling that the disasters which lay ahead were being unleashed, not by those responsible for established injustice, but by those preening themselves on being champions of the unity and freedom of the working class—which class they were about to divide more murderously than ever.

Marianne and I, having learned that we were expecting our first child, were in Belfast for Christmas. The phone buzzed with marching 'veterans' wanting to know whether I thought we should march. My answer was a most emphatic 'No', that we could not march for one man, one vote when the overwhelming opinion and vote of the civil rights movement was for the suspension of marching. Once Long gave permission for the so-called 'People's Democracy march' to go ahead, the second question was 'what should we do if they get attacked?' My answer remained the same, that no number of cracked heads would make the decision right, and that the best we could hope for was that they would learn how hard it was going to be to unite the Protestant and Catholic working-class outside the confines of the McMordie Hall in the Students' Union.

I was relieved when only a couple of dozen turned up for the start of the march. But despite the poor numbers, it became obvious before the day was out that the Paisleyites were not about to let it go. Major Ronald Bunting, Paisley's most prominent supporter at the time, who later left him in disgust, had marshalled his 'Loyal Citizens of Ulster' to harass the march. (Bunting's son, Ronnie junior, had approached me in October, in his first week in the university, to ask whether I thought his presence on a civil rights march would be a good thing or not, given his father's position: I told him to make up his own mind, that no-one should use his presence one way or the other, but to take his time and weigh it up for himself. Bunting senior had actually campaigned for Gerry Fitt a few years earlier, before coming under the influence of Paisley. The son was very like him, both physically and in his innocent susceptibility to a cause. In the event, Ronnie became a fervent civil rights marcher; then, after things turned violent, he joined the Official IRA, leaving it when it went on ceasefire to join the more militant INLA. He narrowly survived one murder attempt, being shot in the neck, and was finally murdered by Loyalists in 1981, in the wave that almost claimed Bernadette Devlin McAliskey's life. Whichever side they were on, the Buntings, senior and junior, had *par excellence* that innocent sense of militaristic honour by which so many men kill or die, no less truly the victims of our culture and its wars than unarmed bystanders—sometimes more so.)

In January 1969, Bunting senior was bent on showing the steely side of Paisleyism to the straggling bunch of Farrell supporters headed for Derry. And, no sooner did he challenge them, than others went to join them. Dormant Republicans in County Derry turned out to protect them at night. By the time they reached Burntollet, about four miles from Derry, there were over a hundred, and marching along a route dictated by the police, they walked straight into a loyalist ambush of sticks, stones, and clubs with nails driven through them, while the police did virtually nothing to protect them. As such attacks go, compared with subsequent experience, it was a relatively minor affair: but its novelty at the time, and the bully-boy lust with which Bunting's 'men' attacked defenceless students, many of them girls, was terrifying to the victims. They made it, bloodied and bedraggled, hours later, to a heroes' welcome in Derry.

The Paisleyite attack, and the negligence of the police, caused an outcry which predictably overlooked the total disregard for the democratic civil rights movement shown by the march organisers, who were naturally glorified by blood for what was essentially an anti-democratic leap backwards in the civil rights struggle. My own reaction was one of cold despair that the sectarian genie was out of its bottle, and that we were in for a few years of mindlessness which would have to spend itself like a chemical reaction for which Burntollet was the catalyst. I also felt ashamed that many Unionists sympathetic to the broader civil rights effort now felt betrayed; and angry that those unsympathetic to the basic call for justice would feel vindicated, however perversely. Support from the middle ground melted like snow from a ditch as Michael Farrell and Bernadette Devlin became accepted in the wake of Burntollet as the public spokespeople for 'People's Democracy'.

The Burntollet affair marked the end of the 'fermentation': but the only certainty it produced was that there would be widespread sectarian violence, and that a process of constitutional reform would be drowned in the cries and counter-cries of appeasement and repression.

I turned my energies towards the issue of educational opportunity in the south, where I was elected President of USI in January. Even there, the Northern excitement was causing a diversionary contagion. Southern students were only too happy to get up and attack Northern politicians and police, and cry for a thirty-two-county socialist republic—so long as they did not have to make one iota of sacrifice to open up educational opportunity in the South.

A few days after Burntollet, O'Neill's main rival, Brian Faulkner, resigned from the Cabinet, criticising O'Neill for "government by commission", adding that he would have granted one man, one vote. Faulkner, by the reckoning of many, should have been Prime Minister after Brookeborough, instead of O'Neill: there are still people who argue that if he had been, there would have been less talk of reform— and more reform.

O'Neill played his last, desperate card, and called his 'Crossroads Election' of February 1969. By the normal standards of democracy, he won handsomely, the party under his leadership winning 75 per cent of the seats; but in Northern Ireland terms, it was a defeat, for the party was pulled to the Paisleyite direction, and O'Neill had a tough job holding his own seat in a direct contest with Paisley, who was now entering the electoral arena. The preacher's catch-cry became the pundit's prophecy—'O'Neill Must Go!'

On the minority side, several able and younger men were elected, to join Austin Currie and Gerry Fitt. They included John Hume, Ivan

...ho happened to be a Protestant civil rights activist, thus ...playing the cross-community appeal of the issue), Paddy Devlin, Paddy O'Hanlon and Paddy Kennedy. Kennedy later broke from the others to take a position closer to Provisional Sinn Fein.

O'Neill's first serious legislative act in the new Parliament was not reform, but the Public Order (Amendment) Act. It was clearly a measure designed to appease Paisleyism, but it enraged the reform-hungry Catholics, who saw in its provision to have a mandatory six months in jail on conviction of 'riotous behaviour', a measure which would be used against Catholic civil rights marchers.

Politically paralysed after Burntollet, some of us took ourselves up to Stormont to see if we could help with research and script-writing. When Hume (who always wrote his own material) embarked on a filibuster, Parnell-style, on the Public Order (Amendment) Bill, we were there for days, once writing all night, helping others to keep the thing going. The Official Record shows the ludicrous lengths to which we went in support of these weary Members. I can still hear the exhaustion in the voice of poor Sir Robert Porter, a widely respected man then handling the sensitive Home Affairs Ministry, when, ashen-faced at about 5.30 a.m., he rose and asked, "Mr. Speaker, who are these ghosts haunting the lobbies?"

All of Hume's best parliamentary efforts, the support of his colleagues and 'the ghosts haunting the lobbies' were of no use whatsoever. The sleeping Unionist members were summoned by the lobby bell to pass the Bill into 'law'. It went on to create volunteers for the then unformed Provisional IRA, by making convicts out of demonstrators fleeing police batons, often enough after meeting with a Paisleyite 'counter-demonstration'.

From then on, only the most strictly organised and stewarded demonstrations, uncomplicated by Paisleyite counter-demo, had any chance of not becoming 'riotous behaviour', and the sight of helmeted, baton-wielding police became very familiar. The police themselves were becoming desperately stretched to deal with the increasing aggro. In one completely undisciplined display in Derry, police smashed windows and batonned anyone in their way, and Sam Devenney, a man injured in this incident, died later. Following intense pressure from Hume, an enquiry was established under a senior police officer into the allegations that Mr. Devenney had been mercilessly beaten in his own home by police.

O'Neill fell in April 1969, after one confidence vote too many left him with a majority of about three. He was followed by Major James Chichester-Clark (now Lord Moyola), whose accession was as much as anything dictated by the need of the ruling élite to block Faulkner, the logical successor. Clark's one vote victory over Faulkner gave him the embarrassing privilege of reporting to Parliament that the senior police enquiry into the Devenney affair had been unable to penetrate 'the wall of silence' among police themselves, surrounding Devenney's death. This in turn assumed the proportions of a cause célèbre in those days before guns and bombs made death a commonplace currency of 'political' exchange.

Hume and his colleagues worked feverishly to clutch the situation back from the sectarian abyss into the parliamentary arena. The new leader was already winning respect and notice in London, but not enough for his warnings in the summer of 1969 to be heeded, that there would be uncontrollable trouble if the Apprentice Boys march of August 12 were allowed to go ahead. This march was not, as might be imagined, of teenage youths, or junior members of honourable trades, but a commemoration by Loyalists of all ages of the Siege of Derry in 1689: an event, which, in its form in Derry nearly three hundred years later, was rather more of a celebration of the fact that the city's nationalist majority was still in subjection to a minority of Unionists, who let them know this quite formally by firing a ceremonial cannon over their heads and tossing coins off Derry's Walls into 'The Bog'—the Bogside area inhabited by Catholics.

Harold Wilson's Government did not intervene and Hume had to watch in frustration as the Apprentice Boys celebration ended in riot. There followed four days of petrol bombing, baton charging, tear gassing and stoning between uncontrollable youngsters and a police force exhausted beyond discipline.

Then an even deeper fear was realised: the violence spread to Belfast, where sectarianism ran much more deeply, and where the tradition of weaponry is more brutal. The police, apparently led to believe by rumour and political utterance that an IRA 'uprising' was at hand, used heavy calibre, high velocity machine guns, mounted on armoured vehicles, on the residential area of Divis in the Lower Falls. This response was not only horrifically out of proportion and character, and without recent precedent, but was also against the people who were the principal victims of disturbance in Belfast. Loyalists, some armed, had come across in numbers from the nearby Shankill, unimpeded by the police, and proceeded to burn down Catholic houses in an old-style 'pogrom'. Almost an entire street, Bombay Street, was burned out. The residents fled for their lives. The fear and humiliation of that night bred the viciousness of the subsequent Provisional IRA campaign.

Nine people were shot dead in less than two days. In Armagh the B-Specials (a kind of paramilitary constabulary reserve, loosely enough controlled by the RUC) had already shot dead a man called John Gallagher. It was now clear that police guns were out in earnest. The image of a nine-year-old victim, Patrick Rooney, shot dead by a police bullet which went through the walls of his home to where his father was trying to protect him, became a potent part of the supportive mythology of what followed by way of defence or revenge. From the Catholic perspective, Paisleyism, hitherto a minority dynamic of Unionism, was now coming at them officially out of the barrels of police guns.

The IRA, which had only a handful of weapons and barely more than two rounds for each, was stunned and humiliated: in the Catholic ghettos, the grafitti rubbed it in—I R(an) A(way)! It would be four months before the Provisional IRA was actually formed: but it was conceived in Divis Street in the second week of August 1969. The Northern Irish tragedy has a haunting geographical consistency, for Divis Street was the venue of that 1964 riot when the Republican leader Liam McMillen, seeking to lead his followers away from militarism into the politics of social agitation, had flown the Irish Tricolour in his election office window—enough to provoke the Paisleyite reaction of the time. Now, five years later, the police, encouraged to open fire on an imaginary IRA revolt, helped bring one into existence. A man who was later a leading member of the Provisionals recalled to me a few years later: "I was standing there raging, and helpless, and I made up my mind—those bastards will never catch us empty-handed again."

Even Harold Wilson could no longer temporise. But his response was too little, too late. British troops were sent in to protect Catholics, who welcomed them with open arms; the B-Specials were disarmed and disbanded; the RUC was subjected to the Hunt enquiry and report, and later—briefly and partially—disarmed. But the real problem was shelved by Wilson. He set up a constitutional study group, when it was plainly obvious that Stormont could not command sufficient consensus to govern. The logical step of suspending the Northern Ireland Government and starting negotiations before either side began arming in earnest, was avoided, with disastrous results. It was not until Edward Heath, freed from his preoccupation with getting into Europe, and humiliated in almost the same moment by the internationally visible excesses of the British Army in Derry in January 1972, faced up to this reality, that Stormont was finally prorogued. By that time, the infrastructures of mutual paramilitary vetoes had been established on both sides, with fatal consequences which continue to haunt us.

In 1969 we got the best of Wilsonism and the worst of both worlds:

enough action to infuriate the Protestants and strengthen Paisley in his bellowing protests about sell-out and betrayal; not enough to reassure Catholics that they might not need to be well armed if the British troops were ever sent home, or brought under the direct influence of the continuing Unionist government at Stormont.

I was in Dublin during that fateful week, waiting to be present with Marianne at the birth of our first child. It was a curious perspective from which to watch the playing out of what I had predicted nine months earlier.

I found myself deluged with requests for guidance from people wanting to help Northern Catholics. It was an hysterical period, with talk of guns flying about, as well as food and blankets for refugees. Students on vacation were volunteering to go to Belfast, and I tried hard to make sure that fools did not rush in where angels feared to tread.

I asked one student to contact some Belfast friends who would have a grasp unclouded by public or media hysteria. A couple of days later, while I was out, the phone rang at our flat, and Marianne answered: I had told her to expect a call from this student (who had a distinctive County Kerry accent), and she was more than a little suspicious when a Northern voice, aged about forty by Marianne's reckoning, announced himself with the Kerryman's name, and asked for me. Marianne told him I was at a meeting. He then asked if I had the stuff with me, or if I was bringing it up. Marianne asked him, "What stuff, what are you talking about?" The voice, heavily meaningful, said, "You know, the stuff . . ." Well, Marianne hadn't known me for years and married me without knowing that whatever foolish political adventure I might embark upon to our domestic expense, carrying 'stuff' was not one of them; and she told the voice at the other end that she didn't believe he was whoever he said he was. It transpired later that the Kerryman had gone into a telephone box on the Grosvenor Road on the edge of the Lower Falls area, precisely to ring me, was descended upon by the police, arrested, and then questioned about me. They inferred that I was involved in gun-running. When he explained my total opposition to violence, they told him they "had thought that too". Suddenly, everyone was a suspect.

I no longer had much confidence in the police. A few months earlier, when I had gone to Lurgan police station to enquire about students who had been arrested even before a civil rights demonstration, I was attacked by two plainclothes people, in full view of uniformed men who ignored my request that they intervene, and continued drinking tea in the front office of the station, as if this assault was perfectly normal.

I had politely asked to see the desk sergeant, whereupon the larger of the two plainclothes people—I did not realise at first that they were police at all—stood on my foot, and began clipping me on the jaw and nudging me in the groin with his knee—enough to provoke or intimidate without actually being painful. I knew from his size that he could have flattened me if he was seriously going to set about me; what was much more aggravating was that the smaller man kept poking me in the stomach and darting out of range, and it was as much as I could do to restrain myself from letting fly at him, which I also knew meant at least six months in jail. Even so, as they ignored my explanation of my purpose, and the uniformed men went on drinking tea, I found myself measuring the distance between me and the smaller man, the big man's stomach and the door. All my rational training urged coolness, yet every other instinct screamed that I was about to be arrested and probably beaten after a voluntary enquiry at a police station, and my reflexes were keyed to give them a run for their money! Suddenly Mary Holland from the *Observer*, down to cover the demonstration, walked into the station: in a flash, the bigger fellow, who a moment before had been saying, "Who are you, who the hell do you think you are walking in here?" was addressing me with a broad smile, "Who was it you wanted to see, Mr. McKeown? Ah yes, come on in here, they're in the cells for their own protection." I followed him most cautiously towards the back of the station and saw that the students were all right. He then accompanied me out to the street which was packed with flag-waving, club wielding Paisleyites. "See what I'm up against, Mr. McKeown? You understand, it's not easy with this going on . . ."

"All I know is that I went into a police station to make a perfectly proper enquiry, and I was attacked by policemen in the presence of policemen, and I intend to report the matter," I replied. "— off before I arrest you," was the gist of his return to the former attitude. I nevertheless did have some sympathy for his difficulties as I walked the gauntlet of the jeering, triumphalist Paisleyites who had taken possession of the town centre for a 'counter-demonstration' long before the original demo could even begin.

I did publish a statement about the assault, for if the elected leader of Irish students was not going to be able to take the most elementary steps in the judicial process on behalf of students arrested, then anarchy would be more credible to students. Mr. Anthony Peacocke, the RUC Inspector-General (as the Chief Constable was then called, in Imperial style) issued a statement that my allegations had been fully investigated and were without foundation; I issued another statement repeating the allegations, adding that the Inspector General's 'full investigation' had not included any approach whatsoever to me. The second statement was ignored and the matter ended; and along with it, I may say reluctantly, my trust in the RUC. Had I been an unlettered child of the ghetto, I would undoubtedly have retaliated in the station, been hammered, charged, convicted and jailed—and at the earliest opportunity sought violent redress.

Exactly that kind of frustration raged in West Belfast in the autumn of 1969. The IRA found itself torn apart, the lapsed Republicans of the Forties and Fifties re-emerging in angry criticism of the quasi-Marxist social agitators then in control. By December, the 'physical force men' were again strong enough to walk out of a Dublin meeting of the Republican movement, and form a 'Caretaker Executive', which later became Provisonal Sinn Fein, with the Provisional IRA forming in January 1970. Friends, even old jail comrades, were murderously divided by this rift, which later produced fatal feuds. Brendan Behan's old joke—that the first item on the Republican agenda was always 'the split'—was back in business.

The violence also split the Dublin government of Jack Lynch. His policy of appeal to the United Nations, and of setting up field hospitals and refugee camps, was viewed by others in the Fianna Fáil tradition as providing an elastoplast for a haemorrhage. It was never too clear what else he could have done, other than create a formal international incident by sending an Irish army lorry across the Border or some such symbolic act. But within a year, two of his Cabinet were sacked on suspicion of gun-running. They were later tried and acquitted in the famous 'Arms Trial' of 1970. One of them, Charles Haughey, returned humbly to serve under Lynch for years, before replacing him as Taoiseach (Irish Prime Minister). The other, Neil Blaney, a Member of the Irish Parliament, and former Member of the European Parliament, still enjoys a very strong following in Irish politics, especially in the west of the country.

Whatever the facts or otherwise about arms sources from levels in Southern society as high as government, there was absolutely no doubt in the minds of Northern Protestants or in the explicit accusations from Ian Paisley. There was also deep bitterness among those who now became known as the 'Official Republicans' (nicknamed the 'Stickies') who have insisted ever since that they were offered arms and finance from a very high source, provided they contained themselves to the North and dropped their socialism, North and South. They refused the alleged offers, which were apparently snapped up by the emergent Provisional IRA. (Again, whatever the original facts, the three members of the Workers' Party—as the demilitarised Official Republicans have become—elected to the Irish

Parliament in 1982, ensured the election of Charles Haughey as Taoiseach after his own party had failed to win an outright majority. They were almost too late to vote and had to jump over a barrier at some risk to do so: their parliamentary athleticism caused some wry smiles.)

It was certainly a long leap from the emotions of late 1969. Then it was rage, fear, hopelessness: and frustration among Catholic politicians that their wisdom was ignored by people presumed to have a deeper appreciation of statecraft than in fact they had. There remained a weird hope that a better situation must emerge out of the obvious chaos. Catholics tended to overemphasise their own demands for justice as the main cause for the Unionist split: to the extent that they considered the real changes that were happening of their own accord within Unionism, it was to regard Ian Paisley as the best ally Irish republicanism ever had. An unwritten order was assumed that he was not to be touched, but encouraged with his bull-in-a-china-shop job among the respectable Unionist establishment.

Among the dour men who had spent much of their adult lives in prison without trial because of their republican reputations or activities, there grew the firm belief that their time had come, that the unfinished business of Ireland's 1916-22 War of Independence was about to be completed. Joe Cahill, whose 1940s death sentence for complicity in the shooting of a policeman had been commuted to life, was still able to tell me with confidence in 1972: "This time we'll finish it!"

Jimmy Drumm, fiftyish, had spent the Second World War in jail, was then first in and last out in the 1956-62 internment period, and was often held briefly during such occasions as Royal visits. His wife Maire, murdered in 1976 by Loyalists, was a formidable platform orator in the cause of violent republicanism, and served a jail sentence for incitement. I always found Maire a pleasant and hospitable person at home, a stark contrast to the platform persona; I came to the conclusion that much of her anger stemmed from the natural rage of any wife and mother whose family is under constant harassment. One had only to ask her, in the middle of a diatribe against the British, about one of her family, for her entire personality to change to that of warm-hearted, motherly figure. She took part, in 1973, in a televised panel discussion on the extraordinary situation in the Dublin parliament, Dáil Eireann, when the Irish Prime Minister, Liam Cosgrave, voted against his own government's Contraception Bill. Maire, invited to comment as Sinn Fein Vice-President, opened her contribution with heavy wit: "I never had that problem—the British saw to that by locking up my husband for most of our married life!"

The Drumms' sturdy determination to subvert British interference enabled them nevertheless to have five children.

The diehards were bound to seize on the moment of chaotic instability as the great moment of hope, the historic turning-point in their self-perceived history of oppression and exploitation.

A comparable range of emotions was experienced among Protestant Unionists who had been much slower even than the mainland British to realise that the sun had long since set on the Empire. Protestantism, Empire and Monarch were ritually celebrated for much of the year, every year, and would be for ever and ever: suddenly the fears which underlay this extravagant commitment to commemoration were being realised visibly. It felt as if their whole world was crumbling, subverted from within by the typically untrustworthy Catholics, many of whom had had their natural deviousness heightened by free education under a Unionist government—which government had then appeased and softened and weakened before the articulate assault of the new generation of 'rebels'. Then, more horrific still, the British government itself appeared more sympathetic to the rebels, while the world's media depicted themselves, the Queen's most loyal and law-abiding citizens, regular celebrants of civil and religious liberty, as a bunch of dumb bigots. In such a moment of collective humiliation, instead of a healing unity, there was the spectacle of top Unionists vying for power. One Prime Minister had gone, after sacking two ministers and accepting the resignation of his most able man. Paisley, having roared that "O'Neill Must Go", was now bawling that "Clark Must Go", and would later bellow that "Faulkner Must Go!"

In their distress, many Protestants who disapproved of Paisley could nevertheless sympathise emotionally with his aggressive assertions. If they felt ashamed of him on the one hand, they felt at least equally that they were being unjustly castigated by the world's media. Just as Catholics rarely understood fully what was going on among Unionists, Protestants felt that the lot of everybody had been getting better, and considered all the fuss over civil rights as exaggerated, if not downright ungrateful. Moreover, they had no medium other than the dull, sectarian corridors of Stormont, through which to express themselves politically. Many business and professional Unionists who might have had the talent and experience to sit down at a negotiating table with such as John Hume, quite simply opted out and left 'politics' to a tiny number of able men like Faulkner, backed by parliamentarians of less and less ability with each election. Some disgusted Unionists backed the formation of the Alliance movement which became the Alliance Party. This party, presented to and by the media as the 'non-sectarian, moderate party' attracted both Catholics and Protestants, mainly on the basis of this very cross- community dynamic. But its twin policy basis has always been 'strong law and order' and 'firmness on the constitutional link with Britain', virtual code-words for Unionism itself. This excludes Catholics who are not Unionists, as well as failing to attract a sufficient number of Unionists who naturally feel that the 'Union' is best protected by the traditional Unionist Party.

The gleam of hope among militant Republicans refracted as fear and resentment among the Protestant working class who felt doubly humiliated. Though their living conditions were only marginally better than those of their Catholic equivalents, working-class Protestants had always been able, through the collective Orange celebrations involving Protestants of all social levels, to share the feeling of being 'masters in our own house'. Some of the more militant began to realise, as Catholic agitators complained of having no bathrooms, that they had no bathrooms or indoor toilets either. They not only saw progress for Catholics as an ill-defined threat to themselves, but felt that they had been deceived by generations of upper-class Unionist leaders into an illusion of 'first-class citizenship'. In the Belfast phrase, it was 'tuppence looking down on three happence'—two pence looking down on three half-pence. Their reaction was remarkably similar to that of Poor Whites in the Southern United States at the spectacle of Black progress under Martin Luther King Jnr. Paramilitary groups formed, which, unlike the IRA, remain largely unproscribed, except for the UVF (Ulster Volunteer Force) banned by O'Neill in 1966. To this day, men leading organisations known to have planned and been complicit in a whole series of sectarian murders, can openly call press conferences and stroll about as free citizens. In the peculiarly twisted circumstances of Northern Ireland, this is entirely understandable: moreover, banning such groups would be just as counter-productive, if not more so, than banning the IRA has always proven to be.

It is worth noting here that a Protestant paramilitarist has really only one target: Catholics: whereas the IRA may 'hit' soldiers, police, politicians and citizens, and argue, with murderous logic—ultimately no different from Churchill's logic for the mass murder of innocents in Dresden, or Truman's for mass murder in Hiroshima and Nagasaki, or Nixon's in the semi-genocidal attack on the Cambodians—that they are making the British-supported regime in Northern Ireland insupportable.

The Protestant paramilitarist has no such range of outlets for the murder logic of his militarism: nor can he even acquire the glamorous or emotional appeal of being an 'oppressed freedom fighter'. The only tactic open is to murder Catholics as randomly and horribly as possible so as to terrify the wider Catholic population out of support for the IRA at any level. For a time, this was precisely the tactic adopted, and the dumped bodies of shot Catholics were often found to have been stabbed and tortured before the final act of murder. In one case, a pathologist suggested that the victim might actually have died of terror before being shot.

The reaction of many to such events must be to recoil in horror. But I find it understandable, and it is an aspect of the Northern Ireland political disease that must be understood. I may say that my own uncompromising opposition to militarism is strengthened by considering deeply both its nature and the consequences of its logical application. Indeed, failure to appreciate militarism's logic inevitably brings forth its mirror image in oneself: that is self-evident in, say, the disposition of the Russians to be prepared to kill all the Americans because the Americans are prepared to kill all the Russians. It may not be so immediately obvious in Northern Ireland, but it is entirely logical, in terms of conventional militarism, for Protestants to wish to kill large, even decisive, numbers of Catholics. That they have killed so few, relatively speaking, is, I believe, a tribute to them, rather than any consideration that the Catholic minority is just too big, and with too many friends, to make the genocide approach a sound bet. Certainly, I know of quite a few among Protestant murder gangs who have come quite explicitly to the understanding that it was and is inherently wrong, rather than merely counter-productive, to murder Catholics. But one must understand the dynamic that prompts the temptation to such murder, in order to comprehend the situation, and to have a basis for an authentic dynamic of forgiveness—without which, in turn, no political settlement will occur.

Catholic murderers are usually more easily understood, given Ireland's long, subject role during Britain's imperial 'glory', and given the more recent subject role as a minority in Northern Ireland. Catholic politicians like John Hume and Gerry Fitt could unreservedly repudiate the violence of the IRA without having any effect on their cultural support and emotional justification. On the Protestant side, the opposite was happening: Unionist leaders were either dumb about the sectarian murder campaigns, or encouraged it with dangerous rhetoric calling 'Ulster's manhood to arms'. Bill Craig declared that he would have cleared the streets in Derry with a volley of shots. Another Unionist MP, Captain Robert Mitchell, advocated the use of tanks and flame-throwing bulldozers. It was little wonder that the sorely-pressed, ill-trained and exhausted police finally used heavy machine guns, and that illegal Protestant paramilitary organisations felt cultural support for their activities.

Having seen themselves as this generation's 'defenders' in a long line of 'glorious defenders', the Protestant paramilitary organisations eventually found themselves despised by their own community leaders, while they themselves realised that their terror tactics were increasing, rather than reducing, support for the IRA. They had the wit and the courage to call off their campaigns, and to try, however fitfully, to develop a political viewpoint that would be both true to their traditions and applicable to contemporary conditions. For people who had long accepted apolitically that they were masters in their own safe house, this was an admirable effort. Whatever future twists the Northern Irish experience may take, it seems unlikely now that the politically awakened Protestant working class will ever go back to sleep. Like the Catholics, morever, they now have a generation of prisoners whose character is political, whatever their jail status, or the crime for which they were sentenced. And Irish prisons are like poisoned glands in the body politic.

In the winter of 1969-70, politicians scrambled around the implementation of one person, one vote and other reforms of local government. The British Home Secretary, James Callaghan, who was relatively tough within the confines of a weak overall policy, had decided that Unionist power in local government, the source of so much grievance, would best be brought into line, by radical decrease in the number of local bodies and drastic curtailment of their powers. This was the real power decision behind a lot of cosmetic discussion in Northern Ireland itself, culminating in the Macrory Report submitted to the Stormont Parliament by Brian Faulkner, then back as Clark's Minister of Development. The Unionist Cabinet did its best to put a professional political face on such events as the Hunt Commission's recommendation that the RUC be disarmed, even as Lord Scarman seemed daily to be discovering their excesses, in his public enquiry into the disturbances.

But throughout that winter of apparent reform through the parliamentary process, a slow and dangerous shift was happening in the role of British soldiers so recently welcomed as defenders into Catholic areas.

Ian Paisley agitated loudly that the IRA was arming, and Clark came under relentless pressure to search Catholic areas for arms— even though most of the bullets so far fired had been in the other direction. While this pressure was building up, a gunfight broke out, in October 1969, between Protestants and the British Army, at the lower end of the Loyalist Shankill Road. The first policeman to be killed, Constable Victor Arbuckle, died during this affray, which Clark weakly described as "senseless folly".

In spite of the then facts, there was little more than a cursory search for arms in Protestant areas. On the other hand, apparently because of the need, politically, to make Clark appear tough in the face of Paisley's pressure, troops were increasingly ordered to search in Catholic areas. Their methods became more and more robust, and what became known as 'the one-sided arms searches' increased even as Hume and company were endeavouring to upstage the emerging IRA by proving effective on the parliamentary front.

The change was almost imperceptible at first, disguised by the weird uncertainties of the time when momentary flashes of violence alternated with street carnivals, and the whole public was intoxicated with having its trauma televised to the world. Northern Ireland was on the world stage—for all the wrong reasons, but on stage. There was no shortage of opinions ready to feed the media menagerie which settled into the hotels and hostelries. Somehow, within a year, to a background of all sorts of sensational reportage, and shallow commentary, the troops who had been sent in to protect Catholics from the excesses of a shaken Unionist establishment, were firmly fortressed in those same Catholic areas, braced for the old war with the Irish Republican Army (Provisional). The conflicts which lay behind August 1969 were buried by the new mythology, as the 800-year Irish-British struggle mentality blinded itself to the domestic failure of Unionist and Nationalist Irishmen to find civilised accommodation. Irishmen, having failed to agree, prepared to kill each other in the wrong war.

I had started to work for the Irish Press Group in Dublin in January 1970, training as a sub-editor, and writing feature articles. Apart from routine family visits, I was soon being sent North from Dublin for longish periods, and was finally appointed 'Northern Commentator' for the Group. Enjoying collectively, for its daily, evening and Sunday papers, the largest circulation in Ireland, this group had been founded by Eamonn de Valera, for half a century Ireland's most significant leader, survivor, by virtue of American birth, of the 1916 executions, and founder of Fianna Fáil, Ireland's largest political party. His son Vivian, a member of the Irish parliament, Dáil Eireann, was managing director of the group. My job involved political commentary, drafting editorials, writing features, and, willy-nilly, news stories which were not strictly my duty.

My first major task was to cover the June 1970 Westminster election in each constituency in Northern Ireland. The second was to follow up what became known as the 'July Curfew', a few weeks later. These two events together marked another decisive downward trend—this time for London-based reasons, rather than any sudden internal Northern Ireland shifts.

Wilson's government was replaced by Heath's Conservative Party, and Reginald Maudling took over the Home Office from James Callaghan. Although many of the British civil servants seconded to Northern Ireland were from the Foreign Office, Northern Ireland actually came under the Home Secretary, and Maudling duly visited in late June. He went home calling the place 'a bloody awful country', and left the British Army commander, General Freeland, with a vague brief to do whatever was necessary to help Jimmy Clark.

The first noticeable effect of this was the 'July Curfew'. On the weekend of July 3, after allegations that arms were hidden in Balkan Street in the Lower Falls area, the British army raided, ran into local opposition, and promptly surrounded the entire area in a saturation operation, announcing a 'curfew'. Although it was quickly discovered that there were no powers of curfew in operation, troops ordered people to remain in their houses. A gun battle went on intermittently over the weekend, with the Official IRA—not the Provisionals—as the main combatants with the British. Three non-combatants were shot dead by the British. One of them, William Elliman, an asthmatic in his fifties, had gone outside his door to get some fresh air after tear gas had been used, and had had part of his head blown off; he had a habit when he came in, of loosening and removing his tie, and hanging it, loose-looped, behind his hall door, ready for going out again. This tie, still hanging behind the hall door awaiting its owner's social purpose, remains in my memory as a vivid image of unexpected death by violence.

The troops deployed in this action were just into Belfast, did not know the area, and were totally unprepared for the situation. But the die was now cast: British troops had moved from the August 69 position of defending Catholics to the July 70 position of appearing to attack them: the 'old struggle' between British Imperialism and Irish Republicanism rose from its sleep. Although the Officials had engaged the British, the Provisional IRA gained most recruitment in the surge which followed this 'curfew'. In the windows of houses in the narrow streets appeared defiant posters, parodying a current British Army recruitment advertisement: 'Join the Professionals' in Catholic West Belfast now meant 'Join the Provisionals'. That summer, hundreds did.

The cups of tea, the plates of bacon and egg, the furtive dating of local girls gave way to the age-old Irish ability to ostracise and boycott. The young working-class Englishmen who had been given such a welcome were now the highly armed, bullying, weirdly uniformed symbols of imperialist oppression. The parliamentary feet were being cut from under those full-time politicians living and working among their people, who were now patrolled by the British as adversaries rather than protectors.

Major-General Tony Farrar-Hockley, then Commander of Land Forces, Northern Ireland, later confirmed to me, during an interview on the role of the British army at this point in Irish history, that they had no intention of facing in two directions: one side or the other would have to be contained while the politicians sorted things out, and the obvious side appeared to be the smaller, Catholic side. At that time he also believed that the Official IRA was a much greater threat than the 'low-grade guerillas' of the Provisionals, because the Officials had a coherent political belief which the others lacked.

The crude military tactic of facing one side contributed substantially to a much more significant political mistake, that of providing the media and anyone else who cared to exploit it, with the superficial impression that the conflict was 'Brits-v-Provos'. That mistake is still operational: by sheer force of duration, the 'Brit-Provo' dimension has obscured the much deeper problem of internal Irish reconciliation, the *sine qua non* of peace.

Faced with a growth in armed resistance that was bound to turn offensive, the leading Catholic politicians moved to form the Social Democratic and Labour Party, in order to make their parliamentary efforts more coherent and visible. John Hume and Austin Currie already had the support of Ivan Cooper, Paddy Devlin and Paddy O'Hanlon for this initiative, but Gerry Fitt, loner supreme, was fighting a little shy. Finally, Currie announced in an RTE (Irish Radio) interview that a new party was about to be formed, but needed the one man who alone could be its agreed leader, namely Gerry Fitt. In a follow-up interview, the redoubtable Gerry allowed that he was very honoured and flattered, and joined the new party as its leader, the position he held continuously until he resigned from the party eleven years later.

During the Seventies, the SDLP provided the most coherent parliamentary representation that Northern Irish Catholics ever had. The name was chosen as a kind of coalition between the 'Social Democratic Party' favoured by the university-educated breed of Catholic leaders such as Hume and Currie, and 'Labour' as espoused by Fitt and Devlin. They were all, of course, 'left of centre', which was quite fashionable, but it is interesting to note that the 'Social Democratic' tag arose directly from an interest in European developments far beyond the scope of ward politics—and long before the same idea bred the British Social Democratic Party of Roy Jenkins, David Owen, Shirley Williams and Bill Rodgers. What was utterly remarkable was that the new party's title had no hint of 'nationalism' or 'republicanism', the very aspirations long touted as the Northern Irish minority's dominant political principles. It took the confrontation between the British Prime Minister, Margaret Thatcher, and the Provisional IRA hunger-strikers a decade later, to so evoke the nationalist dynamic that the SDLP split on the issue, with Gerry Fitt resigning on the grounds that the SDLP had become too 'nationalist'.

I had deep misgivings of a different sort when the SDLP was formed, and I expressed them to John Hume. I felt that the move would confirm Catholics as such as a permanent minority represented by a party which would have its own inert sectarian base, however non-sectarian its leaders. I also gave John my opinion that it would cut him off personally from future potential support from many Protestants who admired him. But he had committed himself to a strategy for conflict resolution based on demonstrating the strength, in ballot-box terms, of both Northern Irish traditions, each of which would have a consensus veto on the other, and in whose common interest, therefore, mutually respectful negotiations should proceed to produce a solution.

It was logical and based on the generally accepted 'realities'. But in addition to my objection to confirming both traditions for ever and a day in ballot-box divisiveness, my opposition was also based on the fact that the resultant 'solution', however ingenious, would require a substantial degree of enforcement of the vulnerable, mutually suspicious poles of the community. This latter reservation touched directly on my convictions about nonviolence.

Although, uncomfortably, I thus disagree with him on fundamentals and could not join his party, I have nevertheless had great respect for John Hume's clear-minded efforts, and for the courage and ability with which he has persisted. He actually began articulating his approach in 1969, when nobody in particular was listening, yet by 1973, he had had it accepted, under the term 'power-sharing', as the orthodoxy of the British and Irish governments in relation to the Northern Ireland conflict. The 'power-sharing solution' enjoyed a brief period of operation in 1974, following the December 1973 Sunningdale agreement. By any standards, John Hume's contribution to Irish, and even wider constitutional history, has therefore been major; in my view, he is the outstanding figure of contemporary Irish politics, and should rank highly among the politician-statesmen of contemporary Europe, in ideas, if not in power.

Marianne and I settled back in Belfast fully in October 1970, after two years of commuting up and down to Dublin. This was the beginning of that tumultuous and depressing period later described by military spokesmen of the later Seventies as the 'Hot War'. In my own mind, I was prepared for a period of violence and inconsequential politics, which I would endure as a journalist, endeavouring to communicate the feeling of being in one tradition to those of another, and vice versa. At times, this occupation seemed useless, as the mindlessness of militarism and paramilitarism stunned one's consciousness.

Hot War, Hot Air

Besides reporting on the 'Irish thing', I spent a lot of time with visiting journalists, who often sought me out for an instant briefing. Once, I said to a young correspondent from the London *Times*—after a couple of hours' conversation, during which he would suddenly appear to understand, then cloud over again in incomprehension—that "anyone who isn't confused here doesn't really understand what is going on". He used this, attributed to 'Belfast citizen', the following day, and incidentally, Richard Rose, in turn, used the phrase as a chapter sub-title in *Governing without Consensus*—gratifying, but nevertheless a warning about how far a pub comment might travel!

No-one could possibly have had an authoritative grasp of what was happening in a fluctuating situation. It was therefore often difficult to decide rights and wrongs in such confusion. The automatic reflex of the law-abiding that the authorities should be backed, became questionable when the authorities were using legitimised militarism to defend a constitutional status quo that was itself changing: it became even more questionable in situations where the means used exceeded the legitimate norms.

Unquantifiable fears, aspirations, and degrees of alienation make any clear and logical analysis at best a useful tool, as Rose's book was and remains. The 'political process', at another level, may be recorded in terms of statements, negotiations, agreements and disagreements of politicians, even allowing for ambiguities; we may point to this or that decision, or breakdown in decision-making, or to this or that election result, or even opinion poll. When you have a situation where a majority of people opposing the IRA elect an IRA man for reasons which they distinguish from his IRA activity (which he does not—as in the 1981 case of the late Bobby Sands), then understanding of the political process mists up again.

Even more vexed is the task of appreciating the 'security situation': the variable states of hot war, cold war, street violence, guerilla violence, official violence, opportunistic crime are all subjects on which information is often secret, distorted, lied about, propagandised and generally rendered unreliable.

I can understand the passions of a Belfast street fighter: but how, for instance, am I to weigh those when connected to the cold trading intrigues of the international arms market? Again, all governments sound off morally about 'terrorism': yet the British, Russian, French, Italian, German, Israeli and American governments are to the fore in competing for sales of almost every kind of weapon to the highest bidder. Sometimes less powerful governments are used as brokers for deals which do not accord with the political stance of the powerful; sometimes the client governments are buying with money that should be directed to development of their people; and sometimes the very governments most loudly pledged to combating global terrorism are involved directly in funding subversion of those in conflict with their interests. Thus, not only is information unreliable, but standards for moral judgement of legal and illegal militarism are obliterated by the realities of the international arms market, so aptly termed the blood trade. Naturally, small-time operators like the IRA could not care less whether their weapons are Russian, American, German, French, Italian—or British. They had no ideological purpose in acquiring the RPG-47 Russian anti-tank field weapon, which they proceeded to use as an anti-personnel weapon: there was simply a large Libyan surplus from the Six-Day War. Even the Irish have an arms factory.

In Belfast, of all places, where the authorities from time to time announce in jubilation the discovery of 'bomb factories'— assortments of chemicals, timing devices, fuses, wire, etc—the biggest bomb factory of all is the one heavily subsidised by the government: the Shorts Missile Division, which has a very good rating from its sales to large and small governments, and which got a boost for its profits from the death trade as a result of the Falklands affair. It is a matter of acute economic interest to those governments heavily involved in this trade to observe the performance of new weapons systems in such outbreaks as the Falklands or the various Middle East eruptions. The French may be said to have 'won' the Falklands war, as the name of their Exocet missiles became part of the English language.

It is this context which explains the otherwise astonishing momentum with which Belfast's street gangs and defence committees were able to create small armies. The ready supply of weapons, air travel and modern communications have transformed the business of raising guerilla armies. The common motor-car, owned or hijacked, can be both transport and weapon. Any handful of people can create a terror unit capable of disrupting severely any modern, technology-dependent society.

It is difficult for anyone trying to understand and resolve the Northern Irish conflict not to reserve the deepest wrath for the arms supply trade. The people of Northern Ireland—like many other little communities racked by tribal or post-colonial conflicts—are well capable of riot and mayhem without having it made endemic because of the ease of establishing small armies. The psycho-political problems are incapable of solution for as long as fear levels remain high: and they will remain high as long as the levels of armament remain high— that is a simple equation. Disarmament and demilitarisation are intrinsic parts of the peace process, not merely desirable bonuses. This is the only way that the dizzying downward spiral of repression, terrorism, counter-terrorism, more terrorism, more counter-terrorism can be reversed.

What Northern Ireland experienced between January 1969, and December 1974, was such a downward spiral of violence until at least some of the forces realised that a mutual and often murderous stalemate was the most that could be achieved by arms. During that period, no person or agency could be said to have had a firm grasp, let alone control, of what was going on. And in the attendant hysteria of 'hot war', even individual self-control seemed less than normal.

As British troops turned more and more against the population of the Catholic ghettos, recruits flocked to the Provisionals. Contrary to the traditionally puritanical standards of the IRA, the Provisionals were less and less choosy about whom they enlisted. As the conflict became portrayed as the 'British versus the IRA', ethnic sympathy abroad, especially in the United States, ensured an immense flow of military equipment to the Provos, who then went onto the offensive. They began bombing downtown Belfast, and government installations and offices, steadily widening the target range to include almost anything and anybody. (By 1982, the IRA was offering to shoot parents who failed to discipline their children!) In response, the government 'tightened security', meaning more and more aggressive troop activity, wrecking of houses in searches, more brutal treatment of street demonstrations, more arrests—all of which increased recruitment to the Provos, and reduced 'security'.

To their own consternation, the people of Northern Ireland found themselves passing through ever lower thresholds of tolerance. When British troops shot somebody, there was outrage among Catholics, for instance; this would be overtaken by, say, the Provos' murder of three teenage Scottish soldiers after drinking with them, in March 1971. Then troops would wreck houses in a street at night, or shoot somebody else dead, and the ability to condone the shooting of soldiers would be widened and deepened—which in turn increased the scope for heavy government reaction.

This process disillusioned me profoundly with people in positions of authority, whom I somehow imagined to have the concerned intelligence to see what a morass they were creating for themselves.

Gradually I came to the conclusion that if one wanted to predict the next stage, one had only to think of a mistake, and double it.

No greater mistake occurred than the introduction of internment without trial in August 1971. It removed consensus to parliamentary process by the Catholic community at a stroke; it gave the atrocities of the Provisional IRA a post facto emotional justification, and flooded their ranks and coffers with renewed support; and it made liars out of military men blethering about 'getting on top of the terrorists'. It sometimes seemed to me that the military strategists were like frustrated guerilla fighters, playing underground games inside orthodox militarism, and thoroughly enjoying the excitement of an interesting little war, just when it seemed that the British Army, stripped of the last of its imperial functions, would have a difficult time in redefining its role. And to watch the exhilaration of Paratroopers as they raced in open jeeps in and out of internment week gun-battles, was to see the front-line version of the same small-boy excitement of militarism, oblivious, like a fighter to punches when hot, to the anguish, grief and continuing human tragedy unleashed by this lunacy.

The slide had been gradual enough from the days when 'city of fear' stories were inflammatory build-ups to mere marches, to the situation in the winter of 1971 and thereafter, when no street was safe from car-bombing, people could not sleep safely in their beds, and journalism could not do justice to the carnage, destruction, dislocation, intimidation, torture, humiliation, rage, grief and terror. The death-toll, the searing tip of this iceberg of suffering, soared from 25 in 1970 to 173 in 1971 and to 467 in 1972.

In the rapid deterioration after internment was introduced, Brian Faulkner was Unionist Prime Minister, Reginald Maudling was apparently irrelevant as British Home Secretary, and Edward Heath, the British Prime Minister, was preoccupied with getting Britain into the EEC, where the Irish government was also headed. It looked as if the British would soon be faced with no option but to close the Stormont Parliament down, leaving them with two possible directions of policy: an attempt at internal Northern Irish reconciliation, or an outright attempt at an all-Ireland solution involving the sovereign governments of London and Dublin, with the European dimension offering some scope for fudging any disputed change in sovereignty.

The latter option seemed too far-fetched on the surface. But the British knew that the proroguing of Stormont would be as deep a shock as could be inflicted on the Unionist psyche, and therefore the fear of Protestant reaction would have to be faced in any case. The All-Ireland context seemed to be generally accepted as the ultimate destination of British policy—as it was when partition was introduced as a 'temporary' expedient. The code phrase for this interpretation of Britain's reluctant involvement in Northern Ireland was Heath's 'we will not stay in Ireland a day longer than a majority in Northern Ireland wants it'. Speculations on the NATO aspects of the problem weighed the loss of British control against the vulnerability posed by chronic instability anywhere in Ireland.

Heath was apparently adamant not to be seen 'giving in to the terrorists': so that the Provos' campaign for a 'Declaration of British intent to withdraw' was actually damaging to their own purpose, as well as making Protestant opinion more and more recalcitrant and militaristic. I wrote at the time, in an Irish Press editorial on their civilian-risk bombing campaign, 'You cannot bomb a million Protestants into a United Ireland'. The phrase was taken up frequently, almost as a principle, notably by the late Cardinal Conway. Twelve years later, it stands more firmly than ever. But with their military tails in the air, hundreds of their comrades in jail, dozens of them dead (as often as not in their own explosions in the early stages), and their areas constantly subject to the humiliation of patrolling by British troops, the Provos were listening to nobody and to nothing but the sound of their own bombs and propaganda: 'This time, we're going to finish it!'

I look back reluctantly, as if into a nightmare, to that period after internment was introduced. It is almost bizarre to recall some moments of beautiful normality, as when our second daughter was born, in October 1971. Such domestic moments provided the only semblance of normal humanity in an almost continuous memory of shooting, bombing, killing, maiming, rioting, barricading, torture, and the rise of the Long Kesh internment camp, like a still from a war movie, sitting off the motorway outside Belfast.

Men who were significant figures in the conflict were often unobtainable, or only contactable by roundabout methods. To keep any sense of what was going on in the minds of those on the run, one had to be on a kind of 'run' oneself, sometimes being moved around in a mickey-mouse manner from pub to pub to house to taxi to house to pub.

I learned how to see in the dark. Long before the war became really hot, I had a weird experience one night after a riot in the Falls area: things had quietened, and British armoured personnel carriers, nicknamed 'pigs' by army and public alike, had droned off into the night; I went back into town to send over my reports and catch up with whatever might have happened elsewhere. This was at about midnight—we used to send copy right up to 4 a.m.—and I had a feeling that things had gone quiet too suddenly and easily. I decided to go back up and look around. I was fortunate then, and usually, to know a few taxi-drivers whom I could ask for, who were not afraid to go into personal danger or risk their cars: one such friend and I returned to the scene.

Where there had been riot and petrol bombing earlier, all was as quiet as evening in church: unnaturally so, it seemed to me. We drove about, and no-one was to be seen, which was eerie in such an area at that early hour of the night. It was dry and dark. I decided to get out and walk about, on some hunch that something was going on, and that people had been told to stay in. By this time, I had learned to make some noise, and not to pad about as if I were a sniper or a soldier. I also kept to the middle of the street, hands out of pockets so that night-scopes (devices which can differentiate brightly between shades of darkness and thus illuminate the night for snipers) would show that I was carrying nothing. Suddenly, as I approached the junctions of Cyprus Street and McDonnell Street, I saw the tip of a rifle pointing at me from a corner; immediately I saw another at the other corner of the junction. I kept on walking, just a little more noisily in my steel-tipped shoes, and when I was almost on the corner, I could see several other soldiers pressed into doorways on the other side of the street. I walked over to the first soldier and said quietly, "I'm a pressman, is there something going on?"

"You'll have to speak to my officer!" came an exasperated whisper.

"Your officer? Where is he?"

"Over there!"—even more exasperation as if I was some kind of fool who might get him shot by indicating his presence.

I turned and saw a soldier, carrying no gun, standing in the street and scanning the roof-tops with a cylindrical object which seemed to have a dull red glow at the end—one of the night-scopes of which I had heard the talk, but which I had not seen in action.

I went over and started chatting to the officer about his interesting toy, asking also why they were out there patrolling, since they were sitting ducks for any snipers who would see them before they could see anybody, scopes or no scopes. The officer was not about to debate the matter, saying "Just a routine patrol", so I returned to the night-scope and asked to see how it worked. He muttered something about regulations, but proceeded to show me how when you pressed it into your eye, the device was activated and intensified the available light. He then allowed me to try it.

I was absolutely fascinated by the way the line between a black roof and a midnight blue sky became the jagged and precise outline of ridge tiles, black below and brilliant green above, so that if the snout of a weapon had appeared, it would have been more vividly outlined than in daylight. I looked around the rooftops for some moments, standing in the middle of the street. When I turned to thank the officer, he was yards away, his colleague's rifle following the direction in which I had been pointing the night-scope. I had forgotten the little glow, and felt a right patsy: a sniper might have blown me away like some decoy, and disclosed his position to eight ready self-loading high-velocity rifles, and I would have been a twenty-eight year old father of two, dead, 'caught in cross-fire', a line I would subsequently hear for people shot dead well out of cross-fire.

It is perhaps a measure of how strange the time was, that my reaction, after I returned to the taxi, was still not so much that I might have been shot, but that it was incredibly stupid for these soldiers to be out on foot, with no support vehicles, given the feelings in the area.

"Are they mad?" I asked the taxi-driver.

"You're learning," he replied.

I tried to work it out: if, as was very possible, a soldier was shot, the only 'gain' was to provide an excuse to go into the area as heavily as possible—which in turn would only increase the number of volunteers to the IRA. If, on the other hand, the idea was to 'flush out snipers', the odds were that the snipers would get the soldiers first. The soldiers were exposed, the very walls seemed to be listening to them, and they were an alien provocation. I decided to go to this foot-patrol's base and talk forthwith to whomever was on duty. So the ever-willing taxi-driver and I went to Hastings Street army post where I was introduced finally to the captain in charge. (It was interesting also to see the cramped, unpleasant conditions in which the squaddies were billeted: physically healthy young men surviving on the degrading comfort of girlie magazines.)

The captain said, when I asked him why an unsupported foot-patrol was in the streets at this hour, that it was "just a routine patrol". I put the various points to him in different ways, that his men were sitting ducks, and provocative ones at that, given the feelings earlier in the evening; he responded cheerfully that they were soldiers, that was their job. I could hardly believe his attitude.

When I finally put it to him very strongly that one of his men could be carried in dead, and that the only effect would be to increase the tension so that more citizens and more soldiers would die, he became very frosty, and repeated almost self-hypnotically that soldiers were soldiers, that they had a job of soldiering to do, that's what soldiers are for, they were on patrol, this was just a routine patrol.

I rejoined the taxi-driver. "They *are* mad, their own men are expendable flesh," I said.

"You're learning," he said again, with an even more laconic tone. Then he changed gear: "I'm learning too." I wondered if he was trying to console me in my naïveté.

Thereafter, I learned to scan corners and rooftops and chimney junctions with my naked eyes in the dark, as well as for forms pressed into doorways and against walls, for I knew that much of my life for the foreseeable future would be spent walking in the dark in areas peopled by highly armed and nervous madmen. Once, having become too used to the experience, I was in a house during a gun-battle, waiting for it to ease off, and when it sounded safe, I went into the dark street, glanced up and down, and started to walk briskly towards the main road where I had left my car. My pipe had gone out, and I put my hand in my pocket to rummage for matches. I paused and had just lit a match which was half-way to my pipe when I saw that I was looking down the barrel of a soldier's self-loading rifle, and beyond into the terrified eyes of the soldier himself. As far as he was concerned, I might have been lighting a crude grenade, or lighting him up for someone else. "Oh sorry, didn't see you, good evening," I said as I passed on, lighting my pipe, my eyes skirting the doorways on both sides. For the next hundred yards, as I walked on as if nothing had happened on this delightful evening, I felt as if eight SLRs were trained on my back and head, and that any moment might be my last. The relief of getting to the lit main road and around the corner was considerable.

I used to stand and watch the reactions of people who lived in the highly patrolled areas. When feelings were high, there was always the chance of some wee woman abusing soldiers as she walked defiantly past them, or of youngsters throwing things at these unfortunate young men. But the most bizarre aspect was how accustomed everyone became to the whole situation of patrolling and being patrolled, even if at any moment gunfire might break out. There must have been a great deal of subconscious stress, however calmly people seemed to take it. I am aware of a number of young men of that time who died suddenly (of natural causes) in their thirties, as well as of men whom I saw age visibly, sometimes becoming burned out shells of themselves in a couple of years.

In one way, while much of my life was lived almost outside the 'war zones', the movement in and out of 'safety' was perhaps worse. One might be reasonably safe at home at noon; in the protected comfort and often jollity of politicians' company in the afternoon; and then have to go into the middle of trouble in the evening. Occasionally, when I felt that I did not want to drive into I knew not what, and that it might be wiser and certainly more comfortable to stay in town—as most journalists increasingly did, relying more and more heavily on telephone information and handouts—I had to be certain that I was not chickening out. Often I made a point of going out, for I was afraid that if I let myself get scared off, I might as well pack it in. At the same time, one had to be careful not to get stuck in one riot situation, with no telephone handy or in working order, and then miss deadlines with other important stories.

It was an impossible position for our tiny, overworked, and at that time, badly paid staff—which was later augmented and better paid than almost anybody else. But I was gaining invaluable experience, and I got to know many of those involved in paramilitary organisations; and they got to know me, know my nonviolent opposition to their various campaigns, that I would write whatever I judged I should regardless of their opinions, but that I would never use my privileged position to set any of them up.

I was also learning on my feet what journalism was about. Journalists are the most extraordinary mixture. Some who are bone idle may be well known and respected; others who are unknown may be indefatigible hunters of the facts. Some care deeply about the subjects of their material, others could not care less if their stories inflamed people. In these ways, they are like the members of any profession. But people come into journalism in many different ways, and with widely differing personalities and motivations, and without the very specific ambitions that might move, for instance, a lawyer, or a doctor. A man may start with an interest in sport and become a news editor or political correspondent. Or he may want to be the crime reporter and end up as the soccer expert. Some level of egotism is necessary, and G. K. Chesterton has referred to the 'rough humility' of journalists. All journalists must develop an appetite to get the story first and more fully and with better 'angles' than any opposition: or for the lazy, have the most talked about, well-turned version of what everybody else has discovered first. A bar full of journalists is a bar full of experts: yet the same people must often, at a moment's notice, listen respectfully and humbly to the utterances of some whom, they know, do not know what they are talking about, or how to say it.

It is also true that a 'press corps' in a small place can create illusions without even trying to: by talking to each other and to an equally small circle of politicians or other opinion-shapers, they can begin to believe that what goes round and round among them is *the* vital material in a society's experience. Similarly with reputations: labels such as 'right-wing', 'hard-line', 'left-wing', 'controversial', 'outspoken' or 'crafty' are stuck on early, and usually nothing the victims of this process say or do thereafter has any effect on all subsequent perception of them. Journalism is, in short, professional gossip, a lubricant in the substantial life of a human community.

There are a few people who are instinctive newsmen, people with a nose for trend and personality and angles of interest; and even more rarely, there is the 'born' editor. But most tumble happily along with a pocketful of labels and clichés, eyes fixed firmly on the next deadline.

Under the pressure of covering violence and politics from morning to early morning, I discovered an unsuspected talent—an exceptional memory for telephone numbers and an almost videotape memory for events and comments that I needed to remember. I first became aware of this after I had been stopped and searched by a military patrol: as my contact book was being examined, I was apprehensive that I might be questioned about some of the numbers and their significance. I decided to try and work without a contact book, and found that I very easily could. I also found that the long telephone credit card number which I used for phoning copy from pay-phones, sat perfectly in my memory for the year of its operation—then became irretrievably scrambled within a few weeks of memorising the new number each year.

The same ability applied in situations where notebook and pen were inappropriate. I even found that it worked in covering parliament, where I could recall quotations more accurately than reporters who had taken them down in shorthand: the reason for this, I suspect, is that I would actually have listened much more intently than would a person constantly taking notes, and thus recorded the relevant matters mentally, whereas note-taking can distract the concentration on substance.

It was also very reassuring to one who had had experience of nervous stress to find that I could remain calm in very disturbing moments, even if I were inwardly frightened and afterwards shattered. Early enough in the 'Troubles', as I was standing one night at a street corner during a lull in rioting, I noticed an excited group on a corner diagonally opposite, at about twenty yards. I had a feeling that they were preparing to do something unpleasant about an army 'pig' which was whining up towards their corner: but just what, I could not guess, for the armoured vehicles seemed pretty impregnable. As the 'pig' passed the corner, blocking the group from my view, I saw something with a blue flame curl over the top of the vehicle, and about a second later, it landed at my feet and rolled into the gutter. It was a small bomb, probably a stick of gelignite with a simple burning fuse. I do not know whether I turned and ran backwards or simply backpedalled madly, but seconds later, I was about twenty yards from the corner, with a deafening explosion in my ears, glass falling around, and a feeling of having had every hair on my legs singed off. I felt myself all over and was perfectly intact. I examined my shins, which were as hairy as ever, yet the feeling of having been singed persisted for a couple of hours. I was almost smiling in relief when I returned to the corner and started to walk towards my bomb-throwing neighbours. When I was about half-way across the Falls Road, somebody shouted, "Get back, get back!": but I could see an army vehicle disgorging soldiers further up the road out of sight from the corner, and I was not about to hesitate. I kept on walking firmly towards the corner, where I was suddenly grabbed and pulled into the group: a piece of fuse was lit and thrown into the air to act as a crude smokescreen, and then a man stepped forward and fired rapidly at the roof of the building on the corner from which I had just walked. At the sound of the gunfire, the entire group, preceded by youngsters, began running like hell down the street. I ran or was half-pushed for several yards, then resumed walking. This disposition of deciding my own pace has always been my practice, usually to my advantage: but not invariably. On one occasion, when I decided to go in a different direction from a curious crowd being cleared from the presumed site of a car-bomb, I was lucky not to be evaporated—for the bomb was in a position different to the reported warning, and was around the corner which I was approaching. Seven people were killed by it.

I never became totally accustomed to these deaths in the streets. Once after I had been very moved by a particular tragedy, I thought that I would nevertheless be able to suppress the images and get my normal sleep. This was in September 1971. I had been standing talking to a man whom I met frequently enough (who had no need to be 'on the run', but was in touch with what was happening) when we heard a muffled explosion close by. "That's funny," he said. "That sounds as if it's inside somewhere." He was quite expert at locating the direction of gunfire and blast-bombing, both of which echo a lot. Moments later, a wee lad shouted to us, "Hey, there's a house blew up!" We ran to the corner of Merrion Street, about fifty yards from where we had been standing, and saw smoke drifting from where windows had been, in the first house. I pushed open the door, and it looked as if a girl, in a rust wool dress, was lying asleep. Then I saw that her hair had been wizened, and beyond her, lying stretched out, blackened and in a grotesque shape, was the body of a young man. Both had died instantly in the explosion, and it looked as if they had been carrying something, for the centre of the explosion was between them, by my impression. A crowd was gathering, and already army vehicles could be heard approaching. Someone called an ambulance, another got sheets and blankets. A man, who seemed to be acting with some kind of authority, stepped past the bodies, then cautiously up a few of the shattered stairs, looked around briefly, and then withdrew. I helped to hold people back and to carry the grim sheet-loads into the back of an ambulance, which quickly removed to the nearby Royal Victoria Hospital. The crowd was now getting hostile towards an army officer who was bustling around the front of the house, asking questions. I suggested to him very strongly that he withdrew before anybody else got hurt, and told him that the only people in the house were the two dead and that they were away to the hospital. He did withdraw almost immediately. It is a great pity that many more officers did not behave similarly in such highly charged situations.

I went to a telephone, made my report, checked on the wider state of things, went home in due course, and went to bed. By this stage I was already fairly numbly used to death, murder and mayhem; and having accepted my own mortality as a possibility in any one day, felt able to sleep at night, grateful to be in the relatively safe comfort of my suburban home. But on that night I could not sleep: the images of Rose Curry and Gerry O'Hare lying dead in the dark kept floating up, and through them I could see the friendly face of young Gerry O'Hare who had waved hello to me in the street a few days earlier. Eventually I sobbed like a child: but this produced no relief, and I felt grim for a long time afterwards. It was not until 'McGurk's Bar', an atrocity that claimed the lives of fifteen people in one blast, including one of the bar-owner's children and his wife, that I finally came to working terms with bomb carnage.

On that appalling night of December 4, 1971, much of the cruel insanity of Northern Ireland's conflict was vividly demonstrated. I was driving at about 9.00 p.m. in the Antrim Road area of Belfast, when I heard a heavy, loud explosion: even with the car windows up, I was sure that it was no 'blast bomb'. It also sounded fairly near, though I could see no smoke plume.

I drove down the New Lodge Road and went into a pub which was likely to have citizens who might know more than I did. There had been a cheerful atmosphere, and one man, who was well-disposed to the local Provisional IRA, had been quite certain that the bomb which all had heard, must have been an attack on the local army post: in that bar, a popular target, since this was one of the centres from which the New Lodge area was raided and patrolled.

The mood had changed utterly moments later when a man had burst in, shouting wildly, "McGurk's is blew up, everybody's dead". There followed an exodus in the direction of McGurk's, a distance of a few hundred yards, on nearby North Queen Street. An angry crowd of Loyalists, who had also imagined that the bomb had been an IRA attack, had gathered at the junction with Duncairn Gardens, just a couple of hundred yards in the other direction; and a sectarian confrontation was developing, with Catholic youths jeering and taunting from the bottom of Spamount Street and Hardinge Street. The two crowds exchanged moods when it became obvious that it was a Catholic pub that had gone up, not an army post.

People had been killed in ones and twos in various explosions, and there had been 'miracle escape' stories for months, especially in the bombing of crowded bars. But here, there was no miracle escape: an apparently solid, three storey edifice had collapsed, and was lying, like sand dumped in a corner, in its own smoking rubble. Only about six stanchions of an upstairs bannister remained incongruously intact of what had been a thriving pub, and the upstairs home of the owner, Patsy McGurk, his wife and children.

Already everyone who had arrived was pulling at bricks, smashed timbers and anything else, to try and rescue anyone possibly alive in the smouldering heap, through which gas from a burst main was still burning. People wept and tore frantically at the debris, regardless of cut hands or any other hazard. There were occasional little screams from someone who had a relative in the pub. Soldiers, policemen, firemen, nurses, neighbours, clergy, known republicans, journalists, and local MP Gerry Fitt, who arrived at an early stage, worked feverishly to get out the living. Spotlights from army Land Rovers lit the scene. Somebody got the gas turned off.

A fleet of ambulances queued up to remove the dead, the dying and the injured. Here and there an arm or a leg or half a human torso or a head would be found, with that awful blasted-on mixture of dust and blood that can make the human litter from an explosion look like something left on a dump. For hours, the work went on, and some people did survive. But fourteen were counted dead by 4.00 a.m. and another died later, making the atrocity the worst single event to date: it remains in the first half-dozen single-incident atrocities of the entire war, ranking with Derry (1972), Dublin (1974), Birmingham (1974), Warrenpoint (1979) and Ballykelly (1982).

About half-way through the grim rescue work, when it began to seem that no more survivors were possible, or that any would be suffocated if the heavy load of rubble were not removed, the police asked everyone to move back, while troops gingerly ran the teeth of an earth mover under the pile and began scooping it up onto removal lorries. At each scoopful, the scoop would be stopped at hand-height while it was examined for human remains, and presumably forensic evidence. Now and again, something would be carefully removed and placed in a plastic bag. The whole scene was too awful for anger. People stood dumbly about, some weeping. Gerry Fitt, soft-hearted humanitarian at the core of a tough political personality, was standing with tears running on to his mud-stained white shirt. There was a hope that this atrocity, in a pub known for its quiet, good order among the more senior dockers and pensioners, was beyond political argument, and might 'bring people to their senses'.

Any such hope was being snuffed out a few hundred yards away, even as presumed adversaries were co-operating frantically in the rubble of McGurk's. Police and troops had intervened between the rival crowds. In the middle of all the taunts and jeers, shots rang out from the Catholic side: Major Jeremy Snow became the first British officer to be shot dead on duty in Northern Ireland (an officer named Alers-Sankey, wounded earlier in Derry, died later in England); and a young policeman was wounded.

From hundreds of people standing merged in the common humanity of helpless grief to four hundred yards away where hundreds of the same kind of people were engaged in the most ghoulish exchange of taunts over the dead, then scattered by an act of murder, was, in a single scene, the range of feeling of this unnecessary war.

I found myself able to report the event quite calmly, once there was nothing further citizens could do, and walked from McGurk's to the riot, to the phone and backwards and forwards through the night until the last body count and the last deadline. By that time, there was all manner of speculation on who might have been responsible, from a rumour that a Provo volunteer might have failed to collect a primed bomb, to the possibility that it was an army 'dirty tricks' operation. Seven years passed before a Loyalist, a member of the Ulster Volunteer Force (UVF), confessed to the deliberate attack, and laid rumour to rest long after it may have done its own insidious damage.

The following day, when I had to 'wrap up' the weekend's events, and comment on McGurk's, I found myself somewhat choked after the first few lines. But the feeling eased off, and I began to feel as if a weight that had been sitting on me since the Curry-O'Hare deaths was lifting, as if an undetected depression was clearing up. I knew that no atrocity could ever shock me again: even the thought of my own remains lying in blasted pieces, exposed to public view and handling, did not concern me.

I felt myself understanding that such events present everybody with a choice: they either make us more sensitive to life, or they brutalise us—and we may coolly choose which. One can live with carnage with a full and clear appreciation of its enormity, choosing with greater determination than ever, a commitment to life; or one may come to terms by becoming more brutalised, accepting the 'necessity' of any and every level of atrocity to get one's way, or to get revenge.

Such threshold moments were experienced also at community level, moments of collective hope that a limit had been reached, that we must pull back from the abyss, and struggle for a more human politic. Several such threshold moments were breached—and lost—in 1971/72.

In those dark, bitter—and exciting—months of December 1971 and January 1972, there seemed to be no way out of further atrocity. The Catholics, totally and collectively alienated from the Faulkner government's policy of internment and torture, and seemingly blind-eyed to Loyalist assassins, nevertheless did not want to give collective support to the Provos, however much they 'understood' their motivations. Quite a few of the Provos had neither wish for nor anticipation of any prolonged murder campaign: their policy was self-consciously one of regular attrition against the British, whose dubious will to stay they sought to break publicly—regardless of, even ignorant of the real problem of accommodation with the Unionists, and of the effect of their campaign on the future requirements of reconciliation and compromise.

Faulkner, for his part, kept telling himself and others that internment had worked in the Fifties and would work again: he seemed incapable of understanding that it was the non-support of the Catholic community which had frustrated the IRA of a decade earlier. Now he was driving the Catholics into support for the IRA, his policies recruiting people who had no tradition of support for militaristic republicanism.

The Official IRA, considerably re-armed from the humiliated group of social agitators of two years earlier, was going through the agony of reappraisal on its feet. Its leaders felt a responsibility to defend against sectarian attack, yet were inhibited from doing anything which might later impede the unity of the Protestant and Catholic working class which was an essential part of their political programme. At the same time they were being subjected to at least the same degree of pressure by the British as the Provisionals, since the British feared them more. A ceasefire, which they were contemplating, would be very difficult to maintain among young volunteers who would then be called 'yellow' by the Provos without any decrease in harassment, internment or torture by the British. While they were trying to consider these problems, on the ground they were being sucked deeper into an unwanted militarism by the offensive pace set by the Provos.

To create an alternative outlet for the deep frustration of Catholics at the deteriorating situation, a massive anti-internment rally was called for Derry on January 30, by the civil rights association, now heavily influenced by the Official Republicans and the tiny domestic Communist Party. Despite its sponsorship, and the misgivings of representative Catholic opinion about any mass demonstrations in the circumstances, the unaligned marching potential of the civil rights movement felt that this was one acceptable way of showing detestation of internment, torture and violence. One such was a young relative of mine, who, like myself, had not participated for a long time.

By a coincidence, that very weekend my virtually apolitical father was at Chatham House, the curiously English establishment in which the British Foreign Office is wont to hold informal conferences, by which to get a feel for what might be politically or diplomatically possible in a situation under consideration for a policy change. It was clear that a radical re-think of British policy was under way, and that Heath's government was determined to get a much wider expression of political opinion and intelligence than that forthcoming from the insular recesses of Stormont.

In mid-afternoon, Sunday, I heard that there had been shooting at the Derry march. Details were imprecise, but indicated that there were several dead. First reports suggested that the army had opened fire, Sharpeville-style, on the marchers.

I found this hard to believe and easy to believe almost in the same moment. I also knew that I would be taking my mother and sister to the airport to collect my father on his return from London, and had little enough chance of finding out if our relative was safe. I rang every conceivable contact and source, trying to get a picture of what had happened, and by the time we left for the airport, it seemed clear that British Paratroopers had indeed been shooting unarmed people—in an action later described as 'bordering on the reckless' by Lord Widgery, in that eminent judge's official report to the British government, and as massacre by most ordinary people.

I tried to prepare myself mentally for any possibility, but found myself getting angrier. I knew that our young relative was well able to take care of himself, but I also knew him to be very protective of people weaker than himself, from a childhood image of him carefully nursing an injured blackbird back to health, to memories of him taking on bullies bigger than himself as a kid when they threatened others. These qualities would make him vulnerable to paratroopers whom I had seen in action in Belfast more than once: I could see him going back to help someone and being hit himself.

I tried to think of how my family could handle such a possibility.

In one moment, I felt myself capable of killing. I could hear words like 'if those bastards have killed him' running through my head. I also felt I was capable of organising cold-bloodedly if I turned in that direction. In another moment, I could feel how utterly broken my family would be, but that they would not be vengeful.

It was a particularly slow journey to the airport, for it had begun to snow. But by the time we greeted my father, I had made up my mind firmly that no matter what lay ahead, I would adhere utterly to my belief in nonviolence. In those few hours, everything I had believed in was threatened and tempered: at the same time, my appreciation of the murderous rage which grips people after such events was deepened to the same degree.

Late that evening, we heard that the relative in question was safe. It was an enormous relief. He had been very close to being shot: people had run at the sound of gunfire, while he, typically enough, did not, and a man pulled him to the ground and told him, "Son, them's real bullets they're firing". They got to a house where people let them in, and gave them tea.

'Bloody Sunday' was an immense and reverberating boost for the IRA, especially in Irish-America, where the date is staked out like a baleful beacon in their mythic understanding of Northern Ireland. World opinion was horrified by the British action. But viewers of the subsequent David Frost programme were shocked to hear Bloody Sunday described as 'Good Sunday for Protestants' by John McKeague, a leading Protestant paramilitarist of the time. (McKeague, whose militarism and politics mellowed through the later Seventies after he broke from his early association with Ian Paisley, was murdered in mysterious circumstances in 1981.)

I suppose the truth will never be known of what caused the highly disciplined Paratroopers to open fire 'bordering on the reckless', especially in the presence in Derry that day, of the British Commander of Land Forces, General Ford. Paras are exceptionally well trained to obey orders, whether the orders are to shoot, or not to shoot: even if all the alleged provocation that the army immediately claimed had taken place, Paras above all would have reacted with discipline. The army press officers also had a blatantly false propaganda line ready for the British press, which had been such a sucker for their press-desk guff, but it was blown apart by the *Guardian*'s Simon Winchester, a man normally well-disposed to them.

Simon, who used to turn up to cover riots in a helmet and combat jacket, often only distinguishable from troops by his white slacks as he chatted behind army lines, was clearly shocked and frightened by his experience of seeing the army of his own country open fire on innocent people, and said so, whatever his friends at army headquarters in Lisburn thought of it. It was the chance ignorance of one of his compatriots that had left Simon out in the firing line, for he had endeavoured to get behind army lines, but was told by a soldier closing the lines, "No, you bastard, you stay there and take what's coming to you."

Winchester's account was all the more compelling because of his patently honest, authentic tone of outrage and disillusionment. Other sections of the British media, which had been poised to support the army, (*The Times'* John Chartres talked of 'a jolly good show'), were forced to ask if there had not been some mistake, and were these really terrorists who had been shot, and had the army, at a high officer level, lied?

Thereafter, some English journalists became truculently sceptical, and often more searching in their questions than native journalists. Some, at risk to themselves, took the trouble to go into possible danger and make contacts, and were frequently better informed than anybody in , say, the *Belfast Telegraph* or the BBC's Northern Ireland news desk. The Belfast papers, much praised for the very fact of doing their jobs in the situation, did not in fact distinguish themselves. The *Irish News*, often literary and enlightened in its editorials, was otherwise very much the Catholic paper for Catholics, while the *News Letter* was the Protestant morning for Protestants, and both were decidedly lightweight in news coverage. The *Belfast Telegraph*, which saw itself as 'Northern Ireland's national newspaper', is an evening paper with the largest circulation and advertising revenue. It was O'Neillite Unionist during the Sixties, under the editorship of the late Jack Sayers, and became a target for Paisleyite abuse. But when things became hot, the '*Telly*' played safe, its editorial line fluctuating mildly between respectable Unionism and a soft-liberal, bleeding-heart, hand- wringing approach. In sixteen years of turmoil, no-one could accuse the *Telegraph* of being at the heart of any heated controversy: perhaps that may be taken as a compliment.

With Bloody Sunday, the propaganda war began in earnest. The media-backed 'Brits-v-Provos' myth suited almost everybody in its simplemindedness, except the SDLP, because it helped distract from the complexities and challenge of the main problem, which was the creation of a just regime enjoying widespread and enthusiastic consensus. Support for the myth has correspondingly lengthened the war and made it more atrocious, especially as internment removed the more mature republicans, leaving less restrained spirits increasingly in charge of local units.

The daily bombing campaign in Northern Ireland, the overnight corpse-count, and the destruction bills might gradually have bored the British public, and the government itself might have been able to lower the international profile of the 'Troubles', had it not been for the outcry, not so much over the IRA's campaign and the sectarian murders, as over the use within its territory of internment and torture by the British themselves; and finally, the event of January 30, 1972, on the landscape of long-suffering Ireland, looked too much like a flash of the old imperial Britain, using the methods so lustily employed formerly in her colonies for dealing with native majorities. Such an image pierced the confusing murk of the more complicated issues, and gave propagandists abroad an irresistibly familiar handle on the problem.

Edward Heath's triumphant joy at joining Europe, and his genuine sense of idealistic statesmanship in that achievement, were shot to bits on the streets of Derry by his own paratroopers, and would shortly be dragged through the European Court of Justice on torture charges.

In March 1972, poor Brian Faulkner, Prime Minister of Northern Ireland for a mere year after so much effort, found that his imagined relationship as a fellow professional politician with Heath, was more like that of tenant to nineteenth century landlord. He was summoned to London, given enough time to resign, and the Stormont Parliament was prorogued. Heath, now focussing his single-minded attention on Northern Ireland, sent in his deputy, William Whitelaw, with a full government team, which hit the place like a whirlwind. Whitelaw set about reconstructing Northern Ireland as if working to an election deadline.

It says a great deal for Brian Faulkner, whose world had been shattered, and who had had the further humiliation of having signed authorisations for torture actually sanctioned much higher up, that he only allowed himself one brief moment of barely parliamentary behaviour by speaking to a Stormont demonstration heavily redolent of paramilitarism. He then swallowed the pill and returned to the job of politics. Over the next two years, he won something of a reputation for statesmanship, gaining respect at home and abroad for courage and ability. Tragically, he was killed in a riding accident in 1977, before he could begin to enjoy or use the peerage he had then recently been granted. The personal tragedy was also political tragedy for it deepened the leadership vacuum in the Unionist community, allowing increased influence to the ultra position of the Rev. Ian Paisley. There has yet to be any convincing sign that accommodation with the latter can be on anything other than subjection.

A one-month ceasefire, with its inherent potential for indefinite extension, would have been welcomed ecstatically by the Catholic community after eight months of continual mightmare. And at a time when the Provos were reasonably disciplined, it might have held them within the constraints of community influence for the future. It would have provided a little balm for most Protestants, and helped them to accept the formal end of ascendancy. It would have annoyed only those Paisleyites who needed the Provos to prove their rhetoric for them.

But Provisional IRA chief of staff Sean MacStiofain said no, and the violence became more vicious and bitter. Protestant killing of randomly abducted Catholics increased, activity sanctioned culturally, almost openly, by some leading Unionists.

So a moment of great potential was severely compromised. But people still clung desperately to hope, and Whitelaw generated a momentum that kept hope alive, a dynamic which has unquantifiable value even when progress is not obvious.

The Official IRA was already strongly disposed to ceasefire, and discussions to that end were under way when, on April 15, one of their Belfast leaders, Joe McCann, was shot dead in the centre of Belfast. He was unarmed, walking in broad daylight on that early Saturday afternoon in Joy Street when he was shot in the back. As he went down, with his hands up, soldiers fired again. This killing on sight enraged the younger volunteers and delayed the ceasefire.

I knew McCann fairly well. He had acquired something of a hero-aura while on the run after internment, adopting disguises which fooled even his acquaintances. While I liked him, and was distressed at the manner of his death, I had found that he was becoming more and more addicted to the role of gunman as the essential function of the revolutionary. Perhaps, having killed already, and been, according to folk-intelligence, the principal in the attempted assassination of the Junior Minister of Home Affairs, John Taylor (now a Member of the European Parliament), he could not easily set his militarism aside in favour of nonviolent revolution. Moreover, he knew that he was a 'marked man', young volunteers having been told during interrogation to tell McCann that the authorities were not going to arrest him, which was generally interpreted as a threat to shoot him on sight, as indeed he was. He must have been very close to being public enemy number one at the time of his death.

Something of the reason that senior British officers still feared the Official IRA more than the Provisionals was demonstrated in the few days after McCann's death. While his remains lay in a house in Turf Lodge in West Belfast, the entire area was taken over by 'The Stickies', as the Officials were nicknamed. They operated checkpoints, à la British Army, at the entrance and exits to the estate, as well as patrolling in open Land Rovers with 'Official IRA' painted on the side.

Also, in fulfilment of the chilling graveside pledge of their normally restrained Chief of Staff, Cathal Goulding, to make the British "pay richly in their own red blood", they clinically shot three soldiers dead.

Fortunately, within a month of this disciplined militaristic display, and after their Derry outfit had alienated people by murdering Ranger William Best (a soldier on leave to visit his family), they did call a ceasefire, which they maintained, with occasional lapses, thereafter.

The Official Republicans, today known as the Workers' Party, resumed their Sixties-style political agitation where they had been interrupted, and demilitarised completely in 1977. It is still possible to hear jokes about the Provos not wanting to attack the Officials without anti-tetanus injections in case they get shot by rusty guns. If there are still 'pikes in the thatch', they are deeply hidden. This is a remarkable achievement, given that the Officials, after their ceasefire, continued to be subject to harassment by the British, and much more murderously by the Provos and the INLA. The latter outfit began largely as a splinter group refusing to accept the Officials' ceasefire. The Workers' Party has won considerable political respect, if not corresponding support, North and South in Ireland, for their persistence with the political process; and they do not like to be reminded of their militaristic roots.

I have been, and will again be tackled by some of them for calling attention to their movement from arms to politics, and subjected to tirades about not letting people forget. But not only do I refuse to pretend that I did not see what I saw with my own eyes, but I insist that the example of what they have done is important beyond the destiny of this particular group. Their achievement is something they are entitled to celebrate rather than conceal. Almost everywhere that an armed revolutionary organisation has settled down to the practice of conventional politics—the United States, France, Russia, Zimbabwe, Southern Ireland, to name a few—it has been *after* they have won, or at least staked out some measure of victory. In the case of the Stickies, they have achieved political respect while their members were still being harassed in their native streets by the British, the Provos, former comrades, and an often hostile press; and most telling of all in the necromantic traditions of Ireland, while their comrades lay in recent graves, or in jail.

By the time the Official IRA dropped out of the war in May 1972, Whitelaw had already begun to release internees, and he now stepped up the pace, regardless of howls of protest from Paisleyism and Unionism alike. In June, in another briefly hopeful initiative, the new Northern Ireland Secretary of State organised a meeting with

Provisional IRA leaders, flattering them with a special RAF lift to London, and including such as the youthful Gerry Adams, then held in Long Kesh. A ceasefire with the Provisionals was negotiated, which appeared to give them good reason to hold fire.

Whitelaw was on a tightrope. In the background was the shadow of Bloody Sunday and the torture litigation in Europe, both damaging to Britain's international prestige and therefore to inward investment and external trading. In the foreground was the Ulster Defence Association (UDA), a large loyalist paramilitary organisation which had already been responsible for a number of assassinations of Catholics picked up at random: it was openly organised, and unproscribed, and had been out showing its considerable numbers, blocking roads and even engaging in open-air, hand-to-hand training. No-one could be entirely sure whether an organisation which so many had joined, more out of protest than out of any deeper sense of insecurity, would have the stomach for more than demonstration and random murder: but out of so many men and boys, it was certain that enough would take to more coherent violence, if they were publicly humiliated. It was therefore important that the deal between the IRA and the British (which had been initiated by politicians actually opposed to the IRA, John Hume and Paddy Devlin of the SDLP, and an Independent Unionist MP, Tom Caldwell, an art dealer who had met the IRA's national leaders, David O'Connell and Sean MacStiofain), should not be trumpeted.

But its terms leaked immediately. Although another ten days would pass before the famous Lenadoon incident brought the thirteen-day ceasefire to an end, I had an overwhelming sense that the Provos in Belfast's command had no basic understanding of the nature of ceasefire politics, and that the deal would collapse at the earliest test, in spite of the good sense that it made on the surface.

Lenadoon was a mixed Catholic and Protestant estate at the south-west extremity of West Belfast, its Protestant population declining because of fear of proximity to republican Andersonstown. ('Republican' Andersonstown merely indicates that a significant IRA presence existed there: the overwhelming majority of the population was by no means steeped in the ethos of Irish physical force traditions, and voted massively for the SDLP which openly condemned the IRA. But, in any such situation where the emotional choice was between the neighbour's children on the run and the highly armed, patrolling British in uniform, the neighbour's children, however atrocious their activities, were usually going to win. The longer in fact the British stayed, the more actually republican Andersonstown would become.)

It was understood that a number of Catholic families would be moved into houses close to the dwindling Protestant enclave at Horn Drive, at the lower end of Lenadoon. The UDA warned that any attempt to move the Catholics in would lead to their being burned out again.

There had been some rioting at this new flashpoint: I recall one evening, when it had calmed down, and British soldiers had created a no-man's land between Catholic and Protestant rioters, the crowds had begun to disperse fairly peacefully, with no bones broken and nobody retching with gas, when I noticed that there seemed to be some hitch on the Protestant side.

I sauntered over the rubble-strewn patch between the two crowds, and as I approached a barricade of two army vehicles, I heard a raised and agitated voice, and some lower, more persuasive tones. There, behind the vehicles, was the late Rev. Robert Bradford, MP, then a Methodist minister in the area, shouting and gesticulating at a senior army officer and a senior police officer. The officers were appealing to him in his office as a Christian minister to withdraw and to encourage the good people behind him to retire to their homes. Mr. Bradford's reiterated reply to this was that the good people on his side would retire when the army had "cleared that rabble off the streets"— pointing to the Catholics.

The unfortunate Mr. Bradford, who advocated both capital punishment and summary execution for terrorists, and at that time inclined to the view that Ulster's Protestants were the 'lost tribe of Israel', was a curious mixture of genuine, hard-working servant of his people, and bigot: the kind of 'Christian' which Northern Ireland's sickness misguides into a belligerent exclusivism. He was murdered by the IRA in 1981 while working in his constituency advice centre.

The housing issue, one of the main grievances of the original civil rights agitation, was about to be made the test of the British government's good faith in the ceasefire, as judged by the Belfast IRA commander, Seamus Twomey, a man committed to the present campaign as the last phase in the 800-year struggle with England, as he described it to me during a ceasefire interview. Was Whitelaw, in the person of the local British army officers, going to allow Catholics to have the houses, or would he bow to UDA threats? Within the twenty-four hours which the local British army officer desperately sought to review the delicate situation, a crowd of Catholics marching with a lorry load of furniture, and with the IRA both very much in the open and staked out around the area, began to make their way towards the sixteen disputed houses. There was no no-man's land for negotiation, and hand-to-hand fighting broke out between soldiers and civilians. With Seamus Twomey shouting about 'truce violation' and withdrawing, whistles were blown, gas was fired, then rubber bullets, then bullets. The truce was over.

The breakdown was partly a function of the political adolescence of the local Provos, which included their conviction that "this time they would finish it". David O'Connell, had he been on the ground in Belfast, might have handled it better: but the indigenous Provos who could hardly believe the changes of the previous two years and attributed it all to their own violence, were profoundly mistrustful of 'politics' and 'politicians'. Indeed, at that time, they might even have been very wary of O'Connell himself, and their loyalty was instinctively to MacStiofain who, as an English 'convert' to the cause, was even more fanatical than themselves.

In the crude perceptions of that hysterical period, a recent diplomatic resolution of a confrontation between 5,000 UDA men and the British army, with General Ford in evidence again, was taken as proof that the British were not about to be even-handed. Of course the British had *not* been even-handed: but any reasonable person would have been glad that Ford backed off with reasonable honour from the UDA, otherwise there would have been many more dead than on Bloody Sunday and the UDA would have had no honourable choice but to move to far more intensive murdering in response: an interesting reflection in itself on what militarism does to the meaning of words like 'honourable'.

Moreover in the context of the British government's open parleying with the Provisional IRA within months of proroguing Stormont, an IRA politico, had such a person any real influence, would have appreciated that the foregoing substantial reverses for Unionism should not have been weighed in the same scale as street brinkmanship games with the UDA. But the Brits, as the Provos saw it, had not backed off in Lenadoon as they had on the Springfield Road against the loyalists in ranks, and that was that.

The war was on again, with a vengeance. On July 21, a Friday, the Provos planted more than twenty bombs in Belfast, timed to explode within about an hour, and the only subsequent surprise was that only eleven people were killed in the horrific blitz. Little or no warning had been given, or such as was was inaccurate or too late. In any case, it would have been impossible, even if the army, police, fire and ambulance men had been handed a ground plan of the bomb locations, to get around to deal with them, for they affected all the main traffic routes, and were set to go off within such a limited time scale.

As well as eleven dead, over 100 were injured, some maimed for life. I drove straight into it, on my way through the city centre, being re-directed this way and that. It seemed to me that there was an explosion going off in every main street that I had just passed. It crossed my mind fleetingly that this might be the Provos' way of asking for a renewed ceasefire—like the Nixon-Kissinger strategy of bombing their way out of Vietnam, a prelude to diplomacy, terrorist style—but while they may have been capable of such a thought, it died with the realisation that the British could have only one reply to such a concentrated attack.

I was due on duty at 4 p.m., and this was some time after two, so I sought my colleagues. (Our office had been bombed—while two of us were in it—and we operated from home or from pubs frequented by journalists, politicians and other contacts). In the course of looking for them, I met a terrified freelance visitor who wanted to get out of Belfast as fast as possible, and another equally terrified reporter who, that morning, had been threatened with a punishment shooting by the Provos. Bombs were still going off every few minutes, and I could understand their mounting hysteria, which was not, however, being calmed by the rate at which they were downing spirits. No-one had any idea of the 'score' at that point: there were queues for phones, and constantly engaged press-desks. I felt certain that the town would be seized up very quickly, and that I might be better to get home to my own phone.

I offered the freelance a lift to his hotel to pick up his things and see him to the station, and told the other man that I would be back shortly to give him a lift. When we were about 100 yards from the freelance's hotel, the Hamill—across the street from both the station and the much-bombed Europa Hotel—in Great Victoria Street, we were diverted by the police: from all the signs, it seemed that there was a bomb in one or other of the hotels or in a nearby car. I told my shaking friend to wait a moment while I checked with the police, and got out to walk towards them. A moment later, I heard the car starting behind me, and I stared in no little surprise as it reversed past me and set off up the Grosvenor Road at a furious rate! He took the car and did not stop until he reached Dublin! (He had been under continuous strain, for he too had been threatened indirectly; after a brief holiday, he recovered sufficiently to return for another stint.)

Most of the press reports of that day refer to panic and hysteria. I saw little enough outright panic, except from a couple of journalists. I walked back through the city centre, sometimes through parts that were deserted, sometimes milling with people, moving away from bombs. Explosions were still happening, eliciting momentary screams, then hesitation to decide by sound or plume where it was. Sirens were so frequent that one almost ceased to hear them, and the whining, racing bomb squad vehicles were the most natural sight in the circumstances.

I was angry, without any particular focus for the feeling, when I caught up with the other journalist, who had meantime decided that he might be better to stay where he was, in case the Provos were watching his car. I insisted that there could be no real authority for the threat, and that we should go at once and face it—otherwise our job would be made impossible, if any local cowboy thought he could scare journalists off. Given the Provos' mood, by his reasoning, they would not have threatened him if they did not mean it. His were the knees in question and he was reluctant to leave the illusory comfort of the pub. I became very impatient and said finally, "Right, I'm going." He then asked me to come with him to get his car.

We went round a few back streets to get his car, and I got into the driving seat and headed straight to the area from which the threat had come, reckoning that there would still be somebody 'in command' in spite of the day's operations. After the usual mickey-mousing from house to pub to house, we met two local Provo officers: my friend was not sure whether to be terrified or whether to apologise for inconveniencing them. I suppose my rising anger must have been coming through for I told them bluntly that whatever about their policy of blowing up the town (at this stage we had no accurate picture of casualties and half-imagined that such a big, well-planned operation would have had warnings well built in, which would also have explained the quick response of the bomb disposal squads), what was the idea of threatening people without any cause? "Here is this man, has he been tried, has he been found guilty of anything? Yet here he is running about scared out of his wits because some cowboy starts throwing his weight about."

"They were only threatening to wing him, as a warning," one of them said.

"Only wing him!" I practically shouted back. "Wing him for what?"

"He was shooting his mouth off." At this point, I sensed that they were both acutely anxious to be elsewhere, and at the same time, felt I was letting myself into a stupid 'yes you did no you didn't' type of argument would could become very counter-productive. One of them said, "We can't hang around, the place'll be crawling with Brits", and then, "Yer man'll be alright". In other words the threat was off. I had a strong hunch that whoever had offered to 'wing' my friend had been acting outside of orders.

I felt oddly sorry for those two young men as they disappeared round a corner of Hardinge Street: history and local circumstance had sucked them into a situation where they were expected to be soldiers, policemen, officers, responsible defenders or ruthless terrorists by different sets of people. Coming from deprived backgrounds, their lives would be taken up with running from authority, killing or being killed or going to jail; and in the meantime, imagining that they were winning something . . .

The appalling details of the blitz were being certified, an hour after the last explosion when I finally got down to detailed checking. I had a feeling of being degraded, a clinging sense of sordidity, as I put the story together. It clung like smoke around me, a palpable disgust that was beyond anger.

One part of me knew why people did what the Provos had just done, knew the dammed up historical resentments that went into such atrocity, the decades, or even the centuries as some felt it, of humiliation at being treated as less than human. Another part of my mind was noting that their atrocity was now living up to and appearing to justify anti-Catholic prejudice, for this was less than human. What, moments before, had been innocent human beings, were now human litter, being shovelled into plastic bags.

The Catholic population had been enraged at the Bloody Sunday massacre by British troops the previous January: now the same population was being humiliated by this grisly attack from their own people on what was now Bloody Friday.

Distanced as I may be by thought, background and education from the ghetto mentality of feeling 'like a Catholic', I felt strangely ashamed as I arrived home that evening. The city was deathly still within a few hours. Friday rush-hour traffic had dispersed early, premises, including even pubs, closed early, and the roads were almost eerily empty by about 7 p.m. on this weekend summer evening. From where we lived, it was possible to see down over broad swathes of the town, and plumes of smoke were still visible here and there. We had moved into our house less than two months earlier, in a predominantly Protestant neighbourhood. My neighbours were standing out at their gates in groups, obviously discussing the events. I felt too degraded to converse with any of them, went indoors and stayed in.

During the next few days, loyalists killed four stray Catholics, picked up at random, but no-one fussed: it was 'understandable' in the circumstances. In fact, more people were killed around that time by loyalists, but no-one appeared to notice. The Provo bombing atrocities were highly visible, dramatic, media-visible: loyalist victims were dawn-light lumps on waste ground.

I remember raising the matter at a Stormont briefing for lobby correspondents by Whitelaw's press secretary, former *Daily Mail* man

Keith McDowell. I was fairly disgusted at the cheerfully vigorous way in which the authorities had cobbled together a propaganda poster based on Bloody Friday, and were presenting it to the select lobby, to encourage a special mention of it. When I asked what pitch was being made for information about sectarian murder, McDowell looked at me as if I had two heads: the reaction to the question, including the response of some fellow-journalists, was that I was behaving like a republican propagandist to raise such a matter at such a time. While I admired the skilful way in which the good-humoured McDowell cheerfully manipulated an often docile lobby, I resented being regarded and almost openly treated as a republican propagandist for trying to bring in all the facts, and not simply those which supported the 'British-v-IRA' mythology.

The fact that I 'represented' the Irish Press Group predisposed quite a few to expect that I might be more pro-Provo than any other journalist, because of the group's direct control by the de Valera family. Moreover the editor of the *Irish Press* was Tim Pat Coogan, author of *The IRA*, and the editor most often regarded as closer to the Provisionals than any other. Though I did have a difference of opinion with Tim Pat Coogan on the issue of propaganda—he felt that with the British spending so much, especially in the US, on propaganda, an Irish editor had a responsibility to restore the balance, while I felt that the simple truth was the most powerful propaganda—I always found him most kindly disposed to me. I appreciated this very much as a blow-in graduate to journalism, liable to be resented by those who 'came up the hard way'. He is a big-hearted man, whose father did Trojan work in restoring the morale of the unarmed Irish police in the wake of the Irish Civil War, and whose mother Beatrice won the Frankfurt Book Prize with *The Big Wind* in the late Sixties.

Right up to the time when I quit the Irish Press Group in the autumn of 1976, I must record that my stories on the Provisionals or anything else, were not bent in their favour—and I wrote some of the most damaging articles about them, all the more so for being true rather than propagandist. Sometimes I was angered, occasionally disturbed, when editorials I had been asked to draft, were altered significantly: but that was an editor's duty and responsibility; and often enough, my editorials were printed verbatim even when they did not coincide with Dublin's assessment.

1972 was relentlessly dazing in its complexity and horror. 467 people were killed by gun or bomb, thousands injured, many grotesquely maimed. There was an enormous population shift, whole areas rapidly becoming totally Catholic or totally Protestant, sometimes almost overnight. It was the year of greatest political shock with the suspension of Stormont, the introduction of Direct Rule from London, and early manoeuvrings for a new settlement to replace the fifty-year old failure. It was a year in which confrontation alternated with ceasefire, the process punctuated by atrocity, not only the named events like Bloody Sunday, the Abercorn, Donegall Street, Bloody Friday, but the steady stream of sectarian killings and daily bombing. I once got headlines for a story, 'Belfast has quiet evening'.

One odd event was 'Operation Motorman', in which the British brought in huge tanks in a massive operation to break down the permanent barricades that marked the 'no-go' areas in republican 'strongholds'. This was very much an in-and-out-again demonstration of strength by Whitelaw in the wake of Bloody Friday, and a measure also designed to discourage loyalists from establishing their own 'no-go' areas, which would have forced the British to 'face in both directions'.

Down in South Armagh, cheeky daylight gun-battles took place, as Belfast men on the run took advantage of the countryside to operate openly, in contrast to their experience of dodging around the back alleys of Belfast. That stretch of countryside had no great tradition of republicanism as such: it was rather more familiar with smuggling and passionately interested in Irish national culture, especially Gaelic games, and Belfast was a relatively foreign place to its people. But the John Wayne-style cowboy activity aroused the young bloods in places where it would have been difficult to raise a civil rights committee a few years earlier. This in turn drew in a larger British presence which was profoundly resented, especially when it took over a Gaelic football ground in Crossmaglen. This sleepy little border town was suddenly a 'legendary heartland of Irish republicanism', nicknamed 'bandit country' by the Northern Ireland Office, a grotto for every touring journalist, with a chat and a jar in the company of knowledgeable publicans providing the ritual 'colour piece' for every paper in the world, it seemed.

The legend became self-fulfilling. When the 'score' had reached about twenty soldiers or policemen killed in the vicinity, a journalist friend of mine, down doing the ritual feature, asked one of the knowledgeable publicans about what the attitude to the police might be, when the troubles inevitably came to an end: "After all, you're going to need police," he said, innocently.

"What do we want police around here for?" the publican asked.

"Well, for ordinary crime and so on," my friend replied.

"There was never any crime around here," was the reply.

In spite of the turmoil, the constant humming of grapevines and propaganda machines, and the fluctuation of the public temper, people did not polarise as totally as they had done during previous upheavals. I experienced so many conversations in which people were obviously determined not to lose grip of the progress of the Sixties, that I never lost confidence in the underlying desire of the majority of people in Northern Ireland for some kind of enduring accommodation.

By the autumn of 1972, I was ragged with exhaustion. Life seemed to have become one long, worsening nightmare from the beginning of 1969, with each moment of hope being transformed rashly or stupidly into deeper despair, both at home and in the outside world. One could only shrug at the main news as Nixon and Kissinger became more murderous in South East Asia: the killing of hundreds of thousands of Cambodians from the air, when the Americans were not even at war with them, seemed a normal sort of thing at the time. British dithering in Rhodesia made that country seem doomed to much greater suffering than Northern Ireland. Such news as one noticed from Latin America indicated chronic instability, with vicious militarism as the standard response. Tragic human disasters like Biafra and Bangladesh, and natural disasters in India and China were about as intelligible as statistics on what would happen in a nuclear war: one simply could not take them in at the level of individual human suffering.

When it was clear that Marianne was expecting our third child in the spring of 1973, I began to feel that my life had been taken over by a war that I had tried to prevent, but was perhaps unwittingly instrumental in helping to unleash. I felt a strong responsibility to stay close to things, but also to begin to have some sort of personal life before my children got much older. My life seemed to consist of struggling blearily out of bed, taking coffee or the lightest of breakfasts, and heading into the office to send the overnight horrors, read the papers, check around various contacts to see if anything was cooking; then over to McGlade's Old Vic lounge, which in those days was packed with press, politicians and 'contacts', including police and army chappies from time to time; have a beer and a sandwich and a sniff of what might be doing, then off to cover the Stormont politics in the afternoon; back at teatime to catch up on the afternoon's violence, statements, charges and counter-charges, court cases; then McGlade's for a bite and sup, then perhaps off to meet those who could not or would not come into town; back into town later, maybe to the Europa or the Hamill where politicians or spokesmen might be pushing lines, or themselves looking for information. These places were swap-shops for people with different series of contacts, as well as useful spots for journalists who never stirred near danger but waited for those who did. With so many visiting journalists, it was at times like a kind of media market.

We had three papers to cover, a morning, evening and Sunday. There was a stretch of some months in 1972 when colleagues in Dublin had banned members from coming North on relief unless management agreed to special overtime and expenses conditions. In any other situation, I might have been down there with them to campaign for better conditions, for we were the poor relations by a long way among journalists at that time, especially when expenditure was greatly inflated by freely financed visiting journalists, and some permanently based correspondents with few-questions-asked expenses arrangements. To provide cover for three papers, with an 8.30 a.m. start and a final deadline of 4.00 a.m., there were, for months, only two of us, and not surprisingly, my colleague, who was not in the first flush of youthful enthusiasm, was frequently ill. Like the war and political situation itself, our office situation was simply crazy, and finally, after I had been on duty alone for weeks, I advised Dublin that if they did not send people up, I would quit: I could not carry on, and at the same time, I could not relax while stories were left uncovered. They had not seemed to appreciate my earlier requests, in spite of the obvious continual supply of copy from one person; now, in a couple of weeks, they sent up two full-time people, including a reporter with desk experience as resident news editor.

I was very relieved, and both Michael Keane and Laurie Kilday, who joined myself and Paddy Reynolds, were well able to look after themselves and settled in with a relish. Michael, after his first break home to Athy in Co. Kilkenny, came back with one of the best yarns of the time. A woman neighbour who had heard he was posted to that terrible Belfast, met him in the local newsagents, and asked him how he was getting on, poor thing, in that terrible place. Michael told her he was in great form, that he was enjoying it immensely. She was determined that it was otherwise and persisted to know how he managed to get on with those awful people: Michael reassured her that they were the friendliest you'd meet anywhere. But she went on about them shooting and murdering and bombing each other, it must be savage. Michael again told her how terrific the people were and how he'd never enjoyed himself more. Finally, the lady turned to the shop owner and said, "Of course, they say it's not as bad as they say it is!"

I then had more time to talk to politicians and others as the build-up began towards the 1973 attempt at a solution, which culminated in Sunningdale, Berkshire, England, in December 1973. Part of me really wanted to retreat to a much more personal life; and it was no joke for Marianne at that time, with me out in all sorts of places, in every kind of company at all hours of the day and night. I made several attempts to establish a new pattern, and to get physically fit; but each new step of the political initiatives and the changes in the tempo of the violence were like a continuing attraction and distraction, feeling at times like an addiction.

I was frequently called on to broadcast, and felt the need to float around and keep in touch with various people who would know the changing patterns in the underground war. A couple of older journalists, whom I respected, advised me on occasion, not to be too intense about the thing, that it would be a "running story for a long time". But the only way I felt I could be 'objective', was by thinking endlessly about it, and keeping in touch as continuously as possible.

Through all this period of press agentry and the planting of bum steers on journalists by officialdom and underground alike, the one outfit I came to trust more than any other was the RUC press office. They put out their information as if it were something they would stand over in a court. One striking example of this was on March 4, 1972, when a bomb exploded without warning among Saturday afternoon shoppers/diners in the Abercorn Restaurant in the centre of Belfast. Two girls, Ann Owens and Janet Bereen, were killed instantly, and two sisters named McNern were dreadfully mutilated and carried all but dead from the wreckage; over 100 others were taken to hospital in various states of injury and shock. By early evening when I had sent over initial reports and reactions, our news desk came back to query my 'two dead, two very seriously injured' with word that the agencies were saying 'four dead'. The army believed there were four dead, but the police insisted on two dead. I can recall the anguished tone of hassle in Jim Taggart's voice telling me, "I know the army are apparently saying four dead, and I know that the other two may be dead even as I'm speaking to you, but my information is two dead, two very seriously ill: I know that two very seriously ill girls are very bad indeed and have apparently lost limbs, but as of this moment, as far as I'm concerned they're alive, Ciaran, and let's hope it stays that way." The McNern sisters made astonishing recoveries to live full lives, bravely coming to terms with maiming.

Through thick and thin, even when they were obviously aggrieved at the deaths of their own colleagues, or at stories which did not reflect well on the police, I found the police press office the most reliable. Other journalists have told me that they have had things suggested to them by the police that were not one hundred per cent, rather as the British army tended to slip stuff over. But as far as I'm concerned, even their off-the-record tips were good, and I covered the war longer and more intensively than most. After my earlier experiences with the police, that was a consolation, and corresponded to a generally improving situation with the police altogether.

Apart from a period when they would be taking over the front line from the British Army in the later Seventies (when Sir Kenneth Newman was in charge and Roy Mason was Secretary of State for Northern Ireland, and the Northern Ireland Office consistently described obvious *prima facie* evidence of interrogation brutality by the police as terrorist propaganda) the police recovery from 1969 has been steady, and often marked with outstanding courage. Policing, in its quality and its acceptability, is a crucial issue in the Northern Irish conflict; it is also a difficult problem for the pacifist who sees a need for the protection of the vulnerable from the deviant, but cannot in conscience give unqualified support to an armed force. My attitude to the police and to policing would be significant later in the Peace People experience, and that will be the appropriate place for a more detailed observation; but in the middle of the 'hot war', it was reassuring to note the progress being made by the RUC, and the fact that, by contrast with the crude, often brutal, 'police' actions of the army, they were a civilised force, with every prospect of becoming the civilianised service which could win the required consensus.

Back in 1972-3, I think my growing desire to have some sort of life other than a second-hand connection to a nightmare, corresponded to the mood of many trying to get on with their lives regardless of the Troubles. With pubs and restaurants dangerously vulnerable to no-warning attacks, social life patterns began to change. Since I spent a substantial proportion of my time each week in what were considered danger spots, I did not share this fear of downtown establishments; but our friends did tend to keep out of town, and a new pattern of dinner parties developed among old graduate friends, with various spouses of both sexes becoming quite expert in cooking. Belfast's culinary tastes in general widened, an inevitable Euro-process accelerated by the pressure on social life by bombers and late night assassins. New little quaint restaurants flourished in out-of-the-way spots outside Belfast.

On the occasions when I took an evening 'off', I rather wanted to stay in, whereas Marianne, virtually house-bound with three young children, would have liked to go out more often than we did. Often arrangements were changed at the last minute, for events had no regular schedule, and I felt very much at the mercy of sudden upsurges of political or violent activity or both—and even the expectation of such had to be 'covered'. One might plan for a day away after a period of anticipated trouble, only to find that the expected trouble did not materialise—and then it would erupt shortly afterwards.

Media build-ups to Easter, when the Republicans held their commemorations and the five-month Orange marching season commenced, often proved unjustified. Then a week or two later, over some trivium, prolonged rioting might break out. Similarly the big July marches, when tens of thousands of Orangemen took over the towns, city and villages for marches which might, by tradition, pass by or through Catholic areas, usually passed off peacefully. But late July and early August began to be real trouble times.

Troubled summers also put off holidays altogether, even if we could have afforded what most people took as a natural annual right. But we were constantly broke, for I was spending a lot of our money running about: the expenditure in Stormont, downtown and in wee pubs here and there made nonsense of my kind of journalism as a serious source of family income. Nor could I come to terms with the tradition of charging expenses under headings which were different from the actual expenditure. When we were negotiating changes, I asked for a differential for those working in Belfast, plus a weekly fixed expense amount. I was most agreeably surprised with the Irish Press agreed terms in 1974 which put its journalists among the best paid in the British Isles: and the Belfast staff were paid a 12.5 per cent differential in recognition of the special demands. The latter was not 'danger' or 'stress' money: the simple fact was that the time and motion study which had delayed the negotiations, had established that a reporter in Belfast was generating as much as five times the amount of copy produced by the average reporter in Dublin. Generous hours and expenses were also agreed: and I had not realised the degree of stress our financial difficulties had been causing until I found, by contrast, that I was able to pay bills with a light-hearted sense of relief, instead of the usual frantic juggling about. This financial relief coincided with a determined effort at change of life style in 1974, which is a little ahead of this point.

In 1973, the main preoccupations were the attempt to create a new Northern Ireland Assembly, and the conduct of local government elections under a new, reduced structure. All elections, except to Westminster, were to be by Proportional Representation; a Border Poll was to gauge public opinion on keeping or removing partition (a two-to-one foregone conclusion for partition, but an irritant to Unionists in even opening the question seriously). Continued violence by the Provisionals was intended to force the British to declare their intent to withdraw from Northern Ireland; continued violence by the

Loyalists, in the form of a relentless series of murders of randomly abducted Catholics, was intended to express their determination to resist anything that weakened the British link, or increased the possibility of an all-Ireland solution. One could not help having sympathy for the British in their post-imperial difficulty: they had no great will to stay, but could not be seen to be giving in to those Irish wishing to drive them out; yet those Northern Irish who wished to remain British also kept them in by their responsibility to defend Catholics against the murder campaigns of the pro-British factions. Whitelaw skated for all he was worth to avoid being sucked into the contemporary Irish bog.

When elections to the Assembly and new local government structure had been successfully held by June 1973, attention focussed on two central constitutional issues: a 'power-sharing' Executive which would somehow involve Catholics in Ministerial responsibility for the first time, and an all-Ireland institution which would reflect the 'Irish dimension' so important to the Nationalist aspiration. Whitelaw sent written invitations to all the political leaders to enter into negotiations on these two themes, and they duly began in the autumn. Vanguard Unionist leader William Craig ignored the invitation, and the Rev. Ian Paisley rejected it, loud-mouthing his opposition to these attempts at political progress. The Provos threatened to destroy any such possibility and the connection between 'political violence' and political development made any kind of coherent reporting a function of both. The high visibility of Provo violence, and audibility of Paisleyite polemics—underpinned by the regular finding of dead Catholics on waste ground in the mornings after what the police used to call 'apparently motiveless killings'—tended to dominate the 'top' of the news bulletins, which would then continue into the 'political' news.

This gave the damaging impression that political development was either impossible because of the violence or irrelevant if it made no immediately visible difference to the level of violence.

Whitelaw swept on with the political programme as if the violence were a separate phenomenon, even while he acknowledged the need to deal with 'politically-motivated violence', as he called it. With John Hume's 'power-sharing' strategy as a basis, the more able politicians took their cue from Whitelaw and negotiated determinedly, in spite of the hysteria being generated outside. Both local government and Assembly elections returned clear majorities in favour—when the possible coalition partners were added up—of the package that would become the power-sharing/All-Ireland Council 'Sunningdale Agreement' signed by the Irish and British governments at the Sunningdale British Imperial Civil Service College in December 1973.

I was virtually in a minority of one among the Belfast press corps in predicting regularly and confidently from the June elections onwards that such an agreement would be reached: just as I would be in a similar minority in refusing to believe that Harold Wilson's new government would, five months after the historic agreement, betray the entire experiment and allow it to founder under Paisleyite pressure.

My reasoning was simple, which was why it was thought to be simple-minded and wishful. Out of seventy-eight seats in the new Assembly, a clear forty-eight to thirty vote majority was held by a combination of the SDLP, Faulkner's Unionists and the Alliance Party, with Paisley controlling a mere 10 per cent 'ultra' vote, corresponding to a 10 per cent or less 'ultra' abstentionist vote in the Catholic community. The middle ground had got a clear mandate to find a solution; the British wanted it; the Southern Irish wanted it; and there was a general feeling that the fighting had gone on long after the original passions had abated, and was going nowhere, murderously. Moreover, with power and other inducements in sight, including the disposition to end internment as soon as was emotionally feasible, and tackle the rapidly rising unemployment, all pointed to a positive result to admittedly difficult talks.

It was also appreciated that such a solution would be given a cautious mandate and that it had three years in which to prove itself—provided, of course, it got the required three years.

This prospect moved steadily closer through the second half of 1973 and the power-sharing Executive was duly installed on New Year's Day 1974, in the presence of the new Secretary of State Francis Pym, Whitelaw having been recalled to help Heath with his third major item, the British miners. Like an unsteady colt, the new Executive began to find its legs. I retain the opinion that it would have survived the predictable opposition of both Paisley and the Provos, had it been given three years.

But despite Whitelaw's explicit anxiety about what it might do to the new coalition's morale, a general election was called in February by Edward Heath with the purpose of obtaining a mandate to confront the British trade unions, and in particular the powerful miners. The issue was extremely important in the wake of the Yom Kippur war and the rocketing of oil prices, but that had not penetrated to the electorate and Heath's mistimed election ended his premiership and returned Harold Wilson's Labour government.

Whitelaw's fears for the power-sharing Executive were well-founded. In the straight vote Westminster election, subtleties of preference could not be made obvious, and Faulkner's somewhat limited candidates ran nervously against Paisleyites in full cry. But it was by no means mortally dangerous, and the Executive survived its first battering and got on with its work.

Merlyn Rees had been an attentive Shadow Secretary of State, and now got to grips with the real job more thoroughly than his shambling manner often suggested. He did not have Whitelaw's brusque, county-establishment confidence, but he did have a thoughtful and intelligent grasp of the complexities of the situation. I think he was rather underestimated as Secretary of State, and got the 'mumbling, bumbling' image treatment from the media, which might, in terms of real decision-making, have been more accurately applied to the media-smooth Wilson in the background.

Paisley had gained a psychological advantage from the February election, and he assiduously added to his constituency of discontent many traditional Unionists who were not really ultras, but who naturally felt more than peeved that the land of their forefathers was now being run by an odd-looking coalition with prominent and decidedly uppity Catholics, some of whom were clearly too clever by at least a half. The sense that the coalition had come about without their full and free approval rankled deeply, even though the coalition had not been 'imposed' in the manner that Paisley insisted in media interview after interview without ever being challenged. When Paisley said that 'Loyalists' had been 'excluded' from the negotiations, not a single interviewer in my recollection pulled him up to remind him that he had been invited, and that he had refused the invitation and thus excluded himself.

The bulk of the media had been predicting the collapse of the talks leading to the settlement, on an almost daily basis; now, when it was actually in operation, the same process continued. While it was fair enough for the media to examine continuously the difficulties facing such a unique constitutional experiment, there was an aspect that was less than balanced. The utterances of the new Executive had to be carefully worded, then processed by the Government's information machine before release in this dry form to the news desks, which then immediately asked reporters to get Paisley's reaction.

There developed a kind of 'Paisley slams Faulkner' syndrome, in which a couple of polemical sentences from Paisley became the news story-line over the more thoughtful statement, which itself would be only partially reported further down the columns, as 'Earlier, the Executive stated that . . . ' And Paisley, who represented 10 per cent in the Assembly, was getting equal air-time in the studios as if he were the Leader of the Official Opposition and potentially alternative Chief Executive.

This imbalance, which arose partly from the needs of what are called 'news-values', troubled a number of serious journalists to the point where, the following year, we actually held a couple of weekend conferences about the problem. This was an unprecedented and interesting initiative by the Corrymeela Reconciliation Centre; it was widely supported by journalists, aware that communicating across a divided community, in often divided readerships, posed very difficult ethical and practical problems.

It was obviously much easier to report the gross acts of assault, spitting and riot which characterised the Paisleyite revolt in the hallowed Stormont chamber, than to note the lines between the lines in the various Coalition speeches. And when Harry Murray, a hitherto unknown shipyard worker, announced that there would be a general strike organised by the Ulster Workers' Council—an unrepresentative group of Loyalist workers—the diversion value was enormous. This is an overwhelming problem for a free press in a free society where 'news' has also become a perishable consumer product. It is not a new problem in principle: a murder, for instance, is always good for 'news', whereas normal, restrained human behaviour has no news value whatsoever. Journalism has given way to the 'news industry'.

The power-sharing Executive did not always help themselves. Frequently, they allowed headlines to go by default. Many of Faulkner's backbenchers shivered in fear of Paisley's tongue, and were forever looking over their shoulders lest they draw a Paisley challenge into their own constituencies. This Faulknerite nervousness, so unlike the ebullient courage now consistently shown by the 'wee man' himself, prevented those supporting the Executive from doing one thing which would have clearly demonstrated their decisive parliamentary majority: they never once held a joint back-bench meeting. Such an obvious initiative would also have helped them to decide on positive ways of taking their policies to the people, and to appreciate thoroughly which lines should be emphasised and which might cause great embarrassment if over-trumpeted. The back-bench solidarity would have demonstrated the reality of Paisley's minority position, and might have inhibited some of the more appalling gaffes.

One such gaffe was a statement by a young enthusiastic SDLP representative, Hugh Logue, who, in the culturally encouraging atmosphere of a nationalist constituency in Southern Ireland, mistakenly described the fledgling—or rather, still-born—Council of Ireland as "a vehicle trundling towards a United Ireland". Lesser polemicists than Ian Paisley could sharpen a stick like that to deadly effect.

The UWC strike began on May 4, 1974. For a while it had a slightly embarrassed, almost carnival atmosphere about it. The screw tightened when people going to work found themselves harassed by paramilitary gangs at road junctions, apparently unarmed but nevertheless intimidating. The British TUC General Secretary, Len Murray, came over for an attempt by the legitimate trade unions to lead people back to work in spite of the obstructions. If anything, this effort increased the sense of loyalist solidarity, and its failure was counter-productive. The UWC announced that 'UWC passes' would be needed for those who would be on 'approved business'. What was appalling about this flagrant usurpation of public authority was not, initially, so much that they did it—that was almost comical—or even that the government adopted an early softly, softly approach, but that the business and professional class, like housewives hearing a rumour of a bread shortage, rushed to queue up to get their passes.

I found myself in a very unpleasant exchange with several journalists who had gone to get passes, making the excuse that they might need them so as to keep people in touch. I refused utterly to have such a pass, and reminded them of the occasions when we had refused such intimidation from the Provos, when the latter had told pressmen to collect their 'passes' to cover the Easter republican parades.

The mood slowly became eerie and frightening, as the community began to cave in to what was essentially street fascism. I had taken Marianne and the children to the presumed safety of Monaghan at the beginning of May when I had to go to Brussels for a three-day Euro-briefing: we had been petrol-bombed two weeks earlier, and Marianne could hardly have coped with another attack in my absence. So I found myself living alone, going out through the gauntlet of the threatening lines of men, to work, both downtown and up to Stormont. I honestly felt that we were passing through the climax of the entire war, and that if everyone held their nerve, we would come out into a much clearer prospect of peaceful progress than ever before, and that the long nightmare would fade into memory. In the early days of that 'constitutional stoppage' as the UWC coyly described it, few would seriously have contemplated the possibility that Harold Wilson's government would give in to such intimidation, and that therefore it was only a matter of time before the crunch came, and a question of skill and diplomacy to undo bluffs as honourably and peaceably as possible.

There was very little explicit violence, compared to the usual level. There was one murder in North Antrim by loyalists, while the Provos seemed happy to let the Loyalists get on with wrecking Northern Ireland, and found themselves in the rather novel role of helping to organise siege supplies, including petrol, to the Catholic ghettos. The

Catholics were also generally confident, in the ghettos at least, that they could outlast all other, even if, as it began to be predicted, sewage were to come up on the streets. No-one put it more graphically than a little old woman reported in the *Observer*, who said, "We've been eating shit all our lives and we can eat more of it than them."

The major violence of the period was an attack by Loyalists on Dublin and Monaghan in Southern Ireland: twenty-six were killed in Dublin and seven in Monaghan—where Marianne and the children were staying for safety!

The strike became serious in the second week, as businesses started to send home those workers turning up. Shop supplies were cleared as panic storing began, and transport was increasingly disrupted. As energy supplies dwindled, it fell to John Hume—who, like Paddy Devlin in Health and Social Services and Austin Currie in Housing, had made a most impressive start as Minister of Commerce—to prepare contingency plans for soldiers to man petrol distribution: an extraordinary irony for a man who had sat down in front of British armoured vehicles in the Bogside three years earlier.

BBC Northern Ireland seemed to have entered totally into the spirit of tension-building rebellion, with the electricity service spokesman, Hugo Patterson, being interviewed almost hourly, and later, almost continuously, as he explained how the electricity power stations could gradually be closed down to a point beyond which it would take weeks to restore normal supplies. This became known as the 'point of no return', which gave the uncertain rebellion a specific focus in the public mind, and a kind of reassurance that the revolt had a limited time-scale, whatever the result.

Rees held firmly to the 'softly, softly' line, and then, as the crisis deepened, Prime Minister Wilson began to surface. At first, it seemed that he would be very tough with the 'bully-boys' and that the resources of the British Army, which had been demonstrated in spectacular fashion in Operation Motorman in 1972, were being prepared for deployment. But nothing significant happened, and now the Loyalists really began to sense, to their own amazement, that they were able to get away with it, with scarcely a shot fired. Amid reports that Ian Paisley was about to go to Canada on a private visit, the Loyalists actually leading the strike made contingency plans for a second line of command when, as they expected, the British would arrest them. It was an unnecessary precaution in the event. Nor did Ian Paisley go to Canada.

The great confrontation seemed about to peak when it was learned that Harold Wilson was going to make a Prime Ministerial broadcast on the biggest constitutional crisis ever to embroil the internal authority of a modern British government. I remember listening to it while having an evening meal by the light of emergency candles in a downtown hotel occupied mainly by journalists. There was a momentary sense of almost Churchillian conviction, before Wilson insulted the Loyalists' self-respect by referring to them collectively as 'spongers'. When he resorted to this abuse, I felt immediately that he had no firm purpose. Even though I could not see how he could give in to the UWC, I felt a surge of sympathy for the men of real character who had painstakingly, and at great risk to themselves, put together such a brave effort at constitutional resolution of an almost intractable problem. I also felt genuine fellow-feeling with my Loyalist neighbours in their outrage at being called spongers. When they turned up at Stormont in their lorries and tractors, wearing pieces of sponge as badges of honour, I could almost have cheered their defiance, had it not been for the quasi-fascist nature of the entire rebellion.

Despite the sense that the 'spongers' speech indicated a lack of stomach for this kind of struggle, it still remained, for me, impossible to believe that the entire authority of the British government was about to surrender before street intimidation and loyalist paramilitarism, especially when there would be no reasonable alternative in terms of a solution. The only result of such pusillanimity would be an indefinite prolongation of war. In thinking it through from the position of British policy-makers, I imagined that they would understand that any future attempt would be prejudiced, in advance, by failure at this point: and that failure now, when the exercise of the mutual political veto had a chance of being turned into positive co-operation, could only bring forward the exercise of paramilitary vetos, and a corresponding increase in the political status of both the Provisionals and the Loyalist paramilitary organisations. However difficult the sweat might be, it seemed by my analysis to be as nothing compared to the endemic struggle that would follow collapse at this point.

One of the ironies of the entire stoppage was that two days before it began, the British authorities had summoned lobby correspondents to Stormont to explain, with the aid of maps and experts, how the IRA planned a civil war, through which they would make Northern Ireland ungovernable, and how the authorities, having captured both the plan and its mastermind, would be able to deal with such a vicious threat!

Morale among the Executive fell sharply, and there was some feeling that Ministers might be getting unduly pessimistic reports from the Civil Service, which in turn put Civil Service loyalty to the new regime in some doubt. Such observation as I could make of the civil servants did not substantiate this suspicion: my impression was rather that they enjoyed both the novelty of the Executive and its talents, and the fact that they were serving fellow Ulstermen rather than Englishmen from whom they felt real or imaginary contempt.

Very trying indeed was a loss of trust within the Executive itself. Roy Bradford, the smooth-tongued Minister of Development, projected an impression of being trickier than his leader, Brian Faulkner, and expressed a position that might allow him to co-operate with the winners of the strike, should the rebellion succeed. When he next stood for a Stormont election, he lost his seat, having lost the support of Loyalists and middle-ground alike.

But the Executive's main frustration was that authority to direct the security forces was in the hands of Wilson and Rees and not in theirs. There is no doubt whatever in my mind that Faulkner would have been far more decisive in dealing with the situation long before any winner momentum developed in Loyalist ranks. Needless to say, he would not have called anybody 'sponger'.

Finally, the Executive was advised that the falling electricity supply would shortly cause sewage pumps to fail, bring sewage up on the streets and make plague a real danger. The Faulkner Unionists handed their Warrants of Office back to Rees who then recalled the rest of the Executive Warrants. That was May 28, 1974. Now, 1984, there has been no political progress since. Violence is endemic. Unemployment is about 25 per cent, with over 50 per cent in the aggrieved areas. A new British initiative, the third since 1975, is dying on its feet. More than another 1,000 people have been murdered. Thousands more have known jail, injury, emigration and every other kind of depression and hopelessness. My anger and contempt in this process of recall has, if anything, 'matured' from the time when I reported in disbelief that the British government had allowed the Sunningdale agreement to fail.

For me, the lesson is that politicians, however agile in balancing pressures, are dangerous if they lack the vision and character to go with authority and responsibility.

The victorious Loyalists soon learned a similar lesson, when the results of victory were hijacked and rendered useless by their own politicians.

It can be argued with some validity that the UWC victory restored pride to Northern Irish Protestants after years of humiliation: it was a kind of *quid pro quo* for the prorogation of Stormont in the first place. On the other hand, if it had not happened, we might now be enjoying self-government in which there could be common pride.

That period was decisive for me personally, partly because of a deepening, tempered commitment to nonviolence, and partly because of my conviction that the party-political structure had too great a capacity for confirming tribal positions, and trapping non-tribal men.

My nonviolence had been tested yet again in that year, when we were petrol-bombed. I had gradually and fitfully been trying to reduce my almost addictive preoccupation with the politics and violence of the situation, and had been spending more time at home and in the garden. On Saturday April 20, having prepared the ground over the preceding weekends, I planted two different varieties of potato in hitherto untilled ground. It was a long, hard day's work, and I finished in the deepening dusk, creaking slowly into the house to sink before the television to watch *Match of the Day*. Marianne went to the phone in the little cloakroom at the front of the house to talk to her sister in Monaghan. Just as I was making my virtuously exhausted frame comfortable, I heard a noise of breaking glass at the front of the house: it sounded as though a cat or a dog had tripped over a milk bottle, and I glanced round casually to look through the hallway in the direction of the noise. The whole front of the house was a sheet of orange flame. We were being petrol-bombed.

The reaction of this total pacifist was illuminating in its divergence from a sensible course. It was one of reflex aggression. I ran to the front door, pressed myself to the wall, flung the door open and dived through the falling petrol flames to get at those attacking my home, with my bare hands. A motorcycle with two young men on it was revving in the middle of the street just down the hill from our house. I raced towards it with the crazy intent of pulling them off it. They took off, leaving me standing stiff with rage. Only then did I look back to see the damage.

The first two petrol bombs had failed to go through the bedroom window at which they had been aimed; one was burning harmlessly away on the side of the wall, the other little more than a sputtering flame on the window-sill. If the attackers had succeeded in putting them both through the upstairs window, two of our children might have been burning to death as I chased the bombers; I might never even have known about it, if, as was often the case, they had turned and opened fire with guns.

I became aware of another petrol bomb burning away under my car. Again I ran, got a brush and a bucket of earth, threw the earth at the flames and pushed the half-full bottle away from under it, to burn out harmlessly in the drain: at any moment the car might have burst into flame; but in my impulsive anger, I was more concerned simply to beat off the attack.

Neighbours came out to express their shock and offer help. We cleaned up quickly, and the whole affair was over in about ten minutes. I felt very calm, but angry and curious at my own impulsiveness; for some reason the neat rows of freshly planted potatoes kept coming to mind, suggestive of my Irish peasant roots! I felt vaguely degraded by the mere fact of having been attacked, but basically relieved that an attack had happened and had failed.

We were quite relaxed by the time the police came, and later, military police and a civil representative of the Northern Ireland Office. No, we did not want protection, I would not apply for a gun, no, we would not have protective grilles put on the windows of our home. Did I think there was any particular reason for the attack? Had I any enemies? It might have been a simple sectarian attack by Loyalists, or it might have been Republicans determined to button my lip: I simply did not know.

I told the police that I did not wish to make any statement, I did not wish any attention whatever to be drawn to the event, and I did not want anyone to go to jail for an attack which in any event had failed, and had given me an incentive to paint the house. The police respected this, but made their own point that unless such persons were apprehended, they might attack again with more serious consequences. This police point was brought home to us forcefully some time later when a pub less than a mile away was bombed without warning, leaving seven people dead and many others badly injured. Things found near my house the morning after the petrol bomb attack indicated that Loyalists from Donegall Pass had been responsible: and it was a gang from this area which had bombed the Rose and Crown.

While we adopted this attitude to the authorities and scrubbed the charred marks from the walls and eaves of the house, Marianne and I nevertheless had to reflect deeply on how our personal convictions could bear on the survival of the children, for whom we were obviously making the choice. It is not a light thing to weight whether one's pacifism might amount to a death sentence or maiming for one's children.

We were certain we would not have a gun. Even if that were not a matter of principle, the facts of gun possession were not reassuring: 50 per cent of American homicides are committed by people using guns bought for protection, often in situations of domestic trauma (not that that was any immediate threat!); moreover having the thing invited its theft and the risk of accidental discharge. We just would not have one about the place. For me, it would have been no less than a symbol of evil, and would have meant the end of everything I believed in.

We considered emigration. We had been married in September

1968, now had three children with every hope of having more; yet our lives had been sucked into a stupid little war which we had tried to avert, which was using up our youth and might even claim our lives. We were still hopeful about the Executive, but for the foreseeable future, we could anticipate that our children's openness and experience might be corrupted by the oppressive bigotry that was like a malignancy in the community soul. We had no right to make them hostage to that closed-in fate, just because we, or rather I, had been involved in the situation in one way or another.

We finally decided to stay for two more years: and if our lives could not be lived with a more hopeful prospect by then, we would reconsider emigration, young enough to start again, and to give the children indigenous roots wherever we went.

Sometime after this, there was a knock at our door one evening, and I opened it to Mrs. Pat Morrow, a neighbour whom I knew to be involved in such things as the New Ulster Movement, an active, middle-ground sort of person. She wanted to talk to me about the local community association. The brunt of her message was that the local association was running out of Catholics! Every Catholic member of the brave little band of mixed neighbours trying to hold the line against polarisation and intimidation, had either been driven out, burnt out, shot, shot at, had a relative shot, and in the case of the last remaining member, nearly frightened to death when the gun of a would-be assassin jammed at point-black range, causing the would-be victim nevertheless to leave town forthwith.

The deliberate assault by Paisleyites on such community initiatives had already been effective in other places, and looked like closing the local effort down. And apart from anything else, to qualify for a governmental community relations grant for any substantial project, an association had to be able to point to a genuinely mixed association.

Pat knew that I had a very busy life and that we had recently been attacked. She asked if we would not mind even signing on as members of the local association. I felt very strongly, in the light of our decision to give the place another two years before reconsidering emigration, that I should not sit back and wait for others to change things for us. So I agreed to come to the next meeting. Before long, and in spite of my determination after three sabbatical years as a student leader never to sit on any committee ever again, I was an active member of the Ballynafeigh Community Development Association, helping to organise a local community festival, bringing out a local newspaper for the festival, and helping to develop a local community house.

The middle of 1974 was a turning point in our lives in several ways. I gardened more and more, painted the house, wrote a little in terms of short stories and even verse, and generally tried to have a life that was half-normal. In July 1974, two days before Marianne and I planned to have three days away together for the first time since our wedding, our car was blown up in a bizarre circumstance. I had arranged to meet Tommy 'Tucker' Lyttle of the Ulster Defence Association at the Europa Hotel at about 3.30 p.m., along with the Dublin poet, Eavan Boland. Eavan, who, with other members of the Irish Academy of Letters, had been exploring the aspirations and self-perceptions of Ulster Loyalists, was at that time composing her collection *The War Horse*.

We were sitting in the ground-floor Whip and Saddle Bar, near the door, and with a good view of the security box at the Europa gate, where I had parked my little yellow Triumph 1300 TC De Luxe, in great shape after recently having had a reconditioned engine put in. We had only been there about ten minutes on this pleasant day, when a large Transit van, its windscreen wipers incongruously working, drew up beside my car. The driver got out and hurried into the hotel, leaving his van door open. He came bursting into the bar shouting "bomb", and there was no mistaking the genuine tone. People hopped over the bar counter to escape the back way. Tucker Lyttle had stood up and back from his chair when the man had burst in and was looking watchfully about him. "C'mon, Tucker," I said, "I'm not hanging around, it looks real." With a last backward look, Tucker turned and we followed the rest through the back and into the street. When we were about fifty yards away from what proved to be a large proxy bomb (a bomb delivered by a blackmailed innocent whose mate or relative is held hostage pending the safe delivery of the bomb), Tucker seemed satisfied that the van did represent a genuine bomb threat. I asked him why he was so suspicious, and he said, "I thought we might be getting flushed out for a hit!"

There are times when nobody is quite sure who is killing whom (is it undercover soldiers? Republican terrorists? Loyalist assassins? inter-faction feuds? racket job?) and Tucker had a naturally suspicious disposition. I remember thinking it must be an awful way for a hard man to live, always wary of potential assassins; and in that afternoon's circumstance, it might have caused his death.

We proceeded to the nearby Washington Bar to wait out not only the Europa blast, but four other big ones in the immediate neighbourhood. The attack had cleared offices and blocked thoroughfares, so that the Washington, one of the few available refuges, was packed out. When I managed to get to the bar to order three beers, I found myself looking at the early evening news on television, with a long view of Great Victoria Street to the Europa, and my little yellow car shining forth. A moment later, the five hunded pound bomb went up, and when the smoke cleared, there was little sign of the car. I said to the citizen beside me, "That was my car, the yellow one that just went up, gives you a funny feeling when you think of the plush seats, solid body, and now rubbish," and I shivered.

"I've been closer to a bomb than any man alive," was the reply.

There was something in this citizen's demeanour which arrested my attention rather than causing me to say, "Mmm, imagine" and escape with the booze. I looked at him, a quiet, slightly sad-eyed man, in no way the cut of a bar-counter mouth. "How was that?" I asked him, just a little warily.

"Oxford Street, Bloody Friday," he said.

I suddenly remembered the extraordinary story of the bus inspector who actually lifted a suspect suitcase which blew up immediately, killing several people, but lifted the inspector in one whole piece on to the roof of the station, from which he had been rescued without even losing consciousness.

"Were you the . . ." I started to ask, and he was already nodding.

"Did you have any after-effects?" I asked him, knowing that people close to explosions often suffered clinical shock or depression, sometimes unconsciously.

"If the weather's wet or if it's going to rain, I get pins and needles in my feet," was the incredible reply.

"Why?"

"Well, the bomb blew a lot of wee bits of stuff into my feet, and they just couldn't get it all out, and they thought it better just to leave it. It's all healed over, but it gives me the pins and needles sometimes."

I expressed my amazement and asked him if that was the only effect?

"When I go up the stairs too quick sometimes, I'm out of breath. But the heart's sound, it's just the blast put a lot of fertiliser dust in my lungs, and there's nothing can be done about it, just makes me a bit short of breath if I go too quickly," he told me, in the most matter-of-fact manner.

As we were talking, large bombs had been exploding nearby, but there was not a start or a flicker from this man. He clearly understood his incredible luck, but was not making any big drama out of it: the claim to have been closer to an explosion than any man alive, would do. His escape is all the more amazing when it is remembered that people a good distance from a blast can be killed by a random piece of debris, sometimes even by suffocation by freak blast-wave effect.

By this time, I was utterly determined that my life would be lived as far as possible as if the continuing violence was no more than an inconvenient interruption in normal urban services, when I was off duty. So I borrowed an old car, and Marianne and I spent three days in Achill Island on the west coast of Ireland. My friend John Healy of the *Irish Times* had been telling me over the years about this place, and I fell in love with it immediately. Those three days were like a month's holiday, and we decided to return there the following year for a proper family holiday.

Marianne's father died suddenly in August that year, leaving her as the last of her family in Northern Ireland, so that any hold on emigration on his account disappeared altogether.

The Troubles settled down to an intermittent pattern of bombing and murder campaigns, which had little or no effect on politics, of which there was also less. Rees began to talk of another Stormont, this time a 'Constitutional Convention' instead of an Assembly. After Green and White Papers and appropriate legislation, the one million voters of Northern Ireland would be summoned once more to the ballot-box to repeat the 1973 returns, this time to a far less hopeful institution.

But Rees did proceed with one major initiative, master-minded by his astute principal secretary, Frank Cooper, later knighted. Quite a number of the Provos had begun to appreciate that continuing violence for its own sake was going nowhere but jail or the graveyard. The UWC strike showed them that the Loyalists could turn off the electricity at any time in the Northern part of a United Ireland: some of them began belatedly and dimly to realise that some accommodation with Loyalists might after all be needed.

But perhaps more important than any explicit political perception, was the fact that the heat and passion of a couple of years earlier had abated. The trauma and losses of the campaign still bonded this coalition of old die-hards, '69 Republicans and the children of internment and torture. While they were by no means ready to call the whole thing off, they were looking for some new direction. They were relieved of the blank militarism of Sean MacStiofain when the latter had given up a hunger and thirst fast to the death and lost his entire status. The more intelligent influences of David O'Connell and Ruairi O'Bradaigh, whom MacStiofain had earlier undermined, began to be felt.

There was also considerable pressure from within the Catholic community for an end to evidently purposeless violence, and there had been a highly negative reaction in Southern Ireland to a bombing campaign in England, where so many Irish *émigrés* live and work, often to support native Irish families.

Amid speculation on a 'fifteen-point ceasefire' plan, there emerged what the Provos referred to as a 'Truce' and the British government called a hoped-for 'genuine and sustained cessation of violence'. In real terms, what it meant was an end to shooting British soldiers, an end to car-bombing of town and city centres—and a gradual end to internment without trial. There was also an extraordinary arrangement whereby the Provisionals controlled 'Incident Centres', which had a kind of authority to arbitrate on what were called police matters and what were, in a broad sense, 'war matters', which might involve the ceasefire arrangements. The idea of this was to prevent a breakdown of the ceasefire over some disputed incident: but it also gave an odd level of civilian authority to the Provos, and the centres began to be used as social and complaints services not unlike politicians' constituency advice 'clinics'.

The ceasefire came into effect on December 22, 1974. I remember Marianne and I were in town with the children doing some late evening Christmas shopping—an extremely rare occurrence at any time of the year—when a spate of bombs started to go off, creating the usual chaos. I was well used to this on my own, but it gave me a shivery feeling having my family with me, with the odd notion that it would be cruel luck to get injured or worse at this point, just as things really seemed to be about to get better.

The Provos blasted away right up to the deadline, almost as if they were getting rid of the stuff instead of having to store it. Then the ceasefire held.

But this was Northern Ireland. Instead of a discreet welcome for the improvement in everybody's lives, the Paisleyites reared up in anger over a secret deal with the Provos. Rees began releasing internees, and with each batch the Paisleyite rhetoric charged British treachery. If a secret deal was on with the Provos, a United Ireland and Rome Rule were obviously next on Wilson's agenda . . .

Naturally, this was accompanied by more killing of Catholics, and such violence was paradoxically seized upon to challenge the government's claims of a 'genuine and sustained cessation of violence' as the basis for continuing to release internees.

A subtle change in the meaning of words was also under way: 'terrorist violence' meant strictly the Provisional variety; 'sectarian killings' or 'apparently motiveless killing' were not 'violence' for the purposes of interpreting the government's policy. Rees pressed manfully on, his agonised and seemingly shambling manner being eminently suitable for the fudging job that this delicate exercise required. By and large, the requirements of 'GSCV' as it became known (genuine and sustained cessation of violence) were met for long enough to get rid of the embarrassment of internment without trial.

Frank Cooper earned his knighthood, but Rees deserves more bouquets than he got for the fronting job.

If it was a novel phenomenon for the Provos to be seen in a political, almost a social worker role, it must be said that that was not the only changing perception around that time. For all the ranting by their politicians, the Loyalist paramilitary men did not want to be manipulated by nods and winks into another all-out spate of sectarian assassinations of Catholics. Over the previous couple of years, they had experienced internment for the first time, as well as the treatment that goes with being picked up under the emergency powers, and they did not like it. Moreover, they accepted for the first time that all the Catholic complaints about the injustices involved were not just a lot of whinging, or republican propaganda. Yet they found their own politicians unwilling to help any of their men once they were caught, whereas they saw the sustained efforts by many on the Catholic side to struggle against the whole apparatus of emergency law. Being a loyalist paramilitary man was fine when you were up-ending the power-sharing Executive: otherwise you were regarded as a thug, and a political leper, with no compensating 'freedom-fighter' mythology.

They did have common cause with Ian Paisley in opposition to the old Unionist Party—but with great wariness. When in 1975, Ian Paisley and Ernest Baird announced that we would see "decisive Loyalist action", I asked Andy Tyrie, Supreme Commander of the Ulster Defence Association, if he was going to allow the UDA to be manipulated again after what had happened in 1974, he replied: "Oh, we'll follow him alright, provided he's up on the front line where we can see him."

The common jail experience had also produced a reluctant respect from the Loyalist hard men towards the Provos, for whom they already had, to an enormous degree, the gunman's respect for gunmen. They had seen the Provo internees burn down their section of the Long Kesh prison, even though it meant hardship for themselves, and they saw their physical courage in hand-to-hand fighting with heavily armed and protected soldiers. In the words of one Loyalist who watched the Provos' resistance from their side of the fence: "They *were* men: you couldn't but admire them. We had to be opposed to them for all the usual reasons, but we had no time for the screws or soldiers either. All we could do was throw them over fruit and tobacco when they were getting punished."

If they were slow in developing new directions, the Loyalists were increasingly sure that their main function in life was not to murder Catholics simply to keep middle-class Unionists in power.

This awakening did not happen without accompanying feuds as

old loyalties were questioned, and areas of territory disputed. With so little room for manoeuvre, and with a self-reinforcing siege mentality in which open-mindedness is akin to treachery, the pilgrimage of the Loyalist working class to political self-respect has not been, and is not, an easy one. But they have persisted, trying out such ideas as an independent Northern Ireland, and putting forward candidates for elections in the orthodox manner. Their 'independence' idea, while structurally unlikely, contains the dynamic of self-respect and may be ignored by the wider community only at the risk of alienating a large section of the Protestant working class who do not have anywhere to go. Lacking the profile of the Provisionals, they also tend to be ignored generally; or it is presumed simply that they follow Paisley, which of course they often do—but with substantial reservations.

The Provos, meanwhile, were seeking to consolidate their new community role, and were less than happy to note how much progress the long-ceasefired Official Republicans had made while the Provos had been bombing away. Rivalry turned to feud, and one night, there was an all-out attempt by the Provisionals to destroy the Officials' leadership. Within days, several Provisionals were also dead, efficiently murdered by the 'ceasefired' Officials, and local mediators had to work hard to bring the feuding to an end. As far as the wider public was concerned, of course, there was no anguish at the prospect of gunmen killing each other. Nor did it have any effect on 'GSCV'—it did not, for that purpose, count as 'violence'. Similarly with the feuding that developed between the Officials and the INLA, the military wing of the Irish Republican Socialist Party. The latters' leader, Seamus Costello (later murdered) was a highly intelligent, articulate and bitter man, who had been on the council of the Official IRA but left after the ceasefire. His new party attracted the support of such as Bernadette McAliskey and Ronnie Bunting, Jnr. Its combination of a coherent socialism, inherited from the Officials, and espousal of the nationalistic militancy of the Provisionals, attracted a number of impressionable idealists of the militarist type.

But the IRSP/INLA volunteers were not of the same calibre as its articulate leadership: a sizeable number had been kicked out of either the Provos or the Officials for indiscipline, including robberies carried out with weapons belonging to the 'cause' but whose proceeds were not for the cause. Bernadette McAliskey went so far as to refer to 'tuppence-hapenny hooligans', the sort of language once used by the establishment about civil rights marchers. Bernadette left the organisation at an early stage.

So while, for the purposes of government policy, there was very little 'violence', there was a lot of murdering going on, in patterns markedly different to that of the previous years. In addition to inter-republican and inter-loyalist feud killings, there was also sporadic sectarian murder. And here the Provisionals began more openly to retaliate against the Loyalists. Sectarianism has always been regarded as alien to the Irish republican tradition, which lauds what it understands, however mythologically, as the sacred non-sectarianism of the eighteenth century figure, Wolfe Tone. But increasingly, they defended clearly sectarian retaliation as steps to defend the 'nationalist people', or to attack the supporters of the 'British war machine'. So sacred is the principle of not attacking Protestants *as such*, especially among the old guard, that, for long enough, such activity by the Provos was not claimed by them, but under such names as 'Republican Action Group'.

Merlyn Rees had read some Irish history, which may have made him sensitive to the Irish weakness for anniversaries: anyway he called the election to his new Constitutional Convention at Stormont, for May 1975, which pre-empted any celebrations of his government's defeat at the hands of the Ulster Workers Council (which had all but disappeared). The election showed that the political arithmetic had not changed very much from the wrecked Assembly. But as Wilson and Rees could have been told, the parties had had to stake out more explicit positions, and for all the openness of the Convention's procedures, the parties went into it fairly well shackled by pre-election manifestos. The various shades of Unionism had ruled out 'enforced power-sharing', and any whiff of an All-Ireland Dimension; the SDLP, returned overwhelmingly for the Catholics, made power-sharing the *sine qua non* of any agreement, and was more insistent than ever on an Irish Dimension.

The SDLP took comfort from the improvement on the internment position, for they had been sharply reminded of their failure to honour a pledge in 1973 to refuse to talk while internment lasted. This also encouraged Rees to go on releasing internees even on days when 'GSCV' seemed to be in tatters. On the other hand the Unionists kept on demanding 'more security', and an 'end to violence' before they could move. In short, Rees had to do a Whitelaw, but in a far more complex, if less heated, situation than that which the Conservatives had faced.

He had another major problem left by Whitelaw: the latter had granted 'political status' under the name of 'Special Category Status' for those sentenced on conviction for 'politically motivated' crimes. Whitelaw's June 1972 concession was in the middle of his rush to generate political movement, and in particular to get an end to the hunger strike of leading republican Billy McKee, former Belfast leader of the Provos, in advance of the ill-fated 1972 ceasefire. Whitelaw had also, in a wave of more cosmetic exercises, renamed Long Kesh as The Maze Prison, and internees as detainees; and in a move that fell somewhere between the cosmetic and the substantial, abolished the Special Powers Act, and substituted the 'Temporary' Emergency Provisions Act, which he admitted "altered the traditional liberty of the subject in serious and fundamental ways".

Rees had an obvious personal distaste for both internment and Whitelaw's interim measure, the 'Diplock Commissioners'—a quasi-judicial procedure held within Long Kesh itself, in which an internee, who might have a lawyer speak for him, had to prove his innocence against the evidence or opinion presented from behind a screen by unidentified intelligence or Special Branch officers. To Rees' credit, he resumed executive responsibility for internment, abolishing the internment camp Commissions, which were such a degradation of the judicial system that all but a handful of lawyers boycotted them, in spite of the inflated fees for appearing at them.

His task was then to consider how 'political violence' could be dealt with by judicial process as understood in a free society, even as he was proceeding to end internment: and dealt with in such a way that the Unionists could not point to a decline in 'security', while international opinion, already enjoying Britain's discomfort on torture charges, could be satisfied with its justice.

This major task was assigned to a special Commission, to which Rees appointed as chairman, Lord Gardiner, a distinguished Law Lord, understood to have been appalled not only that Britain became liable to torture charges, but that British soldiers were being trained in such barbarism. Gardiner's Report was doubly significant.

In the first place, it provided the germ of an actual policy, that of establishing the normal rule of law, whether or not political consensus was forthcoming, on the very grounds that a community enjoying and giving its free consent to fair rule of law, would be more likely to proceed to creating political and constitutional consensus. So 'restoring the normal rule of law' became a policy goal.

In the second place, the Gardiner Commission specifically recommended the ending of Special Category Status, i.e. political status, for prisoners, as soon as possible. This, in the context of progress on the first principle, would underline the perception that in a free society of whatever structure, providing its citizens had equal recourse to the due process of just law, there could be no such things as 'political violence', as applied to the 'special category' prisoners.

Gardiner's judgement was, in principle, wise and far-sighted. Unfortunately, the *political* judgement on when to end 'special category status' for conviction on crimes arising out of a situation of chronic constitutional and political instability, has proven far from wise. With almost indecent haste, while his Constitutional Convention was still dithering, Rees announced that Special Category Status would no longer be granted to anyone convicted of crimes committed after March 1976. Maybe Rees was clutching at something to prove toughness to the Unionists over 'security'; maybe he was anxious, with internment being ended, to be rid of the whole sordid business; maybe he wanted to clear the decks for the local politicians to arrive at some kind of agreement. But that fateful date arrived at a time when the Constitutional Convention had broken down, sectarian tit-for-tat murders had increased to a frightening degree, and no amount of fudging could disguise the fact that 'GSCV' was well over. Internment had been brought to an end, but the insidious 'Temporary' Emergency Provisions Act went on and on making its contribution to the cycle of dissent and violence.

Merlyn Rees bore more real weight and had to endure more substantial failure during his relatively long, two-and-a-half year period than any other Secretary of State for Northern Ireland. Whitelaw had used up most of the possible initiatives, including cosmetic bluffs. Rees's position had to be that most difficult of all policies, the policy of having no policy while encouraging the locals to devise their own solution. This was especially difficult when he was actually exercising the full sovereign power of the government in a more substantial way than any other departmental minister in the Cabinet.

One small cosmetic effort he allowed himself was to change the system of security gates in Belfast's 'control zone', a segment of the city centre into which access was more strictly controlled after the devastation of the car-bombing campaign. He called us lobby correspondents, in batches, to his Ministerial office, and with senior police and army officers in attendance, explained his new gates system—essentially a smaller area, more tightly controlled.

As someone who worked daily inside and outside the security gates, and knew how derisible the slap and tickle security searching actually was, I started smiling at his explanation. He wanted to know why I appeared sceptical. I told him that the changes would have little or no effect on security, but the very fact of publicising changes would attract the attention of bombers who would work out how to bomb inside the new gates, and then feel obliged to demonstrate this.

"Well, what alternative have *you* got?" he asked. I suggested that it might be better to remove the gates altogether, on the grounds that they were not particularly useful and were hindering commerce needlessly, and that if people chose to take advantage of this to bomb places of work in the community, the government would see to it that premises were rebuilt every time and that the government's will to have a creative community was stronger in the long run than the will to destroy.

I was really surprised when he responded that there was a lot to be said for the 'psychological approach'. But he added, disappointingly, "But the government has to be seen to be doing something".

I replied again that if I were a betting man, I would bet a fiver that within a month of the gates being changed, there would be bombing inside and outside of them.

I would have won my bet. The Provos bombed shops with incendiaries right at the gates themselves as well as deep inside and outside the gates. They capped this by having the biggest bomb of the decade in Belfast, an 1,100 pound proxy bomb on a lorry, delivered right to the front of the British Army's Belfast headquarters in the old fortified Grand Central Hotel.

Not only did this shatter the inside of the army's downtown fortress, but it tore out the inside of Newell's, one of Belfast's oldest department stores, on the other side of the street.

What made this even worse I discovered the following morning as I strolled up Royal Avenue to take in the daylight state of things, while cleaning up was still in progress. Standing in the roadway, quietly fuming, was Reg Empey, an old acquaintance from student days, who had been prominent in the Unionist Club, had acted as election agent for leading Unionist William Craig, and had himself been elected to Stormont. Beside Reg, who was manager of Newell's, a chute was noisily delivering the remains of Newell's stock from an upstairs floor to a rubbish skip in the street.

"Morning, Reg," I said, "the store took a terrible hammering."

But Reg, normally a most cheery customer, was staring fixedly across the street at the army's blasted headquarters, oblivious, it seemed to me, to the whoosh and clatter of his wrecked stock hitting the skip. It took a while to discover the reason for his out-of-character mood. I started to say sympathetically that I had told Rees that his new gates would attract trouble, when the source of Reg's anger came out: what was grieving him most was that soldiers, after the blast had gone off, had looted stock that could have been salvaged, and that the booty was obviously hidden in the blasted post across the street. Looting by soldiers was by no means unknown, but given their thankless role, no-one had so far charged them. Some were later charged and convicted, a rather pathetic side observation on the whole war of the 'brave chaps against the thugs and terrorists'—both groups being from the same socio-economic backgrounds.

1975 was a much happier year for me personally. I built a glasshouse, developed much more of my garden and resumed playing the piano after a lapse of fifteen years. We were expecting our fourth child in September, and did not get that holiday: but life was increasingly a holiday, even as I continued to cover both politics and violence, and involve myself in the local community. Life was much more 'normal', and solvent. I began to reflect much more on my own on the underlying problems of violence and politics and how they might be resolved enduringly.

While I observed the ongoing efforts at Stormont with a sympathetic eye, I was more and more persuaded by my original feeling that John Hume's strategy was fundamentally flawed, in that it was based on almost permanent division of the Northern Irish people, and would therefore always be vulnerable to sectarian demagoguery and attendant paramilitarism: and that therefore any solution which did not quickly transcend or outgrow the sectarian 'realities' would require enforcement rather than relying on a richly enthusiastic consensus.

I was returning with deeper conviction to my original instinct that the most important goal was to make the common humanity of the contemporary generation of Northern Irish people the most true reality of all, and that only in that perception could there be creative stability and mutual celebration of diversity.

I had already found in practice, as in my university days, that people in the community field engaged in a common project developed real friendships in which the prior perception of Catholic, Protestant, Unionist, Nationalist, artisan, rich business, unemployed, skilled, semi-skilled, male, female, tended to dissolve in favour of co-operation among real friends focussing on the common purpose.

The community association network, loose and varied though it was, provided a vital means of communication which was used effectively on occasions to bring spates of sectarian tit-for-tat murder to an end. Moreover, in contrast to party politics which understands democracy simply in terms of ballot-box numbers at once-in-five-years intervals, community development politics understood another vital democratic reality—*demos-kratis*—the strength of the people themselves, the ability of people to get together and do things for themselves, and for their own self-respect.

Community-based activity also provided an outlet for the patriotism of not a few former paramilitarists on both sides who wanted out of 'the action' whether for reasons of conscience or safety or simple change of conviction: their involvement led some members of the 'strong law and order' Alliance Party to charge on occasion that the community movement was being used as a 'front for gunmen'.

Certainly, I did meet men, on the community network, whom I knew to be killers, and who knew that I knew it, including men who, not so very much earlier, would have cheerfully plugged such as myself and considered it their patriotic duty. But I felt that this process was vital in itself, not only as a way for former killers to recover a better way, but for the wider society to exorcise its own guilt of mutual neglect and suspicion.

I felt that a society in which the less pressured did not make the great effort to establish the basic law of love, was as guilty collectively, by omission, as those, more pressured, who collectively took up arms to give the divisions their visibility. When the 'condemners' invoked the Bible, or promised eternal damnation for those whom they publicly judged as the sinners, they reminded me of the Sanhedrin who could never have understood what Jesus of Nazareth meant by 'love your enemies'.

Knowing my own aggressive reflexes, and capacity to wish to kill, I came to understand the commandment 'Love your enemies' not as some *extra* dimension for the specially saintly, but as the very *first* step in being able to love oneself in spite of one's own propensities and weaknesses. Loving one's enemies therefore did not come *after* loving one's neighbour: one could not love oneself or one's neighbour, unless one could love one's enemies—starting with the enemies *within*.

However, I knew, and know, how difficult it is for anyone reared in our culture to repudiate once and for all the 'security' that its militarism or paramilitarism professes to offer. In this context, I again came to the conclusion that the development of 'community politics' was essential to provide the confidence among self-respecting people that might enable them to opt for the disarmed, nonviolent possibility. Rooted in my own understanding of what is sacred, this conviction even caused me to wonder whether a power-political 'solution' at the Stormont Constitutional Convention was entirely desirable. I could envisage situations where I might feel conscientiously obliged to refuse to co-operate with a power-sharing regime which applied force to command allegiance in advance of building up substantial consensus from the community.

Hope did spring briefly in the Stormont Convention. At one point the now veteran negotiators, John Hume and Paddy Devlin of the

SDLP, appeared likely to make progress with Ian Paisley: the latter having talked of leaving Ulstermen behind closed doors with no outside interference, in which situation they might hammer out a deal. The bizarre talk went around that Ian Paisley, hitherto regarded as the born wrecker, was the man to talk to, the man who could deliver the deal. Then Bill Craig, Paisley's rival for the soul of traditional Unionism, offered 'Voluntary Coalition'—an ill-defined power-sharing not imposed from London. Craig delivered this with memorably enlightened rhetoric about living together with common consent as Ulstermen. The Home Affairs Minister of 1968 had come a long way, and Catholics were prepared to listen. But Ian Paisley was not. He proclaimed loudly that 'the loyalist people' would never share power with 'the enemies of Ulster'.

It was all pretty disgusting and disappointing, but nothing like the traumatic collapse of the earlier Assembly. The Convention tottered on with its debates, no-one wishing to be seen as the final wrecker.

I became more detached about reporting the killing, although occasionally the horror would break through, as when the riddled body of one victim lay decomposing for days, because of suspicion that it had been booby-trapped to kill security forces drawn to its location.

One death which will live long in my experience was that of a three-year-old girl. One morning, when I was off duty, I was out in the garden, putting in the first large pane of glass in my newly erected glasshouse. Two of our children, Rachel, then not yet four, and Susan, just over two, were standing on the path, watching the excitement. Just as I was setting the glass into its position there was a large explosion, right behind me. It seemed so close that I half ducked, still holding the glass. Rachel shouted, "There's a bomb", and I looked round to see a plume of smoke about two hundred yards away. Our garden, which looked out over much of the city, was above an area which the Department of the Environment was converting from an old river valley leading to the Lagan River, into all-weather playing-fields. There were workmen's huts at the edge of this area, and I immediately assumed that this was yet another sectarian attack on workmen. I left the glass down, put the children into the house and went around to see. In fact, the explosion had happened in a booby-trapped car in the street behind the proposed playing-fields. A man was lying badly injured on the road, with several neighbours tending him before the ambulance would arrive. From experience of such sights, I reckoned he would recover, for, to put it crudely, nothing had apparently been blown off. He was trembling with shock, but there did not appear to have been any great loss of blood. I was making this instant lay assessment, as I began talking to a grim-faced man standing nearby.

"I thought it was the workmen's hut round the corner at first," I said. "Does he live about here?"

"Aye, John O'Connor, he lives around the corner," replied this neighbour, obviously deeply shocked.

"I think he'll recover alright, mostly shock, doesn't seem too bad considering the way his car is," I went on, almost by way of comforting the man.

"Aye, he'll probably do all right, but the wee girl had no chance," he said.

"What wee girl?" I asked, looking all round.

"His wee girl, Michelle; took her to school every morning in the car; blown to bits," the man said, throwing his arm towards the blasted car. He then choked up and retired towards his own house. I looked around and could see no sign of any little girl, and I wondered immediately if this was a rumour and if anybody had actually seen the little girl; then, up against the wall of a house in front of where the bombed car was parked, I saw splattered against the wall what looked like a doll's golden wig. Again, I thought, maybe it's a doll that was blown out of the car, and the neighbours have taken it to be Michelle and in their concern for the living were gathered around Mr. O'Connor. I walked over towards the 'wig' not daring to believe what was getting clearer: it was the scalp, with beautiful hair, with blood and bone and brain smeared down the wall and licking around the edge of what might otherwise have been a doll's wig. Three-year-old Michelle O'Connor had been blown to bits in a quiet neighbourhood on her way to nursery school. I went home. As I came through the back door, Rachel greeted me, "What's wrong, Daddy?" I looked at her bright little face, her ash-blonde hair neatly done up, and I couldn't answer her. I went to the phone and reported the 'story': I think it was the only time that I ever really 'broke down' while reporting such things: it had taken me by surprise, I was out of touch with daily murder, and my normal feelings were operating more freely than for a very long time past.

I went back out and finished glazing the glasshouse, and found ways of explaining to the children without too much fuss what had happened and why I was so upset, for they were amazed to see Daddy crying. For a long time afterwards, Susan, who was then only learning to talk, would say, when bombs were heard going off, or were mentioned on the television news, "Bomb, Daddy, bomb, poor wee Michelle, bomb."

The local community association had long had great support from the Ballynafeigh Clergy Fellowship (Church of Ireland, Presbyterian, Methodist and Roman Catholic) who in this area at least, co-operated as if the God they worshipped were one and the same. In this moment of tragedy, they went round together to speak to neighbours. This practice of jointly visiting the bereaved and other neighbours was an important factor in preventing the spread of sectarianism in our area, where, the previous year, some streets had changed their demographic character, in terms of denominational label.

Organising festival events and functions for pensioners took on an extra relevance in our area. When the first festival office was bombed, the committee decided to go for better accommodation, a three-storey house on the main road. Despite threats, this was fully developed as Ballynafeigh Community House, with Pat Morrow prominent in the effort. We were ultimately faced with the decision of whether to open quietly or with a few trumpets. I was PRO for the association, and I felt very strongly that we should make our presence felt, and that to open quietly was a silent way of giving in to the IRA or UDA. We decided to invite the Lord Mayor of Belfast to open the Community House, to have all available media coverage, an open day for all local residents, and fulsome announcements in all the local churches. We also decided that if we were bombed, we would seek compensation and build a bigger and better community house.

On the appointed day, the Lord Mayor, Sir Myles Humphries, duly came, we had a perfect launch, and everybody was in great spirits. As it happened, that was March 16, 1976, the day Harold Wilson made the amazing announcement that he intended to resign as Prime Minister, and our event was squeezed down by the local reaction news. But it still featured with surprising prominence for a 'good news' story, as opposed to a good 'news story'. Some journalists were surprised to find me involved in this 'do-goody' role. I was duly interviewed. "Do you not think, Ciaran McKeown, with community workers getting shot and community centres attacked, that you are all in danger here of simply being targets for the bombers and gunmen?" The question was almost made to sound as if we were guilty of some kind of criminal incitement. I answered that I was aware of attacks elsewhere on community centres and workers and that we had heard rumours that we too would be attacked; but that we were confident that when people found that this was a useful centre of service in the community, those who saw themselves as local defenders would want to wish us well; but that in any case, people would have to stop hiding in their houses for fear of being attacked by other neighbours with guns, and that if it took a Gandhi-like courage for unarmed people to face up to such threats, then so be it.

Another initiative on this front, in April 1976, was a conference in a Carmelite monastery in Tadcaster, Yorkshire, England, organised by the Northern Ireland Community Development Committee. The conference invitees included a wide spectrum of community leaders from Northern Ireland, as well as some politicans. Some of the community leaders present had intimate connections with members of paramilitary organisations, and there was an attempt, untraced, to sabotage the effort with a 'flyer' story in the press about 'IRA and UDA in secret peace talks'. This caused the politicians to change their minds about coming.

The conference was nevertheless a very fruitful experience, strengthening friendships across very wide gulfs, and increasing the cross-community communication network. This could not have happened at a more necessary time, for sectarian killing had increased frighteningly from the beginning of the year.

Internment had ended completely in December 1975, and with it, 'GSCV'. In early January, Loyalist assassins killed five Catholics in one night, in Co. Down, in revenge for a recent killing of Protestants. The republicans retaliated. They stopped a workers' minibus at Kingsmills in South Armagh, ordered the eleven occupants out, and held them at gunpoint at the side of the bus; they asked if there were any Catholics among them, and one man stepped forward. He was told to walk down the road, which he did, expecting every moment to be his last. But the bursts of gunfire which broke out behind him, left him unscathed, and left his ten Protestant workmates dead on the road.

This set the pattern for a tit-for-tat war that stuttered on for months, pushing the murder rate up to levels reminiscent of 1972. People were in despair, war-weary, almost unable to be angry any more at the carnage; depressed and apathetic about the latest Stormont political failure; entirely unimpressed by the ending of internment or of 'special category status'; wondering where—or if—it was all going to end; fearful that the Provos and loyalists alike were getting ready for the 'final crunch'; even in some cases, wearily hoping that if the final crunch, that is, all-out blood-letting, 'had to come' then let it happen and get it over with, and then let the rest of us who survive get on with living in some kind of peace.

Having reconstructed my own life and happiness over the previous couple of years, I was convinced that the same attitude could lift the whole community out of its misery, through development of the community approach, regardless of party-political failure and its attendant violence. Only such a collective self-respect could produce the courage to overcome apathy, violence, political and economic stagnation; and I felt that the task would have to be tackled, whether or not there was any 'final crunch'.

This was the nature of my commitment as we took ourselves off to Achill at last in July 1976, for the first full holiday since 1968. For the first time since our honeymoon, we listened to no news, took no newspapers, confined ourselves almost totally to ourselves, the sea, the sky and the mountains, hearing only by accident about the mid-July murder of Christopher Ewart-Biggs, the British ambassador in Dublin.

After several days, I began to write down what I was calling 'The Philosophy of Peace'. I wrote for a couple of hours every afternoon. I did not think too much about the community development programme which might lie ahead of us, but I was very relaxed and confident about whatever the future might hold. I was also strangely certain that I would not be a journalist for much longer, though I would be writing more.

We came home on August 4, and still kept away from news and the rest of the human race. On Sunday, August 8, we turned on the radio to find out what time it was. It was a beautiful day. We were amazed to hear interviews with leading politicians, talking of the extremely tense situation, appeals for calm, grim outlook and so forth. It was a measure of how restful our holiday had been that, far from looking at each other and saying, 'Oh God, no, we're off again', Marianne and I looked at each other and laughed. Marianne said, "I don't feel tense. It's amazing how the media can announce that everybody is tense."

I looked out from the large window at the back of our house, across the clear sunlit view of Belfast, over the Lagan, over to West Belfast and round towards the North and the Cavehill where I grew up. Birds floated lazily over the river. I looked forward to getting back into the garden, and finished a second coat of paint on the woodwork on the outside of the house. We now knew we were expecting our fifth child in the early Spring, and were thinking of moving to a larger house, so there were a lot of jobs to be done.

I imagined all the other parents and children and grandparents in the city on such a day. They would want to enjoy it. They would not want to be tense, and they would not want to be told that they were tense. In the hazy sweep that was West Belfast, known to the world in terms of its strongholds and trouble spots, most people would be much the same. Soldiers too would want to enjoy the sun, maybe wishing that they were stretched out in one of those places suggested by the recruitment advertisements.

Some people, however, would be raging that relatives were in jail on such a day, or in recent graves—recent being the longer for those who lived in the tunnels of their own memories and restricted experience. Somehow the wounds would have to be healed, horizons widened; it was time people learned to live their own lives, instead of living out myths imposed by history on a lifetime, or on days by a news bulletin . . .

But the holiday was over, nevertheless. And since I was due back at 4.00 p.m. on Tuesday August 10, I began listening to news bulletins, and 'catching up'. I rang a few people, but did not stray from my home or garden. I heard that Provo Sinn Fein Vice-President Maire Drumm had harangued a demonstration in Dunville Park, and threatened that Belfast would be pulled down stone by stone if prisoners were not granted political status; heard how the demonstration passed off peacefully enough, but that youths had stoned Springfield Road police and army barracks; watered my vegetables, smoked my pipe, went to bed.

Next day, I resumed painting the window frames, switching from concerts on Radio Three to listening to news programmes and back to the music; heard how rioting in West Belfast was widespread, with much hijacking of vehicles on this August 9 anniversary of internment, recalled that terrible day five years earlier. But now there were no internees: instead the cause was the demand of prisoners sentenced under the 1973 'Temporary' Emergency Provisions Act for political status. I got a good deal of painting done and all the routine gardening. My crop now included tomatoes, cucumbers and peppers from the glasshouse; several sowings of lettuce; three sowings of potatoes; sweet corn; two kinds of cabbage; beetroot, broccoli, brussels sprouts, peas, beans, french beans, parsley, a divider richly coloured with sweet pea, a new border of roses grown from carefully rooted slips. Life was full, peaceful, solvent. Another beautiful day.

I lingered in bed on the morning of August 10, in spite of the holiday habit of getting up at 7.30, for I would be on the 4 p.m. to midnight shift that day, and I was startled when the phone rang at eight o'clock. It was RTE from Dublin.

"Ciaran, will you come in and talk to us at eleven o'clock about your story on Maire Drumm's arrest?" asked Brian Reynolds, producer of the mid-morning current affairs programme *Here and Now* to which I was a regular contributor.

"Brian, I just go back to work today after nearly four weeks, I haven't a clue what's going on," I said. "If you like, I'll talk to you about my first break in eight years!"

"But that's your story in the *Irish Press!*" Brian explained.

"Impossible, Brian," I told him. "I haven't sent copy for nearly four weeks."

"Wait a minute till I get the paper," he said; and I asked Rachel who had just bounced into our room to run down and get the paper from the front door. She arrived just as Brian returned to the phone, and there it was, 'Maire Drumm arrested' by Ciaran McKeown in Belfast.

"It is your story", Brian was saying. "Please, can you get in about 10.30?"

"But I didn't send that story!"

"It's got your by-line."

"I can see that, but I did not send that story. I have not sent a story for four weeks—maybe they're trying to sell papers!" I cracked with customary modesty.

"Will I call you back?" Brian was asking, aware that I was still not up, which may have been accounting in his mind for my inability to see that I had written the story on Maire Drumm's arrest.

"Look Brian, I'll ring around and come in via a trip round. But I'd rather talk about what it's like to get a holiday from here after eight years."

I got up, read the paper, listened to the news, rang a few colleagues and set off to take the long way round by West Belfast to RTE, which was actually only about ten minutes from home. I stopped at a garage on the corner of Finaghy Road North to get petrol and matches (for my car and pipe respectively). I chatted to such citizens as were about. There was a tone of seething anger about the previous day's rioting and hijacking, which surprised me. The rage centred around the fact that youngsters could take cars from adults who felt powerless—"you never know who's behind them with guns," or if they had guns themselves, "you can't argue with a young one the way you can with an older man, they'd shoot you soon as look at you". This entirely random encounter confirmed what I had been listening to on the phone and detecting from the bulletins and papers. Nobody wanted to know much about the prisoners, and certainly not about hijacking cars or burning Belfast stone by stone, and there would be little sympathy for Maire Drumm's being arrested.

The tone of the anger was different to that observed after events like the July curfew of 1970 or the milling, barricade excitement and panic of the first internment day. The wheel seemed to be coming full circle: the total rejection of the police in August 1969 had given rise to the Provos, internment in August 1971 had confirmed them; now there seemed to be building up a frustrated desire to reject the violence of the Provos—frustrated because the Provos were indigenous, they were of the people, and the prison issue still held a root of communal, cultural legitimacy. This rooted connection did not, however, justify the hijacking and burning of their own neighbours' cars and commercial vehicles supplying the area.

I told presenter Rodney Rice in the live interview that I felt that the Provos had gone too far, that they were alienating potential sympathy on the prison issue, that Maire Drumm would get little sympathy unless the authorities pressed charges to conviction. I gave my opinion that arrest was probably cosmetic and that she would be released: she would only arouse sympathy if convicted, for her rhetoric was scarcely different to that from some leading loyalists who would not be arrested or charged under the useless Incitement Act. Rodney Rice reminded me that I had said before that the Provos would lose support over various atrocities, but that they still came back and did worse.

I repeated my view that this was a cumulative process, and that they were often rescued by over-reaction by the authorities; but that unless the authorities were stupid enough to go on a rampage of harassment, the Provos were putting themselves close to the kind of rejection by the people that had befallen the police and the army in the past and given rise to the Provos in the first place.

I got home about noon, and resumed painting my window-frames. It was yet another sunny day. My *Irish Press* colleague Alan Murray rang about 12.30 to say that Jimmy Drumm, Maire's much-interned husband, had been on complaining belligerently, and that I was going too far this time with my criticisms of the republican movement.

"Needless to say," Alan added, "I did not enlighten him that that was my story that got your by-line this morning!"

"Yes, what about that?" I asked Alan. He had no idea, and we never did find out how I got a by-line for a story, when my name had not been on anything for a month.

"Well, see you about four, or a bit earlier maybe," I told him, and went back to painting, after some lunch.

Alan rang again at about 2.30. "Thought I'd better give you an earlier call. Some shooting up at Finaghy Road North. May be a kid killed. I'll give you a shout if I hear any more."

I had got about another twenty minutes' painting done when Alan rang again. "Seems there's definitely one man dead, definitely one kid dead, maybe two, looks bad, maybe even more dead."

"Look Alan, I'm covered in paint," I said. "I'll just get cleaned up and come in about four, put over the early stuff and then go up and have a look."

I put the paint brushes in a jar of spirit and put the lot under the bottom step of the stepladders on the extension roof, to keep them from blistering in the hot sun, until I could get back to it.

I went down to the kitchen and told Marianne I'd have to go in early. "First day back, two stiffs, looks like couple of kids dead," I said as I washed my hands. The brushes sat in their jar under the ladders on the roof until November, when I finally accepted that I was not going to be able to get time to complete the job.

By then, moving house was out of the question, as was emigration. I was no longer a journalist and my whole life had turned inside out.

A Turning Point

On that August 10 day, there had been little or no hijacking. In the early afternoon, in the Tullymore Gardens area of Andersonstown, snipers opened up on a British army patrol from nearby Glassmullan Camp (whose look-out posts stared down into the Drumm home in Glassmullan Drive). They missed, and were seen escaping. Soldiers radioed descriptions and two army Land Rovers converged on a Ford Cortina, carrying two men, speeding down the Stewartstown Road and into Finaghy Road North. The car was being driven by a former internee, nineteen-year-old Danny Lennon.

The pursuing soldiers opened fire. Danny Lennon was shot dead. The car swerved out of control.

Anne (Corrigan) Maguire was walking along Finaghy Road North with her children. Joanne, aged eight-and-a-half, was on her bicycle; Mark, who would soon be seven, and John, aged two-and-a-half, were walking; Andrew, six weeks old, was in the pram. Nearby was Anne's sister Eilish (Corrigan) O'Connor, whose eldest child, Michelle, had been killed by a car, driven by a frightened motorist fleeing a riot situation, on this same road, about a hundred yards further down, eight years earlier.

In the middle of this sunny afternoon, a Ford Cortina suddenly tore into them.

The world would see the railings and the pram and bicycle. Joanne and Andrew were killed instantly; doctors would stand by helplessly for hours before pronouncing John dead.

For weeks they would work on Anne's injuries, relieved when her deep unconsciousness proved to result from brain bruising, but not permanent damage. Her broken legs and pelvis would heal, and she would give birth to two more children. Then Mark, who was the uninjured witness of that first horror, would find his mother dead from the wounds that would not heal, forty-one months later.

Those forty-one months would see Anne going to the other end of the world in search of peace of soul, while her sister Mairead would do the same in search of peace for this world. But that could hardly be foreseen on August 10, 1976: on that day, Catholics in West Belfast, who had exploded in anxiety for their lives against the police in August 1969, in anger against the British army in August 1971, now erupted in anguish against the very people who were the product of these earlier traumata—the Provisional IRA.

Violence was consuming itself, it seemed, and could beget no more violence. In the length and breadth of the Falls area, people gathered to talk about it, or stand silently about in the summer evening air, as the shock sank in, then released a great wave of feeling.

Women grouped at street corners to weep or say the Rosary. Chapels filled for the evening Mass. On Finaghy Road North, a little shrine with fresh flowers was already in place in front of the twisted railings. People stood staring at the spot or walked about aimlessly; cars slowed down as they passed, passengers looking out in a mixture of curiosity and awe, at times it seemed almost in reverence.

There was something unmistakably different about this tragedy among all the tragedies we had lived through. The arguments would quickly start over whether the Provos or the pursuing soldiers should be blamed, or the British in general for being there at all; or 'fifty years of Unionist misrule' for stoking the fires; or whoever you thought were the 'real' cause of all our agony. But even the most intransigent seemed to sense that there was something obscene about trying to blame either a dead youth or the soldiers who killed him, while the mother of the dead children was lying seriously injured in hospital.

There seemed to be nobody to explode 'against': and the immense frustration of this anguish coming on top of the previous day's fury meant that something had to break somewhere. A volcano working up from the depths of the communal soul was looking for an outlet. While men stood about speechless and impotent, women marched here and there in small groups and prayed. One woman rang the *Irish News* and gave veteran reporter Tom Samways information on a petition that had been collected; she also gave her name and telephone number for others to contact, an unusual thing to do in a town where you keep your head down. Her name was Betty Williams. The volcano sensed an outlet, and Betty Williams' phone 'never stopped'.

A rally was announced for the afternoon of August 14, when Finaghy Road North would see the first expression of what would become the Movement of the Peace People.

On the afternoon of August 10, with the sun gleaming down over the bay at Keel on Achill Island, Mairead Corrigan regretfully cut short her holiday in order to accompany home a friend who was grieving over a recent bereavement. On the way home, she heard about a tragedy in which two, and perhaps three children had died, with their mother seriously injured after a Provo had been killed in a car chase by soldiers. Hours later she accompanied her brother-in-law, Jackie

Maguire, to identify his children. Then, as Jackie numbly told reporters that there was no use in appealing to 'the gunmen', as they were asking him to do, Mairead Corrigan made an appeal which moved people around the world. There was not a trace of bitterness in it; it lost no dignity for being made in tears; it spoke of bringing up children to love their neighbours— "it did not matter if they were Catholic or Protestant, that's not what Anne and Jackie were telling their children and now they're dead, oh God, it's awful". The volcano sensed another outlet.

Throughout the days following August 10, I was almost continuously engaged, along with the normal duties, in doing two special features on West Belfast, to put the events of the week in perspective, I debated with a colleague, freelance photographer Brendan Murphy, who was with me much of the week, whether to go near this woman Williams. The dailies were quoting her, and one English paper, the *Daily Express*, featured her on page one with the headline 'Why I must stop the IRA' across the top, and her signature on the bottom. That in itself was enough to sicken me, for it seemed to combine the cheapest sensationalism with *Daily Express* jingoism. Moreover, throughout my reporting of the Troubles, I had always found talking with women after a tragedy to be the most difficult and hapless exercise—unable to say anything much if they weep, perhaps wanting to comfort them, yet professionally restrained from stopping to hold a hand.

Finally, at about 11.00 a.m. on August 12, in Brendan's house, I decided that we should at least ring her, since she had taken the unusual step of giving out her number. I did so, introduced myself, and asked if she would mind if we dropped round to see her briefly?

"You might as well, cocker, one more won't make any difference," came a strong earthy voice from the other end. I thanked her and put the phone down, and turned to Brendan, relieved: "Well, she sounds alright, not a weeper anyway."

We presented ourselves at Mrs. Williams' house about twenty minutes later. There were newsmen sitting on the wall outside, and a taxi had just arrived to take her off to Ulster Television studios. We went in and Betty Williams was answering questions by others from the English dailies. I could see that she was not going to have time to talk, nor had I any indication that she had anything to say. So I told her that we would not hold her back, but would she mind if Brendan took a snap or two?

My telephone impression was completely confirmed, and any nervousness of being caught in mid-story by a weeping lady, especially one who was not a relative of the bereaved, was dispelled.

On Friday August 13, the Requiem Mass for the three Maguire children was held in the chapel of St. Michael the Archangel, on Finaghy Road North, where the little table shrine at the railings had been enlarged. The Chapel was packed. I will not easily forget the sight of those three little white coffins in a row. I went home directly after the Mass. I have read reports, including one in a book, of how I was seen standing, in a white suit, weeping at the graveside as the children were being buried. They are not accurate. I did not attend the burial. While that was happening, I was in my garden at home with my own children.

About mid-afternoon, RTE rang to ask me to come in that evening to the BBC studios to talk about the significance of the week. Paddy Devlin, the local parliamentary representative and then SDLP chief whip, would also appear, as well as Betty Williams and Mairead Corrigan. I agreed.

RTE's interviewer, Forbes McFall, kept us engaged while the BBC floor personnel set up shots being suggested from the Dublin production end, which was getting agitated as transmission time approached, with no sign of Betty Williams or Mairead Corrigan.

It was a hot evening in the studio, the lights adding to the summer heat. Paddy Devlin had taken his jacket off.

"What do you think, Paddy?" I asked him. Paddy Devlin is a large character, volatile, compassionate. I had a great regard for him. He has since attacked me on several occasions, in his colourful way. I still have a great regard for him, and always will.

"Nine-day wonder," said Paddy, to the point.

"I don't think so, Paddy; I think this is a real turning-point," I replied.

"Nine-day wonder," Paddy repeated, "The Provos will lean on those two women and they'll fade away."

"I don't agree, Paddy," I replied. "I hope we won't be disagreeing too violently, but I will be saying that the feeling is such that people are prepared to speak out in spite of threats or guns, that this really is the time for Gandhi-like courage."

"Of course, I'm not going to say that, I'll give them every encouragement, but the important thing is our talks with the Unionists," Paddy replied.

Transmission time, and still no sign of Betty or Mairead: so Dublin signalled the go-ahead, and the programme went off as the pre-show chat had indicated, with Paddy and myself talking about two totally different things, he about the SDLP—Unionist Party talks, myself about a turning point, that people knew there had to be some other way, that what was required was a peace movement of people prepared to challenge violence without the protection of guns.

As I was talking, and as we came downstairs afterwards, I began to realise that I was standing on, if not already across, the line generally accepted as lying between journalistic 'objectivity' and 'involvement'.

When we reached the ground floor, we met Betty Williams and Mairead Corrigan who had arrived just as the programme ended. With them was Maureen Joyce whom I had known ten years earlier, when I worked on a student vacation in the tobacco shop where she was employed. Paddy and Mairead already knew each other. The other mutual introductions were made. Mairead Corrigan said to me: "Oh, Ciaran McKeown, I've always wanted to meet you."

I was, naturally, flattered: especially as these words came out of a face dominated by two large, direct eyes and a broad smile. She was explaining that she had read this and that article that I had written.

Before we left the building, I said to them both that I thought there was a chance to create a real peace movement, and that if there was anything I could do to help that, I would do it. I explained to them that I was a pacifist apart from my journalism, and gave them both my telephone number at home, which has always been ex-directory.

I went home that evening feeling very relaxed and at peace with myself. The intuition which caused me in Achill to feel that I would not be working much longer in my current job was about to be proven, and the ideas I had been drafting were about to be tested.

Saturday August 14 was another splendid day. The Finaghy Road North demonstration drew about 10,000 people, which in a way was rather small, especially in the light of the larger rallies which would follow, when the memory of the Maguire tragedy was fading. Nevertheless, it was a remarkable occasion, not least for the fact that it had no particular focus, no platform, no speaking equipment — and no speeches.

Women with placards and banners turned up from Twinbrook, a nearby Catholic estate in which some women on a bus about to be hijacked earlier in the week had shown that courage of exhaustion that made Rosa Parks refuse to give her bus seat to a White passenger in Montgomery, Alabama, USA, nearly twenty years earlier. "I was tired," Rosa explained later, when this otherwise forgotten lady was asked about the incident that effectively launched the Black Civil Rights movement and rocketed Martin Luther King, Jnr., into the leadership of that great struggle. These Twinbrook women simply said to the youths taking over the bus: "If you're going to burn this bus, you'll have to burn it with us on it, for we're not getting off!"

In my mind, that was the first real act of the 'peace movement': but no 'personalities' emerged from it, and media concentration on the Maguire tragedy meant that it was ignored. Nevertheless, they got a great cheer as they arrived. Even bigger welcomes were given to women who had bussed over from the East and Ormeau areas of the city: and a group had come from, of all places, the Shankill Road, home district of Loyalism down the generations, and traditionally hostile to the Catholic Falls district in which they were now standing.

There were also more men, proportionately, at this rally, than at most later rallies. There were also quite a few public figures and politicians, mostly from the Alliance Party, but some from the SDLP. I noted particularly the presence of those I sometimes characterised a little cynically as 'the professional peace people': people inclined to issue condemnatory statements and gather petitions, but whose concern for peace rarely indicated any concern for the justice that might ultimately guarantee a dynamic peace. I was a little apprehensive that such people might compromise the quality of innocent, simple humanity of this beginning.

In the centre of the crowd on the lawns of St. Michael's, some nuns began to sing gentle hymns. On the roof of a nearby garage, some Provo-supporting youths began to jeer and shout and wave the Irish tricolour. When some of those near me began shouting back, I pleaded urgently with them to ignore the youths, and to keep things dignified. The youths seemed to lose heart at the lack of response, and their protest faded. Later, when the almost silent demonstration broke up, a large section accompanied the Shankill contingent back down the Falls Road to the top of the Donegall Road where they would get a bus home. There was some shouting and throwing of rotten fruit at them, but nothing serious.

The rally had been an expression of feeling, but it was not yet a 'movement'.

That weekend Mairead Corrigan rang me several times with queries on what to say if the media asked this or that or the other. My response was invariably: "What do you know about it?"

Usually, the answer was "nothing".

"Well, then, answer 'nothing'," I would advise. I pointed out then and frequently to Betty and Mairead in the following days and weeks that the truth comes through the media more powerfully than anything else, especially since people everywhere were sick to the teeth of the half-truths of politicians and the careful phrases of clergy and other public people.

I was becoming puzzled a couple of days later to know what had

144

become of Betty Williams, since only Mairead was ringing, when Betty suddenly cut into a conversation I was having with Mairead to say, "Can you get over here, cocker?" The term 'cocker' was a familiar one which she appeared to use to everyone: it was unusual in Belfast where the words 'mate' or 'squire' were more common at the time.

I dutifully 'got over there', and discovered that Betty had been away for a couple of days, and that Mairead had been very busy with newsmen, and with people suggesting rallies here, there and everywhere.

I had already made up my mind that I was ready to pitch everything into what I felt was a unique moment to launch a peace movement proper. What was concerning me was how to proceed with Betty and Mairead in such a way that they could really grow without losing anything of the authenticity with which they had begun. In a vague way, I felt that they would learn from my experience without being 'briefed', and that I could protect them from self-serving interlopers and bandwaggoners. The difficulty of doing this invisibly eventually proved too great.

On this Tuesday, August 17, just after noon, I wanted to be sure that they were of a similar conviction to myself before so much would be put at risk. So before any questions started, I simply said: "Look, I think we can start a real peace movement, but there are a couple of things we have to be clear about: first, do you trust me—after all, you do not know me and I could be a journalist with no real interest other than getting on the inside of a story?"

With immediate, total conviction, both answered 'yes'. I asked them if they trusted each other. The response was the same. I explained that I thought trust was the most vital element: internal bickering would be a far greater threat than any external danger.

The second thing, I said, was that this was for life: "You cannot go asking people to dedicate themselves to working for peace, risking their homes, careers and lives unless you are really dedicated yourself, and that means, literally, being instruments for peace for the rest of your lives."

Again, the response was totally convincing. The little scene surprised me, for I had not anticipated asking these questions. There seemed to be an immediate empathy between us, three people who had met only a few days earlier.

I then said that there was no need to be worrying constantly about what to say to the media: "If you do not know the answer, just say so, your honesty will be appreciated, and as time goes by, you'll pick things up without even noticing. In the meantime, we will have to think of a name for the movement, announce a rally for the Ormeau

Park and stop all these random rallies dispersing people."

We agreed that I would organise a press conference on Saturday's rally, and that my involvement would be kept private, but not denied if anyone asked directly: there would be no lies, diplomatic or otherwise . . . .

From that point on, there was a specific movement whose authenticity I would guard jealously, yet which would appear as 'spontaneous': there was a great deal of spontaneity about much of what happened, and in what we did. But 'authentic' is a more appropriate word in many cases, for what followed did not just happen unaided out of thin air. We began to get a little bit organised. People ringing in to see what they could do were either invited for telephone manning duty or asked to organise a group in their own areas, hire a bus for the next rally and await word on future rally plans.

I envisaged a rally phase that would enable us to mobilise people, then encourage them to organise in their own areas, from which, after the rallies, they would travel to visit others for socials and debates, and so, slowly, create a new community network. I discussed the prospects with Marianne, then expecting our fifth child. She could see that I was already committed, knowing whom she had married eight years earlier. Much of our conversation was taken up with the nature of the possible movement, its name, the personalities of Betty and Mairead, whom Marianne had yet to meet. We both felt that the media's various labels, 'Ulster Women's Movement', 'Mothers for Peace' etc. were misleadingly sexist, since it was not specifically a 'women's movement', and that the last thing we needed was to become vulnerable to a sexist battle in the middle of beginning. Marianne favoured my old joke phrase about the 'peace people': and as I mused somewhat wryly on it, it grew on me forcibly.

I put it to Betty and Mairead the next day, and both liked it; both agreed that we did not want to exclude men either in reality or in image. The three of us had met in the sacristy of St. Michael's the Archangel, where they were to meet Father Agnew, who, with Father Malachy Murphy, had been so helpful to the Maguire and Corrigan families and everyone else during that terrible week. Betty and Mairead produced a statement which they had written as a kind of all-purpose draft to give to newsmen pestering them to say things.

They were uncomfortable about it: it contained such sentiments as 'we say to the gunmen, get out, we don't want you'. There was clearly a growing need to say something in answer to all the queries.

"What do you think, Ciaran?" Mairead asked.

146

"I don't think it's really what you want to say. Here, lend me your jotter a minute," I said. Mairead had a blue jotter, in which to note names and telephone numbers. I scribbled out a statement of purpose, and read it aloud. Betty and Mairead agreed that it was exactly what they wanted to say. This was it:

We have a simple message from this meeting, and from this movement for peace.
We want to live and love and build a just and peaceful society.
We want for our children, as we want for ourselves,
our lives at home, at work and at play, to be lives of
joy and peace.
We recognise that to build such a life demands of all of us, dedication, hard work, and courage.
We recognise that there are many problems in our society which are a source of conflict and violence.
We recognise that every bullet fired and every exploding bomb make that work more difficult.
We reject the use of the bomb and the bullet and all the techniques of violence.
We dedicate ourselves to working with our neighbours, near and far, day in and day out, to building that peaceful society in which the tragedies we have known are a bad memory and a continuing warning.

I suggested that we might call it our 'Declaration', to be read at rallies. We agreed on the name 'Peace People', and the lines scribbled in a couple of minutes in the St. Michael the Archangel's sacristy became 'The Declaration of the Peace People'.

The Saturday August 21 rally in the Ormeau Park was, in my opinion, the biggest of the entire movement. Women from East Belfast, notably such veteran community organisers as Winnie Jordan and Isobel Bennett, had duplicated thousands of leaflets to put through doors; and Pat Morrow from our local Ballynafeigh Community Association had also been busy with typewriter and duplicator. Thousands of people from North and West Belfast had gathered in Ormeau Avenue and marched up with Betty and Mairead leading under the new Andersonstown banner. We had decided that the only banners in this much bannered city would be simple white cloth with the district names in blue letters, and some were already appearing. Many more would show their areas in the coming weeks, and we would be indebted in particular to the sisters of the Good Shepherd convent in Ballynafeigh for their help in making some of them.

As the marchers poured into Ormeau Park, they could be seen by thousands more already gathered into a large open space from the South and East of the city. The huge park stretches from the predominantly Protestant East Belfast into the mixed Ballynafeigh area.

There were also people from the South of Ireland, including Judy Hayes from the Glencree Centre of Reconciliation outside Dublin: she and her colleagues went back home to organise huge demonstrations in the South. It was another sunny day, and faces were happy and open even as they were weeping: people hugged each other like long lost friends, or long-estranged relatives embraced in reconciliation.

Somebody began singing 'Abide with me' even while people were still arriving. It was taken up by those around, and by the time it reached the back edge of the arena, the first group was into the second verse, so that an extraordinary and haunting choral effect was created. There was still no loudspeaker equipment, but Mairead had a transhailer and spoke through it to the relatively few who could hear, and to the radio and TV. Betty also spoke and the Declaration was read for the first time, many reading it from newspaper clippings. Then, with Mairead announcing, to a great cheer, that the next rally would be up the Shankill, the short rally was over, and people began dispersing—even as some were still arriving!

The numbers were important for another quite mundane reason: a group of journalists, including myself, met in the middle of the throng, and tried to agree on the size. One reporter suggested that it was like a cup-final crowd; I thought 50,000 was a reasonable figure by that standard; another pointed out that there were far more present than when Bill Craig, the traditional Unionist leader, had addressed an estimated 60,000 loyalists lined up in ranks. There was a lot of head-scratching before the man from the Press Association, whose figure would reach all news desks, said he would say "over 30,000". The word 'over' could cover up to twice the number.

When I was reporting, I said, "countless thousands, in a crowd so large that it defied estimate by experienced reporters . . ." I was contacted twice in the next hour by the Dublin news editor, querying my report and quoting the PA 'over 30,000' line. I stuck to my version and the *Sunday Press* added its own bit to the numbers game with the headline '50,000 Answer Provos'. I was not pleased with that headline: not because of the 50,000, but because the movement was not out simply to answer the Provos, although that was obviously what many felt. Later the Provos would seize on my involvement and point to that headline to show that I had been manipulating the media.

The charge of media manipulation got another boost because of an event two days later. I received a call from Ulster Television to appear on their tea-time news magazine and talk about the peace movement.

"Are you well clued up on it?" the reporter asked.

I said yes, that in fact, off the record, I was up to my eyes in it. The programme involved Derek Brown of the *Guardian*, and myself, talking to Betty Williams and Mairead Corrigan, with Colin Baker as presenter/reporter. The very strong opinions I expressed in favour of the significance and future growth of the movement happened to coincide with my occupational judgement. But later Provisional Sinn Fein complained to UTV about my participation. A senior UTV staffman phoned to advise me that UTV would be issuing a statement that the station knew nothing about my involvement at the time when I was asked to take part. I said that was fine, except that I had pointed the fact out to the person in question. This surprised UTV, who issued no statement: all of which undoubtedly encouraged the Provos to believe their own propaganda that we were part of a co-ordinated establishment propaganda campaign.

But by this time, August 23, I was merely wondering when to submit my resignation, for the work ahead was clearly going to require total commitment. The Shankill rally, on August 28, would be, symbolically, the most significant of all the rallies, for Belfast's torn people. It was the one they said 'could not be done'.

The mid-August 'volcano' had produced an enormous spout of energy which had every chance of going straight up in the air and spending itself inconsequentially. It might even if wrongly inflamed, do great damage, or leave people exhausted and more despairing than ever. What had to be done was to 'bend' the gush into a network of activities and groups. Had the Christian Churches not been so divided, they might have provided the appropriate network.

I was under no illusion that the community association network had any kind of monopoly of people of character and humility on a level superior to that of the party-politicians. Many of the 'community' groups were riddled with personality and ideological crises: a lack of clear vision encouraged rivalries and cliques; in a few cases, the age-old phenomenon of one-person empires was the reality parading as 'community organisation'. Under-funded, over-worked, the community network was as demoralised as any in the wider community. But it was committed at least rhetorically to community development whether or not any 'political' solution emerged. And community development seemed to me the best way to invest the sudden supply of emotional energy, and the safest way to avoid the party-political and sectarian minefields. I saw the task ahead roughly as follows:

1. People needed an extended, visible opportunity to articulate the cry that they wanted an end to war, and a beginning to some new accommodation;
2. They needed a boost to their self-respect, having lived under an internal and external perception of themselves as savage and incurable bigots;
3. They needed mechanisms by which such expression could continue to develop, after mass rallies would inevitably dwindle;
4. They needed to feel that such activity and expression were substantial, and corresponded to the highest spiritual and intellectual aspirations;
5. They needed, in the short term, a form of leadership that inspired them with the confidence to do things for themselves, thus creating an upward spiral of self-confidence;
6. In a situation where fear of local intimidation meant that people kept to themselves—'whatever you say, say nothing'—it was important that people were enabled to see, in the various 'strongholds', that there were more of those who wanted an end to killing, than otherwise, and that there were people who would say, out loud, what they thought, regardless of real or imaginary threats; and
7. They needed to feel that an enduringly stable and loving society was out there at the end of the process then beginning.

The process had to get a bold, clear start, and to avoid becoming bogged down in self-appointed committees, which might reduce the whole enterprise to the lowest common denominator of caution and fear. It was therefore vital that Betty Williams and Mairead Corrigan be protected from the matrix of established jealousies and animosities, and get a clear run at presenting a new vision, with clarity, confidence and authenticity. In an initiative marked by the intervention of many, especially women, who were novices in the public arena, it was important that they they be seen to grow steadily out of their own roots.

It has been said, sometimes almost malevolently, that I briefed Betty and Mairead intensively, that I was some sort of cross between Machiavelli and Svengali—names actually invoked—to enable these 'two ordinary women' to perform in public in the effective way that they did. At the early stages, such charges usually amused us, with

Betty joking 'wait till we ask Gandhi', or 'let's ask Machiavelli'. There
was also an embarrassing attempt to deify us in some circles, to suggest
that we were 'divinely sent', that we were some kind of reflected
'Trinity' in which Betty was the heart, Mairead the soul, and me the
head, or sometimes it was guts, heart and head in the same order.
Certainly it was an astonishing relationship, which in itself attracted
a great deal of attention, since its empathy, at times telepathic, was
instant, deep and powerful. It echoes in me still, seven years later,
though I have scarcely seen Betty Williams for four years, and rarely
enough see Mairead Corrigan.

I am therefore not entirely sure that I can write about it with the
kind of detachment which I would like to command. In the first place,
these were not 'two ordinary women', two 'average Ulster
housewives', two 'mothers for peace'. They were quite unusual, as
was obvious to people in general, the 'ordinary women' mythology
notwithstanding. Betty Williams, then thirty-three, had behind her
a turbulent and tough life. She had two children, a boy, Paul, then
coming into his teens, and a daughter, Deborah, then four. She was
married to Ralph Williams, an easy-going marine engineer who spent
much of the year at sea. She had lived briefly in Bermuda and had
seen rather more of the world than any 'average Ulster housewife'.
The details of her biography, however, are not relevant to this
consideration: I sensed immediately that she was a fighter, that she
was tough enough to take a lot, and still come up for more; that she
had a quick and shrewd intelligence; that she was impulsive but could
live with the consequences of her own impulses and, if necessary, spit
in the world's eye; and that far from recoiling from performing on a
wider stage, she would have felt herself perfectly entitled to do so. If
she were an actress and I were a director, I could have seen her roles
ranging from street fighter to prima donna to genuinely noble, regal
persona. In the event, she did demonstrate some aspects of all these
possibilities. Without knowing anything about her, I had an instant
sense of who she was: and apparently, she had the same intuitive
recognition of me.

Mairead Corrigan, then thirty-two, had a background that was
more like mine, in the sense that her activities had prepared her almost
directly for the role she would now carry out. Coming from an
orthodox Roman Catholic background, she had joined the 'Legion of
Mary' as a teenager, and her work for that lay Catholic organisation
included working with local community groups, broken families,
alcoholics and prostitutes. The 'Legion' sometimes has a reputation
for being that extreme expression of Mariology, of primary devotion
to the intercessionary function of Mary, mother of Jesus, which some

Catholics and almost all Protestants find unbalanced; and girls who go on in it indefinitely are likely to be thought of as 'Holy Marys', either in the genuine sense of being like lay nuns, or as girls disguising a repressed or sublimated sexuality. But the 'Legion' in many places, and certainly in Belfast, was much more a dedicated organisation of practical people helping the poorest of the poor, physically and spiritually. I spent two years in the organisation when I was a teenager, and helped out in hostels for alcoholics and other broken people: and there is nothing like the smell of vomit, accumulated excreta and long unwashed flesh to remove any incense-and-roses spirituality from the soul; and nothing like the colourful language of those in despair, with barely the spirit left to abuse those caring for them, to keep things in perspective.

The practical dynamic predominated in Mairead. She was vitally charged, rather than vivacious, and very determined, very much her own mistress. Like Betty, she had left school at fourteen, but had spent a year at commercial college acquiring the skills which would help her rise to the position she held in August 1976, of personal secretary to the managing director of Guinness (Belfast), the large brewery so closely identified with Ireland's drinking habits. She also continued to read and study in the area of theology and the renewal movement in the Roman Catholic church. It is a measure of how far from 'ordinary' she was, that she had been the first woman to address the Chapter of Clergy in the deeply conservative diocese in Belfast. She had also been chosen as a lay observer to the World Council of Churches in Ulan Bator.

Again, I felt an immediate affinity with Mairead, and that it was reciprocated. When I had explicitly asked about trusting each other in that first meeting, the response between the three of us was immediate and authentic: it was a sensation, like people in love, of having known each other all our lives. A few months later, the well-known English disc jockey, Jimmy Saville, who did a fund-raising sponsored walk with us, remarked that he had not seen that kind of empathy in a group since the Beatles.

The strength and energy that this relationship gave us was a powerful source of the same confidence to many people. It was an equal source of frustration to those who resented it, or who sought to come between us, or felt that they were better qualified to do what Betty and Mairead were doing before the world. Naturally, I was seen as 'manipulating', but in my observation, that charge tended to come from would-be manipulators. Reactions to the 'trio' were intense, at times reaching the extremes of wanting to see us either as a Christ figure with Mary and Martha, to a Rasputin figure with a ménage à trois.

As this personality cult, so useful in launching the initiative, began to mushroom to a level of hysteria, it was obvious that it would need to be earthed. There is a line between inspiring people with enough confidence to get on with what must be done, and a dangerous mass hypnosis in which people expect leaders to 'do it for them', or believe that success will be inevitable provided that those particular leaders are there. Ireland, moreover, has a diseased appetite for dead martyrs, the living version of which is tearing leaders apart while they are challengingly still alive.

While we did not deal with this problem satisfactorily, we were nevertheless acutely conscious of it: our failure did not result from a lack of foresight. I understood clearly and specifically that too strong an identification of the nonviolent society we were advocating, with this cult leadership, would leave it vulnerable on several points: it could undermine the self-respect and growth of those inspired; it risked sudden reversal if the leaders were killed, as happened with such movements as Gandhi's and King's—and cult leadership invites assassination; it would impose upon the leaders intolerable burdens of expectation from the led—and any shortcoming would carry with it the burden of scandal or profound disillusionment.

We tried to take account of the latter by warning of how long and difficult the effort would have to be, and that we wanted 'a world fit for sinners'; and Betty was often quite cheerfully rude. But the cult just grew and grew. It was a function of our remarkable relationship, certainly: but that in itself was merely a focus for a deep public need at home and abroad for an image of heroic leadership at a time when wars and scandals and disllusionment with politics in so many places had generated widespread apathy. For a while, we fitted the bill: and particularly in the Decade of Women, the visibility of Betty and Mairead on the landscape of Northern Ireland—itself hitherto a symbol of primitive savagery, and now for a few moments to be the venue for a renewed presentation of humankind's most ancient vision—was irresistible.

We could not simply shut up, close down, or back off: part of our very purpose was to proclaim, in prophetic rhetoric, that a different world was possible. We were saying and doing things that rightly inspired people, and we knew in advance that the universality of this vision would touch people everywhere.

Despite my discomfort with the more cultish aspects of our leadership, I felt that so long as the three of us respected the relationship in which we found ourselves, our mutual irreverence and laughter would keep us sane and balanced. In due course, we would constitute the movement democratically and provide the mechanism for elective leadership and earth the cult by the voluntary withdrawal of the 'leaders'. For a long time, my confidence seemed to be justified. But in the end, its failure, and the rupture of the 'trio' relationship, caused very great pain and damage; while the democratic structure, which should have carried the original inspiration, all but choked it to death.

The seeds of both creative and destructive possibilities were present from the first days. Indeed the 'trio' relationship almost foundered in the first week, after an incident involving an invitation to meet Secretary of State Merlyn Rees. This invitation had been relayed by a man called Jones, who was the local Civil Liaison Officer in Andersonstown, a functionary with some of the duties which might have been carried out by a Member of Parliament, had we had a normal Stormont parliament: he liaised between the local community and the Northern Ireland Office, and was recognised generally as a person who might mediate between army and community in the heavily patrolled areas.

I felt very strongly that this invitation should be refused, on the grounds that our entire initiative came from the spontaneous reaction of unattached people, and excluded nobody of any allegiance. The British government had been saying, rightly and for long enough, that the 'solution' must come from the people of Northern Ireland themselves: therefore any involvement with government would shatter its indigenous quality.

Betty was in favour of going, and said that no-one need even know about it. I argued that no particular good could come from it, that it could prove divisive, and that people were bound to hear about it. If we were asked if we had any contact with the government, at this point, we could say no: but, if the Rees invitation were accepted, we would have to say yes, for a nonviolent movement had to be totally truthful.

Betty said that Jones had assured her that Rees could keep it secret. I said that we did not want to be involved in secret meetings, and that in any case such things were almost impossible; and that I knew Rees, and felt he would not lie if he were asked directly by journalists if he had met the Peace People. Betty's information suggested that he would deny it. I insisted that Rees, for instance, asked in Parliament, would not lie to Parliament; but that even if he would, we would not. Betty felt that if one little white lie helped to save lives, she would not feel the slightest bit guilty about it. I said that if we allowed ourselves to think like that, we would have to forget the whole thing, for we would end up in no time enmeshed in a weave of diplomatic lies, and that the trust which was the most important thing we had, would be finished: I personally would have nothing further to do with it. It was a fundamental confrontation between us, although it was conducted without the slightest degree of rancour or anger. But it was almost final: I said I would discuss nothing further until it was settled.

Mairead did not contribute much to the discussion, but was clearly troubled by both the dilemma and the implications for our further progress.

The meeting with Rees was confirmed for 11.00 a.m. Monday August 23. I was due at the *Irish Press* office at 8.30 a.m. I rang Betty at about 7.45 a.m. and said I was coming over to her house. She still felt very strongly indeed that meeting Rees was the right thing to do. She said unmarked cars would arrive at 10.30 and bring them to Stormont and back, and that no-one would know. I told Betty I was very sorry indeed, that I still hoped she would change her mind. But I repeated that if she and Mairead went to Stormont, I was out. I would wish them well, but apart from any contact as a journalist, I would not be back. I went to the office, still oddly confident that the meeting with Rees would not occur.

At about 10.40 a.m., the phone rang. It was Betty. "We're not going, cocker," she said.

It transpired that Mairead had gone to nine o'clock Mass, ready to go to Stormont, but very troubled and unsure what was the right thing to do. She hoped to find her answer in prayer. The gospel at that morning Mass included the lines, "If you tell a lie before men, it shall be known before the throne of God." That was enough for Mairead, and she went round to Betty's and told her of her decision, which decided it for Betty also.

The little crisis was over, and we felt that our relationship of trust had been confirmed in this trial over 'truth'. I even allowed myself to believe that it was an essential part of the process, putting an early and explicit end to any notion of diplomatic or 'white' lying.

The irrepressible Mr. Jones came back to try again. Since he was known in Andersonstown, I did not want him running around with this project, and certainly not running back and forth to Betty Williams's house. I told him that we had been through this already and that we were clear that we were not going to have any appointments with the Secretary of State. From his 'think about it' response, and the very fact that he had come back, I could see that he was admirably persistent, and must have been a very good Civil Liaison Officer. I contacted Stormont and spoke to a senior civil servant, explained to him that we wished to have no contact with the Northern Ireland Office at this time, and could not foresee any such need: but that if we ever thought it right, we would take the initiative;

and could he please see to it that we were not plagued by invitations from Mr. Jones. I never saw Mr. Jones again.

The question of contact with the British government (in the Northern Ireland Office) arose again when a senior civil servant approached me and told me that the government had been planning a propaganda drive with the theme '7 years is enough'. The advertisements would be mounted like graffiti, scrawled writing on a brick wall background. There would be a television version in a comparable mode. The whole operation would cost about £90,000. He wanted to know if I thought this government drive would affect the Peace People, and if so, how? Although this was an informal approach, I felt that it was dangerously close to involvement, and I got the impression that if I had strenuously suggested that it might damage us, the government might have cut its losses and cancelled the campaign. However, I merely said that the government would have to make up its own mind on its own programmes, and we would continue with ours, regardless. I offered my personal opinion that they would be wasting their money.

The government's propaganda campaign duly began with suitable co-operation from the local media. It was aimed at war-weariness, and presumably hoped to ride the tide made visible by the Peace People, though it had been planned before August. But the Provos, in a rare moment of humour, widely appreciated, scrawled up, with the same kind of pseudo-graffiti care as the government-employed artists, '700 years is too much', making nonsense of the government's slogan in the target area.

Another problem struck the trio in the second week when we came under considerable pressure from the group known as 'Women Together' to call off our Shankill march, due on August 28. After unsuccessful telephone representation, the legendary Saidie Patterson, Women Together chairperson, arrived with several of her colleagues at Betty's house. Saidie might fairly have been described as Belfast's leading female activist over the previous forty-five years, following her role in the organisation of women textile workers for decent wages and conditions in the days of the tuberculosis-inducing mill conditions. Women Together had grown from the initiative of a woman called Ruth Agnew, who worked in the gasworks. It had a number of branches, doing good work, but not capturing the public imagination in any forceful way. Saidie had also been co-chairperson of a short-lived initiative called 'People Together' which had gathered a big petition for peace, which it presented to the Northern Ireland Office. Such initiatives tended to invoke the common Christianity of Protestant and Catholic, and urge a collective condemnation of men of violence: the Peace People was sharply different, in deciding to march, Protestants and Catholics together, through such as the Shankill, as if centuries of self-reinforcing bigotry had not happened. We were going to proclaim with our bodies as much as our mouths that our common humanity transcended all historical and denominational divisions, whatever the threats or risks.

Naturally, with a lifetime of tough experience behind her, Saidie felt that this could not be done. Moreover, she felt that it *should* not be done, and when her telephone persuasion came to nothing, she arrived, so to speak, with the troops.

Betty sat in her favourite fireside chair throughout the three hours of the persuasion. Mairead sat among the ladies, discussing the points backwards and forwards. I moved in and out occasionally with cups of tea, answering the phone, writing, making calls, staying on hand.

Years of union negotiating, firm insistence alternating with nostalgic reminiscences about the organising work of the Thirties, were brought to bear on Betty and Mairead by the redoubtable Saidie. At times, I could hear her telling them that they simply could NOT march, and giving reasons from experience; at others, her approach was, "I'm old enough to be your grandmother . . ."

Mairead was countering with the good that could come of the march. Betty was dangerously silent, and came into the kitchen occasionally to release some suppressed expletives. I was afraid that she might explode, and that a very counter-productive animosity would develop not only with Saidie Patterson, but with some members of Women Together who might justifiably feel peeved that these two unknown women were receiving so much publicity while their years of efort had been largely ignored.

I went in and stood by a chair, like an interested bystander: although rumour had been flying about, it was still not public knowledge that there were three of us, not two, at the heart of this enterprise.

After a while, Saidie sought to enlist my support: "Son, you know what it's like, you know what I'm saying. There could be people shot. Tell them."

"Saidie," I said, "I know that everything you're saying is perfectly valid. But sooner or later somebody has to stand up and say, we are not afraid of your guns, we will not live in terror. And that's what we're trying to do. If others don't want to come, we won't mind. If the three of us go up the Shankill and get shot, then everybody will know it can't be done. But if we get away with it, everybody will know it can be done."

Saidie argued back and forth on the point: but Mairead and I persisted with the line that until we, as unarmed people, faced down armed people, the trouble would continue. Suddenly Betty said, "Goodnight ladies!" There was an embarrassed shuffling, and one lady began saying, "Ach, Betty, there's no need . . ." but before she could finish, Betty, sitting in an attitude of dangerously imperial majesty by her fireside, said, "I don't say goodnight twice in my own home!" The embarrassed shuffle accelerated into a nervous kefuffle of straightening hats and coats, and exodus with as much dignity as Betty's disposition would allow.

Saidie started on me again in the hall, reminding me that she was old enough to be my grandmother, and asking me, since I seemed "to have a lot of influence over those two girls" to get them to call it off, or even just to have a rally in the Woodvale Park, but no march up the Shankill. She also warned heavily that there would be terrible trouble if the Irish Congress of Trade Unions turned up on the Shankill with ICTU banners, as had been suggested. I tried to reassure her that I did not think anybody would be hurt in the end, but that we could not let the fear of fear defeat us for ever. She went off, warning us to mark her words, and that we wouldn't listen.

When the door closed, Mairead turned to task Betty about being so abrupt. But Betty would have none of this: her rage which had been simmering for hours, now exploded. Waving Mairead's protests aside with a "I can say what I like in my own home," she started on me and said, more colourfully than I record, "You're talking about forming groups and democratic meetings and all that; well if this is anything to go by, count me out, I'm not sitting for three hours through that sort of stuff, Ciaran McKeown. You can put me up in front of a row of Provies with machine guns and I'll face them, but I'm not going to sit through that again for anybody or anything."

I just stood smiling at her while she raged, and then said, "Yes, Betty, you're going to sit through meetings and longer and more boring meetings than that, it'll be harder than getting a dig on the jaw or a stone on the head, but you'll do it and come up smiling because you're dedicated!" Betty just burst out laughing at me: her fierce rages, which could be frightening, could vanish in a fit of giggles just as quickly as they arose.

I said she could miss the next meeting and "take the night off" (it was 11 p.m.) while Mairead and I would go and deal with the other emerging problem, the proposal of the Irish Congress of Trade Unions Northern Committee to join the march with Union banners. Despite the hour, we could not risk this issue mushrooming the following day.

The trade union movement in Belfast had always been vulnerable to the sectarianism of our politics. Workers joined trade unions to get union cards and rates, but the UWC strike of 1974 confirmed the historical split. Rising unemployment notwithstanding, the political loyalty of Protestant workers was not to their unions, but their Ulster Unionism. Despite its docile, easily split support, the trade union movement had fought gamely over the years to improve rates and conditions. Now, with support from British and Irish unions, they were trying to get 'A Better Life For All' campaign for peace and jobs off the ground. It was making little impact, and the temptation to ride in with ours was very strong; and I wish there could have been some way for us to help. But it was vital that the general spontaneity of ours as an across-the-ground people's movement was not compromised by any sectional, denominational or confessional interests which might automatically draw forth an adversary.

We went to see Terry Carlin, the young hard-working secretary of the ICTU Northern Committee, to ask him that his members desist from displaying banners at our rally. Terry was naturally most keen that their banners should be displayed and was reluctant to bow to any pressure on the score. But he acknowledged our point that it was our march and rally, although the unions had been planning something of their own for that Saturday. He undertook to raise it with his colleagues, and we left it at that. In the event, many trade unionists turned up to march, some with their families, but without banners. I pay tribute to their magnanimity, in suppressing their own identity in our favour: they were a long established and indigenous structure in the community, whereas, for all that anyone might speculate, the Peace People might be a nine-day wonder.

I now felt so confident that the Shankill march would be an enormous success, with no-one injured, that I phoned a message to Professor Adam Curle of the Bradford University Department of Peace Studies, whom I had met earlier in the year at a community conference, to advise him to fly over, to see an historic occasion. I also prevailed on Marianne, who has retained an intense dislike of large crowds ever since the civil rights days, to come, although she was now three months pregnant.

It was another sunny day, and it was truly historic. Although it lacked the drama of other marches, and some of the subsequent glamour, it was the most significant symbolically, and its success meant that we could proceed later with other deliberately symbolic marches across territories presumed by centuries of prejudice to be impassable by one section or the other.

While marchers were assembling at the Catholic Falls Road end of Northumberland Street, which connects the Falls with the Protestant Shankill, Marianne, Adam Curle and I went on our own up to the Shankill Road end. I noted with relief and respect the presence of many trade unionists, minus banners. There were quite a few police about, looking very relaxed, and well outnumbered by the people gathering in an almost carnival atmosphere for these strange Catholics to come across.

One gentleman in a dark suit, with a bowler hat, Orange sash and white gloves came marching down the road carrying a large Bible. He was giving forth, in a loud voice, sentiments clearly designed to remind the assembling Protestants of their faith, and the unbiblical nature of the Roman church. He disappeared into a small group of men who emerged, and I later heard that local paramilitarists had locked him in a toilet of a pub while the march passed by! A paramilitary interpretation of nonviolence, I suppose . . .

As the marchers came up Northumberland Street, with Betty and Mairead visible at the front of the throng, people surged forward trying to get a look. I found myself shoulder to shoulder with a gentleman in a combat jacket whom I recognised as a member of the outlawed Ulster Volunteer Force: he recognised me simultaneously.

"Great crowd, isn't it?" I said.

"Great," he said. "I'm on the welfare side of the UVF, you know, and if they'd leave it to the women, the trouble would be cleared up in no time."

Before I could respond, the crowd heaved again, and he was gone. I turned to see the Falls contingent, which also included people from many other parts of the city who had chosen that end to begin. It was less than a hundred yards from the meeting for the joint march: and there followed another symbolic moment.

Reporters, photographers, television crews, all laden and coiled, jostled for vantage points between the Falls contingent and the Shankill people who surged forward to meet them. For perhaps a minute, people struggling to get forward and embrace their fellow citizens could not reach them because of the crush of media men: it was as if the media were keeping the people apart! I'm not among those who blame the media for all our woes—but I thought it symbolic of that aspect of our reportage which constantly reminds people of their divisions, reinforcing rather than removing the points.

Some media people in Belfast liked later to claim that the entire phenomenon of the Peace People owed its power to the media: that moment showed no-one posing for angle-shots, but thousands of people stretching forward to express the powerful emotion of the moment in heart-felt embraces.

Quickly enough, the media-men dispersed to race in search of new forward positions, and after a momentary halt while the contingents mixed, the procession started up the Shankill. The pavements were lined several deep with people who had come to watch: they found themselves stepping off to embrace the marchers and being drawn in to the great occasion. Strange apparitions like Catholic nuns in full habit were embracing and being embraced on the most Protestant of Protestant holy ground, down which, earlier in the day, the Royal Black Preceptory, an organisation of Protestant lodges like the Orange Order, had marched for their annual parade.

Marianne and Adam and I were at times anywhere from twenty to a hundred yards ahead of the march. I looked down side-streets, and saw women chatting at their doors, some in curlers ready for the Saturday night out, some obviously taking a break from their Saturday housework. From street after street, they moved up to the main road to watch the approaching march. I saw their faces, at first curious, then transformed into expressions of inspired friendliness as they leaned out to welcome, and then to join in. I watched the bemused yet respectful faces of many of Belfast's hardest men standing, pints in hand, outside pubs directly associated with loyalist paramilitary organisations, others leaning from upstairs windows. Tommy 'Tucker' Lyttle, spokesman for the Ulster Defence Association, was to the fore, and I saw a reporter peel off to ask him for a comment. I recall the slow smile on Tucker's face: later I read a report quoting him as saying, "I don't suppose it'll do much harm!"

By all that was mythologically holy, there should have been a riot, with people getting shot dead or beaten to death or worse. Yet here was one of the happiest sunlit expressions imaginable, of humanity in the mass.

I went on to the top of the Shankill, to try to get to the Woodvale Park in advance of the march and make sure everything was in order, with no last-minute hitches that the march might suddenly meet. I met Saidie Patterson, waiting to welcome the marchers. In her seventies, and with hip trouble, Saidie had been unable to march: but having accepted the inevitable, had rallied round and was now ready to play her part.

The marchers poured into the park and settled themselves in front of a natural mound on which the loudspeaker equipment had been mounted. Saidie took the microphone and made a speech of welcome and then broke into 'Abide with me'. Then Mairead spoke, followed by Betty, who had found the hymn-singing a little doleful, and called on everyone to join with her in 'When Irish eyes are smiling'. This burlesque touch put the crowd in the best of humour to disperse in linking groups, and was added to future rally programmes.

We could now look forward to the symbolic double-march in

Derry/Londonderry the following Saturday, when Catholics from one side and Protestants from the other side of the River Foyle would meet on Craigavon Bridge.

Into Orbit

The Shankill march had been an unqualified success in its essential purpose, but there was an actual fall in numbers. The accepted figure, in the region of 27,000, included people who had been swept into the march, but who had not set out deliberately to demonstrate for 'peace'. Those who had made a prior decision must have been considerably fewer than any of the reported figures: so some initiative was required to ensure the four-month momentum of mobilisation I had in mind, and which would require much more organisation than we had so far developed.

I had asked some volunteers to look for office space for us, but nothing had transpired, and there were signs that while business might vaguely wish us well, prospective landlords were dubious, fearing that we might become high-profile targets. Eventually, I went to see the Rev. Ray Davey, founder and guiding spirit of the Corrymeela Reconciliation Centre, at its headquarters in 8 Upper Crescent, Belfast. Ray himself opened the door: "Ray," I said, with my hands open and extended, "we have no room!" I explained that all we needed was one room with enough space for a couple of desks, telephone, and so on.

"The only thing I have is a room at the top," Ray said. "It might be too small for you, come up and take a look."

It was a relatively small, L-shaped room. "We're renovating the whole house, as soon as we can get the go-ahead." The house had been a university property. "But you can have it in the meantime, if it is any use to you," Ray said.

I accepted it gratefully. A call to the Post Office accelerated the process of installing the phones, we moved in with a desk and a chair given by Ray Davey, and that little room was seen in the following nine months by thousands in the flesh, and by millions on television. So many TV crews visited in the coming days that a permanent beam for lights was erected near the ceiling.

Corrymeela, in Belfast and in the residential centre at Ballycastle in North Antrim, have hosted many initiatives, but usually for an evening, a weekend, or perhaps a week: they hosted the Peace People organisation for nearly nine months, and they must have read the gospel line to 'forgive seventy times seven' every day in order to have sustained patience with the turmoil of that experience. Their ground floor enquiries and administration office was constantly disrupted by people seeking the top floor circus; and not everybody associated with the Peace People had learned how to close doors behind them, or the words 'please' and 'thank you'. The Peace People phenomenon, moreover, happened like a comet, and as it tails away, the Corrymeela initiative goes on quietly, its facilities at Ballycastle a kind of haven for internal refugees and an ideal setting for many reconciliation-orientated conferences. While the Peace People had a more dramatic impact, with, I hope, some longer-lasting effects, Corrymeela is the more enduring initiative, and the concrete evidence of Ray Davey's vision will be seen for generations to come in both Ballycastle and Belfast. Perhaps some such understanding gave Matthilde Stevens and her colleagues the patience whose example I will not forget.

We moved in the day after the Derry rally on Craigavon Bridge. It was the same kind of big, emotional success as the Shankill, and the organisation of bus-groups, which reminded some of the King campaign, helped compensate for what might have been a momentum-sapping drop in numbers. A new Derry peace group was formed, including some of the women who had reacted in 1972 to the killing of Ranger William Best, and new volunteers, including some former supporters of Ian Paisley, Loyalist stalwarts of the 1974 UWC strike.

It was time, with groups forming and an office established, to declare more specifically our longer-term purpose. I typed out a rally programme which would take us close to Christmas, as well as all over Northern Ireland, to key cities in England, Scotland and Wales, and finally Southern Ireland. The immediate reaction of Betty and Mairead was laughter and cries that the programme was impossible. But there was no disagreement: 'It's impossible, therefore we will try it!' was the attitude.

We announced it right away, so that people could look forward to an entire programme and avoid dispersing into random initiatives; and with London, and the Boyne at the end, and the Falls rally in the middle, there were high points to encourage people to keep up the momentum on the less 'glamorous' marches. This was the programme:

September 11: Antrim (town about 20 miles north of Belfast): Betty and Mairead present

September 18: Newry (border town about 40 miles south of Belfast): Mairead
Liverpool: Betty

September 25: Dungannon: (mixed town in the middle of Northern Ireland): Betty
Glasgow: Mairead

October 2:	Ballymena (nearly 30 miles north of Belfast, heart of Ian Paisley's constituency): Mairead
	Birmingham: Betty
October 9:	Downpatrick, south of Belfast: Betty (I also spoke at this rally)
	Leeds: Mairead
October 16:	Enniskillen (far west of Northern Ireland): Mairead (Betty also came after re-arrangement of that week's British rallies, and all three of us spoke)
October 23:	Falls, Belfast: all
	Cardiff: Ralph Williams (representing Betty)
October 24:	Newcastle-upon-Tyne: Mairead
October 30:	Craigavon (new town south-west of Belfast): Mairead
	Manchester: Betty
November 6:	Omagh: Betty
	Edinburgh: Mairead
November 13:	East Belfast (Victoria Park): Mairead
	Bristol: Betty
November 20-21:	Peace Weekend—events to be organised everywhere, and opportunities created for people to sign the Declaration, join or form groups.
November 27:	London (Hyde Park to Trafalgar Square): all
December 5:	Boyne, Drogheda: riverside rally near site of symbolic Irish battle, commemorated annually by Protestants for victory over Catholic King of England, by William of Orange, 25 miles north of Dublin: all

This programme gave people all over Northern Ireland, and in the rest of the British Isles, an immediate sense of the comprehensive nature of this peace initiative. We were deluged with calls from people in all the places specified, for information on those organising the rallies in those places. To their surprise, some of those phoning in found that *they* were the organisers, if they were willing and able: for the whole programme hinged on the gamble that people would respond as they did.

The sense that there was going to be intense rally activity culminating in two major, symbolic rallies, one in London and one on the banks of the River Boyne, galvanised the efforts anew, brought a new wave of recruits to office work, and another wave of media attention, now probing more deeply into our purpose.

I had already had to draft a couple of press statements to clarify distortions, and by now accepted that my role could not be hidden. The local BBC had started a ten-day production schedule for a thirty-minute documentary, during which they proposed to be constantly in the company of Betty and Mairead. It became obvious immediately to the producer that I was taking many of the decisions. I said to him that I would appreciate it if he could keep me out of camera shots, and that I would endeavour to avoid crossing them as his team was working. I became uneasy that this amounted to a deception, and that the 'two ordinary women' line was becoming a lie. Marianne, while she was reluctant to see me committing myself for the two-year period I proposed, felt that if I was going to be so far committed, there should be no deception about it. I had rationalised that since media reporting was *de facto* distortion, then allowing our message to ride piggy-back on a media myth was fair enough. Marianne also felt that I was much more effective behind the scenes and that, inevitably, if it became known that I was directing operations to the extent that I was, then people would divide, some strongly for, others virulently against me. These considerations were batted back and forth between Marianne, Betty, Mairead and myself, with Betty and Mairead increasingly insisting that I should not be 'hiding'.

The BBC documentary effectively decided the issue. Its producer, Robin Harris, was a man whose integrity I respected, and I had no wish to exploit my friendship with him to compromise the truth of what he was doing. After a few days, I went back to him and said, "Robin, forget my request: if I happen in the course of things to become visible, so be it, it's entirely up to yourself, I don't want you to feel remotely obliged."

Robin replied, "I'm glad you raised it first, Ciaran, because I was asked that very question this morning by the BBC programme board, 'What are you going to do about McKeown?'"

By the end of September, my news editor gave me a straight choice—strongly advising me to hold onto my career, and that I was very likely to be shot—of staying in the peace movement and resigning, or keeping my job. I resigned.

This decision gave rise to the idea that I had either a messianic complex or a death-wish, and is worth a little observation. It would naturally seem that for a married man expecting his fifth child, with a family entitled to a life-style expectation indicated by a total income then approaching £10,000, that my action was either grossly irresponsible, or that I was about to use my wits to make even more money; or that I was indeed suffering from messianism or a death-wish. The truth is much simpler: while I had no idea where my future income might come from, I had every confidence that I would survive, and that my confidence would be shared by my bank manager; and that even if I slipped deeply into debt, I could recover on the same level of journalistic salary, with a frugal life-style. But the deciding factor in my judgement was that there was no-one else with the training, experience, willingness or opportunity to do what I was attempting to do, and that therefore I had no real choice but to do it. And I also believed that whatever deprivation this decision might cause my family, it would be compensated for by the example of being true to oneself.

I should add that the confidence with which I risked family security took quite a beating in the following years. The bank manager did indeed share my own attitude, and allowed my overdraft to grow merrily. But the commitment dragged into four years rather than two, with correspondingly deeper debts and loss of earnings; I then discovered that I was unemployable in 'mainstream journalism', having made my views so widely known, and displayed an independence of mind that would not encourage any prospective employer to see me, to use Reaganspeak, as a 'team player'. I found that very hard to accept for quite a while, but am now reconciled to the price one pays for independence. Moreover, loss of career is not the disaster that even those concerned about me imagine; and I have found the humiliations of penury and signing on the dole an irreplaceable experience. My family have never been without food, shelter and relative comfort, and are therefore better off than most of the human race. We have also learned about true friendship.

If the *Irish Press* had not given me a straight choice, I would have resigned shortly thereafter, in any case, for the work-load was becoming intolerable. I was also at that time the honorary editor of *Fortnight*, the Northern Irish independent review magazine; and was prepared to launch a fortnightly newspaper for the Peace People. I wrote *The Price of Peace* in late August, in snatched moments. And in general, had to be on hand for all sorts of decisions.

Work began each morning between 7.00 and 8.00, and went on all day, with occasional, irregular meals. It was usually at about midnight that I would deal with such mail as I might have selected from the piles that arrived each day—ranging from messages of goodwill, or occasionally of hate, to serious offers of help, and sometimes useful advice.

Many of those who thronged the office each day were simply attracted to be there and unable to tear themselves away: but were not always of any particular use as worker-volunteers. But one morning a woman walked in and offered to help, and became a great asset: Ann Campbell, softly spoken, English, married to an Ulsterman, and mother of three children, had the vital gift of gentle discretion, patiently putting up with endless phone calls, noting those messages that really needed urgent reply, carefully trying to ensure that appointments for Betty, Mairead or myself did not overlap.

In the early weeks, this was an immense problem, with different people making appointments, often leaving us double-booked or triple-booked. This gave rise to the opinion that we were hopelessly disorganised, and I would certainly concede that there was a lot of inefficiency. On the other hand, as one sitting in the eye of a storm of demand, I had to ensure that nothing interfered with the efficiency of what I had to do myself, even if it meant being unable to attend to what others regarded as vital.

Naturally, that disposition aroused the charge of aloofness, arrogance and 'not listening'. Ann Campbell absorbed a lot of the pressure from many, near and far, who were insisting that the presence of one, two, or three of us was absolutely vital in such and such a place at this or that time. Appointments with new peace group leaders, schedules for visiting new groups, making speeches on week-nights, and endless media demands not only had to be dealt with, but Ann also had to pacify those kept waiting: here, I must confess that we were not punctual.

Betty was the best at punctuality, on time if at all possible, and having the sense not to overload herself with duties. I was invariably running at least twenty minutes behind, and sometimes much, much longer: this is a failing which I have still not fully overcome. Mairead was fairly hopeless in this regard, trying to make time for everybody and being dreadfully late for almost everybody, sometimes giving hours to people with no appointments, and holding back those who had made them.

But even if we had been as conscientiously punctual as our rhetoric on the consideration of others should have demanded, the pressure to have a bit of our time could never have been met. People landed in on us, from parts of Northern Ireland, or as far away as America or even Australia, and expected our early, if not immediate attention: if we stopped to talk to them, we were inefficient for others; if we insisted on going on to other appointments, we had become aloof, or arrogant or bureaucratic.

Throughout this hectic period, we retained an irrepressible sense of humour, sometimes mimicking the less justified complainants. Visitors remarked on how cheerful we were, usually in an agreeably complimentary tone; but some felt that we should not be so full of fun when our business was so serious; then again, there were complaints from some if either Betty or Mairead were seen publicly in tears!

On the financial side, where we would have to be more correct in our arrangements than any group in Ireland, we had the invaluable help of Patricia Knox, the wife of a local Methodist minister (John Knox, later Peace Education Officer of the Irish Council of Churches). Pat had knocked on Betty Williams's door in the first week, and offered to help, and became treasurer. The honesty, integrity and openness of our accounts throughout could not have been bettered, a statement I can make without fear of contradiction, and by reference to the audited accounts. Yet no organisation that I know of was subjected to so much abusive gossip about money as the Peace People, including even public statements by people who should have known better.

In September 1976 we already had Ann Campbell and Pat Knox doing two vital functions. And in the evening, as well as for much of every day, people like Margaret Watson, Maureen Joyce, Tom and Brenda Conaty and many others, manned telephones and replied, in standard form, to as many goodwill letters as possible. By the end of each day and first thing every morning, there were piles of letters ready for signature. Later difficulties with several of the initial volunteers can never erase the value of the great teamwork of those months. Those involved in that unsung work may fairly feel that they saved lives.

The Price of Peace which I published in mid-September was like an expansion on the Declaration. I had decided never to get into the position of writing scripts, which would have compromised the immediacy of style of Betty and Mairead; but I felt that this document would give them, and members generally, a grasp of the situation and a range of nonviolent perspectives from which they could make their own judgements and utterances.

Not only was it useful to them, but the booklet had an amazing little history of its own. It was taken back to Kristiansand in South Norway by a young Norwegian who gave it to Gunnar Borrevik, then foreign editor of *Faedrelandsvennen* and later founder/director of the Norwegian Journalism Institute. Gunnar and his news editor colleague Oddvar Munksgaard read it, and in consultation with the paper's editor took a decision which would transform the future of the Peace People. Gunnar, a strong supporter of NATO, especially in its role of protecting Norway's most northern border with the Soviet Union, is no pacifist. But like Oddvar, he is a deeply compassionate man and took the trouble to consider carefully what we were attempting, rather than dismissing the initiative as a short-lived burst of emotionalism. He concluded from *The Price of Peace* that we knew what we were talking about, and that nonviolence was *tactically* right for Northern Ireland. So *Faedrelandsvennen* decided to launch the 'People's Peace

Prize', a populist alternative to the Nobel award, with the aim of raising the same amount as the Nobel Prize. The award would be made in Oslo in late November, with due ceremony.

The booklet also prompted Kevin Done of the *Financial Times* in London to write a serious article about the function of the Peace People, and Jonathan Power commented favourably in the *International Herald Tribune*; and it provided the 'peg' for a PBS New York television programme on the movement. This level of coverage altered the perception of the Peace People internally and externally: somewhat incredulously, serious journalists now had to ask, is this phenomenon more than a passing source of heart-warming interest? Hardly: but if there was even a glimmer of such a possibility, it would be a story that might give hope to the whole world.

This deepening external response was very encouraging, and since outsiders had nothing to lose, their expression of support for us was almost uniformly positive. But domestically, the Northern Irish, accustomed to failure, were rightly wary of investing too much hope, and looked increasingly askance at the international attention being paid to the Peace People.

Marianne's prediction on my 'divisiveness' began coming true: some who read *The Price of Peace* became totally dedicated to its purpose; others asked who did Ciaran McKeown think he was, 'telling us what to do'? One clergyman publicly repudiated nonviolence as "alien to our Western way of life", while another invoked the now firmly Trotskyite image of 'People's Democracy' when referring to the community politics aspect of our initiative, at one of our own meetings.

Nevertheless, the booklet gave at least some of our members much-needed guidance and stimulus, and a sense that the Peace People were intellectually defensible. I was sufficiently encouraged to circulate it to some bookshops: one mounted a window display, then quickly removed it and put the books under the counter after a visit from local IRA members.

It also gave British pacifists considerable comfort. They had been troubled by the presence of British troops in the Northern Ireland conflict; and my argument that the removal of troops without an advance constitutional solution would actually be a constitutional act as much as a military one, helped them to perceive the simple-minded 'Troops Out' slogan as potentially violent. Professor Adam Curle described the thinking behind the Peace People as the clearest and most correct that he had encountered in thirty years of both studying and mediating in some of the world's seamiest conflicts. But some British pacifists, as well as a few domestic ones, continued to regard my 'pacifism' as corrupt, since I would not support 'Troops Out'. I told such as Pat Arrowsmith that the task of British pacifists was, so to speak, to get British troops out of Britain. Not having our experience, they did not have the same appreciation of the living connection between demilitarisation and the development of constitutional consensus.

In Norway, as the People's Peace Prize was taking off, a translation was made of *The Price of Peace*, and published along with brief resumés of the historical background and the current conflict. Norwegian television's foremost current affairs presenter, Franz Saksvik, came to Belfast, and conducted a half-hour interview with Betty and Mairead. I saw the programme later in Norway, and felt that it was probably the best they ever did: the authenticity of the original impulse was still vibrating through the programme, and was fleshed out with more substantial answers to gently probing questions. After the programme was broadcast, the contributions to the People's Peace Prize, already £15,000 and now backed by some twenty of Norway's papers, shot past the Nobel £80,000 target in early November and reached £201,000 by the end of the month when we arrived to receive it.

All of these developments confirmed the conviction that people everywhere were feeling a great need for something more than a vision of 'the growth economy' with its intrinsic arms race, and widening rich-poor gap. The response evoked by the Peace People was not merely a warm-hearted hope that the bewildering Northern Irish might break out of the straitjackets of their own murderous history: what came back to us time and again, through public, private and media contact, was a sense of gratitude that we were calling for a new way of expressing our humanity politically. We had somehow touched the deepest chords in the human soul. For instance, I will never forget a Norwegian who told me in tears: "When I read the Declaration of the Peace People, I said to myself, this is exactly what I believe for myself, for the Norwegians, for the Irish, for all peoples."

While the effect of the mushrooming initiative was not always so straightforward at home, it was certainly having a stunning effect on public morale and on the rate of violence. It is impossible to quantify any claim for the effect the Peace People were having, and no such claim was made by us. What I would simply note is that talk of the 'final crunch' disappeared; storing of supplies in anticipation of trouble following the collapse of the Stormont Convention ceased; the descent into violence of an ever more sectarian kind halted and reversed; the rate of killing and the motivation for killing eased noticeably; community support for violence dropped sharply; confidence of investors increased; there was a marked improvement in the life and quality of life prospects for the people of Northern Ireland in those early months, and for quite a long time afterwards. Indeed, apart from the damage done at the time—and for future prospects—by the H-Block hunger strike period, the retreat from savagery has continued ever since: 1983, for instance, had the lowest death toll since 1970.

Any judgement of how this came about would have to take into account some intangible, but *real* factors. The underlying feelings of the basically decent and sensible people of Northern Ireland were bound, in unquantifiable measure, to be against the slide towards ever more sectarian violence. War weariness, and a sense of futility over the endless violence was a latent, inert factor, awaiting expression. The courage observable in many daily lives was there to be expressed, but hitherto had no effective way of finding voice. Also, for all the abuse that the Northern Irish get about being divided over 'religion', the fact is still a fact that many are *actually* religious in the real sense of believing in and praying to God and had prayed privately and in various groups for 'peace'. That spiritual disposition also needed a unique non-denominational outlet for expression.

The factors therefore, which could give real force to such a phenomenon as the Peace People were there already. Our job was to help create the opportunities for such factors to come into play—and to stay visibly, audibly in force long enough for their reality to be appreciated as more than a sudden gush of grief at too great a single atrocity.

We were no more, but equally no less, than instruments in leading a collective expression which was waiting to be made. We understood this quite consciously and, once committed to the responsibility, we were aware that if we did not live up to this duty, we would not merely have destroyed one particular opportunity, but effectively have prevented a further opportunity from occurring with any prospect of success. The commitment, therefore, had to be total, while trying to avoid the tones of fanaticism and the manners of zealotism. In undertaking this personal commitment, we were taking upon ourselves the identity of a presumed majority of the people of Northern Ireland, that they also were ready and willing to find some other way of living together.

We therefore took the view that for such people, and for this effort, everything had to be done with courage, vision, intelligence, style and genuine love. We had to give this initiative a name, a face and a quality of expression, in as extended an opportunity as we possibly could; and in such a way that it would create a structure which could work indefinitely for the generations that it might take to have a thoroughly reconciled and nonviolent community, true to what we were presuming to be the deepest aspirations of all people.

By projecting the rallies forward in time, and outwards throughout the British Isles, the purpose was to accelerate the process *at home in the first instance*. People would realise that every Saturday was a peace rally day somewhere for four months, and that this would be followed by a more enduring and detailed campaign worthy of the initial success. The plan also provided the opportunity for other people in the British Isles to express their feeling; and for us to express to them a heart-felt wish for neighbourliness.

I cannot over-emphasise the critical psychological significance of this. When people are demoralised and begin to believe their own media and cultural myths about themselves, they begin to behave accordingly; if they have the opportunity to present themselves as much more truly human than the image would suggest, and then find that people elsewhere and everywhere respond instinctively to that, the effect is powerful. If the opportunity can be sustained, it can have a lasting effect. By thus creating the opportunity for the people of Northern Ireland to look outwards instead of glaring suspiciously at each other from fortified trenches of heart, mind, soul and physical territory, and for their neighbours to respond with affection and support, we made such effects possible.

The point was surely proven to many. The deep *political* significance of this, in a conflict as psycho-political as is Northern Ireland's, is not easily appreciated by political commentators conditioned daily into regarding the party-political apparatus—its labels, slogans and symbiotic violence—as the totality of politics. We will never learn to live with, or heal, the misshapen, handicapped Northern Irish 'body politic' until we attend to the deeper realities of the Northern Irish 'psyche politic'.

We could not have had even the temporary success that we enjoyed if the right disposition had not *already* been there, awaiting expression. Betty, Mairead and I were often called 'opportunists': in the sense in which I have outlined this conscious strategy, I accept the charge as a compliment. My only regret is that we were not sufficiently successful opportunists.

The emergence of the Norwegian People's Peace Prize sharpened another question: how to deal with the flood of invitations to visit both European countries and North America, and later, Australia, New Zealand and South Africa. At first I resisted these, agreeing only a trip to Germany by Betty as a direct response to the visit to Northern Ireland by Erica Voges, a leader of WOMAN (*Welt Organisation*

Mutters Allen Nationen: World Organisation of Mothers of All Nations), set up by Germans after the Second World War.

But I argued against accepting others until we were satisfied that the operation within Northern Ireland and in the British Isles was running smoothly. We had to ensure that we did not 'balloon' early and burst by Christmas. If we started 'running around the world' too early, people would naturally say our 'heads were turned', and that the work was on the streets of Belfast and Northern Ireland; if we left it too late, we would miss a tide that would not return, and neglect a significant aspect of our entire strategy. We were the only people who could decide, the only people being invited, and the only mechanism for making decisions. The timing, before the easy media visibility of the rallies would fade, was crucial, and difficult to judge.

By the first week in October, the organisation was coping with rally preparations and pressures almost routinely; the first edition of the newspaper, *Peace by Peace*, was almost ready; and the Norwegians were showing that we would have sufficient resources to establish a permanent organisation in the Spring. I felt that we had about two years in which to create a network of friends before the energy of the initial impulse ran out—this was like an intuitive fuel-gauge calculation.

I was to be proven quite wrong in one aspect of this anticipation, in that I expected not only the violence to drop, but that its media visibility would also fade, and that the longer, slower, media-opaque process towards a deeply, creatively peaceful society would have begun irreversibly by the passage of about two years. This prediction depended on the prison issue's being handled with at least the same ingenuity that had characterised the ending of internment by Merlyn Rees and Frank Cooper. I made the prison issue a key theme in the first editorial of *Peace by Peace*: since we would have no direct contact with government, I imagined that they would not miss this 'signal'; much later, I discovered it had not even been read—even though the Peace People were the dominant political reality at the time.

What I certainly did *not* expect, in spite of my considerable experience of governments, was to hear Roy Mason, who had succeeded Merlyn Rees as Secretary of State, regularly repeating the aggressive line, 'there will be no amnesty for these criminal terrorists'. I knew, as a lobby correspondent, that it had long been accepted wisdom that the prison situation would be very 'favourably reviewed' when there had been a 'genuine and sustained cessation of violence'. However appropriate the government's 'not-an-inch' attitude might have appeared at other times—indeed, however appropriate for a government *never* to deviate from rule of law by using internment, torture *or* amnesty—a period of unprecedented public expression in favour of reconciliation, with communal support for paramilitarism dropping like a stone, was not the time for an exhibition of third-rate Churchillianism. In my opinion, that is what we got in the years of Roy Mason's Secretaryship of State.

Then, as now, I isolated the prison issue, with its roots in the 'Temporary' Emergency Provisions Act (a 1973 Westminster promulgation with fifty years' antecedence in the Stormont Special Powers Act) as the only vehicle which might carry the motivation and opportunity for continuing violence into another generation. I believed that our efforts could provide the cover and incentive for the Northern Ireland Office to begin dismantling the apparatus of emergency, especially those provisions which alienated young people in all the heavily patrolled areas. If the 'Temporary' emergency powers could not be dismantled at the moment of greatest opportunity, then they would become permanent, and a community which had lived with a period of passionate violence, would have to learn to live with endemic violence made logical by laws that bore little resemblance to 'the rule of law' and 'due process'. I would have thought that plainly obvious to any student of the conflict.

Even as Roy Mason talked of restoration of the rule of law as being the best way forward, his ground policy of 'rooting out the terrorists' conveyed the more tangible impression that he was more knuckle-headed than any military brass-hat. His opposite number, Conservative Shadow Secretary of State, Airey Neave, who was otherwise a most thoughtful and courteous man, was forever demanding the use of the British army's 'specialist services', the SAS, for covert operations, a potentially sinister approach in what remained ostensibly a situation of civil unrest, with the police still publicly accountable. Both Neave and Mason seemed impatient to 'clean up' the Northern Ireland mess, rather than solve the Northern Irish problem, and it was deeply disappointing eventually to hear Airey Neave express satisfaction after a briefing from the Northern Ireland Office on the undisclosed security measures authorised by Roy Mason and involving the SAS.

Of course, they may have had a more cynical assessment of the nature of the Peace People phenomenon than I had, and decided to cash in, since the Peace People were bound to fade. They would have been encouraged in that view by the attitude of quite a few 'Peace People' who were merely anti-Provo, or anti-terrorist-on-all-sides, but firmly pro-status quo—by which they understood pre-1968. While such 'peace at any price' people were, I know, a minority, their 'Backward, Christian soldiers' attitude was occasionally vocal. I was a little shocked at their opposition to my proposal at an early meeting that we should raise funds for a holiday hostel for house-bound relatives of maimed people, since such relatives were neglected victims of the terror. The idea that republican, loyalist, service and uninvolved relatives might have a lot in common in such a grim situation, did not transcend a feeling of self-righteous vengeance among some. One woman asked, as if pointedly, how we might feel if somebody belonging to the Maguires had to share facilities with those belonging to the people who had "killed those three wee children"? I asked how many in the crowded room could remember the names of the Maguire children? A very small number of hands went up, and a half-angry, half-sheepish atmosphere hung for a moment: then Pat Morrow, of the Ballynafeigh Peace Group, settled the matter with a decisive observation on what Jesus of Nazareth would have done, recalling his attitude to so-called outcasts of his society. A majority present thundered their agreement in applause. But it had been a warning light that great waves of crowd emotion would not translate easily into Christian forgiveness in this allegedly Christian society; and perhaps the government accepted this as an unchangeable reality.

As for the Churches themselves, my initial impression was that most churchmen were delighted, and many were happy to march with the people, without seeking any kind of special platform notice. There was visible unity as all marched together (in most cases) whereas platform performances might have emphasised differences, as well as embarrassing those of no persuasion that they might be swallowed up in some kind of evangelistic hysteria.

But church support, while genuine, was surprisingly superficial. Years afterwards, the understanding of churchmen of what we were trying to do remained media deep. Even enlightened churchmen like the Rev. Eric Gallagher and Dr. Stanley Worrall, in their book on the Christians of Ulster, relied largely on media reports in their section on the Peace People. While they drew attention to the Declaration and allowed that I appeared to have a coherent philosophy, they certainly did not ask me for any explanation of what we were about, and for quotation, relied on a derisible media report, using an out-of-context quotation about the Nobel Prize. My insistence that the 'community politics' of which we spoke so much, could be understood by direct reference to the early Christian communities, seemed to pass them by.

My repetition of the line that Christianity was explicitly nonviolent until the Constantine conversion produced the 'just war' aberration, either passed most by, or caused outrage. One otherwise friendly clergyman was extremely angry with my assertion on television that I could not imagine Jesus of Nazareth looking down the sights of a rifle to kill anyone for any reason whatsoever, and that if I was right, "how could anyone be a 'Christian' and a soldier'?" He came to see me, which I appreciated, to denounce me as intolerably aggressive towards many sincere Christians.

The 'Christians', Catholic and Protestant alike, seemed enthusiastically to support the superficial aspects of the Peace People phenomenon. But I would be dishonest if I did not concede that that clergyman did indeed represent a majority who see themselves as followers of Jesus, and can imagine Jesus shooting people in a 'righteous' cause. Some Christians who justify 'killing in certain circumstances', allow that Jesus himself would not do so: but that he was divine, while we are human. I find this profoundly self-deceptive and dangerous, especially in a society so confessedly 'Christian' as Ireland's. It means in effect that our humanity is defined as murderous and otherwise corrupt: we kill *because* we are *human*—Jesus wouldn't because he was divine.

Since I know that individuals can only embrace personal nonviolence through a deep intuition of its truth, the superficiality of the ecclesiastical response did not impinge on me too depressingly in 1976. I imagined the Churches would grasp the opportunity to move more rapidly towards the nonviolence that is becoming orthodoxy for many Christians elsewhere, stimulated by the threat of nuclear war to rediscover their theological roots. In the interim, there have been some stirrings in that direction. But the violence of power politics is so deeply and insidiously interwoven into the Christian tradition since the Fourth Century, and almost nakedly so in Irish politics, that it is difficult to anticipate anything other than generations of struggle within the orthodoxies themselves before the theological licence to murder in certain circumstances is exorcised.

Ironically, the greatest block to this will most likely come in Southern Ireland whose theocratic constitution inhibits an all-Ireland democratic consensus. Were there a commitment to Christian nonviolence, then the Irish army would become an unconstitutional institution! Impossible though that may seem, that day will have to come if there is ever to be an end to Irish ambivalence on the issue of 'violence'. Until that day, 'violence' will be 'political' and morally tolerable for every group of Irish Christians, Protestant or Catholic, which has 'God on our side'.

Every military or paramilitary group, in Ireland as elsewhere, *has* to have 'God on its side': otherwise, the human psyche could not live with the overwhelming guilt of militarism. The late Cardinal Conway said that the Northern Ireland conflict had "nothing to do with religion". While superficially correct, that statement is actually an indictment of 'religion' in Ireland. So long as 'just war' theory provides the 'holy war' justification and mentality, the healing value of the Christian understanding of redemption will not be available to nurture political peace. I may digress to observe that since Christianity, and the other Semitic religious traditions, are the dominant underlying influences, however submerged or contorted, in the Euro-American militaristic culture which so threatens the earth, there is no hope of 'peace', or 'justice', or even mere disarmament, until the orthodoxies face up to the 'just' or 'holy' war lie to which they attribute divine authority.

Although I was surprised at the vehemence with which some attacked our espousal of nonviolence, I would have been disappointed if it had not produced a great deal of questioning: for the very essence of our initiative was to encourage people to be less sheep-like and more truly conscientious in shouldering their individual and communal responsibilities. But, by and large, in our early declarations of purpose, we were benignly dismissed as naive idealists, who might be forgiven such aberrations as nonviolence, in favour of the excellent promotional job we were otherwise doing. It would be much later, as it became clearer that nonviolence was the be-all and end-all of our commitment, that benign patronisation would give way more generally to irate opposition.

Our direction set, our organisation adequate, and authority at its height, we were ready in early October to move outwards. We had already given our good wishes for the establishment of a sister organisation in the South of Ireland, the 'Southern Movement for Peace'. The indefatigable Dr. Brendan O'Regan, of Shannon Development and Bórd Fáilte fame, had put his considerable organisational ability into this, setting up groups all over the South, anywhere that peace demonstrations had been organised, and liaising with county councils. Later, when it became obvious that our concerns would also be 'political', he established 'Co-operation North', a 'non-political', economic co-operation effort which has continued to be a productive 'grandchild' of the Peace People impulse. In all the fuss and excitement over the peace movement in the North, it tended to be ignored that even more people demonstrated for peace in Southern Ireland than in the North: for example, while we had 27,000 on the Shankill, a Dublin demonstration drew an estimated 50,000 on the same day. It has been calculated, even allowing for those who might have attended several or all of the demonstrations, North and South, that one in ten of Ireland's entire population marched for peace in the autumn of 1976. That is the most conservative estimate: the figure has been put as high as 750,000—almost twice as many. The Southern expression, even if it did not get the media coverage it warranted, gave frustrated Southerners an opportunity to express their feeling, and to demonstrate that Southern Ireland was not simply one big bolt-hole for IRA operators in the North.

On Tuesday October 12 Betty, Mairead and I flew together to the United States, on separate missions: Betty and Mairead to take part in an hour-long TV programme called *Woman*; and myself to take part in the *McNeill-Lehrer Report*, similar to the BBC's *Panorama*. Both programmes were on the PBS network.

It was in a carefree spirit that I fastened my seat belt on the plane, and, apart from the TV programme, prepared to regard the next seventy-two hours as a holiday from telephones, typewriter, meetings, interviews and appointments. We thoroughly enjoyed our trip out, being received most warmly at Shannon Airport by Brendan O'Regan, and his peace movement colleagues, Billy Keane and Kate O'Callaghan, and treated like celebrities on the Aer Lingus flight. A rather different version of the same thing awaited us at the New York end, where we were hustled apart into security rooms. Then Betty and Mairead were bundled into one car to be taken to Buffalo, New York, with armed security very much in evidence. They were accompanied by the Rev. Dave Bowman, an American-based Irish Jesuit, who was anxious to brief them, and to get them to announce the account fund number of 'Reconciliation Ireland', the fund sponsored by the American National Council of Churches, should there be the opportunity to raise funds.

Disappointed media people, who wanted to avail themselves of the PBS-paid visit, to interview Betty and Mairead, had to make do with me—those, that is, who realised that the bearded guy looking in astonishment at the car disappearing with Betty and Mairead had anything to do with the operation.

Betty and Mairead had originally been scheduled to do their programme in New York, and we had looked forward to the opportunity to get together alone and review our progress at this remove; but death threats had been taken seriously and they were removed to Buffalo, where I tried in vain to contact them from New York. The following day, as I was discussing the set-up of the *McNeill-Lehrer* programme with the New York studio, we tried several times to contact Betty and Mairead. I eventually told the people in Buffalo that I would consider acquiring injunctions and filing charges of kidnapping if necessary if I was not allowed to speak to them, and a few moments later, Betty and Mairead were magically available: they had been given none of the messages left, and were surprised that they had been kept incommunicado without their knowledge.

This high-security management of us became a familiar feature of overseas visits, and our personal repudiation of armed protection made little difference. Apart from this security making nonsense to people whose very prominence was due to facing armed threat unarmed, there was the vital necessity, in New York, of getting together, to have the same 'tone and pitch' like a musical trio, if not the same line: each of us had different emphases, different ways of expressing the same impulse.

The programmes were successful enough. But while we were busy in the United States on our first overseas trip together, the British army was becoming involved in controversy back in Belfast: rubber bullets had been fired by troops at close range at a crowd of youngsters in the Turf Lodge area of West Belfast. One boy, Brian Stewart, had his skull fractured by a rubber bullet, and was critically ill. All I could get in New York were the usual contradictory reports, the army claiming minimum force, the residents claiming the army running amok. There was nothing we could do until we got home to make a first-hand investigation: regardless of our growing prestige, it was vital that what we were doing was not used as cover for military excesses. This consideration was all the more acute since our Falls march and rally was due the following week, when a repeat of the Shankill experience on the Catholic Falls could have immense effect.

I was exhausted on the trip home. Like someone who has been on his feet all day and does not realise how tired he is until he sits down, I felt the tiredness of the previous two months sweep over me. But there was no time to be exhausted: in addition to work which would be waiting for us, we needed to consider in much more detail how to respond to questions on the security forces, 'informing', likely political or constitutional prospects, and so on. Our basic position of promoting the creation of a horizontal consensus, and discouraging efforts to solve the problem from the top down, was sound enough, but needed fleshing out. We reviewed the abrasive way in which we had been separated and manipulated, and Betty in particular was most anxious that I should adopt a more vigorous front-line profile. I remained convinced that they were far more acceptable, and were doing a first-rate job, whereas I would arouse too much suspicion and hostility. People who were not actually trying to muscle in and take over were quite happy for me to be directing the operation: but they might take a different view if I moved ahead of Betty and Mairead in the public articulation of policy. Betty said she was tired of seeing me being treated like an extra, and added bluntly: "You're the leader of this thing, cocker: get out there and lead!"

A press conference awaited us in Belfast. The media were only interested in their own stock questions on stopping the flow of arms and cash to the IRA: our actual method of doing that, beyond hand-wringing, bleeding-heart appeals, of offering Irish America a genuinely contemporary nonviolent example with which to identify, and of evoking the nineteenth century example of Ireland's undersung nonviolent organiser Michael Davitt in historical connection, did not fit deadline or category needs, and was duly ignored.

At one point, a TV man, summing up the media's lack of interest in anything substantial in our replies, said politely, "Ciaran, do you mind moving out while we get a shot of the girls?" (I was sitting in the middle.) "No he will not move out!" Betty said defiantly. "Leave it, Betty," I said, "we'll talk about it later, I couldn't be bothered right now," and moved out. We were starting to pay the price for the initial deception, and I did not wish to arouse undue resentment among the press.

For the first time also, we found that people had such a glamorous notion of overseas travel that they could not imagine that we had been to the States and back in seventy-two hours: the impression among some was that we had been away for weeks. The 'tripper' charge was off and running, faster than us.

On the second day after our return, we went up to Turf Lodge to investigate the riot that had resulted in Brian Stewart's skull being fractured by the firing of a rubber bullet. A meeting had been called for 2.30 pm in the Turf Lodge Community Centre, and we decided to go up well before that to consult with local leaders, and then to attend the meeting. All three of us went, along with Ralph Williams, recently home from sea, and Margaret Watson, a local teacher's wife who had, in the first week, come to criticise and stayed to organise.

With that dramatic timing of so many events in Northern Ireland, the news came through that Brian Stewart had died in hospital. Feeling in Turf Lodge was feverish. Under pressure from responsible local leaders, the British army (which, lest awkward parliamentary questions be asked, had to record a number of patrols to prove that this was not a 'no-go' area) had kept out of the area during daylight for several days, running its 'political patrols' quickly through the area at night, when kids were asleep.

We visited the local curate, Fr. Paddy McWilliams, to get a detached account of what had happened. We had been spotted, and two leading Provisional Sinn Fein people came to the priest's house to advise that we should not show our faces at the meeting. I was determined that we were there to get at the truth, and that if the truth was that troops were responsible for Brian Stewart's death, we would say so, however much trouble it caused us. The Provos clearly did not want us anywhere near the protest meeting: they were genuinely afraid we might be lynched, for their propaganda had depicted us as British agents; and they did not want us disturbing their self-image as local defenders and representatives. We decided to attend the meeting, despite the opposition.

We went into the already-packed Nissen hut community centre, to one of the most charged atmospheres I have ever experienced. We walked up the centre aisle and stood to one side of the platform—there was no room anywhere else. The chairman called the meeting to order: it was so packed that people were literally edging up the walls, and the only form of amplification was a transhailer, a battery-powered bull-horn. This latter feature, more than anything else, convinced me immediately that we were in for mayhem: for the only way to be heard over a crowd with a transhailer is by shouting, and the effect, as I had seen years earlier in a civil rights situation, is to increase hysteria, rather than to command order.

This is exactly what happened. The more the chairman shouted for order, the more some incensed women near the front shouted back at him. He was trying to insist that it be a democratic meeting, where everyone would be heard; they were shouting that we should be thrown out, that we were 'army-lovers'. The hysteria increased. The spot at which we were standing adjoined a back entrance. The diminutive Fr. McWilliams had appeared there, and was standing beside Ralph Williams and Betty. Some men beside Ralph were trying to provoke him by making abusive remarks about Betty, and Ralph soon took Betty out the back way and over to the chapel.

Meanwhile, three men had arranged themselves in front of me, and the middle one was shouting in my face, phrases like "Turncoat, McKeown, you should know better, traitor", his mouth barking out the insults at nose-biting range: once or twice, I think he just about resisted the temptation to bite my nose off or butt me in the face. The two on either side of him took up the abuse any time he paused for breath: they obviously wished me to respond, so that they might have an excuse or signal to attack me physically. In this constrained position, I noticed Mairead moving forward, appealing to the chairman to be allowed to address the meeting, through the transhailer, to explain our presence and purpose. Mairead, who had spent years doing things for people in Turf Lodge, could not begin to appreciate that instead of being loved, she was now the object of greater hate, firmly identified with the alien world outside the ghetto.

She began pleading with the women in the front row, who were screaming at her. Over the top of this din, the chairman continued howling for order through his counter-productive bull-horn. Without wishing to insult my current interlocutors, I suggested quietly to Fr. McWilliams that the meeting be adjourned for a few minutes while we withdrew, and that we should get Mairead out. The same idea seemed to occur to members of the platform party, and somehow over the next few minutes, Mairead was edged away from the platform and we slowly withdrew by the back entrance while the mayhem milled on. People then poured out of the side entrances as we moved towards the chapel. Fr. McWilliams put his arm around Mairead to protect her from a few tentative attacks, and I put my arms around both of them as we proceeded. The following group of women became more emphatic in their abuse as we reached about half-way to the chapel, as if they sensed that the quarry was about to escape. Their pulling and kicking at me was merely to get at Mairead, who was much more the target of their anger. I saw some men coming towards us, led by the man who had been questioning my parentage minutes earlier. He was carrying a hurley stick, and I braced myself for a heave to the chapel door, which seemed to be receding instead of getting nearer. As if by a collective instinct, the women launched themselves at us. Hands flashed past and under me to grasp Mairead's hair and skirt. Their faces, almost beside us, were oblivious of both myself and Fr. McWilliams.

I looked up again and saw the hurley stick coming down—but not on our heads: the man shouted, "Quick, get them in here, the women are going to kill them."

He brought the stick down to act as a bar to push the women back, and then cleared the way towards the chapel. Once we were inside, the hubbub subsided, and the crowd retreated to the back of the chapel and started to stone the rear door, and the roof of the sacristy. We settled down to wait for a quiet moment before going home: but it transpired that our cars had been wrecked, the crowd had laid siege, and were waiting for us to emerge to stone us.

I felt oddly relaxed in the peace and quiet of the chapel, where some elderly residents started to come in for the afternoon 'Holy Hour' service at 4.00 p.m. Mairead's face was a picture of puzzled and aggrieved anguish. Betty was completely cool: she could understand what Mairead could not accept. Fr. McWilliams would be taking the service, and he began to put on his vestments.

The Provo Sinn Fein leaders who had earlier tried to dissuade us from coming in, were now trying to figure out how to get us out of the area in one piece. They posted volunteers in the chapel and sacristy

to 'protect' us. I found this amusing, with the memory of the New York
police so fresh: it's amazing what a threat unarmed people can be! I
began talking to these volunteers, going back over the origins of the
Troubles, right through internment, up to where we were, recounting
things they were obviously too young to have known about.
Eventually, when I said to one who appeared genuinely interested,
"Do you not agree?", he said, "I'm not too sure what you're talking
about, but you certainly have the courage of your convictions." A
teenager in such a situation clearly has to identify with what is seen
as courageous—right or wrong: come to think of it, few enough grow
out of that.

We had suggested speaking to representatives from the protest
meeting, to explain our purpose in coming up: unfortunately, along
with the three or four people allowed in, was Brian Stewart's teenage
sister, who was in a deeply disturbed state of grief, and who almost
seemed to see Mairead, who began talking to her as one who also knew
bereavement, as if she had murdered Brian herself.

I wandered out into the chapel proper, and down to the front doors
to see what was happening. There was no-one about down there, and
I came back up to suggest that we might simply walk out the front
door. It was then I learned that the cars had been wrecked, and that
we really were going to need help to get out quietly. There was
something hilariously 'Irish' about the situation, which kept me in a
wry humour throughout: stuck in a chapel sacristy, with rocks hitting
the roof and the door, local citizens outside waiting to lynch us for
our supposed 'army-lover' attitude, Provos inside protecting us,
Provos outside trying to organise a 'Black taxi escape plan' for us,
other residents in for the Holy Hour, as if all was well with God in
His Heaven in this best of all possible worlds. I observed to Fr.
McWilliams that there was nothing to stop the crowd coming through
the chapel to get us, and why didn't they just do that, since they had
no respect for his cloth, the back door or the roof? "They're too
superstitious," was the brief reply of this hard-working curate.

Eventually the local Provo Sinn Fein men returned with their
strategy, and their leader said: "Now, when we open that back door,
run towards the black taxi, and when you get in, lie down."

"I walked in here, and I'm walking out," I said. He looked at me,
as if trying to satisfy himself that I was all right in the head, then turned
and said, "C'mon, there's no time to waste", with which he ran
towards the taxi. Betty and Mairead followed. I stopped at the door,
turned to thank Fr. McWilliams, then turned cheerfully towards the
taxi. There was another taxi in front of the one we were to take,
whether as a decoy or for a more forceful purpose, I do not know.

The crowd was now standing, several with bricks and stones at the ready, puzzled at the manoeuvre. I walked briskly to the taxi. This was not any kind of crazy bravado or carefully worked out nonviolent tactic: every instinct and experience I had with regard to crowds commanded me to behave 'normally'. Not a stone was thrown. As soon as I got into the taxi, the driver shouted, "Keep your heads down." We kept them up. The taxi suddenly accelerated away— exactly the signal the crowd needed and down came the barrage of stones and bottles.

But we got away in one piece and were brought over to Betty's house, where the Sinn Fein men, in some embarrassment, allowed themselves to be persuaded to have tea. We also had a longish and reasonable chat. They had perhaps good reason to have been afraid for themselves and for us, and we were grateful for their courage and concern for us.

When they had gone, we discussed the new situation. It was clear, from the calmer sources of information, that British troops were indeed responsible for Brian Stewart's death, and that we should say so. It was also clear that we had a major communication problem with republican West Belfast. The fact that Mairead, a long-time lay church worker in the area, had been the prime target to the women, with myself a close second to the men as a 'turncoat', suggested that the people of Turf Lodge were in a deeply demoralised state, in which anybody from outside the area was an 'enemy'. There had also been cracks about 'glamour girls' from several of the women.

I had detected one persistent line in the shouts: anger about their menfolk in jail, and how dare we call them 'criminals' and 'scum'? This was both a reference to the Northern Ireland Office's 'criminalisation' policy for those convicted under the emergency laws for crimes committed after the previous March; and to Betty's remark about 'scum' in the first week.

"Some day, and soon, Betty, you're going to have to apologise for calling them scum," I said to Betty. I had suggested this before, and Betty had said "Never!" For her to call anyone 'scum' was authentically Betty Williams, but it could not stand as she increasingly became a symbol of nonviolence. It was not, as has been strongly claimed later, that I was trying to 'change' Betty: she was as capable of generous warmth as of fierce anger, and I did not feel that apologising required a 'personality change'. She did apologise, publicly and fulsomely, about a month later.

Marianne had prepared dinner for all of us, and I rang to advise her that we were all in one piece, in case she had heard anything on the radio about the mini-siege. She had not, and was therefore more annoyed that dinner might be ruined. We decided to forget everything for the rest of the evening, have a good dinner, relax and get a night's sleep before tackling what looked like a busy week leading up to the Falls rally.

By mid-evening, we were all in pretty jovial form in my home, joking about the star treatment in New York versus the star treatment in Turf Lodge, comparing protection from the Provos in New York with protection by the Provos at home. But the prospect of even a few hours' respite was interrupted by media phone-calls. Sinn Fein had issued a statement about how we had been 'chased out of Turf Lodge by local women . . .'

We did not want to react. But we could not allow 'no comment' to stand against that statement, since we wanted to criticise the army's responsibility for the death of Brian Stewart, without its appearing that we had been intimidated into such a posture. Briefly dismissing the 'chased' line, we explained that we had gone to Turf Lodge to investigate the trouble leading to Brian Stewart's death, and that we were convinced that the army was responsible. We argued that these useless, politically dictated patrols, which acted as 'Aunt Sallies' for kids, should be cut out altogether; and that our entire policy was one of demilitarisation of the conflict.

Some early reports came out as 'Betty and Mairead were attacked in Turf Lodge' . . . while 'later, Ciaran McKeown attacked army policy'. The fact that Mairead and I had been attacked and that all three were criticising the army did not quite fit the mythological labels ordained for us—Marianne's prediction was being steadily fulfilled.

When the media arrived in inevitable droves the next day, I stayed mostly out of it, despite the previous week's discussion of re-adjusting our front-line profile. The Peace People image, near and far, and especially of Betty and Mairead themselves, was radically altered on the teatime local and network bulletins, when they answered questions about 'security' matters in a firm manner, acknowledging the difficult situation in which the army and police were placed, but pointing to the importance of their obeying the law, and avoiding over-reaction. They voiced the need to begin the whole process of demilitarising the heavily patrolled areas. The 'two ordinary women' were suddenly 'controversial'.

This caused some consternation among the Peace People. It also caused commotion in the BBC: I have never heard the full details of what transpired that day, but plans to transmit the full fifty-minute *Panorama* report on us were hurriedly reviewed and the commentary hastily re-written. The fifty minutes were cut to twenty-five, and a fair slice of that now taken up with that day's news interviews. The prepared material showed Betty and Mairead in the full sunlit glow of the earlier rallies, while I, neatly labelled as a former civil rights activist, surfaced gradually like a Machiavelli figure in the background; the last part, showing Betty and Mairead on the demilitarisation line, seemed to suggest to some that their innocence had been corrupted.

The reaction of most of our serious volunteers to the *Panorama* programme was interesting in itself, for we had all regarded *Panorama* as the BBC's most serious current affairs programme: they were uniformly disgusted at the output. Some were also a little disappointed in that they had given interviews, in line with our hope that it might become obvious that more than three people were involved: but these interviews were not used. Marianne hardened in her view that a minute given to the media was a minute wasted, or worse.

But we were not about to let one television programme, whose prestige we had hoped might be seriously helpful, to put us down: we nicknamed it *Panarumour* and used that description to anyone ringing in to complain or enquire about aspects of the programme, and got on with our work.

The programme produced one unexpected row. At about midnight, I received a call to the office from Paddy Devlin, then still Chief Whip of the SDLP.

"Right, young fella, when are we having talks?" Paddy asked. He always called me 'young fella', and I couldn't understand the aggression in his tone.

"Talks? What are you talking about, Paddy?" I asked.

"C'mon , young fella, I watched *Panorama*, you've gone political, and we're a political party and I want to know when you're having talks with us?" Paddy was shouting already, and had put his request more colourfully than I have recorded.

"Ach, Paddy, you know we can't be having talks with political parties, certainly not in the current situation, we can't be getting involved with any one section or party," I explained.

Paddy exploded at the other end, repeating his request with even more punctuation than before. Had it been anybody else, I would have told him to call back in the morning, and put the phone down. But I knew Paddy well, and knew to ignore the bluster. So I suggested to him that he and I might have an informal chat as old friends, but no party talks.

"Right, when?" Paddy replied, as if to nail me down.

I had walked away from one desk to answer the phone Paddy was on, and I started to say to him, "Hold on a second, Paddy, till I get my diary."

"—you and your —diary, I never reached for a —diary anytime you asked me for an interview," Paddy was expostulating at the other end.

If Paddy could not begin to appreciate the time pressures apart from all the others, there was not much point in trying to have an 'informal chat': so I said to him, "Look, Paddy, I don't need that kind of abuse right now, you can call me back when you've calmed down". He was still erupting at the other end when I replaced the receiver. Maybe I should have erred on the side of long-suffering patience, but I felt he was beginning to bully as much as bluster. He did not ring back. Later he suggested to journalist friends of mine that I was an agent of British policy, and stated publicly that the entire Peace People phenomenon was a 'con-trick'; later still, he came as near apologising as a politician can, and I would still look forward to co-operating with him in something, someday. In spite of this hiccough in our relationship, I still feel close to him politically, and never at any time lost affection for him. As a senior civil servant once put it, "Paddy's heart's in all the right places!"

The word 'political' now began to cause real problems. Already there had been representation from some women in East Belfast, whose basic position was that they were 'following the lead given by Betty and Mairead' but wanting to know who gave authority to Mr. C. McKeown. This theme was taken up more and more, some people genuinely worried that a 'political' person would wreck the Peace People, others more visibly using that line to manoeuvre themselves into positions of prominence. The most awkward version of the unease was probably also the most authentic: it was expressed by a man from North Belfast at a representative meeting of groups: :"Why can't we stick to the simple message of our Declaration and not Ciaran McKeown's complicated policies?"

The fact that the Declaration implied a potentially massive cultural shift in various forms of support for violence, demanding action as well as rhetoric, seemed at times like a sneaky trick: as if people had been conned into repeating something and accepting it, without reading the fine print.

There began to be debate on the phrase 'all the techniques of violence' in the Declaration: some wanted it made 'clearer', to mean terrorist violence only, or 'all violence, but with support for the security forces', or 'forces of law and order'. I flatly refused to define the phrase, on the grounds that people were coming to the movement from widely different backgrounds and traditions, and that there must be no orthodoxy, no narrow sectarian pacifism. People must individually take the trouble to think about what 'violence' meant, in their own conscience.

I hoped that this approach would cause a gradual shift towards conscious nonviolence, all the more enduring because it arose from deep conscientious consideration. Moreover, I did not want our members divided 'for' or 'against' any armed group, legal or illegal, but to see us all, in the first place, as historically predisposed to attitudes which were part of our communal and cultural violence. It is not surprising that the label-prone media found this 'woolly': when I suggested that it would be more accurate to describe the approach as 'Socratic', they asked me what I meant.

This approach was rooted in the conviction that people finally accept nonviolence through an intuition of its truth rather than by any clever intellectual analysis. It dictated the policy of asking people to inform on the whereabouts of weapons and explosives, but to avoid informing on persons or adding to the numbers in jail. The nonviolent society which we foresaw would be one in which the prisons were progressively cleared, and in which the motivation to violence was inhibited instead of expressed; and where the community concern of many people, otherwise drawn to violence, would find creative outlet in what we called 'community politics'.

The more we were quizzed on 'politics', the more we tried to explain not only the 'neighbourhood politics' concepts, but the need for the 'communitarian approach' to be a significant element of any *constitutional* solution. By this theory, no local community could be pushed around by central government, but would always have a veto with which to defend Swiss-style 'cantonal rights'; and equally, local communities would be encouraged in a much less explicitly violent society, to co-operate enthusiastically with neighbouring communities on decisions of mutual interest, such as universal services like roads, telecommunications, industrial development, social services, marketing. In direct contrast to the original British decision to emasculate 'local government' as a source of abuse of power, we were proposing a substantial increase in the sheer number of local governments, and that they should have a measure of outright autonomy: by having enough, numerically, no substantial number of people could be made hostage to a sectarian majority on either side. The central agency of government could then emerge only as an agency of service enjoying the free and full consent of local governments.

This approach was never seriously considered by government or academia, beyond a superficial dismissal by one or two academics using the loaded word 'soviet'. In fairness to them, it received almost no local media coverage.

This neglect of a serious proposal, which aroused interest abroad as an advance on contemporary forms of parliamentary democracy at a time of anxiety over democracy's future, did not worry me in the short term. It was not until I listened to silly radio arguments years later trying to decide whether the Peace People had failed because they were 'too political' or 'not political enough' that I realised that we should have pushed our ideas much more energetically at established policy-makers and opinion-shapers: far from understanding them better after a few years, they still had not heard them, it seemed.

Our more immediate concern was with the low-level application of these ideas in the wake of 'hot war', when neighbours were afraid to talk to each other, or sat dumbly in their living rooms while young bucks strutted in the paramilitarism of the IRA, UDA, UVF, INLA, Red Hand Commando, or one of the more minor outfits, dominating various neighbourhoods, and giving whole areas the 'stronghold' character of their particular violent expression. Our purpose was to encourage such neighbours to take an active interest in the quality of life of their own streets and districts, to feel that they had friends in other communities busy in the same genuine patriotism, and that together they would defeat the deepest law of repression, 'whatever you say, say nothing'.

For many, this was exciting, even if some remained uneasy about the very word 'political'. Ironically, it caused some resentment among 'established' community organisations. As a community volunteer myself, with many friends on that network, I tried to persuade them that the new 'converts' needed their help and advice, and in some cases, the people newly activated were both welcomed and welcome. But some of the 'new' Peace People were a bit of a pain in the neck to the 'veterans', for they seemed to carry with them an evangelical 'we are the Peace People' triumphalism.

All these tensions, problems and propositions boiled away throughout the early months of debate and activity. It was like a surfing exercise to keep our board sweeping onwards while the waves broke here and there. A degree of arrogance, otherwise incompatible with either democracy or good manners, was inevitable. Even to announce a four-month rally programme without consulting anybody implied this. Often, when people asked such questions as 'why are we going to all these places?' or 'why no rallies after Christmas?' or 'why go to Britain?' or 'why go South?', all we could reply at times was 'it's necessary', or 'we can explain afterwards, there isn't time now'.

We did, however, take a very great deal of time to explain ourselves: in spite of all the other pressures, there was scarcely a night when one, two or three of us was not out at some meeting somewhere in Northern Ireland. This intensive work, like a long, drawn-out election campaign, was not media-visible, nor particularly visible to our own members in general: if a group only saw one of us in a month, it would feel neglected—yet there were over a hundred groups in the process of forming at that stage. Some of those demanding most attention were quickest to fade away; others demanding little attention are still going.

When we began going overseas, in one, two or three-day trips, rarely longer, the joke went around, 'The Peace People visit Northern Ireland', or 'Peace People: today, the World; tomorrow, Northern Ireland'. Usually we found this popular abuse amusing: it had its own dynamic, its own way of communicating that a Northern Irish group could have that kind of global appeal, its own way of making the Peace People part of the fabric of Northern Ireland's daily conversation. It was different from moaning about the Troubles, and that 'this place'll never change'. If we did nothing more than give people a harmless target for abuse, it would be something! When office staff got weary of these complaints, I would invoke Micheál Mac Liammóir's famous remark about the gossip which Oscar Wilde enjoyed about himself: "Not to have been widely talked about would have seemed to Oscar the most ostentatious form of obscurity!"

Such levity did not always relieve the difficulty caused to our volunteers on the ground. I remember one man saying to me, "It's all very well for you spending weeks in Paris explaining what we're about, but that gets us a bad name here!" I had to point out that I had done a full day's work from 7.00 a.m., flown to Paris in late afternoon, taken part in a three-hour TV special on Northern Ireland, and flown back the following morning to do another full day's work—so that the Paris visit in question was squeezed into two full days' work—at home! But people domestically could not adjust easily to thinking of places as being hours away, rather than the distances associated with long holidays.

We never successfully overcame the 'tripper' charge, although I think we would ultimately have been forgiven this apparent aberration if everything else had been handled properly. Certainly, enough serious members appreciated the value of this overseas work, and also the wear and tear on us, of such activity, which gave us little time for relaxation or reflection at home or abroad.

This overseas dimension was designed to confirm in a positive mode the distinct, though not separatist, 'Northern Irish identity' born of our shared experience over two generations. I endeavoured to reinforce this distinctive sense by reiterating an old dictum of

European law, that 'two generations of a custom make that custom law': and that therefore, no matter how passionately anyone might feel about the circumstances in which Ireland was partitioned, or the unstable consequences of that decision, the sheer fact of Northern Ireland's existence for over two generations had created a distinct experience and identity by the actual passage of time. A sign that we were succeeding in this came, not as might be expected from a republican attack, but in a front page local Sunday paper story containing a decidedly odd charge from one of Ian Paisley's leading supporters in the 1974 UWC strike. Mr. Jim Smyth accused the Peace People of 'trying to brainwash the people of Northern Ireland into a Northern Irish identity'. The story claimed that 'thousands of loyalist women' had succumbed to this brainwashing. This was good to hear, even if the word 'brainwashing' was an echo of the 'communist' charge. The word brainwashing surfaced quite a lot: rather than argue against it, I took to saying that there were a lot of dirty brains about in need of a scrub—which did nothing to reduce the charge of arrogance.

It may surprise some who remember the early months of the Peace People as a period of remarkable public solidarity, that the day-to-day reality for us was relentless work, often with a considerable swamp of resentment and hostility around us. After one meeting, at which the questioning and ear-bashing had been particularly inconsiderate, Mairead turned to me with an almost hopeless look in her eyes, and said, "What do they want, Ciaran, blood?" This was a meeting of supporters, incidentally.

Just as some quickly forgot the very names of the Maguire children, so they readily forgot that Mairead, while coping with the immense recent pressures, was also grieving over the loss of her sister's children with whom she had been close from their births. To relieve the public pressures on her family, she had also moved out of her parents' home to live on her own for the first time in her life, sharing accommodation first with one girl-friend, then with another.

At one stage, Betty had said to me that she thought Mairead might crack under the strain, and I too wondered if her great energy was a function of grief. But, as she told me herself when I once mooted the idea of taking it a little easier, she was very tough, and that so long as she got time for prayer, she would be alright. She is indeed one of the toughest people I have ever met. It would be some time before her steely strength would surprise those who regarded her merely as a very sweet little Irish girl.

But she found it hard to accept the constant quibbling and questioning, which she was at pains to answer, whereas Betty simply derided it. Mairead's disposition and mine were similar in insisting on trying to trust people even when we were dubious about motivations, whereas Betty's instincts tended to be quick and decisive—and often correct—about whom she trusted and whom she would never trust.

Mairead seemed to take reactions as a matter of personal hurt: she had a belief in the power of her own love, which was admirable. But sometimes, as for instance in the Turf Lodge situation, a judgement could be made in the interests of love, that is, consideration for the aroused feeling of the local people, which would dictate a withdrawal until a more amicable meeting could take place. Another such incident occurred when we protested in February 1978 over the booby-trap murder by the Provisionals of a UDR man, William Gordon, and his ten-year-old daughter, Lesley. About a dozen of us held a silent, placarded protest outside Provisional Sinn Fein headquarters on the Falls Road. As the situation threatened to become counter-productively violent, I said to the Sinn Fein people that we had made our point, and that they had made theirs, and that we would withdraw quietly before anyone got carried away or got hurt. I began to lead the group away, cautioning everyone in our group not to look back or trade arguments with those shouting abuse. We were almost successfully away, when Mairead turned to try to persuade a group of hostile young women following us, of our reasons for the protest: it was the unwitting signal for an attack, in which one of our number, Edwin Graham, was severely kicked while defending Mairead, and spent the night in hospital under observation for a very nasty injury close to his eye.

In other situations, the power of one's love might well dictate staying to endure whatever may be inflicted, such as in confrontation with all-out official repression. But in the complicated matrix of violent forces and passions in Northern Ireland, decent people who otherwise feel *themselves* to be the aggrieved parties, might actually be confirmed in a deeper commitment to violence if drawn into violent expression by a nonviolent protest. I believe there is a fine line to be judged between a necessary demonstration of unprotected courage in protest over injustice, and allowing such demonstration so to inflame the subjects of the protest to the point where they are confirmed in violence or prejudice. In Northern Ireland, this judgement is far more difficult than, say, in situations of actually black and white clarity, as in racism, or situations of visible imperialism and tangible slavery.

Moreover, to meet the complexities of the Northern Ireland conflict, we were concentrating on nonviolent community development, rather than traditional nonviolent protest, associated with confrontation and civil disobedience.

The people who flocked to the Peace People were largely people who had never marched about anything in their lives. These were not students, or hippies or nostalgic flower people, or trade unionists or radicals or 'politicals', even though they came otherwise from every conceivable background. I would have liked to have seen rather more trained talents than we attracted, but this category obviously elected to wait and see, lest it turned out to be the mere emotionalism at first suggested. Some such did come along later; others told me much later still—too late—that they had not realised what we were attempting to do, or they would have joined; still others told me that they 'always knew it wouldn't work' and were surprised at a chap of my intelligence ever thinking that it could . . .

There was also a disproportionately large number of hurt women in our ranks, people scarred by Northern Ireland's male-dominated ethos, which had itself been accentuated by the militarism of recent years, and expressed in increased wife and baby battering, drunkenness and broken families. Many such women sought self-respect and comfort among the Peace People: and while we had to strike a balance between the forward momentum and tending to the needs of the walking wounded, we had a rule that no hurt person be turned away. For many women in this society, the ability to put on hat and coat on a Saturday, every Saturday, and announce that they were 'going to the Peace', was the height of liberation. A number of chronically unhappy marriages were resolved during this period of 'liberation', either healed, or finally and cleanly separated. If not a 'women's movement', it was more that than most peace movements, though not in the sense understood, perhaps, by radical chic feminists.

The 'women's movement' aspect often put me in an odd position, to say nothing of wild gossip. It had its amusing facets: few men have had the experience of reading long articles about themselves giving the impression throughout that one is a woman: to read of Mrs. Ciaran McKeown, the 'third' peace woman, the 'organiser' woman in the background of Betty and Mairead, appealed to the wry streak in me. It was interesting to experience the vicarious feminist thrill of an American feminist journalist who wrote such an article, she being particularly thrilled about my philosophical writing—as a woman. The other side of that coin was the merciless vindictiveness of at least one Irish feminist journalist, for whom the truth was no barrier in her war against males of the species. And another journalist simply would not believe Marianne that I had written the Declaration—it could only have been written by a woman, he insisted, it had that gentle touch!

All these matters were the reverse side of the public tapestry, the endless stitching, unthreading and rethreading while we maintained the main show, the programme of weekly rallies, with Betty and Mairead alternating Saturdays at home or somewhere in England, Scotland or Wales, but all of us present for such rallies as the Falls, which was the only occasion of serious rioting in the entire programme; and even that was minor by Belfast's riot standards.

It was held on October 23, the week following both the Turf Lodge incidents and the '*Panarumour*' programme, both of which had raised the 'political' profile markedly. And that week was not without another revealing 'political' conflict.

A former Unionist MP at Stormont, Peter McLachlan (who, in the short-lived 1973-4 Assembly as a Faulkner backbencher, was given to asking endless parliamentary questions, contrary to the Unionist backbench tradition of being lobby-fodder), came into Corrymeela House to warn me of a death threat emanating from the Ulster Defence Association. He seemed to take the threat very seriously, and was apparently close to the sources from which it had come. I did not take a serious view of it, for I did not sense any overwhelming hostility from such sources at that time, and I was not unfamiliar with the UDA myself. I assured him that we had already decided long since that neither assassination nor the threat of it would deflect us in the slightest; that we would behave as if such dangers did not exist; and that, in any case, assassination was much more likely after the rallies, when our public visibility would have dipped, and even then from some disturbed individual rather than an organised source.

Incidentally, we had given serious consideration to assassination, not in the usual sense of how to avoid it, for that is impossible (and in any case, no adult can be fully alive and mature without accepting his or her own mortality), but on how we should react. We wanted to inhibit two things: any stall in the forward momentum over such an event, and the self-indulgence in grief that the death culture enjoys over such events, and which breeds mere vengefulness. Since one's death is a matter of real grief and loss only to those with a real flesh and blood closeness, it should be mourned privately only by them: as for the rest, the appropriate advice was that of Joseph Addison in his meditation in Westminster Abbey, 'what folly it is to mourn those we must so quickly follow'. There were to be no martyr's funerals, and I certainly made up my mind that I would not attend any such event. We would proceed almost as if it had not happened, just as we would live as if the threat of it did not exist.

Rather than debate the matter with Peter McLachlan, I recalled his association with the work of Corrymeela, and with community housing projects; and the fact that he and his wife Jill had fostered young offenders in their own home—an action one did not tend to associate with even the most enlightened of Unionists. I gave him a copy of *The Price of Peace*, asked him to read it and to tell me what he thought of it; and if in that light, he might be interested in helping us. I felt that someone like him, with considerable experience of business, politics and community affairs, might well be needed in the immediate future, and more so when my two years' commitment was up.

He rang me the following day to say that *The Price of Peace* was the nearest thing he had ever read to what he believed himself, and that he would be happy to help in whatever way he could. I asked him simply to drop in whenever he could.

A couple of nights later, I came into the office to find the makings of a full-scale revolt. Margaret Watson told me that the Falls Road members would have nothing to do with a Unionist because of Faulkner's internment policy five years earlier. This view appeared to be shared. I argued that nothing anybody did, said, or was before they joined us had any significance, that we were a reconciliation movement and that no-one was to be excluded.

Later, when the pressure on time was making it impossible to fulfil all the speaking invitations, I suggested that the load be shared with such as Pat Knox, Pat Morrow and Peter McLachlan. Almost immediately there a public row. 'New fears for peace movement', 'Row over appointment of politician' were the headlines. It seemed that the Catholics were opposed to Peter over internment, while Protestant Shankill Road members resented having, as they saw it, a 'middle-class Unionist foisted on them' as a spokesman. Peter was shocked and came in offering to put out a statement saying that he had no association with the movement, if that would be helpful. I told him that we would not put out any such statement, since that was not the situation, and advised him to sit tight, get on with the work, and that people would accept him for his work; and that the papers would quickly pass to new sensations.

The media found their new sensations, and Peter McLachlan became so popular around the groups that Margaret Watson was among those encouraging him within months to organise a change of leadership while Betty, Mairead and I were out of the country on separate speaking engagements. Peter backed off that ploy at the time: but it was one of the delightful features of the early Peace People that those immediately disposed to distrust each other on tribal grounds, wondered within days how they could ever have had such feelings about their new friends. People came in as 'Protestants' or 'Catholics' and quickly became 'Peace People', almost scratching themselves to understand how they could have thought *like that* 'before'.

These transformations were, in many cases, genuine and lasting; in others, they were a function of the sustained heightening of consciousness of the rally phase, and were severely tested when the lower-key group discussion of issues began in earnest. Many did not survive the test.

Every week, we found that all the little frictions, which are part and parcel of any large endeavour, dissolved when a rally was imminent, and for the day or two of afterglow. The Falls rally, for all its unpleasantness, had this capacity for creating solidarity, to a marked degree. Everyone knew that it was now the most likely to be dangerous. Apart from the widespread view, shared and promoted by the Provos themselves, that we were nothing more than an anti-Provo reaction, the Falls Road had suffered more from the Troubles, and from what had preceded and precipitated the Troubles, than any other part of Belfast: there, more than anywhere, people could say with passion, 'Justice first, then peace'; and there is no doubt that many 'Peace People' would have put those phrases in the reverse order.

It was quite a relief to wake up to pouring rain on the morning of October 23. Feeling for the march was high enough to guarantee a good turnout, regardless of the weather; and the decision of Sinn Fein to have a march before ours, made it a day not to be missed by any serious member. But the rain would dampen trouble, and provide many with the reasonable excuse for carrying the protection of an umbrella!

A more uncomfortable worry for me that day was whether the Bishop of Down and Connor, Dr. William Philbin, might turn up, and what my meeting with him might be like. Unlike other church leaders who had marched among the other marchers regardless of ecclesiastical rank, Dr. Philbin had not attended previous rallies, and his secretary had rung the previous day to announce that His Lordship would be "at the platform". Mairead, who handled the call, asked if he would be marching, as we knew the Church of Ireland (Anglican) Bishop, Dr. Arthur Butler, would be. According to his secretary, Dr. Philbin had a previous engagement, but would certainly be "at the platform".

We were a little annoyed by this, for we had already come under some pressure from Tom Conaty, a prominent local Catholic businessman/politician to have Canon Pádraig Murphy, the local parish priest on the platform. Canon Murphy (the same who had the previous year declared me 'persona non grata in any Catholic institution' over my writing on the schools issue) and the Vicar-General, Monsignor Patrick Mullally, were generally regarded as two very tough, arch-conservative priests who ran the diocese very much their own way under the Bishop, who was an academic, a poet, and an outsider to the diocese.

As well as my previous differences with the Bishop and the Canon, I had also fallen foul of the Monsignor the previous year, for not taking his side in a dispute with the so-called 'rebel priest of Ballymurphy', Fr. Desmond Wilson: I had not taken Fr. Wilson's side either, but in my following phone-call to Mons. Mullally, he cut the interview short with, "It's easy to see whose side you are on, Mr. McKeown, good-day."

I did not want any 'conflict baggage' from my past to influence any possible meeting at a peace rally, and I was well disposed to civilised greeting, should the occasion arise. But I was equally certain that I did not want our platform hijacked, for the first time, by robed churchmen, of any denomination. Since some leading Catholics had been saying with triumphalist vanity that 'the peace movement was started by three Catholics', I was particularly wary, on that day, of ecclesiastical manipulation.

The Shankill contingent, and people from various parts of the city and further, met the Falls and other groups at the Northumberland Street corner from which the August 28 march on the Shankill had started. We met under the shadow of an old mill, burned to a ruin during that 1969 August week which had led to the sending in of British troops. With the Shankill and Falls well mixed in the front rows, we set off. This time, I was there in the front line, rather than walking around and ahead, as at the Shankill; and two Shankill women linked my arms.

We had hardly gone twenty yards when a rock whizzed past my head and landed in front of me: it had been so accurate that it passed cleanly between myself and Florence McCormick on my left—if either of us had turned our heads, we would have been struck. I looked around and could see no sign of any stone-throwers, and concluded that it was a one-off effort by someone particularly angry about the 'turncoat' McKeown.

Moments later, something very hard struck me behind the ear, and I staggered. People around closed in to protect me a little more, and again, when I looked to see where the attack had come from, could see no-one: the derelict houses and fencing from which direction it had come, and which would have made perfect sniper cover for a serious attack, looked deserted.

We marched on in the rain, and the expression of those lining the pavements here and there was markedly different from the Shankill experience. There was a frightened look on the faces of those who wished us well, and warned us to look out, they'd heard there was going to be 'trouble'. There was no mass pouring off the pavements to join us as on the Shankill, although some bravely did. After those first two stones, there was no real sign of trouble, other than this marked fear among the residents we passed. We were not even seriously heckled anywhere. About four hundred yards from the entrance to the Falls Park, where our platform had been arranged, we were informed by people who had been up to the park that 'the Provos' were waiting for us with piles of bottles and stones. As we got closer, this warning was intensifying into 'Don't go up there, they're waiting for you.'

Several of those around were asking what we should do: the only possibility for turning away was at the Donegall Road and a few side-streets beyond: after that, there was a straight stretch of three hundred yards along which we would be walking straight into trouble.

I made up my mind what to do, but could not tell anyone, lest word get back to anyone waiting. I gambled that those who wished to attack us would be inside the park, where the missiles had apparently been assembled; I also reckoned that the actual Provos, as opposed to their supporters who might give us some aggro, would be opposed to our being attacked for their own propaganda reasons at least. But in any case, this was one occasion where we could not turn away, despite the potentially great risks. So I decided that we should march on, as if going into the park, and at the very last moment, if real trouble was in the air, when we reached the park gates, we could march on past. We would thus run a dangerous and unpleasant gauntlet to prove our point, but avoid the all-out ambush trap of being enclosed in the park.

It might seem to some a strikingly arrogant and autocratic disposition to be taking decisions involving the lives of any of the thousands of people present: but in such a situation, any pause for consultation would have been dangerous, and any prior instruction running through a crowd might actually reach would-be attackers, who could then change tactics. So I responded to the now panicky warnings that we were walking straight into a trap, by saying, "Keep walking, keep your heads up, dignity and courage no matter what, and don't stop the march for whatever reason."

I retain a respectful memory of the large figure of Canon Pádraig Murphy, standing massively in the middle of the Falls Road under a banner of welcome, and his huge frame bearing down to shake hands with the first marchers. Wary though I was of any media manipulation by this formidable priest and his colleagues, I admired the physical courage with which he was standing out there: for he was by no means popular, and stood a very good chance of being attacked—which is exactly what happened moments later.

As we marched along the railings outside the Falls Park, I could see people up near the spot where our platform had been arranged; it had already been hijacked by Sinn Fein and People's Democracy members. Many more were just inside the railings: some did not have the tactical sense to let us walk into the park and were already throwing stones and bottles. I also noticed some very alert young men at various points outside the park, and my strong impression was that they were Provo volunteers with instructions, as in Turf Lodge, to make sure that nothing serious befell us. Further up, about a hundred yards beyond the park gates, I could see British troops in riot gear, with both riot guns and rifles at the ready. It would only have taken one shot, perhaps, from one of the young men in the less obvious uniforms, to have created a Bloody Sunday situation, if that had been anybody's intent.

The air was fairly full of bottles and stones as we approached the park entrance. Just as it would have looked that we were about to turn in, I told everyone near me to keep marching, and to stop for nothing: I got Betty beside me, and we almost pulled people forward to keep them marching ahead of us, advising them constantly, "Courage. Dignity. Don't stop for anybody, if you stop there will be greater danger for everybody."

At this point, a group emerging from the park grabbed Mairead, and again I saw the distressing sight of hatred in the faces of quite young women, as they gripped Mairead. One had a death-like grasp on her hair. Several people rushed to Mairead's aid, and there was a real danger of the entire march being halted in a very ugly ambush situation. I told those about to add to the stoppage to keep moving, regardless: and as soon as Mairead had been loosened from her attackers, got those with her to take her forward quickly.

Betty was still standing very coolly urging the other marchers through as I rejoined her. I looked up again towards the army positions, then around towards the nearby cemetery, to check that there was no other ambush position. The gates of the cemetery were closed, but through them I could see Bishop Philbin and his vicar-general. I have to say that the image of the apostles in the upper room came to mind: later I recorded this, in an article on church attitudes to violence and nonviolence. It caused great offence, which I deeply and sincerely regret. It is a measure of my feelings and attitudes at the time, that I could not decide whether I was right or wrong to have written such a thing. It may seem that I am compounding the matter by raising it again; but it would be dishonest for me to edit out in my own favour what I now clearly feel to have been an arrogant, angry, self-indulgent, indiscreet and even cruel observation. I did not stop even to observe, as my father pointed out to me, "Ach, Ciaran, after all, they are elderly men."

For thousands of those on the Falls march, this was their first experience of riot at first hand: or rather, of being stoned—for it was not a riot in the sense of two groups of people having a go at each other. They came through it with dignity and courage, and when we finally held our rally nearly a mile further on, they were in the highest spirits imaginable: they had been 'through the fire'.

Among those present was Anne Maguire, just out of hospital. Virtually no-one knew her, of course, for no photograph of her had appeared since the tragedy. Still unsteady on her healing legs, she had gone to the park in advance of the march, and had been attacked there. Now she was at the rally, taking part in the reading of the Declaration, which was read with deeper feeling that day than perhaps on any other occasion.

Among the sea of wet and happy faces in the crowd, I observed Peter McLachlan, and with him Geoff Martin, a Queen's student leader from the Sixties, now EEC Information Officer in Belfast. Tom Conaty was in tears of shame that peace marchers, who had been welcomed on the Shankill, should have been attacked on his native Catholic Falls Road: but Tom soon accepted that that day was a victory of the majority of the Falls people; and it was not too dangerous a humiliation for the Provos. It was no surprise to hear a few months later that actual Provos had been under orders that nothing was to happen to us: the attack had been by undisciplined supporters; had it been otherwise, I might not be writing this.

People dispersed in great good humour, comparing bumps and scratches. Betty had got off almost scot-free, in spite of standing right in the firing-line, and Betty is not tiny. Mairead had been scratched and had hair pulled out by the roots. I had a swelling lump behind my ear, and various other bruises and scratches which I had not noticed receiving. My general impression was that no-one had been 'seriously injured' as the media label goes, but that several had been taken to hospital. From Betty's house, the hospitals were telephoned and it was established that a mere nine people had been treated for various minor cuts and bruises, but that no-one had been seriously wounded, according to the hospitals. The worst casualty, in fact, had been Canon Pádraig Murphy, who had to have several stitches in a deep head cut. With Tom Conaty and Betty Williams, I went to the

Royal Victoria Hospital to visit anyone who might still be there, but all had been discharged, a little more than an hour after the rally.

We went to see Canon Murphy, and I shook hands with him. By the end of that wet, early winter day, the throbbing pain in the back of my head was almost like a glow of satisfaction at a good day's work. We were over, physically and emotionally, the most dangerous rally, half-way through the mobilisation programme, and morale was so high that there was no danger of any deflation in the last run-through to December. Proof of this came immediately with the numbers applying for tickets to London.

Yet another wave of media people arrived, and overseas invitations increased. The strange, nine-day wonder of August 1976 was not about to fade away; yet no-one could quite label the phenomenon that one day seemed anti-Provo, another day anti-army, and to have a will, a mind and a character of its own.

Cruising

The November rallies went off successfully amid mounting excitement over the London and Boyne events. Betty and Mairead were rapidly becoming international household names—Mairead's name causing considerable pronunciation problems. Betty used to joke that "They only keep me in this movement because I'm the only one with a name people can pronounce!" But even her name came out sometimes in European mouths as 'Beetee Veelyeems', while Mairead was variously, 'More-aid', 'Marrad', 'Moyrad', 'M'rade', 'Marryad'. Of course, even within Ireland it was variously pronounced because of the regional Gaelic dialects. My name suffers the same variation and even wilder distortions overseas: my favourite was one Norwegian's effort: 'Carryon McGoon'. I pronounce Mairead in the Ulster dialect as Mahrade, and Ciaran as Kee-ah-ran. McKeown is approximately McKeeown. I've often wondered about the difficulty faced by, say, a Vietnamese Buddhist monk like Nhat Thanh, in front of a CBS presenter. With English virtually the first official language of the world, Indian and African names have the hardest time of all, I suppose.

To domestic amazement, the Peace People were reaching into the realm of star glamour. Joan Baez rang and offered to come in support, asking if she should come quietly or singing. I said to come singing and talking, and she came, with Ira Sandperl and Molly Black, and they talked and she sang, delightfully.

Lord Longford came, and was worried that our espousal of nonviolence or of 'pacifism' might be embarrassing to Cardinal Hume and Archbishop Coggan, if we were to utter such sentiments on the Trafalgar Square platform which they would be sharing. I told him that we would most certainly be talking about nonviolence on the platform in Trafalgar Square, and that if that would be embarrassing to the Church leaders, we would not take any offence if they stayed away. Lord Longford was very anxious both that they should attend and that they should not be embarrassed, and while he allowed that pacifism had an honourable tradition in the Church, it might make it very difficult, if the Church leaders were to feel that they were being identified with pacifism. We spoke about nonviolence at Trafalgar Square, and I did not detect any ecclesiastical embarrassment: but I detected the absence of Dr. Donald Soper, President of the

Methodists, who had, we were told, decided that we were not pacifist enough.

By the time of the London rally, November 27, we had a formidable network of friends in Britain, not merely among the famous, but among the established peace networks, as well as many people newly inspired to the idea of *working* for peace. Suggestions were made of getting together in the Spring to form a British branch. (Monsignor Michael Buckley of the Wetherby Ecumenical Centre took the initiative for this in February 1977, and on his nomination, Mrs (now Lady) Jane Ewart-Biggs, widow of the British ambassador murdered in Dublin in July 1976, was declared President of the Peace People of England, Scotland and Wales; it continues under the guidance of Northern Irish *émigrée* Anne Strain, of Sevenoaks in Kent.)

On the weekend of November 20-21, we held a membership drive, which consisted of local groups throughout Northern Ireland asking people to sign individual copies of the Declaration of the Peace People and forwarding their names and addresses where possible to our office. Over 105,000 people signed over a two-day period. Anne Maguire was attacked yet again at Finaghy Road North, having eggs thrown at her.

By this time, too, the significance of going to so many smaller places was dawning: not only were local people in the smaller towns gratified to be involved, but city people, many of whom had not been out of Belfast for years, were reminded of a forgotten graciousness, the old decencies and hospitality that were the day-to-day reality in rural areas. Northern Ireland was indeed a diverse community of villages and towns, not merely a crude demographic entity with a sectarian flaw.

The days leading to the London rally were different in character to our previous experience. The London organisers were concerned with detailed preparation, and were slightly out of tune with our more cheerful dependence on spontaneity. This was London, we were told, things had to be well organised: the police, media, churches and others had to be catered for, whereas we had been inclined to expect such bodies to look after themselves.

The London organisers were a mixture of such dedicated peace workers as Mark James of Pax Christi, who were absolutely delighted with the visibility given to the nonviolence movement; and rather more establishment figures who were at times patronisingly tolerant of this pacifist aberration among otherwise quite admirable Irish people.

Contingents arrived from Norway, Germany, Holland and the United States. Special trains were laid on from the North of England.

Over a thousand travelled directly from Northern Ireland on November 26, to join thousands of emigrants. We visited the incoming groups in the various hotels.

The actual rally was very enjoyable. We left Hyde Park almost deliberately a few minutes late. Betty, Mairead, myself, Joan Baez and Jane Ewart-Biggs were in the front line: at Westminster Abbey, where the robed churchmen joined us from the front, we had to skip around the ecclesiastical party. It did not seem right to us that the march in London should be led by church leaders, when the character of the Irish rallies was otherwise. No offence was taken there, or at the platform, where Derek Hobson, the TV personality (and a Queen's University contemporary of mine), was entertaining the waiting crowd. Among those introduced was Diana Rigg, the actress originally best known for her *Avengers* role!

So it was certainly a more glamorous rally than others, but it retained its populist flavour, not least when Betty Williams offered a quasi-Churchillian gesture to a group of chanting 'Troops Out' people. The singing of civil rights songs by Joan Baez, who harmonised with the throng's rendering of songs made familiar by Martin Luther King's campaign, gave us a linking echo with that great struggle.

It was a very emotional time for us. I felt deeply grateful that we had arrived so successfully at the symbolic final week. The French journalist, Richard Deutsch, the *Le Monde* correspondent in Ireland, had committed himself to writing a book about us, which was very much centred on the relationship of the 'trio', and he had been snatching odd minutes in car-rides with us to glean material. I sat up late that night with him and Mairead, reminiscing on the progress to date, and looking forward to the rest of my two-year commitment. In the middle of such a period, when we had made so many friends, when celebration parties were going on in the various hotels, and we had 'the world at our feet', there was an element of sadness in discussing my inevitable and necessary withdrawal, and the step-by-step process by which the organisation would achieve a democratic basis and a direction of its own. The forthcoming spring convention, the establishment of the Charitable Trust and Company to disburse the capital funds, the putting of the newspaper on a steady footing, and the gradual shedding of responsibility and authority were discussed: and implicit in the whole proposed development was the end of the 'trio', whose seemingly magical relationship was the vibrating centre of the whole thing in the minds of many. Thus, at the very height of our achievement and profile, I was feeling a kind of nostalgia for its inevitable passing.

Richard understood and respected this. He assisted me considerably in the pressures of my continuing editorship of *Fortnight*, providing articles on international affairs, and detailed guides to the European Common Market and Community. Typical of him the following day was to accompany us to the airport and take back to Belfast, for *Fortnight*, an article which I was finishing in the taxi out. By this time, I was really looking forward to the peace and relative solitude of getting inside an aeroplane.

But it was no disappointment when we were actually applauded on board the Scandinavian Airlines jet for Oslo: the captain welcomed us on board during the fasten seat-belt routine, and many of the passengers were people returning from the London rally, who sang such songs as 'We Shall Overcome', and created quite a party atmosphere. There were no 'angles' to the Norwegian support, and we appreciated the open, warm-hearted friendship and gaiety of that flight.

People had gathered at the airport, with flags and flowers. Television lights lit the gangway from the place, and we were filmed from the steps to the terminal, like celebrities, with interviews starting at once. Inside the terminal, there was even more of the same; and here, as I began to see to the bags, I found myself being as much in demand as Betty and Mairead—my profile among Norwegians was much higher than elsewhere.

I felt touched, and suddenly guilty that I had not taken time to become familiar with at least a smattering of Norwegian, for the Norwegians had already guaranteed the financial basis of our organisation through the populist People's Peace Prize, and the warmth of this reception was the visible vindication of the conviction that our message was universal. It was the overwhelming answer of real, unprejudiced people to all the doubts and criticisms of sceptics and cynics alike.

We were installed in style at the Hotel International, where Gunnar Borrevik and Oddvar Munksgaard briefed us on the schedule for the following two days. It would include an audience with King Olaf of Norway, and various functions of that kind, before the formal city Hall ceremony on Tuesday evening, November 30, when we would receive the prize; and conclude with a torchlight procession to a square near the city centre.

Next morning before we got into the roomy Mercedes car which would take us about, I bought *Teach Yourself Norwegian* in the hotel shop, to the amusement of all concerned. To learn Norwegian in snatched moments over the next 30 hours seemed too outrageous even for one of my arrogance: but what I had in mind was to be able to make a 'thank you' speech of some substance, and with a credible sense of knowing what I was saying. So I pestered the driver and Gunnar and Oddvar with questions on how to pronounce the road signs as we drove along, while shooting through the basic grammar. Norwegian is actually very easy to read, in that every single letter is pronounced, and there are no silent or oddly different effects. Moreover, I had spent four months as a student labourer in Iceland in 1964, and while there is no helpful linguistic comparison, there was an echo in the sound. A bit of a mimic, I began at odd moments to speak English with a Norwegian accent, which was fun without being offensive; and as the day wore on, I became confident that I could indeed deliver a speech in Norwegian.

It was not expected of us, for there are only four million Norwegians, and while they have something of a chauvinistic rivalry with the much larger thirty-million Swedish nation, they understand that people taking a Scandinavian language inevitably take Swedish.

Gunnar Borrevik was prepared to humour me, and he obliged most readily when I asked him to translate into Norwegian the speech I had written in English. Franz Saksvik arrived as Gunnar, with increasing enthusiasm, was coaching me in the Norwegian speech. Franz coached me in the equivalent of BBC Norwegian. I then rehearsed for a couple of hours in my bedroom before the ceremony.

By this time, I was extremely glad that I had made the effort: our programme had brought us into contact with a wide variety of Norwegians: royalty, leading businessmen, politicians, media, churchmen, but also schoolchildren and people in the streets and restaurants who recognised us instantly, wished us very warm support and sought autographs. We were better known, and our progress and purpose had been more deeply, minutely and regularly charted in the Norwegian media than anywhere else—including Northern Ireland. Already the Peace People's Venner (Friends of the Peace People) had been formed to continue support after the ceremony was over. They are still active over seven years later.

By happy coincidence, Dr. Hilda Armstrong, then International President of Inner Wheel, was present at the Oslo City Hall on the evening of November 30. Hilda, from Northern Ireland, had lost her son, Sean, murdered in the Troubles, the first direct victim of the campaign against community workers. She was an active supporter of Harmony House, a reconciliation project for children, and was in Oslo to receive a cheque for this initiative, another example of Norwegian generosity towards the Northern Irish. We joined in her ceremony in the Lord Mayor's parlour before our own in City Hall.

The Peace People's ceremony, televised live, began with a

programme of music by young musicians and singers. (The attention given to children and young people in Norway is noticeable: on their National Day, for instance, they parade their children, not their armaments.) Then Gerd Benneche, Chairperson of the Norwegian Press Association, read the citation for Betty and Mairead, with honourable mention for myself, and we were called to the platform. Betty and Mairead were presented with the cheque for £201,000, made out in their names, and with gold medals bearing their likenesses, specially struck for the occasion.

I then moved to the microphone and delivered my speech in Norwegian. I cannot think of any situation in which such a small effort was so appreciatively received. We were particularly glad that the tens of thousands of Norwegians whose contributions made up the prize, and who were watching the ceremony on television for up to hundreds of miles away, were able to hear our appreciation in their own language.

There was only one drawback to this effort: as we moved out of the hall, to join the seven thousand people waiting outside for the torchlight procession, people grabbed my hand to shake it, and spoke rapidly and expectantly to me in Norwegian: but I could hardly understand a word they were saying! I felt embarrassed as I nodded in appreciation of the goodwill in their expressions, whatever it was they were actually saying.

The torchlight procession was a unique experience in the entire campaign. By the end of the evening, people were unwilling to leave us, and we were unwilling to let them go.

I explored with various Norwegians, especially the leading journalists, why there had been such a response to us. The Norwegians are highly conscious of the Russians at their Norwegian frontier on the edge of the Arctic. They are supporters of NATO, but refuse to have nuclear weapons on their soil. They value their independence, and stayed out of Europe in order to protect the small crofters and fishermen on their bleak western flank. They have big ship-building and forestry industries; they are oil-rich and are pacing the oil revenues from the North Sea to prepare for its running out. They are Lutheran, slightly repressed perhaps, but tolerant, and have a small, unthreatening Roman Catholic community, with good ecumenical relations, which were further enhanced by our presence. One of the country's best-known theologians was a Dominican priest, Fr. Halvard Rieber-Mohn, who died in 1982. As a small, rich, relatively secure country, with a strong memory of the German invasion in the Forties, and just a little nervous of its being forgotten that they share a border with Russia, they exhibit enormous concern for faraway places of suffering.

Their effort on our behalf was by no means an isolated endeavour. Oddvar Munksgaard told us with tears in his eyes of the experience he had had in directing their efforts for the starving people during both the Biafran and Bangladesh wars and attendant famines. When he had delivered a planeload of supplies at Lagos, he had asked the Caritas representative for guidance in selecting forty children whom they could bring back with them in the empty plane, and care for in Norway. The weary Caritas man had waved him hopelessly in the direction of a camp, some miles away, where about 3,000 children were in various stages of malnutrition. "How can you pick out forty who are to live?" Oddvar asked, still choked by the memory eight years later. Painfully, they selected forty; by the time the plane stopped to refuel in Geneva, fourteen had died.

In Bangladesh, he had watched children just fall into ditches and die, on the refugee columns. These compassionate journalists, men toughened by the cynicism-inducing practice of their profession, but with an incorruptible humanity, have developed a unique approach to foreign news coverage, which involves their readers. They send reporters to cover the story, and if they find that there is something they can do, even if it is simply to supply money, they launch a campaign among their readers. They have found that there is an upward spiral in this process: as people begin to give money, they want more news, they buy more papers, the papers increase circulation and revenue, and therefore advertising increases, the ability to cover the story increases—and the subjects of the coverage benefit as well.

It is a remarkable form of creative journalism: it is also more accurate, and Norwegians are better informed, in detail, and have a higher readership of newspapers than any other country. There are many anonymous people in Northern Ireland, Brazil, Nigeria, and Bangladesh who are alive today because of these newspapermen. There are also hospitals in the latter two countries, built, equipped and staffed by Norwegian newspaper readers. The same applies to a number of enterprises to which we directed funds, and to the Peace People headquarters in Belfast, named *Fredheim*—Home of Peace—as an acknowledgement of the Norwegian support.

If such an approach were adopted in Irish journalism, the already considerable generosity of the Irish would be multiplied; and the process would also inhibit domestic self-hatred.

The more we expressed our gratitude to the Norwegians, the more they insisted that they were grateful to us, and they meant it: they genuinely felt that the efforts of such as ourselves to attempt a nonviolent resolution of Northern Ireland's problems was a source of botn inspiration and security to themselves. While we appreciated this, it added to the sense of responsibility we felt for such a sacred opportunity to be carried by three fallible and vulnerable people, to whom so many looked in expectation for more than we could deliver.

The Norwegian visit was a high point, but it was not the only peak around that intensive period. We flew directly back to Ireland to receive another award: we were among those elected 'People of the Year' in Southern Ireland, and the citation was made by none other than my former editor, Tim Pat Coogan, who paid a warm tribute to the 'peace ladies'. The award itself was a solid silver disc, of simple, elegant design, inscribed in Irish and with our three names on it. It was one of two of all such awards which I retained, and I gave it to Anne Maguire, perhaps the most forgotten person of 1976, before she emigrated to New Zealand in an effort to start a new life in 1977.

The other award which I still have is a large bronze medal, presented to us in Berlin on December 10, 1976. This is the Carl von Ossietsky Medaille, awarded by the Berlin Section of the International League of Human Rights, possibly the most active section of the league in the world, with the indefatigable Wolfgang Schaar as secretary and led by its president, Edwin Beck.

I had been a little shocked at the intensity and immediacy among some Norwegians of their animosity towards the Germans: anti-German phobia had long eased in Britain, but of course Britain had never suffered the humiliation of defeat and occupation by the Nazis.

There was a curious connection between our reception of the Norwegian People's Peace Prize and the Carl von Ossietsky medal. The Norwegians wanted to give us their own populist version of the Nobel award; the Germans wanted to remind the world of the heroism of von Ossietsky, who had opposed Hitler nonviolently in the mid-Thirties. He was ignored after Hitler interned him in 1935, and released to die of galloping tuberculosis after receiving the Nobel peace prize in 1938. Thus, in an inverted way, the Berlin liberals were also acutely and immediately aware of the Nazi memory: and we had the rare privilege to serve as a dim reflector of this example of German heroism in the cause of nonviolence.

The ceremony in Berlin was marked by an excellent speech by Günter Grass. I replied in German, this time the translation being made by the foreign editor of a leading German paper.

I was becoming quite restless at being 'protected' by this stage: we seemed to be living under an armed guard now every time we stepped out of Northern Ireland. And when 'Death to the Peace People' was sprayed in black paint outside a church headquarters which we were about to visit in Berlin, our already overwhelming police escort was increased by the addition of young 'plainclothes' men in a Mercedes sports car, whom I nicknamed Starsky and Hutch: they wore black leather jackets and jeans, automatic pistols barely concealed, and generally exuded militaristic macho of the kind that would be disappointed not to get in a fight. They smiled benignly at my requests that they be stood down or called off, or whatever the appropriate expression is.

It was an awkward situation: we were being treated like royalty, housed in the Berlin State Guest House, using the very rooms used by John Fitzgerald Kennedy and Martin Luther King, waited on hand and foot, yet subject to an inflexible and armed protection every time we went outside the electrically controlled gates with their military guards. I felt like a truant schoolboy when I finally got away on my own in downtown Berlin. When I protested that we were prominent *because* of our opposition to arms, and had to repudiate such protection, the persistent and polite reply was that they could understand it if we were to be killed in Northern Ireland—but not here, please!

Our German hosts were also anxious that we should not travel to East Berlin, but Mairead and I went over for a few hours, and on the way back, I'm afraid I gave our ubiquitous guards, waiting at Checkpoint Charlie, a bit of a fright by turning left on the six-metre no-man's-land at the Berlin Wall, and using my pipe-knife, hacking a piece of mortar as a souvenir.

Then came the high moment for North-South in Ireland: the December 5 rally on the River Boyne. This had been placed right at the end of the programme because sensibilities can be so acute and perverse in Northern Ireland that if we had gone south without first travelling the length and breadth of Britain, the whole operation organised by these three Catholics might have been seen as a sneaky Catholic Nationalist plot.

The Boyne rally was another great success, the Southern and Northern contingents approaching to meet at Peace Bridge, thus named by the citizens of Drogheda years earlier. The river Boyne is 'holy ground' for the loyalist tradition, and its symbolism had great effect for those present, and even for a group of Americans, who had come on a specially chartered flight, under the auspices of the American National Council of Churches' Reconciliation Ireland programme.

Like so many moments, it had its controversy. I had been troubled about what to say on this last official rally of our declared programme. Since our 'mandate' was based on an assumption of widespread support, expressed in the large numbers at rallies, and the now regular meetings of peace groups, one could legitimately adopt either of two approaches: the more tempting was to cut loose with all the rhetoric at one's command, to inspire with such a sense of purpose and vision that the memory might help to carry people through the long, perhaps boring, wet or even dangerous evenings of local work which lay ahead; or else to speak very plainly, to pose questions and challenges, to set off a chain of debate. Ira Sandperl, veteran of Martin Luther King's campaign, familiar with both the dynamics and consequences of rhetoric, and the need for intelligent, nonviolent organisation, favoured the lower key.

I finally decided, on the platform itself, with Betty and Mairead well able to arouse and inspire, and the singing of Joan Baez adding in that direction, and with the mists over the Boyne having magically lifted as the crowds converged in this historic act of reconciliation, to be very plain-spoken.

We had already been suggesting for some time that the party-political structure in Northern Ireland was part of the problem, that it was a statement of the division, even though some of the best spirits were endeavouring to engineer a 'solution' through that structure. So, noting that the rallies were now over, and that much hard work had to be done far from the inspiration of such events, I asked out loud what we were to do, were we to support power-sharing among the political parties? People were taken aback at this, and a few called out 'yes'. I told them that we should not allow the momentum we had developed to be spent in that direction, or allow ourselves to be divided again at the ballot-box after forming such a network of friends; that our work was to increase that network, to build a new consensus, to solve the problem from the bottom up by relentless work, not from the top down by clever solutions. This was the gist of it, and it was received with respect, but by no means with enthusiasm; and, especially among those active in political parties, such as the Alliance Party and the SDLP, it caused anger: for many in those parties had been counting on the Peace People merely to create the right climate for a second try at a Sunningdale-type solution.

The 'political' controversy among the Peace People was now well aroused, and during the next year there was a sustained effort, partly successful, by members of the Alliance Party in particular, to blunt the nonviolent, consensus-building 'political' function of the Peace People. Some Alliance members felt directly threatened by the Peace People, since they saw their party as *the* party of reconciliation. And of course, Paddy Devlin had already long since signalled the disposition of the party politicians: with Paddy, as ever, I was grateful that the attack was forthright and from the front.

When I argued that parliamentary democracy was a more fundamental concept than the party-political structure, some felt that I was being obscure; others, that talk of nonviolent community democracy smacked of communism or anarchy. The Alliance Party members took most offence when I observed that their twin policy of 'strong on law and order' and 'strong on the British link', virtual code-phrases for Unionism, made reconciliation with non-Unionists, and those who opposed special powers, extremely difficult. There were, of course, quite a few who happily ignored any possible problems in this best of all possible worlds and worked with equal zeal for both the Peace People and the Alliance Party.

After the Boyne rally, we went to a reception organised in a local convent, and presided over by the late Cardinal William Conway, who had been supportive of the Peace People. Over tea and sandwiches, I told him that we intended to intensify our argument in the coming year that nonviolence was the essential Christian position, and our opposition to 'just war' theory; and expressed the hope that we would not get into any destructive polemic with the Church over it. I was sorry to see that this made the Cardinal very uneasy. He suggested that it might not be very wise, for it would be difficult for Protestants. It was my turn to be taken aback: it had not occurred to me that the Catholic hierarchy might have considered declaring for nonviolence, but was being held back by ecumenical considerations —especially since the World Council of Churches had usually been more forthright, until recent years, than the Vatican, in its opposition to armaments. I started to recall the position of the Anabaptists and Mennonites, to say nothing of the Quakers (who for Northern Irish purposes, and against their wishes, are regarded as 'Protestants' by most), when Cardinal Conway pointed out that the Protestants would find it difficult because of such events as the Battle of the Somme in which thousands of young Ulstermen and other Irishmen were mere fodder.

Before I could raise the question of how difficult the Catholics might find it because of the commemorative Masses for the heroes of Ireland's 1916 Rising and War of Independence, we were summoned to say goodbye to the American contingent. Cardinal Conway died the following year and I had no further opportunity to discuss with him how best the difficulties of achieving 'nonviolence as orthodoxy' might be overcome. In the years since, I have had many discussions with clergymen at every level, some inspiring, some deeply depressing. I regard the network of parishes and congregations as a vital structure in our culture through which nonviolence might indeed become the dominant ethic. There is reason to hope that some of the Catholic bishops who believe in private that nonviolence is essentially Christian, or that the 'just war' theory is either an aberration or at any rate a mere abstract that dissolves into irrelevance in the real situation of war, will come out of the closet and say so. More difficult, but not impossible, is the challenge facing Protestant clergymen disposed to nonviolence, but who fear revolt or removal by their congregations.

Another little controversy arising out of the Boyne rally was that an American, inspired by the rally, wrote a cheque for 20,000 dollars for the Peace People, on the flight home. This money made its way into the Reconciliation Ireland Fund account, and no doubt very good use was made of it for the purposes of reconciliation. But the Peace People were thought to have received it, and we were in no position to acknowledge it, or to say what was being done with it.

It would be a recurring feature that money which people imagined was somehow going to the Peace People, never in fact reached us. We were unusually fortunate with funds, and certainly did not worry about money. But it caused embarrassment and in some cases anger. In the spring of 1977, for instance, when Betty Williams made an exhausting four-week speaking trip in Canada and the United States, I got a phone call from her one night, which burned the wires. Betty had been very well received, and her hostess had called on those present to be generous, and had left out documents which would show how they could help. Betty had noticed the thorough distribution of leaflets which bore the Declaration of the Peace People, not only word for word but as a direct copy of the actual design layout I had used on the back of our newspaper. She turned one over, and read, in growing rage, a brief reference to this inspiring peace movement, then the question 'How can you help?', followed by the name, address and account number of an excellent Southern Irish reconciliation project!

There were other occasions when people who visited us asked for literature, and perhaps a photograph of Betty and Mairead, and later used this as promotional material for their own purposes. I felt that this was fair enough, and hoped that it would increase friendship all round, and that struggling organisations would benefit from the attention attracted by our high profile—that the rising tide would lift all boats, as the late Southern Irish Taoiseach, Sean Lemass, would have said. I was disappointed that the opposite was usually the effect: that the Peace People were blamed for 'getting all the money' while other, older organisations lived on the edge of bankruptcy. One organisation actually based a fund raising tour of the United States on an attack on us, which did them no good, and hardly helped us.

What was deeply objectionable, apart from the short-sighted, mean-mindedness of such responses, was a public statement by one of those involved that 'there was a growing public concern about money going into the Peace People coffers'. This 'concern' was never specified, but it fed the gutter gossip about fortunes being made. When our audited accounts were published, and showed the meticulously bona fide nature of our financial account, this fact was not newsworthy . . .

As Christmas approached, we could be satisfied that we had not stepped on any major sectarian or political landmine, no mean feat in itself; violence had dropped dramatically, never—to date—to recover its former intensity, tensions had eased tangibly. We had the resources in personnel and finance to establish an enduring organisation. Our international image and contacts were remarkably good, and Northern Ireland's image had been transformed. The packed concert by Joan Baez in the Ulster Hall in December gave a most welcome super-star touch to Bomb City and brought home something of the glamour with which we had been touched overseas. Perhaps the most important achievement was the invisible one—the 'final crunch' that had not happened.

Now that it was clear that we would not be dominated by any denomination, we called a pre-Christmas rally specifically to invoke the Christian leadership: it was held in Armagh, seat of the Roman Catholic and Church of Ireland (Anglican) leadership, the ecclesiastical capital of Ireland. It was a simple, friendly event, suggesting that we might be able to look forward to a period in which the Christian ethos might be rescued from its ambivalence on militarism.

I looked forward to a couple of days off at Christmas, with no phones, no news, nothing but Marianne and the children. Then, in her Christmas Day message, Queen Elizabeth mentioned the peace movement specifically in example of the reconciliation theme of her address. The phone started ringing again within minutes . . .

Coming Down

Where do you go from here? It was asked many times a day, by members and media alike, for months on end. We outlined the forward programme of development so often that it was like a cracked record to hear oneself repeating it. The question really meant, 'What is the next excitement, sensation, trick, miracle?' and therefore the questioners did not hear the flat reiteration of the need for relentlessly hard work. There seemed to be a need to present and fix us as having our heads forever in some clouds.

The rally phase to mobilise the Peace People had been an extraordinary experience ranging in character from Pied Piper to pilgrimage. Now, with so much more expected, we set out with cheerful confidence on a much less easy stage, but still towards the 'promised land' of peace. I had poured scepticism on the aspirations of those who imagined that a series of marches would bring peace, and had urged concentration on serious, detailed work. But I, too, must have been 'carried away', for I did not fully realise that this message had little chance of penetration; and in any case I have always found it difficult to appreciate the extent to which people find relatively simple ideas baffling or frightening, just because they are unfamiliar. And even to say that gives an immediate impression of arrogance.

People were either content to hear what sounded like an intelligent speech, and relax, because *we* obviously knew what we were doing and that therefore, somehow, it would be done; or they asked with increasing vexation who Ciaran McKeown thought he was, *telling* us what to do. Perhaps, with violence dropping so fast, and the party politicians temporarily in the wilderness, I felt that an unrepeatable opportunity to push out as many new ideas as possible was too good to miss—and overdid it.

Having seen the mortal damage done to the movements of King and Gandhi by their deaths, after over-emphasis on single-focus leadership, having even thought of the splits that had plagued Francis of Assisi in establishing an order of friars under vows of poverty, chastity and obedience, I regarded the careful dissolution of the personality cult leadership into a democratised movement in which the vision and authority were progressively shared, as the key to our distinctive development. At the same time, I recognised that the clamouring egotism of 'the pack' could destroy that possibility if our largely naïve membership were not brought along, gently, but quickly enough to out-pace those already seeking position. In principle, I still believe that this was one of the finest aspects of our strategy: in practice, it failed disastrously; worse still, I refused to accept that for years.

I once outlined my ideas on the nature of both local and global politics in the necessarily disarmed world of the future, at the Max Planck Institut in Starnberg, Germany, a few years into the Peace People development. The Institut director, Professor Karl-Friedrich von Weizsäcker, that most distinguished physicist/philosopher, declared his agreement with all the ideas outlined, including such approaches as replacing the analogous use of Newtonian language in our political jargon (e.g. 'building society on firm foundations') with the language of Relativity and Uncertainty in the politics of the century of Einstein and Heisenberg: but he categorically and adamantly rejected my ideas on the process of rotating leadership, and of creating a tradition in which leading individuals would voluntarily hold *and yield* authority.

He would entertain no argument on the matter: leaders were leaders and that was that. I smugly shrugged off his rejection of an idea which I felt to be important and creative, interpreting his attitude as inevitable in a German of his particular experience. He had been a pupil of Heisenberg, had known Einstein, Bohl and other great intellects of this century, and had grown up in pre-Hitler Germany, his father having served in government in the Weimar Republic. But I saw this otherwise great man as having been marked by the experiences of weak leadership followed by the diabolical strength of Nazi leadership. His orthodoxy, I imagined, stemmed from the more recent experience of the recovery of German democracy, which he has served so well. So I basked in naïve conviction that we would demonstrate the truth of the principle I had outlined, in the experiment still in operation.

Today, I have to cling rather desperately to the idea that people will, with equal serenity, accept or relinquish the authority necessary for the discharge of personal and social responsibilities: but I have to lay alongside that idea the more immediate truth that people do not behave thus, and that it will be a long time before such a mature tradition of democracy is established—as it must be, if the human race is not constantly to be vulnerable to tyranny or slavery.

It has been burned into me most painfully that some people desperately need to feel important and to have position, while others have a comparable need to be led: both dispositions are functions of the lack of self-knowledge and self-confidence, products of ignorance and fear. These deep-seated diseases are characterised by self-deception, which makes the shortcomings invisible to the sufferers.

In a society as deeply demoralised as Northern Ireland's has been, these diseases are acute and widespread, and make people vulnerable either to becoming or to following demagogues. The example of the demoralised condition of the German people in the early Thirties is a powerful one: and that condition drew forth the crippled personality of Adolf Hitler with a sure instinct. What the rest of the world came to regard as a great evil, began as the domestic need for the great good of restoring self-confidence.

Making due allowance for scale and policy, it is possible to see some analogy with Northern Ireland, whose decent friendly folk can turn in their need for identity and self-respect to the hideous violence of self-assertion, or vote, in such numbers, for a figure like Ian Paisley, a man roaring his secular presence, it seems to me, to escape not only the loneliness of an exclusivist childhood, but a spiritual life lived in the baleful shadow of 'the God of Wrath'.

As 1977 dawned, and aware of this disease of demoralisation, I was nevertheless absurdly confident that so long as we remained true to ourselves, our self-perception as instruments, and our willingness to say or do whatever was required, at whatever cost, that nothing but a healthy and creative society could be the outcome. The only possible obstacles were not the 'violence' or 'the men of violence', but any loss of integrity, courage or direction from within—which proved at least partly valid.

The six-month period until June would be in two distinct phases: the first three months would be devoted to preparing for a Constitutional Convention in April, which would decide the structure, procedures and authority with which the Peace People would operate: and with putting the functions of the movement on a more efficient basis. The following three months would consist of putting those procedures into operation, and preparing for the first formal meeting of the, by then, thoroughly democratised movement, in the autumn.

This time-frame was in itself a way of serving notice that we were here to stay after street demonstrations were over. It was also suggestive of the amount of work to be done: and it seemed to me to be a reasonable length of time to allow for all the new groups to become fully integrated, to visit each other, begin the process of earthing cult leadership, and start thinking about the future leadership and direction.

We also wanted to constitute ourselves in a way that might act as a demonstration model for how the people of Northern Ireland as a whole could organise themselves democratically, regardless of past allegiances or present party allegiance. Therefore, if the time-scale seemed long to some anxious to have a more muscular say in the decision-making, it was an ambitiously short one for creating an exemplary structure.

One of the activities in which we were already engaged, and which was a source of some disquiet, was the operation of what I called 'the escape route'. The reason for the dramatic title was to bring it quickly to the attention of those who would need it, namely those living in the underworld of paramilitarism on either side, who might now want to make a fresh start in life, free from the emotional—and stronger—pressures to remain engaged. The degree to which paramilitary organisations coerced internal loyalty varied greatly, and even fluctuated according to the time of year. In some cases, where a member had been reasonably senior, the difficulty could be immense, with the real fear of being murdered; with others, a less justified fear was no less effective. Sometimes a lapsed member, re-establishing family life, might be left entirely alone, then suddenly asked to drive a car, for 'just one wee job'; or, coming up to Christmas, when pressure to provide for prisoners' families increased, asked to assist in a robbery. Such people would note more readily than others what the phrase 'escape route' meant: but to many, Peace People among them, it smacked of assisting terrorists on the run, or aiding and abetting in their escape from 'justice'.

It was in the very nature of such an operation that we did not talk about it other than to declare its existence, and for whom it was intended. While we could not seek formal co-operation with the authorities for such an activity, we had to find a way of doing it which avoided its becoming a mere dodge from arrest. The simple approach was to ask a would-be 'escapee' if he would mind if we checked to find if he was wanted for a specific offence. If he was, we obviously could not do anything like providing him with shelter or a route out of the country; at the same time, we would not 'inform' on a person who had thus come to us in trust. Our advice would have tended to be that such a person might be better to take a rap for a present offence voluntarily, and that we would assist in a fresh start thereafter. If he was not immediately wanted, however suspect, we would be free to assist.

There are people alive today, people who were not murdered, because of this activity: because among the 'escapees' were some who had been ordered to kill and did not wish to do so. There are people living fruitful, stable lives who might have become more deeply involved in violence. The operation had some effect in weakening the internal terror grip in the organisations. It was one of the best things we did.

The high-profile leadership which enabled us to announce such a scheme also made it more difficult to operate. I found myself arranging clandestine meetings to meet telephone callers, in such a way that my easily recognised appearance would not add to danger for the escapee—and I had to minimise the risks of being 'set up' myself; and it would not have been appropriate to get into the habit of having 'escapees' spending the night sleeping on our settee. Sometimes those who had brought themselves even to contact us were in a state of acute terror, and were afraid to talk to anyone other than 'Betty, Mairead or Ciaran'. Finally, we approached two clergymen whom we felt to be sympathetic as well as discreet, and asked them to consider establishing procedures and a network for carrying out this work.

I asked them to try it for a month, and that if it proved too much, or otherwise impossible, we would understand, and try some other way. But no alternative was required: with dedication, efficiency and discretion, these two men recruited to their operation other people with comparable qualities. It will be a long time, if ever, before it is possible to express public appreciation by name to those who did this work, in Northern Ireland, throughout the British Isles, and even further afield. Those who engaged in this potentially dangerous, nonviolent and discreet activity for the sake of genuine peace, were a silent and undemanding source of inspiration: and a comfort, especially, when others who would never have volunteered for such duties, were clamouring for notice and position.

In the first week of January 1977, we participated in a weekend conference called 'Waging Peace'. This had been arranged by Peace Point, a longer-standing group concentrating on peace education, and had been postponed, following the rise of the Peace People, until our rallies were over. I outlined my 'Strategy for Peace', a short résumé of practical elements in the nonviolent, communitarian approach. Rarely has any address of mine been received in Northern Ireland itself with such enthusiasm: it seemed agreed that the strategy was both visionary *and* practicable, and an advance on anything hitherto proposed. I was greatly, but briefly encouraged, for the effect of the address, rather than recruiting more people or groups to work, was to cause more intense questioning of who the hell Ciaran McKeown thought he was. It also increased the fear of various peace and community organisations that they were about to be swamped or absorbed in the tidal wave directed at will by the well-funded, brilliant, high-profile manipulators of the Peace People. That very evening while the 'glow' of the initial address was still dominating the dialogue, a leading politician of one party said to a member of another, "We had better get together quickly, these people are going to take over". This notion, that we were aiming to 'take over', became rooted: the fact that *nobody* could 'take over' in the sort of politic which we sought, was not understood.

I was not unduly discouraged by this response: yet again, whether out of innocence or arrogance, I felt that the sheer passage of time would prove that we were genuine, and not engaged in some kind of peace imperialism. But I found the personal aspect difficult to handle. One leading member of the Peace People expressed to me the extent to which I became more a subject of debate than the ideas I was articulating. He told me that he felt the same as many more, that when he listened to my strategy speech, he felt he would have followed me to the ends of the earth: so that, immediately afterwards, he wanted to be sure what sort of a *person* he was proposing to follow. The personal problem was multiplied by the fact that Betty and Mairead were the symbols to whom people had so massively responded: yet if they had presented the same ideas, they would have received a great ovation—and the ideas would be ignored. Partly this was a function of the inherent sexism of our society; partly it was because they would not have communicated the same unmistakable sense of having thought through every aspect of the proposals in a full knowledge of their context, including the sacrifice demanded. They aroused hope, joy, gladness; I seemed to excite dedication to a cause, and spark resentment of my person in the same moment, and sometimes in the same people. Life can be prickly, sometimes.

Over the next three months, the three of us, separately or together, visited group after group, outlining our strategy, and helping those with no committee experience to develop the rudiments of organisation. At the same time, we kept the international aspect steadily before the public, responding singly, as far as possible, to invitations. This meant better planning than before, especially after I encouraged Mairead to accept a seemingly impossible series of invitations to visit Australia and New Zealand. The public response there, especially to Mairead, had been considerable: marches had been organised, and support groups formed. To deal with the invitations adequately would require five weeks away, and some felt that it was asking too much of Mairead to go so far, for so long, on her own. But I felt that it was to Mairead in particular that the invitations had been addressed, some of the Australian correspondence actually specifying her original broadcast in the wake of the August tragedy, and that therefore the only really effective response was for Mairead to go. There was even a suggestion that such 'trips' should be given in rotation to those doing most work—as if they were in some sense holiday rewards! Now that the rallies were over, those who felt better qualified to represent us than Betty and Mairead, were becoming more visible: while those better qualified to direct things than myself were in great supply.

I advised Mairead, who seemed overwhelmed by the sheer extent of the Australian and New Zealand demands, that if they were refused now, they would never effectively be renewed, that it would be worth the present effort, which would not have to be repeated. One senior member genuinely felt that this was too much after the relentless pace we had set since August, and that we would all crack up if we kept going at the present rate. But wise or foolish, Mairead decided to go, and undertook the five-week tour, which was both fruitful—and physically punishing. She charmed everywhere she went, and enlisted solid support. Most notable was that of the tough New Zealand Premier, Robert Muldoon, who later came specifically to Northern Ireland with his wife, to visit the Peace People, and who offered help in the tricky area of resettling people who needed a fresh start as far from Northern Ireland as possible—despite domestic accusations in New Zealand that he was risking the import of terrorism!

I could hear the increasing exhaustion in Mairead's voice, in her phone calls, as the trip proceeded in February and March: one night, when I asked her where she was, she had to turn and ask her hostess which city she was in. It was Sydney. Yet I am sure that little if any of that exhaustion would have been appreciated by her audiences: for in the years that followed, I have seen Mairead scarcely able to walk or keep her eyes open, yet summon the energy to inspire a waiting crowd as if she were as fresh as a daisy. The phenomenon reminded me of the ability of great musicians like Artur Rubinstein and Pablo Casals, who could cast aside all limitations of great age to invest their virtuoso performances with thrilling energy.

One idea which I tried to launch demonstrated for me the insularity, bordering on hypocrisy, of many 'do-gooders', and simultaneously illustrated to many the fantastic, pie-in-the-sky nature of Ciaran McKeown's 'vision'. It concerned the connection between 'First World' and 'Third World' economies, if looked at purely as an economic matter. But it concerned the equality, the equal sanctity of all human lives, if judged in that light. The proposal was that each peace group should have a 'Third World' function as a regular activity: either fund-raising for a specific project, identifying with a particular village in some situation far worse off than their own; or at least seeking or disseminating information on the plight of the majority of human beings for whom day-to-day food supply is a continuous struggle for mere survival, with over 3,000 million people in recurring difficulty and short life expectancy, and over 300 million in what Robert MacNamara described in a World Bank Report as 'absolute poverty'—already too far gone to be helped in anything other than the conditions for death. I proposed that when each group had established such a function, the Peace People as a whole might adopt, as a 'twin', some place of comparable size or population to Northern Ireland, and work to equalise the levels of human life, in longevity and quality, in both places.

The idea elicited puzzlement and resentment, and finally, outright hostility. The most obvious opposition was, naturally enough, the observation that our purpose was to resolve Northern Ireland's problems, and when we had done that, we could get on with saving the whole world. The second was that other groups, Oxfam, War on Want, Trócaire, Christian Aid, to name a few, were all doing a thoroughly good job, so we would only be duplicating. Next came the suggestion that we were trying to take over every aspect of voluntary work in Northern Ireland, to add to the growing Peace People empire. In general, it was felt that we had more than enough to do, without adding any 'extras'.

I was more than disappointed with the response: the origin and purpose of the idea was simply a consciousness that a movement concerned with cherishing all lives must dictate some effort for those most threatened, wherever they are. The benefits of the proposal seemed to me endless, the objections negligible. Not only was it intrinsically right, and would produce real benefit for actual people, but it would act as a continuous educational factor, reinforcing the belief that all lives have equal rights. A group which had, say on a monthly basis, to concern itself about people in misery far away, might be more likely to find mutual accommodation on the local problems of sectarian or other division. The constant realisation that there were always many more millions of people much worse off, would help to put the Northern Ireland squabble—and the perverse self-indulgence in its own drama—into perspective.

The ability and motivation to help people in distant distress would inhibit the self-pity of the Northern Irish about their own suffering; it would also help to ensure that the 'poor-mouth' dependency of the Northern Irish on the British, would not give way to an even more insidious begging from the other Europeans and the Americans for the poor suffering Irish, and help us to appreciate our intermediate position between the very rich and very poor peoples of this earth.

We could accept help from those richer, but if we were not prepared to help those poorer, then we were merely adding to our coterie of nurse-maids.

It seemed to me that we could not seriously tackle Northern Ireland's problems wth the appropriate nonviolent strategy and determination, if we did not have a constant, relentless appreciation that every human life is sacred: and that understanding dictated an immediate and active concern about 'Third World' conditions.

As well as being rooted in an outward-looking vision, my conviction about this idea was reinforced by another Norwegian practice: once a year, all the voluntary and church organisations combine in a nationwide effort to visit every household for a collection for some specific charity. When this had first been mooted in Norway, the same objections had been raised by individual charities that this might reduce their individual slices of the 'charity cake', and was a kind of duplication. In the event, not only was there the massive annual collection, but each of the organisations found that the public response to their individual collections at other times was greater. This annual event, known as the 'Nodhjulp', being the subject of national media attention in its build-up, and on the day, has increased the Norwegians' outward-looking disposition and reinforced the people's instincts of generosity. I was there on one such occasion when the target was thirty million krone: the actual total was over fifty-five million. Everyone enjoyed the day, and enormous good was done, at home and abroad.

In the last few years, a thoughtful Belfast journalist, Derek Murray of Ulster Television, has quietly established an 'Ulster Cares' initiative, which has some aspects of this idea: but it has yet to make that vital leap into the public consciousness that would make our intimate connection with our far more distressed brothers and sisters on earth part of our self-identity.

Ironically, the most vociferous opposition to this aspect of my approach came from a highly vocal section which vigorously supported our travels to richer places on behalf of Northern Ireland: they praised the 'enlightened, outward looking vision' of our overseas work, but saw the 'Third World' dimension as arrogant, pie-in-the-sky nonsense. It caused so much irritation that I backed off it somewhat, confining myself to occasional efforts, and regular material in the newspaper *Peace by Peace*. Whatever about the movement as a whole, this Third World consciousness provided me with energy at times of exhaustion or discouragement: I only had to think of such as Mother Teresa in Calcutta, or Adolfo Perez Esquivel, an imprisoned nonviolent leader in Argentina, and appreciate the size of their task, and my burdens would seem much lighter.

Most galling about the defeat of this initiative is that I am convinced that it would have found agreement in the hearts of most of our less vocal members: they had that spontaneous generosity which would have caused them to rally round if they knew someone was in trouble across the street—all that was needed was for them to understand that the starving of this moment are just across the street of a very small world. And as I have watched the Peace People in decline increasingly preoccupied with financial survival, I have become totally persuaded that the 'spirit of poverty', without which generosity is compromised, is vital to the dynamics of nonviolence.

So, if I have tempered on some notions, I continue to insist on the essential indivisibility of peace and justice at home and globally, and that we must practise this understanding with regular practical work. Moreover, only a consciousness that the rescue of most human beings from misery and impending death by poverty is the primary task facing our species, will provide the motivation needed to rescue all of us from self-destruction of a more dramatic kind. We will not prevent war, or end the arms race and trade, if our motivation is mere fear of being melted.

Possibly I pushed too many ideas too quickly for popular consumption. But while I remained uncompromising in putting forward ideas and principles for general purposes, the advice I gave to group after group was to find *some* project of practical work in their local community, which would bond them and provide the renewing source of good morale; or where their own community seemed perfectly content, as in the better off residential areas, to find a community which they could help.

We held a large meeting, representative of the groups in late January, 1977, to outline progress and plans. There had been a lot of talk that the media should be kept out, that members might want to say things which they would not wish the world to hear. The *Belfast Telegraph* rang me on the morning of the meeting to ask if the press was to be excluded. I told the reporter that some members were likely to propose that, but that Betty, Mairead and I would oppose it, and would want the meeting kept open. In the event, the meeting rejected our advice, and voted to exclude the press. The *Belfast Telegraph* attributed this decision to me personally, and observed that, as a journalist, I should have known better!

A much worse distortion appeared in the *Sunday News* on the morning after the meeting, with a screaming front page flyer headed,

'Peace Leader Lashes Press'. A *Sunday News* reporter had apparently ignored the decision to exclude the press and stayed at the meeting. Her report described me as launching a 'bitter attack' on local pressmen, calling them 'unprofessional'.

At no point did I criticise local press people: I did say, in explaining to our members the extent and depth of understanding of our purpose in some countries, that this was due to the extent of quality reporting, since some news media had sent over their top journalists to spend days and even weeks going around with us, reporting our activities in depth and detail.

The *Sunday News'* outrightly untrue story enraged some of our members, who could hardly believe that such a thing could happen in a newspaper. My consistent advice was to ignore any such distortion; but some were beginning to feel that our relations with local media needed urgent attention. Before any serious consideration of the possible problem could take place, the Tuesday edition of the *News Letter*, sister of the *Sunday News*, carried a banner-headlined front-page story, with my photograph, announcing that I was to face disciplinary proceedings before the local National Union of Journalists' branch on Thursday, following my 'attack' on local newspeople.

The NUJ-style kangaroo court, two days later, was a farce. The meeting was the most packed that many could remember, for the agenda obviously offered more entertainment than usual. The branch chairman, Bob Rodwell, who was then an active member of a local peace group, withdrew from the chair, which was assumed by the treasurer. When the moment for the 'trial' came, I asked if the meeting was 'open to the press'? There was genuine astonishment at this, one journalist observing in a puzzled tone that we were all journalists, what could I possibly mean? I pointed out that I was only present in the interests of the Peace People, who could be damaged if what I had read in a newspaper about discipline proceedings were true; and that on the basis of this hearsay, I had attended to protect the Peace People interest. Therefore I had to know if the meeting were closed, or if there would be reports published on the meeting.

A short irritable meeting followed, during which one journalist observed that the *News Letter* had been out of order in publishing the agenda of an NUJ meeting which was always confidential. Another pointed out that branch meetings were always 'in lodge' (confidential), and that this one should be just the same. Finally it was proposed and passed that the meeting be closed to the press.

"Now, can we get on with the business?" the acting chairman said, with the air of a patient man who has been unfairly messed about. I then asked if any member to be subjected to disciplinary proceedings was entitled to any kind of notice of such proceedings, since I had merely read about it in a newspaper? There followed a frantic exploration of the NUJ rulebook, which yielded the interesting expression of natural justice that fifteen days' notice in writing was due to any member in such an invidious position.

This spoilsport rule had a most dampening effect, with the chairman observing that it looked as if we would have to postpone the matter. I said that I would waive my rights, adding pompously the hope that the rules be observed in future for any member whose professional standing was about to be impugned.

The chairman then simply outlined the proposal that I be disciplined because of my damaging remarks about the professionalism of fellow journalists.

I said that I had made no such remarks, that I had a tape of the entire meeting, and that I would like to hear the reporter who wrote the story repeat exactly what I had said, and to explain where the attributed remarks had come from, since no-one had made them at the Peace People meeting.

At the mention of the tape, there was some stirring: but nothing like the unease which followed the reporter's reply: "I thought that was what you were saying."

There was a ghastly moment of silence, while the entire meeting realised not only that the quarry had escaped, but that they had a much trickier matter on their hands: the self-confessed unprofessionalism of a reporter who had attributed that very charge to me. They spent the next hour and a half trying to figure out how to save the face of both the reporter and the *Sunday News*. Eventually they decided on the formula that 'Ciaran McKeown was exonerated' but that the branch was satisfied that the '*Sunday News* had acted in good faith'. It is a pleasure to record that some journalists were disgusted at the shabbiness of this, notably two *Belfast Telegraph* men, one of whom said the branch should be ashamed for "bringing a man, half hanging him, then saving their own faces". No retraction of the damaging articles was ever printed.

I did not press for any remedy. I appreciated that the young reporter had been honest within the meeting, and I had no wish to worsen relations with local journalists. But any hope that this little confrontation would have served notice that the Peace People were not to be easy meat for sloppy hacking proved totally misplaced. A general feeling of unspecified annoyance with me persisted sourly among some for years; and misrepresentation of the Peace People was a regular, at times devastating, feature of local coverage.

One journalist friend has attributed this to the fact that I had humiliated the entire branch to their faces. Perhaps. Certainly, I often found myself at meetings with journalists present, when Peace People attacked the media, and I would hear myself saying that we should not worry about what the papers said, that if we simply got on with our work, the truth would get through in the end; it would have been hard for any reporter to ignore the implied contempt. At the same time, I frequently defended the media on the grounds that it was their function to scrutinise what we were doing, maybe even giving us a hard time in the process: but people reared to imagine that what they read in the papers was true, found that difficult to accept.

A much worse media storm broke around my head soon after the NUJ meeting. I had written an article for *Fortnight* on the topic of the Churches, their division, their ambivalence on violence, and on the differing pressures on Catholic and Protestant clergymen. Referring to Catholic clergy afraid of their bishop, and Protestant clergy afraid of their congregations, I suggested that too many were like the apostles hiding in the upper room after the Crucifixion: and here I added that most unfortunate reference to the Falls rally.

The *Sunday News* seized on the offending paragraph to conjure up a personal conflict between myself and Bishop Philbin. Dr. Philbin did not comment, and I later apologised to him both on a public platform at Belfast City Hall, and in writing. But the story had a divisive effect within the Peace People.

Tom Conaty, a prominent and very orthodox Roman Catholic businessman and politician, and then a leading figure in the Andersonstown Peace Group, called a meeting in his home attended by about nine Peace People. They issued a statement saying that unless we gave an undertaking not to criticise the clergy, they would resign. We replied that we could not possibly lead by way of ultimata from behind. Tom resigned and several others with him, some of whom later returned. The *Irish Times*, arguably Ireland's best newspaper, editorialised on 'Mr. McKeown's expulsion' of Mr. Conaty.

I regretted that remark about the Bishop, and also the resignation of Tom Conaty: he had done some excellent work during the rally period, and while his somewhat triumphalist Catholicism was rather at odds with much that we stood for, his was an authentic position. Many Catholics who have started out regarding the ecumenical movement as an opportunity for Protestants to become Catholics, have in the process learned a great deal from Protestants. Certainly, Tom had been surprised by Protestant support at Ormeau Park, and had thrown himself into the organisation after that.

While Tom resigned and some Protestants also seemed to feel that a Catholic who attacked his bishop must be gravely suspect, this remark of mine was actually quite popular with many. Not a few felt that it was time somebody challenged the Churches, and that the sight of a Catholic taking on his bishop could do nothing but good. I might have agreed with such sentiments on some topics: but the fact that I had used a piece of descriptive abuse unrelated to the specific issue was wrong, and the more I reflected on it in the subsequent months, the more it embarrassed me in its unkindness and stupidity. There is a place for vigorous polemics, even in peace writing: but this particular remark was not in the language of a public peacemaker. I damaged the peace movement with it.

By the time we held our Constitutional Convention in April, I had made up my mind on the date of my demise from leadership as October 1978, and announced that forthwith. That would mean, if my ad hoc chairmanship were confirmed in October 1977, as was reasonably anticipated, that I would guide the organisation through one formal year of its existence and have more than fulfilled the two public years which I could give. Since that would be eighteen months hence, no-one was particularly concerned: that is, until the Norwegian journalist, Gunnar Borrevik, who was present, got a phone call from Norway to tell him that according to Reuters (whose stringer, operating out of the *Sunday News* office, was not even at the conference) I was quitting the Peace People following various controversies with local clergy and pressmen. Gunnar later complained formally to Reuters, noting that he would not have credited such distortions on an international wire agency, if he had not been personally present at the meeting. Since we took distortion for granted, we did not complain.

The Peace People Constitution which I had drafted for presentation to the Convention was simple enough: autonomy was built in for every group; delegates chosen by groups in proportion to their registered membership, would vote at twice-yearly Assemblies, and elect an Executive annually. The form was thus the familiar one of parliamentary democracy, but with a vital difference in emphasis, to make it more democratic: the Executive would be the servant of the groups, not the master, and the Assembly could make recommendations to groups but not command allegiance to policy resolutions. The Assembly could, however, instruct the Executive. It was therefore more truly a form of parliamentary democracy than the party-political parliaments which we have come to accept as 'democracy'. The constitution also took the Declaration of the Peace People as the guiding spirit of the new organisation.

Most of the delegates were rather bemused by things like

'constitutions', but there was a small, highly vocal group determined to change the concept. This group was anxious that we should not be 'political', a motivation which we would see more visibly and determinedly from Alliance Party members in October. They wanted to amend the draft so that each group, regardless of size, would have two delegates, thus castrating its democratic representivity, and exploding my suggestion that it could act as a demonstration model for a possible new Northern Ireland constitution.

I had written the Declaration, planned the rally phase, drafted the policies for the Charitable Trust and Company, launched the newspaper *Peace by Peace*, established our office and effectively taken most of the serious policy decisions, and was also the focus for controversy: I now felt that I should leave it entirely to the delegates to make what they liked of the Draft Constitution I had offered, and did not volunteer for a sub-committee which would take account of proposed amendments.

The Convention was generally one of great friendliness, exuding an encouraging sense of a more mature effort to continue the initial success in a more orderly manner. This also contributed to a general willingness, which I rather shared, to accept all sorts of possible suggestions for progress, however ill-thought.

This proved a fatal weakness when the 'two delegates per group' proposal was casually accepted. Steve McBride, a politics graduate who had returned from post-graduate work in California to join us, was very depressed at the damage done by this amendment. I was so delighted with the progress otherwise made that I urged him not to worry about it. But his forebodings later proved justified, when 'groups' of no more than two, doing virtually nothing, or even undermining our efforts, had the same right to speak and vote as dozens in active groups who were too busy with their own work to spend time marking the Executive members or the movement's leaders.

But in April 1977, I was so delighted that our momentum towards the autumn was secure that I underestimated this decision. It seemed more important, and probably was, to ensure that the Peace People would have been the dominant story in the public consciousness for a year: the momentum of war would not easily recover from that. By then, we would have a formally managed, democratic institution carrying an enduring dynamic for peace, with its roots in the original inspiration.

We had also recently been joined by Max Magee, a former Church of Scotland minister, former missionary in India, a member of the Iona community, an expert in parapsychology and an extremely practical man. He helped considerably to establish order in our progress during this period; and relieved me personally of much petty aggravation over administrative decisions to which there were always going to be objections.

In May, after some media huffing and puffing, the Rev. Ian Paisley began organising another version of the 1974 Ulster Workers' stoppage, saying that he would retire from politics if it was unsuccessful. With paramilitary backing, the Paisley operation started, despite considerable opposition from both middle and working-class Unionists who feared that the Paisley thrust could do nothing but damage to an already ailing economy, as well as revive the level of violence after the dramatic decline over the previous eight months.

I felt certain that Paisley had completely misjudged the temper of the time, and that the effort would collapse. But there was always the danger that if people caved in as before, a momentum might develop, especially if some untoward incident were to arouse tribal passions. So we concentrated resources on organising a system of bread and milk distribution, and also began demonstrating support outside shops for them to stay open in spite of intimidation from those supporting Paisley. We did have to run milk and bread on a few occasions, and got a few knocks during the demonstrations; but Paisley's efforts collapsed before they could really get off the ground.

He claimed early successes in numbers not turning up for work, and that the media were not telling the truth on the figures: whatever the validity of his claim, it was quickly obvious that the government was not about to allow the resources of the BBC to be deployed again in arousing public hysteria, and the momentum of 1974 never had a chance of rolling.

I was asked by the police to cancel a rally at the City Hall, since the police might be stretched in the circumstances. I refused to do so on the grounds that it was vital to make visible what had been absent in 1974, namely popular opposition to the bully-boy tactics of the Paisleyites.

The final straw for Protestant opinion in this time rejecting the Paisleyite strike was a confrontation between the RUC and militant loyalists in East Belfast. This was an extraordinary spectacle, for the people of Northern Ireland were used to seeing the police charging republican crowds: yet here they were operating with unmistakable single-mindedness against loyalists. Had it been the British army thus engaged, Paisley might have been able to arouse indigenous support against the London masters. But the RUC were kith and kin, and rioting with them offended everything respected by the Protestant psyche, and lowered Protestant self-esteem to the level with which their prejudice regarded Catholics. To general relief, the farce collapsed. Ian Paisley did not retire from public life.

We developed another new feature out of the episode—the 'flying squad' groups ready to bring bread and milk, now became regular teams canvassing support and selling papers in various areas. Many a citizen was surprised, especially in out-of-the-way places, to answer a knock on the door to find Mairead Corrigan in sweater and jeans on the step. According to the gossip, she should really have been in the Bahamas, or dining out in fur-coated luxury in Europe's more fashionable resorts—yet here she was on *terra* extremely *firma*.

Mairead was superb at this work, the only drawback, as ever, being her chronic inability to leave the neighbour to whom she was giving her full attention, in order to keep up with the rest of the squad visiting a particular street or area.

The response at the doors, then and always, was mostly friendly: abuse was rare, and outright physical attack confined to a few isolated occasions, with usually more damage to vehicles than heads.

Out of this activity, a youth section got off the ground, a development accelerated by the organisation of youth peace camps in Norway in the summer months.

In another event that spring, we were well beaten by John Hume on the BBC's *You The Jury* programme, which was chaired by Dick Taverne. Mr. Taverne was then in political limbo following his defection from the British Labour Party, and I imagined he was a man who, more than others, would know the difference between parliamentary democracy and the party-political structure. The proposition at the beginning was that the Peace Movement was the best hope for Northern Ireland. I led our case, with Mairead Corrigan and Peter McLachlan as support witnesses; John Hume led the opposition supported by Anne Dickson (Brian Faulkner's successor as leader of the fringe Unionist Party of Northern Ireland) and by John Harbinson, an academic constitutional expert.

I had anticipated a really interesting debate with John Hume, the most formidable intellect in Northern Irish politics: what I was not prepared for was a persistent and ultimately successful effort to paint us as opposed to parliamentary democracy, and as vaguely anarchist or communist. I sat helpless as John seized on Mairead's assertion that the party-political structure was a statement of our divisions, to turn this into an assault on parliamentary democracy: "So you are opposed to the ballot-box, you are opposed to parliamentary democracy," he kept saying to Mairead, who had no experience of this kind of hectoring.

What was more surprising was that he was able to do the same thing to Peter McLachlan, pushing this allegedly anti-parliamentary disposition the whole way to suggest the irony that here was a peace movement on the same side as the terrorists in their assault on the institutions of the state.

When John Harbinson, asked for his opinion on our case, simply said it 'smacked' of the Soviet system, one could feel the audience getting offside. It was just a little bit irritating then, when Dick Taverne, in putting the question at the end, altered the wording to make the choice seem as one between the peace movement or parliamentary democracy.

I knew and accepted that we had been thoroughly outpointed; but felt that it had been by cheap debating tactics unworthy of John— the more so since he knew better than anyone that I had taken an almost lone stand at times in support of his efforts at recreating parliamentary democracy in the early Seventies, when Irish journalism generally was writing the possibility off.

Also that spring, I accepted an invitation to be an associate research fellow of the Norwegian Peace Research Institute. It was understood that I would not be able to produce publishable research work for perhaps two years, but in the event I did not get time to produce any, and we were reduced to doing a taped session on a range of questions, to justify the grant which I received and which helped to keep creditors at bay for another while. But I felt that I had given the Institute poor value, and when some leading Norwegians offered to organise another university function for me, to help me financially, but with little work attached, I refused the offer.

I did, however, accept nomination and election to an international committee, based in Antwerp, charged with co-ordinating the international network of nonviolent organisations, an initiative of Dom Helder Camara, the Brazilian nonviolent archbishop. This election of a six-person team took place at a conference of nonviolent organisations in Derry, and it was here that I first heard of Adolfo Perez Esquivel, the Argentinian nonviolent leader, who was also elected, in his absence. Adolfo, artist, sculptor, and former professor of architecture in Buenos Aires University, had given up his career in 1974 to become Secretary-General of Servicio Paz y Justicia, the Latin American nonviolent network. When he went to get his visa to come to Europe for the conference, he was arrested, and jailed without question, charge or trial by the military junta, then led by Galtieri's predecessor, Jorge Videla. Videla had Mass said in private in his palace each day, while his regime systematically imprisoned, tortured and 'disappeared' people. I followed Adolfo's fortunes or misfortunes over the next year, and when I read the writing to emerge from jail, with its extraordinary tone of forgiveness and pity for his torturers, I was convinced that this was a truly great leader in the nonviolent tradition, keeping the torch lit in a situation of desperate adversity.

Later I persuaded Betty and Mairead to nominate him for the Nobel prize, to draw attention to his plight and to his example. He was finally released to house arrest when it became obvious to the Argentinian authorities that the Norwegian embassy was taking a particular interest in his fate. He received the Nobel prize in 1980, which proved a positive morale boost to the Latin American nonviolent forces. It was a moment of privilege to meet him in person during a short European tour in 1980. He remains little known outside Latin America, in spite of the Nobel prize, and even within the sub-continent, where people, like Dom Helder Camara himself, can be made media 'non-persons', an insidious echo of 'disappearing' people.

With an ad hoc Executive appointed in April to assist us through to the first formal Assembly of the Peace People in October, we felt more free to accept invitations in late May and early June, ending the run-up to the traditional July holidays with a reminder of our international perspective. But this caused more annoyance than before among some who felt that they should decide who should go where and when. We began to hear of the 'need to bring the Big Three under control'. Peter McLachlan, while not obviously the dominant force in this pressure, was its focus, as the man to replace me.

The pressure came to a head while Betty and Mairead were in the United States to receive honorary Doctorates of Law from Yale University, and I was participating in a UNESCO conference on community development in Paris. Peter rang to wish me well the night before I left, asking me, oddly enough, which flight I was taking. I told him the early flight. Thanks to British Airways, I was late into Heathrow for the early Paris connection and had to wait a couple of hours before proceeding to Paris.

I phoned Steve McBride in mid-morning to mention a couple of items for the next edition of the paper and was amazed when Steve asked me "what this emergency meeting of the Executive was all about".

Peter McLachlan had called an 'emergency' meeting whose purpose was 'to discuss what to do about the leaders'. What this really meant in the minds of those pushing it was that Betty and Mairead would be safely elevated into a 'special position' such as 'vice-presidents' or 'ambassadors', and, that done, there would be a straight proposal to replace me with Peter McLachlan. The meeting was inconclusive, the presence of those opposed to the idea inhibiting the others.

We had a normal meeting when the three of us came back, and when the 'emergency' meeting was mentioned, I simply said that there had been no authorised meeting and that therefore it was not part of our agenda. I was actually trying to save faces, but succeeded merely in cementing the charge of dictator. However, when Betty, Mairead and I accepted another invitation to go to the States in order to set up Peace People Incorporated, USA, there was no repeat performance.

Another task remained before we could contemplate a summer break. When the Norwegian money had been awarded, I had arranged for it to be held in a Norwegian bank until we could establish two legal entities which would disburse the funds. We had already agreed that this money would be used for local community projects, some of which would have charitable status, while others might be liable for tax. It would have been misleading, and the money would have been taxable, had it been brought into the country in the personal names of Betty Williams and Mairead Corrigan. There was therefore a delay while we established the Peace People Trust and the Peace People Company, and three months passed while the legal and bureaucratic niceties were completed—three months of endless gossip about 'What have they done with the money?' with all sorts of rumours of fashionable houses, fur coats and big cars. The money was finally received by the Company and lent immediately to the Trust, with the Bank of Ireland acting as custodian trustee, and seven people, including Betty, Mairead and myself installed as directors and trustees respectively.

Only then could we turn to the considerable task of processing the dozens of applications for assistance, the latter often coming from people either opposed to our purpose, or very anxious that our help remain confidential. The desire for secrecy arose from two considerations: fear of attack, or fear of damage to business confidence in an enterprise. Over the next two years, dozens of projects received support, ranging from small amounts to thousands of pounds, for anything from hosting a conference to establishing a small craft co-operative.

Our policy, as far as possible, was to make loans, their return keeping the resource available indefinitely for pump-priming new projects, while the vital self-respect of projects would be better nurtured by loans than by grants. This 'circulating resource' idea was crucial for both practical and psychological reasons: and I hoped that if we could show it working, government might assist the establishment of a co-operative bank using a similar approach to the stimulation of intermediate enterprises. I had already responded to some initial, urgent requests, but the sheer volume of work anticipated in this area dictated the need to make a professional appointment.

Peter McLachlan was unemployed at the time. He had had business, political, community and media experience, and had also, with his wife Jill, fostered young offenders. His record and availability, and apparent sympathy for our wider purpose, persuaded me that we should offer him the job of Projects Manager, and I proposed this to Betty and Mairead.

Betty was stunned and vociferous in her opposition; Mairead was unsure. Betty told me in no uncertain terms that she thought I was mad, that Peter McLachlan had been involved in an effort to get rid of me, and that she believed that he would continue to undermine me if he were actually working in the office. I argued for his qualities, pointing out that petty politicking made no difference, that it would always fall flat on its face when confronted by the three of us; and that if he were with us full-time, he would see that there was too much to be done, that the task was too important, and that there would be no scope or inclination for such machinations. As for getting rid of me, I would be going anyway and he would be more acceptable to many people: by that time, the ethos and principles of the Peace People should be irreversibly established.

The 'two ordinary women' were rather less naïve than me, and were less than enthusiastic about the idea: but they agreed 'if you say so': we put the proposal to the Trust and Company, and Peter McLachlan was appointed full-time Projects Manager, the only full-time salaried executive in the organisation.

We also appointed Max Magee administrator, with appropriate authority, although Max's remuneration was mere minimum subsistence. While I felt that by working for nothing, my independence and authority would be preserved, Max was worried that the relatively large salary paid to Peter McLachlan might confuse the perception of authority, that people might imagine he was 'in charge' for the very reason of his salary. Money was beginning to surface as a factor.

During the summer, Queen Elizabeth paid a Silver Jubilee visit to Northern Ireland. She specifically invited Betty and Mairead to meet her on the Royal Yacht *Britannia*—their names had not been on the government's list of persons worthy of this honour, as I discovered later. The invitation sparked a mini-protest from some Catholic members: but our view that common courtesy, and respect for the disposition of the majority of our neighbours, dictated acceptance, prevailed over objections that it would make life difficult in the Catholic areas.

The Queen went out of her way to spend several minutes with Betty and Mairead, instead of the momentary courtesy handshake extended to most: her first question to Mairead was an enquiry about her sister Anne's health.

Secretary of State Roy Mason had staked a lot on the safety and success of the Queen's visit: and a high price was paid in terms of heavy, alienating action by marines, who were stretched to long hours of duty in different parts of Belfast, and finally exceeded the bounds of discipline in Turf Lodge in house and personal searches.

Ironically, the news of their excesses came to me in the first place from Peter McLachlan, one of whose involvements was the chairmanship of the Queen's Silver Jubilee Committee. Peter had been leaving people to Turf Lodge after a 'Family Week' in Corrymeela, and he had been disturbed at the military action.

We issued a statement of protest: but its only noticeable effect was the interpretation that this was Ciaran McKeown doing a clever balancing act with the attack on troops to be set against Mairead and Betty's acceptance of the Royal invitation.

The Royal exchange made no difference to our relations with government, just as a similar courtesy audience with Pope John Paul II, yielded no movement on the ecclesiastical front on 'just war' theory. Although the Pope came to Ireland two years later and made a passionate plea to 'the men of violence', there was no explicit movement from justification of militarism towards nonviolence; and the Pope's markedly less passionate plea to politicians and on the immorality of bad law, received little attention in the general burst of 'Pope Blasts Provos' coverage.

But while we kept our sights on radical movement, these courtesy visits helped in making nonviolence seem a little less 'alien' and a little more 'respectable'—an important consideration much derided by most radicals, but, I believe, vital in establishing nonviolence as orthodoxy in the survival culture of the future.

The first formal Assembly of the Peace People took place on October 7, 8 and 9 in Belfast's Europa Hotel, and, fifteen months on, the media now gave the event the same kind of coverage as party-political conferences in the same venue. It was a very intense meeting, with one particularly robust debate on our 'political' nature. We succeeded, with some restrictions, in getting majority acceptance of the non-party, political function of a peace movement. It was a considerable advance on the attitude that 'peace has nothing to do with politics which only divide people'; on the other hand, the boast of a leading Alliance Party member that they had succeeded in preventing the Peace People from 'going political' had some justification. This battle was made more difficult by the complete innocence of many of our members of what was afoot, and their ignorance of standing orders procedures which Alliance Party members easily dominated.

It was also accepted, again with reluctance, that each group should be self-financing, except for projects, and should make a contribution towards running a central organisation, if they wanted such an agency: the capital funds were not to be squandered on internal administration. The Peace People were really showing signs of maturity and of shouldering their democratic responsibilities.

The Nobel Prize

I was a very contented man when I arrived in the office the following morning, October 10, to tidy up the aftermath of Assembly paper-work, and to prepare for a year's work which, I was now confident, would establish the Peace People as an enduring, leavening, well-funded, well-constructed, well-earthed and well-known catalytic force, transcending all divisions of party, denomination, age and class, while retaining the dynamism, without the hysteria, of the original impulse.

I began to be interrupted by telephone calls, and the arrival of TV crews. We still had a large number of overseas visitors present, and members of staff were hosting them downstairs. Mairead arrived in for lunch. Betty had gone to London to receive an award at a 'Woman of the Year' luncheon.

The media people began asking about the Nobel Prize: apparently it was due to be announced at 3.00 p.m. that day, and they were speculating that it was coming in some way to the Peace People. I told them that they were wasting their time, that we would surely have known something about it, that we had seen no sign of contact or research by the Nobel Institute. But they persisted, and I even allowed them to set up equipment in my office, as a contingency, laughing all the time that they were wasting their time, and that I hoped they would not be too bored while I got on with my paperwork.

It was minutes before 3.00 when I guessed from the attitude of Norwegian journalists present, who were far from pooh-poohing the media preparations now taking over the house, that the whole idea might be serious.

I went into a small office with Mairead, and said to her that it looked as if the Nobel Prize might be about to be awarded in some way to the Peace People, to the movement as a whole, or to the three of us, or to Betty and herself, or to one or other of them.

Mairead seemed quite upset: she had had to overcome considerable hesitancy to accept the Yale doctorate, feeling that it was daft for someone who had left school at fifteen, and not entirely convinced by my argument that she was doing more for the rule of law than many lawyers. In the interim, she had been influential in persuading fellow-awardee, Dr. Irving Shapiro, head of DuPont Chemicals, to favour Derry for a new process rather than Holland, with the result of a 1600-job, £29 million deal much publicised by Secretary of State Roy Mason. Characteristically, and in keeping with many Norwegians, she was also concerned that I might again be excluded. I told her to put that out of her head, that I was freer to operate if I was not involved and that this award, if they received it, which was the most likely form, would put them into the front line as symbols of nonviolent peacemaking, and that they would have the burden of behaving accordingly, which I would rather do without.

Just after three o'clock we learned via a Press Association flash to the media, who had had some kind of embargoed signal not given to us, that Betty Williams and Mairead Corrigan had been awarded the 1976 Nobel Peace Prize, with the 1977 award going to Amnesty International.

The three of us had a telephone conversation: the prize would be accepted in the name of the Peace People, and of all of the people of Northern Ireland in their desire for peace.

Betty's first response to the only question that seemed to interest most reporters, namely what they were going to do with the estimated £80,000 cash, was that the money would go into the Peace People funds.

Mairead began her television interview by saying that she was deeply honoured, that the prize should have gone to many other people, people like Ciaran McKeown: at this point, she broke down and began to cry. I took it on myself to interrupt the interview—to the annoyance of the media people lapping up the human interest tears—and hurriedly persuaded Mairead to straighten up.

In the next 'take', when she was asked about the money, she joked that her mother had always been worried by the way she gave her money away, that she should have saved a little 'nest-egg'; and turning to all the gossip about the Peace People and fortunes and fur coats, she said that maybe now she would buy that fur coat that everyone talked about. It was a light-hearted response. Much later, her joke would be taken seriously when controversy about the money did us enormous, real damage.

I was delighted at the new opportunities which the prize obviously opened up, but I was also embarrassed. Many people seemed to feel that I must be deeply hurt and disappointed, and that if I was not, I could not be quite human: I almost felt obliged to affect some disappointment! But my only concern was that it endangered the long process of earthing the cult of personality leadership, and might weaken the conviction accepted by our members that very weekend that the Peace People must become self-financing, and not expect annual injections of major finance from Norway and elsewhere. (In addition to the Peace People's Prize, a young Norwegian bank official had initiated a 'limited collection' of coins based on the special ones minted for the Peace People's Prize, and the money from this had been earmarked for our administration.)

I did not worry about gossip: I felt that we could handle with dignified disdain the predictable expression of abuse emerging from the politics of envy.

It did not occur to me for a moment that the Nobel Prize, or any other external event, could cause a rift between myself and Betty and Mairead. But I had been getting rather out of touch with Betty. She had not developed any real stamina for meetings, or regular work; she took an occasional dash at correspondence, stayed for parts of meetings, and rarely contributed to such events—her silence at the Assembly had been noticeable. I had had no qualms about this: her forte was to arouse people in a charged address now and again, and I saw little need for her to bore herself to death by attending meetings in which she might merely lose her temper and alienate someone; one such outburst had already precipitated the resignation of Margaret Watson.

But I should have realised that we were drifting apart, when the preparations for the Nobel ceremony began. The Nobel Institute required that two speeches be made, one a short 'thank-you', immediately after the award ceremony, the other, the following day, being the Nobel Lecture, to last forty minutes. The Institute wanted the longer address in advance, so that it could be translated and printed. We agreed that Mairead would make the thank-you speech, preferably in Norwegian, and that Betty would deliver the address.

As the deadline approached, we still had not met, as suggested, to discuss what might go into it. Finally, with a few days to go, I wrote the lecture, and arranged to bring copies to Betty's house, where she and Mairead and I could go over it. I was taken aback when Betty took the draft from me very angrily, and said, "I thought the three of us were going to write this!"

I told her that the deadline was imminent, that I also had a *Peace by Peace* deadline to meet, that this was my draft, and that she could use it or put it in the fire if she wanted to. Her attitude changed totally when she had read it, and was moved to tears. Later, she practised delivering it as she had never practised anything before. She was delighted with its reception in Oslo, and to be told that it was the best Nobel peace lecture in living memory.

We had been determined never to have 'prepared scripts', but felt that the advance printing of the Nobel lecture justified this exception. This may have explained Betty's initial anger at my having written it; but I think it was rather more that, as we saw less and less of each other, she became more vulnerable to those who told her that she was the 'real' leader of the Peace People, and that she should not let Ciaran McKeown manipulate her.

So long as we were together, I never regarded either my direction of the Peace People or the support and encouragement I gave to Betty and Mairead as 'manipulation'. But I was conscious that Betty and Mairead were now, for the rest of their lives, on a world stage, with the Nobel medal around their necks, identified with the whole cause of nonviolence, with a rhetoric they had really only absorbed since the relationship with me. This influenced my decision not to go to Oslo.

The December 10 Nobel ceremony proceeded with warmth and dignity, and was followed by a successful tour of Norway, before the two newly invested Nobelists came home to a welcome rally from the Peace People at Belfast's City Hall. They were studiously ignored by the City Council, with the exception of a hurriedly organised congratulatory statement extracted from the Mayor's office by an Alliance member. With wry courtesy, we conveyed to Belfast's Lord Mayor an invitation to visit Norway as the guest of the Mayor of Kristiansand.

The sour domestic response to this unique honour was probably a good thing, ill-mannered though it seemed. It was a reminder that the people of Northern Ireland could not be embarrassed or flattered into a new relationship; and it inhibited any renewed outbreak of mass movement hysteria. Still, it was a little hard to stomach the expressions of mean-mindedness that abounded: I felt that it should have been clear to any reasonable person after sixteen months of unremitting effort, that we were serious in our commitment, and that we had genuinely put all major incoming resources, after acquiring and equipping our headquarters, at the disposal of a wide group of people, including some hostile to our purpose. The persistent rumours and gossip about 'big cars, fur coats, thirty-four-room mansions' were downright distasteful.

All of which made the shock I received a few days later the most devastating to date. As I was finishing the pre-Christmas edition of *Peace by Peace*, I thought I should lay the rumours to rest, and reassure our overseas friends—for the most extraordinary versions of 'what are you going to do with the money?' had gone out internationally, even through the 'quality' papers—by putting the definitive statement into our own newspaper. This would have been that the bulk of the money, between £60,000 and £65,000, would be placed in the Charitable Trust, earmarked for specific projects, including a 'Third World' programme for our groups and the movement as a whole, while the rest would cover three salaries for one year; it would also cover the additional expenditure involved in the Nobel trip for relatives not covered by the Institute's arrangements. This broad arrangement, which meant that all of the money would in some way have been at the disposal of the Peace People, had been agreed by the three of us, communicated to the Executive and then, to their great relief and encouragement, to the representatives of our groups at the December Consultative Board meeting in Newry. It would enable them, as well as our office and Executive spokespeople, to give a firm and reasonable answer on the phone and on the doorsteps when canvassing and paper-selling, and confronted with the inevitable 'what did they do with the money?'

So I arranged to meet Mairead and Betty at Betty's house to agree the exact wording of this definitive statement. As I began to outline it, Betty said: "I've changed my mind: I have a wee project of my own which I want to back with my half."

She was half across the room with a cup of coffee for me as she said that, and by the time I had taken the cup and said, "What? What do you mean, Betty? What project?", she was on her way back into the kitchen to get her own cup. After sixteen months, I knew every variation of tone in Betty's voice, and I knew that the entire arrangement was off, and that her mind was irrevocably made up to dispose of her half of the Nobel Prize in whatever way she saw fit. She was entitled to do this: but it would have been helpful to have made this clear from the start—she was scarcely entitled to have the rest of us misleading people that the resource would be deployed by the Peace People as a whole as agreed. What hit me most forcibly was the prospect for our members knocking doors, selling papers, and getting the 'what's it for, another fur coat'? response.

Mairead was a picture of consternation: "What do you mean, Betty, what are you talking about?" Even before the row erupted, I made a lightning decision that the only way to protect the Peace People from the effects of Betty's decision was to separate the entire Nobel dimension from our basic work: "Look, you two are going to be Nobelists for the rest of your lives, you are going to be invited here, there and everywhere, and the Peace People will not be able to support you in that. The best thing would be for you to invest the money, it will yield a small annual return, enough to cover your special expenses to fulfill your Nobel obligations. Now I have to go back to work on the paper. Goodnight."

"Wait a minute, Ciaran, this is all wrong," Mairead began, having sat open-mouthed with shock, as this development sank in. "Betty, just what are you talking about? When did we ever start thinking about my 'half' and your 'half'?" They started to argue. I stayed for several minutes while they had a heated argument, then left.

There have been rumours for years about that Nobel Prize money. There have also been stories in the media, as well as statements made to our groups, that Betty had wanted to put the money into the funds, but that she had gone along with a decision made by the Executive to hold on to the money. None of these stories, statements or rumours is true. The decision to keep half the Nobel money was made in the first instance by Betty. That is the plain truth. It would have been a happier, more chivalrous approach in this chronicle to have ignored the matter completely: but that would have been a silent corroboration of the contrary versions of what did happen.

That was not the end of the matter. Next morning, I consulted with Max Magee. My main concern was that Mairead would feel humiliated by appearing to keep the money, whereas if she did not, Betty would be publicly isolated. Max thought that the idea of investing the resource was the best way out of the mess, especially since it would assist Betty to ease her way out of an organisation in which, apart from international representation, she was already playing little more than an occasional, symbolic part.

Mairead was still deeply upset when she came in, and she and Max and I discussed the matter to try and find both the best solution and the best way of presenting what was bound, in some measure, to damage the Peace People. Mairead's inclination was to proceed to put her half in as agreed, and that would relieve the Peace People budget of two salaries, and still leave a substantial amount for projects; and that Betty could fend for herself.

I insisted that I would not take any salary from either the Nobel resource or any other Peace People fund. I suggested that since our members were settling down to real work, a nasty split story over the Nobel money could be crippling for morale, and that maybe if Betty used the near £40,000 to arrange her life to her taste, she might then return to work. Both Max and I felt that if she, Mairead, could stomach the humiliation of appearing to have 'kept the money', then that would be the quietest, least damaging way out of a horrible situation.

Finally, Mairead said, "All right, I'll do it if you two think it is right: but I don't feel it's right, and it never will feel right". I think Mairead was right in her initial reaction: it would have been healthier and cleaner all round to break with Betty then, and better for Betty as well. The consequences were all the more painful for being dragged out over another two years. The big car and the fur coats were no longer a joke.

Our credibility was irreversibly damaged, at home and abroad. The Executive issued a statement 'endorsing' the decision that the Nobel prizewinners would be investing the resource to help finance the responsibilities imposed by the award, and simultaneously thanked them for the large sums hitherto given to them, which they had made available to the funds. This 'endorsement' has sometimes been interpreted in public reports as suggesting that Betty was merely carrying out an Executive 'decision' that she keep the money. That is a misinterpretation. I drafted the endorsement statement and had the distasteful duty of asking the Executive to support it: the Peace People had no say whatever in Betty's decision.

Although it would have been hard to imagine a worse body blow, I remained convinced that so long as we persisted with our work, its truth and justice must inevitably encourage the nonviolent reconciliation we sought. But it was now more vital than ever that progress be relieved of the counter-productive effect of 'personality' leadership.

Shortly after the Nobel crisis, I suggested to Betty and Mairead that neither should stand for re-election in October 1978, and that all three of us retire simultaneously from the Executive. After discussion over several days, both agreed. When this was announced to the 1978 Spring Assembly in Ballymena, Peter McLachlan welcomed the proposal; but many others thought that Betty and Mairead, or at least one of them, should stay on.

A visitor from County Carlow in Southern Ireland, Mrs. Christabel Bielenberg, attempted to have a resolution put to the Assembly to that effect. I pointed out that we were entitled to make personal decisions on whether to stand or not, but that she, as a visitor, did not have the right to seek to make Assembly policy. She described my opposition as 'dictation'; and it was not the last time either that Mrs. Bielenberg would seek to determine the direction of the Peace People, or to classify my opposition to her as 'dictatorship'.

Israeli Interlude

A most memorable occasion for me was to be in Jerusalem in November when Anwar Sadat made his historic visit to that city and to the Knesset. I had been attending a week-long symposium in Tel Aviv, organised by the Israeli liberal intellectual group, *New Outlook*, on the theme 'Can the Guns Fall Silent?'

I include this short report, not merely out of personal interest, but to indicate something of the parallels in all conflicts, and specifically a direct parallel between the Irish conflict and that more globally significant struggle in the Middle East. I must acknowledge that the immediacy of my interest in such matters was not always shared by fellow members of the Peace People, as indeed it may not now be by some readers.

The conference itself was an unprecedented affair, including for the first time in Israel, Arab leaders, diplomats and academics from neighbouring adversary countries. This was such a breakthrough that it was both front and feature-page news daily. There was speculation about a Sadat visit, but few there dared to believe it. As an outsider to the passions of the region, I was convinced that he was coming, for the series of tips and leaks in the international press seemed utterly confirmed when Sadat himself had made the extraordinarily explicit statement that "I would go anywhere in the world, even the Knesset, for peace". The *even the Knesset* phrase could hardly be interpreted as other than advance notice of the visit.

But unwilling to believe in such a possibility, most keynote speakers were concerned with the possible structures of a strategically organised, militarily maintained peace. My function was rather to address the psycho-political aspects of the conflict, to explore what effort might be made in the direction of cultural accommodation, to ensure a lasting peace that need not be fortressed. My main line of argument was that so long as the peoples of a region could not visit each other, socially, culturally, professionally, or even as tourists, because of the strict passport regulations, then armed prejudice must persist, and there could not be peace. It was the need to break through these cultural barriers, more than physical barriers, that would be served by a Sadat visit, which I confidently predicted would occur.

But I went on to warn that if such a psycho-political initiative were taken, it could be murderously counter-productive if not followed up by the most intensive ground programme of mutual visits at every level of society: for time would be given for the most vulnerable— the Palestinians and the Jewish Settlers—to arm their fear of sell-out, just as a comparable breakthrough in Ireland in 1965, between the Northern and Southern Irish Premiers, euphorically received at the time, had heightened irrational fears and expectations, without any capacity being developed to assuage either. The result had been counter-productive within a very short period.

This approach was most warmly received, and a little 'conference within the conference' was held to discuss further how such a lateral peace movement might be started. Then news came through, that afternoon, that Sadat was indeed coming, that very Saturday, and the entire symposium was gripped with delusory euphoria about a possible deal on the West Bank for the Palestinians.

To sit among Israelis as Sadat spoke was an extraordinary experience. People wept with joy, and their eyes spoke admiration for the Egyptian leader's statesmanship. Within an hour, the ecstasy had turned to numb depression, with Menachem Begin's response. The lack of depth in his reply, and the hucksterish strutting at the podium embarrassed Israelis as much in its style as its content: by all that was holy for the Chosen People—even those who imagined themselves free from tribal prejudice—an Israeli leader should always be able to out-do an Egyptian at anything, as surely as Israeli militarism has been the most clinical in the world of our time.

One young Israeli lecturer said to me, "There's no hope—Begin's a land-grabber, he doesn't understand what Sadat is saying." Having earlier tried to restrain feverish speculation on an actual land deal over the West Bank, I now found myself trying to cheer Israelis up, to get them to look at the positive aspect of the breakthrough and to stir themselves to organise a peace movement no matter what Begin did or did not do.

Several different peace initiatives of the populist kind did emerge that winter, and received some attention. Then the work at governmental level took off with President Jimmy Carter's Camp David efforts. Later, the two Middle East leaders were awarded the Nobel peace prize; but by the time they were due to receive it, of course, Sadat declined because of Begin's handling of the Camp David accords.

Then Sadat was assassinated in late 1981; and Begin, at the time of writing, has resigned, having had to deal with the consequences for Israeli honour, credibility and security of his 'Peace in Galilee' operation in Lebanon, which included the Chatili massacre, and had all the hallmarks of attempted genocide of the Palestinian people. The latter's shaky hopes for a West Bank home he further scattered by wanton encouragement of new Jewish settlements.

I have watched all this with a painful sense of sympathy with both the Jews and the Palestinians. Theirs is fundamentally a local Semitic squabble made global by their strategic position, their place in our cultural consciousness, and the grotesque callousness with which the superpowers arm the adversaries.

Another aspect of external fomentation was neatly described by an American Jew with whom I was discussing our mutual ethnic problem of the Irish-Americans and American Jews: "Yeah, American Jews will fight to the last drop of Israeli blood!"

Members of the Israeli peace movement have the agony of not wishing to appear unpatriotic while their kinsfolk are in battle, but at the same time are unable to contain their sense of shame and anguish at the horrors of the Begin initiative, itself so redolent of that great shadow on the Israeli soul, the Holocaust. Israelis have a terrible choice: to react to the Holocaust with unshakeable belief in the criminality of war and attempted genocide, or to use it as the elastic justification for any action that will finally provide an earthly promised land for them.

When the violence is as contained as it ever can be in that uneasy part of the world, and a vulnerable, militarily maintained 'peace' is established, the truth will remain that there will not be peace in the Middle East—or anywhere else—until the peoples of a region, who do not know each other, who fear the unknown in each other, who regard the other as less human, have overcome these springs of prejudice, and begin to find a positive expression of their common humanity.

The world is endangered by the Middle East peoples: but the world has taken much, the very basis of a global civilisation, from the common heritage of the Semitic peoples. I dare to hope that they will give us, eventually, another great example.

Persisting

Five fascinating days in Israel provided a sunlit contrast to a menace on Northern Ireland's winter horizon of 1977-8. The 'blanket' protest by prisoners in the H-Block cells of Long Kesh—H.M. Prison The Maze—was now developing apace, though public figures were doing their best to ignore it. Roy Mason appeared to be becoming as intransigent as the Provos. There was disturbing evidence that the police were involved in heavy beatings and other forms of pressure to extract the confessions sufficient to secure convictions in the no-jury courts.

Seeing these developments as the greatest potential blocks to progress, I drafted a booklet for submission to Westminster on the counter-productive nature of this legislation, appealing for a return to normal judicial process, and raised the topic at the Spring 1978 Peace People Assembly at which the 'trio' withdrawal was announced.

When frightened people demand security, and politicians offer it, they need to be very sure that what is provided actually increases security, rather than reducing it. They might also like to consider whether the form of the security is *just*. Some might even like to think about whether it is moral. The violent history of Northern Ireland makes one clear statement: the use of special powers, of internment, of outright terror tactics, do not bring security but reduce it; they are not just; they are downright immoral, not only in their murderousness, but in their insidiously degrading effect on the entire population. People eventually, and even quickly, take for granted a way of life which is less than that of the free people they imagine themselves to be: they begin to live a lie.

When the British acted heavily, as in the 1970 curfew, they accelerated recruitment to the IRA. When Brian Faulkner introduced internment, young people flooded into the terror outfits. When Rees and Cooper began to undo internment, violence eased. When Roy Mason, and later Margaret Thatcher, began to pose as tough, they ensured a like response. The key factor in all of this is the perception of wide sections of people of what is reasonable or just—and effective. The tragedy is that contemporary governments take short-term views, respond to short-fuse emotions, implement emergency measures— and hope that the long-term dangers will not materialise. Our history demonstrates quite scientifically that the use of 'temporary' measures can and does make the very violence they seek to meet, endemic; and by being less rooted in the original passions, ever more nihilistic, as the very value of life, and all the decencies which flow from it, are diminished. The society not only becomes demoralised—it becomes *de-moralised.*

I had difficulty in believing for a long time that the Northern Ireland Office under Roy Mason was seriously set on an outright victory over the Provisional IRA, to be gained by tough measures. Given the build-up of a wide structure of political intelligence in the Whitelaw-Rees period, I imagined that the government could read all the signals that community support for violence was dropping, and that the situation was ripe for reconciliation towards a just peace, and that they should avoid deploying the apparatus of alienation, and begin to dismantle it.

Gradually I learned that Mason had reduced the breadth of advice to his office; and when both he and the then Chief Constable (now Sir) Kenneth Newman casually characterised those expressing anxiety about police methods in obtaining confessions as either falling for or assisting terrorist propaganda, I finally accepted that they were a double disaster, and that the sooner both went home the better.

Even then, as I listened to Mason unwittingly harden the resolve of Republicans by reiterating that there 'would be no amnesty for these criminal terrorists', I presumed that he must be implementing a short-term policy to end with the appointment of a new Secretary of State. A state of creative peace would have to include undoing all the consequences of emergency, not transform them into a permanent cause. What I found both dangerous and galling was his phrase that these 'criminals' had been convicted by 'due process of the law'. If the 'Temporary' Emergency Provisions Act was going to be accepted as 'due process'—rather than a profoundly unsatisfactory deviation from due process to meet a short-term emergency—then we were in for long-term trouble.

The argument I articulated for acceptance by the Peace People was that we could neither accept the IRA's demand for 'political status' for prisoners, since that would be to give violence a political quality, nor the government's position that the convictions were the result of 'due process'. I therefore advocated that those arrested, held, questioned, tried and convicted under emergency law, and committed to the emergency prisons for activities arising out of the constitutional emergency, should have 'emergency status', to be reviewed when the emergency was over.

In the meantime, we would advocate that a process towards ending the emergency begin, and that the places to start were on the emergency law itself, and police behaviour under it. We pointed to the fact that some 80 per cent of the convictions were through confessions gained during interrogation without access to legal advice. We noted that two-thirds of those in prison were under fifteen years of age when the emergency began, one-third under the age of nine. We emphasised the cyclical nature of the violence, and the place of alienating official action in that cycle.

I appealed to the Peace People to recognise that this was one of those difficult problems which was itself a source of conflict and violence in our society. We had to accept that no established institution in the society would risk tackling it with sufficient conviction, and that it could not be left to prisoners in isolation to tackle it, for their response would merely be more violence, through their alienated families and friends. We had to create some room for the government to act, and the British authorities were not particularly vulnerable to the votes of the Northern Irish. (Unfortunately at that time, the Callaghan government was indeed dependent on Unionist MPs' votes, and often counted also on Gerry Fitt's vote for survival.)

By a large majority, the Peace People accepted this approach: but they did so with great unease, and a substantial minority opposed this approach, with some even adopting a 'let them rot' attitude towards the prisoners. Since the majority approach to peacemaking was mainly identified with me personally, many, even among those reluctantly supporting the policy, were looking forward to my early demise as leader. Peter McLachlan was on record as supporting this policy, and never demurred from it: but people sensed that it would not be a burning priority with him, whereas for me, it was the very touchstone of our seriousness as a peace movement seeking to work at the heart of the conflict.

With 'Betty, Mairead and Ciaran' leaving in the autumn, and Peter McLachlan taking over, it was important to ensure that the policies and programme and character of the Peace People be firmly established before we withdrew. The acceptance of the prison and emergency laws issues on our agenda represented substantial progress in that direction, as well as a degree of recovery from the embarrassment of the Nobel affair. Nevertheless, with Peter McLachlan perceived as 'soft' on the tougher issues, and with people much happier to listen to his glowing reports of how we were disbursing our funds through the Trust and Company, there was perhaps a deeper hope than I suspected that when McKeown left, perhaps the H-Block issue would leave with him, and the Peace People could settle down to giving out money.

Mairead made an exceptionally successful trip to the United States that Spring, when she addressed Senators and Congress members, and later met the leading figures in such large American foundations as the Rockefeller Brothers Fund, the Ford Foundation and the Public Welfare Foundation. When she came back, we discussed the development with Max, our main concern being that yet more money presented us with the challenge of establishing a more professional organisation.

William McGeorge Bundy, former adviser to the late President Kennedy, and then President of the Ford Foundation, had already authorised the forwarding of 25,000 dollars under his immediate disposal, and arranged that a senior executive of the Foundation would come to Belfast to assess our resources and purpose. The Ford report would give guidelines to all the other foundations on our aid-worthiness.

Mairead said that one aspect which concerned them was that I, as the apparent driving force at the centre of the operation, was a married man with a large family and no income, and that their confidence in the survival of the initiative depended considerably on my continuance, with a salary to enable me to do so.

The Ford assessment proved very positive, and we used two opportunities in the early summer to go to the States to follow up this development. Betty and Mairead had been invited to a 'Decade of Women' function at the United Nations in May, and I had been invited to address the United Nations in June, at the Special Session of the General Assembly on Disarmament. Mairead and I had very fruitful meetings with the various foundations, to whom we presented a budgeted programme, and the representations produced over 100,000 dollars over the next couple of years. I agreed to accept a salary from the Ford resource, at a rate of just over half what my journalistic income would have been. It was a decision I later regretted deeply, and finally gave up accepting a salary, and resumed working for nothing until the end of my period of responsibility. But in the summer of 1978, it seemed a logical way of being able to continue to provide drive and direction as the organisation expanded.

The International Fellowship of Reconciliation (IFOR) was one of over twenty Non-Governmental Organisations (NGOs) invited for the first time to address the General Assembly of the United Nations, and the Special 1978 Session on Disarmament. The NGOs were greatly encouraged at this gesture of recognition, which gave them something of the status enjoyed by accredited national missions to the UN for that short period. Jim Forrest, the energetic Director of IFOR, had thought it would be a good idea if I would write the IFOR address, as the author of the Nobel lecture and other things which had attracted some attention in the international peace movement; and that Betty or Mairead might deliver it. I told Jim that the Nobel lecture was the only time we had done the 'prepared script trick', and that I would not do it again. IFOR then decided to ask me to address the UN myself.

I hoped that this unusual honour might encourage people in Northern Ireland to share my sense of privilege as the first and only Ulsterman ever to address the United Nations General Asembly. But I might as well as have been on a free junket to Acapulco for all the interest it aroused: come to think of it, a junket to Acapulco would have attracted more attention at home!

The address was well received at and around the United Nations. Its appeal was partly in its passionate rhetoric in favour of nonviolence; but mainly, I think, especially among professional diplomats, for its scepticism. I argued that if we applied the mathematics of probability which physicists used in developing the weapons which now threatened all life on earth, then we would have to accept that the probability of disarmament tended to zero. I went on to say that it was practically impossible for the larger powers to disarm, for they were locked into a poker game of power politics based on armament, their economies almost inextricably interwoven with the arms industry; and that 'To expect that governments can create a disarmed world is like expecting elephants to cultivate a garden'.

The governmental missions appreciated this unusual realism from a non-governmental speaker: and indeed, the main thrust of my approach was that the peace movement should stop wasting energy in appeals to government, and concentrate its resources on expanding the community of the personally disarmed throughout the world, to create the lateral consensus and leavening power which alone might enable the governments to escape the doom made inevitable by the arms race.

While it attracted favourable attention among serious professionals, the address was not uniformly supported in the international peace movement, or even within all the sections of IFOR. Some felt that its very scepticism was devastatingly depressing to those working for disarmament, and that I should have concentrated on urging specific measures of arms reduction. My view, then, as now, is that everyone concerned knows all the possible options for limiting, reducing or eliminating conventional or total-destruction weaponry: what is missing, and what has to be created, is the consensus of disarmed persons, a process to be developed by dedicated individuals creating disarmed communities, disarming the smaller nations and thus encouraging the citizens of the larger powers in an inevitably long and risky process of demilitarisation and disarmament. I may put this view into an intelligible perspective by this observation: if a small, non-strategic power like Ireland cannot disarm, then there is no hope whatever for world disarmament. The effect of this attitude for peace workers is plain: it would be better to work for the exemplary demilitarisation of Ireland, than to join in campaigns for nuclear disarmament elsewhere.

It is also a view which casts doubt on the value of such initiatives as CND: it is easy enough to arouse millions of people to the fear of being melted, and to create a weak, shivering consciousness of the horrific unthinkability of nuclear war. But it is more immediately difficult and *necessary* to get people to accept that they will not have any form of armed protection, and to withdraw their consent from such: nothing less will disarm the world and save it from the Gadarene rush to race suicide.

Among those to congratulate me on the address was the British Ambassador to the United Nations, Dr. Ivor Richard, now European Commissioner. Availing of the goodwill in his hearty felicitations, I suggested to him that he might ask the British Prime Minister, James Callaghan, to call off, or at least postpone, the government's arms sales fair to begin in England that very weekend. He seemed puzzled, so I explained my feeling that the sensible proposals his mission was making to the Special Session would be compromised by the simultaneous mounting of a major arms fair, aimed aggressively at the smaller, sub-nuclear powers. He still appeared to be taken aback: I suppose he did not anticipate such an instant response to his friendly remarks; but I felt justified in eschewing a more normal diffidence in the circumstance, for it seemed to me to be the crudest hypocrisy to be making disarmament proposals at the UN while focussing much greater resources on the blood trade.

As he continued to respond with diplomatic vagueness, I suggested that at least the arms sellers might stop featuring the 'cluster bomb' a particularly nasty conventional bomb capable of burning down or blasting a city's heart by scattering a large number of smaller bombs from the first blast. Ambassador Richard seized on this to exclaim that it was an American weapon, nothing to do with Britain: I said that I understood it was being made in Huntingdon in England. He said, "Well, good-day," and walked off.

Mairead had stayed in the States for a speaking tour just before this, and we met at the home of Sally and Guy Leonard, in Bronxville, near New Rochelle, New York. Sally was treasurer at the College of New Rochelle, whose principal, Sister Dorothy Ann Kelly, was President of Peace People Inc., USA, and who, along with the College

Chaplain, Fr. Sean Cooney and the Leonards, had been extremely kind and helpful to us ever since Mairead had received an honorary doctorate from the College. The two of us had hoped to meet with Ambassador Andy Young (now Mayor of Atlanta, Georgia), President Carter's close advisor, whom Mairead had already met, and with whom I had had a few words in the UN Assembly Chamber. Along with Jim Forrest, we hoped to enlist the help of the American Mission—which included the movie star Paul Newman—to lobby the Argentinians on behalf of Adolfo Perez Esquivel, as well as to persuade various western powers to stop selling arms to Argentina while the military junta went on 'disappearing' people, and generally disregarding the most basic of human rights.

My exchange with the British ambassador—which also caused me to watch the entire Falklands affair with derision—had already discouraged me about the value of such lobbying at the time. So I was not unduly disappointed when President Carter summoned Andy Young, Paul Newman and company to Washington for consultations. We had instead a very interesting meeting with some of Young's staff, veterans of both Martin Luther King's campaign and the anti-Vietnam war struggle. One interesting observation of these tough veterans of nonviolence, then close to the heart of American power, was their assessment of Jimmy Carter's plight.

Carter, a born peacemaker it seemed, and dedicated advocate of human rights, was trapped in the power politics of the arms trade. He had been under relentless pressure from the Pentagon and the arms industry to develop and produce the neutron bomb, a relatively minor weapon which, however, in its ability to kill living things and leave property intact, had become the symbol of all that is evil about the arms race, and had been nicknamed the 'capitalist bomb'. It also encouraged the lunatic idea of 'limited nuclear warfare'.

Carter, while trying to encourage the Russians without appearing weak, had authorised the development of the delivery system only, not the warhead, and called on the Russians to reciprocate, which they did not do. Carter was hammered by the 'peace movement'—a loose network of disarmament groups, nonviolent communities and libertarian human rights groups—for authorising the delivery system, and hammered by the military/industrial/financial lobby for not authorising the warhead development. He was being squeezed from both sides, a process which continued through the Iranian hostage crisis and finally put him out of office.

Those few days in New York, while socially most enjoyable, were depressing in their illumination of the extent of the problems that the human race faces for mere survival. But the net effect was to deepen determination to make our domestic effort an exemplar in tackling seemingly intractable problems differing only in scale from those exercising the best minds and spirits in the United Nations.

One other event occurred while we were in New York which had a direct bearing on our domestic future. Sally Leonard was receiving regular enquiries from Mr. Carleton Sedgeley, whose agency organises speaking tours in the United States, for celebrities. We told Sally that commercial tours were not really our 'scene', and that we had already ignored an approach from the Royce Carlton Agency. Sally asked us to tell Mr. Sedgeley this directly, so Mairead and I met him in the United Nations Plaza Hotel, close to his offices.

Mr. Sedgeley appreciated our disposition, but pointed to a list of distinguished Europeans and others who were his clients, and argued that we would be enabled to get our message across to wide civic and campus audiences, and the media, as well as earning finance for our work. He offered 2,000 dollars a lecture for Betty and Mairead, and 1,500 dollars a lecture for me. We told him that we would discuss it at home, and decide one way or the other, and that that would be final.

We did discuss it with Max Magee, for its implications went even further than the American foundation resource which was largely non-renewable, whereas this might enable the Peace People to sustain a staff structure of considerable strength for the forseeable future, at a level which would not have our members spending most of their resources fund-raising. Moreover the Sedgeley operation would be no great strain: the basic structure of the programme was a forty-five minute speech at most, followed by question and answer sessions. The same speech, whose précis would be known in advance, and could be used in the promotion, would also make media handout material an easier proposition.

We decided that I would go for ten days in February 1979, assess the demands, the kind of speech and questions and answers that would arise; then Mairead would go in March and Betty in April, each for ten-day speaking tours, with a weekend off in the middle, so that we did not suffer the extremes of exhaustion which we had endured before. We estimated that this relatively minor outlay of time and energy would bring at least 40,000 dollars into Peace People funds each year, and would make good use of the 'personality' factor without stifling the domestic growth of the movement.

By Christmas 1978 it was obvious that I would have far too much to do to give up the necessary fortnight in February, when Peter McLachlan would also be in Salzburg for three weeks. Moreover,

Mairead had received and accepted a number of invitations from leading American politicians such as Speaker 'Tip' O'Neill, to be in Washington and New York around St. Patrick's Day. So I rang Mr. Sedgeley to suggest that Betty go first. He was relieved, for I was not so easy to promote as the Nobel prizewinners, and I told him to liaise thereafter with Max Magee. Max was at this time considering leaving, to take up the position of Principal of the College of Psychical Research in London. He gave the details on the Sedgeley agency to Betty, and that was the end of the connection as far as the Peace People were concerned.

Betty arranged with Mr. Sedgeley to do a five-week tour in February and March, and before returning, made preliminary arrangements for another such trip in October. Before she went on the first occasion, I suggested that she might like to spend some time being briefed on what was going on: she told me that when she wanted my help, she would ask for it. Apart from the loss of anticipated funds for the Peace People, it was worrying that Betty was going all over the United States, not really in touch with what the Peace People were about, and quite unqualified to speak on wider issues. All we could do was hope that she would confine herself to simple lines of rhetoric as in the early Peace People days: we were ready, if necessary, to dissociate the Peace People from any gross misrepresentations which might arise, but were reluctant to do so in advance.

To the extent that we heard reports of her tours, she did indeed appear to stick closely to what she knew; and while the level of interviews given to the media were of the sentimental magazine variety of much of the early days, and far removed from currently more specific positions, they were not damaging. The only gross mistake was to misrepresent 'emergency status' as 'special category status', but that was not until 1980; by which time, it hardly mattered.

Mairead, incidentally, often receives considerable honorariums for her speeches and appearances abroad, and places these at the disposal of the Peace People.

The Peace People were now two years old, well esablished and getting deeper into the real issues of the conflict, and with a better understanding of nonviolent peacemaking. The very word 'nonviolence' became common currency. We had good contacts at the centre of American power and finance, and in Europe, as well as strong connections with the international peace movement. If we kept our heads, it could only go on getting better, and we might be able to prevent a prison crisis before it happened, in a more explicit way than we had helped to prevent the 'final crunch' whose non-happening was scarcely noticed. Rhetoric notwithstanding, the dynamics of much peacemaking are actually silent and invisible—the news that doesn't happen.

It was with relish that I embarked on another project, a pilot experiment for the 'Achill University of Peace'. I had gained so much from our previous holidays in Achill, that I thought it would be a perfect place for people whose work through the year involves so much strain, to relax, and genuinely to 're-create'. The idea was that people involved at the thick end of our work, and others in the community development field, who rarely got more than occasional weekend conferences to sort out their thoughts and feelings, would spend three unpressured weeks in this island of wild beauty, and gentle, sturdy people. The only 'university discipline' would be three-hour sessions each morning of the weekdays, and any other session that the participants felt moved to call. Thereafter they were utterly free to swim, fish, walk, climb, enjoy the singing pubs—or paint, for this is a favourite spot for budding painters. They should go back to their work deeply refreshed, and with the sense that however strained things might become, say in Belfast, Achill was always there to return to, to be refreshed once more.

Calling it a 'university' was not a piece of gratuitous pomposity. I had been struck by the damage done to otherwise enlightened and effective people by their sense of inferiority over not having had much formal education, and their immunity to persuasion that contemporary universities are not the crucibles of intellectual development and enlightenment that they imagined.

They had a real point in observing that I could afford to say that, having had a university education. I therefore hoped that the mutual exploration of ideas over an extended period in such a circumstance would convince such people that their grasp of ideas was as sure as mine, and that they might therefore develop a deeper confidence in themselves, instead of feeling that ideas were 'over their heads'.

We did have a reasonably successful pilot run, though the 1979 session fell through because of internal difficulties in Belfast compounded by post and petrol strikes in the South of Ireland; and we held another session in 1980. The structure exists to take the idea further, when other circumstances permit.

Internal Crisis

Betty, Mairead and I withdrew from the Executive in October 1978, and the new Executive elected Peter McLachlan as chairman. My relations with him had begun to be somewhat strained, over the conduct of the Company and Trust, of which I was still chairman. We had approved the financing of project after project, but it was worrying that few of the recipients were meeting the terms of the standard letter of contract which we had agreed, by which they would begin repayments, so that the fund would remain a renewable resource for others in the future.

This was an absolutely vital element of the strategy from the start, for we wanted to insist, as an aspect of the ethos of nonviolence, on the politics of self-respect. We gave grants occasionally, where appropriate, but preferred the loan system, so that those developing new enterprises would feel confident that they really were responsible for their own initiatives.

But by the summer of 1978, the bulk of our resources had flowed out, with little more than a derisible trickle coming back. I proposed that we freeze on further outgoings and that the Project Manager concentrate on getting the return flow moving, which was agreed by the trustees and directors. But when this was reported to a wider meeting, including Executive members, Peter McLachlan suddenly left as if hurt. I was then upbraided for 'criticising' his conduct of his job, which I had not done in any explicit way: in fact, I had praised his energy in processing projects for approval by the two boards. But I began to be seen as making his life difficult, and after he was elected chairman of the Executive in October, people became understandably confused between the authority of that function, and his lack of authority as the paid officer of the Company, as Projects Manager. The confusion proved dangerous.

The Assembly approved by a two-to-one majority a resolution to campaign for emergency status for those convicted under the Emergency Provisions Act. The concern we expressed over police methods was strongly reinforced by a subsequent Amnesty International report, and the government established the Bennett Commission to investigate. The Bennett Report, albeit in the restrained manner of such bodies, substantiated our legitimate representations and made nonsense of the repeated claims by Roy

Mason and Kenneth Newman that such complaints were terrorist propaganda.

These developments, paralleled by an intensification of the protest activity by the 'blanketmen' in the prisons (which initially included loyalist prisoners who later abandoned it because of its public association with the republicans), encouraged the hope that public opinion might force Roy Mason to accept the counter-productivity aspect of his posture, which looked increasingly Napoleonic: but it was a wary, and ultimately unjustified hope.

Naturally, as editor of *Peace by Peace*, I gave such issues, including the Assembly's treatment of them, the attention they required. But Peter McLachlan began reporting 'bad feedback' from our groups on the H-Block issue. Since I was no longer on the Executive, the focus of this 'bad feedback' was the newspaper: and to opposition on the actual issue, was added the line that I was making it very difficult for Peter McLachlan to 'lead', since he could not control the paper.

I reacted rather sharply to this, making it clear that I did not anticipate that Peter McLachlan would be leading people in any direction other than the policies of the Peace People as agreed by the Assembly, or implied by the Declaration; nor would the paper so deviate. This reassured those in favour of Peace People policy, but confirmed the view of a vocal minority that I was a neo-republican dictator.

My experience of 'bad feedback' (a phrase I learned to despise) did not coincide with Peter McLachlan's. I found that members were able to overcome initial antipathy to considering the issue of the H-Blocks, where prisoners had begun the infamous 'no wash' protest, smearing their excrement on the walls rather than co-operate in the wearing of prison clothes to the bathrooms. Once they had debated the issue, even groups in Unionist areas, with deep prejudices to face, found themselves able to see the point of the 'emergency status' argument. The 'bad feedback' which worried me rather more was the sense that the Peace People were beginning to feel leaderless after the withdrawal of the 'Big Three' and that the whole movement was visibly declining.

Continuing my staged withdrawal from remaining responsibilities, I stood down from the chairmanship of the Trust, and our Treasurer, Jim Galway (no relation of the celebrated flautist), was elected in my place. Jim, a retired businessman in his later seventies, the soul of Unionist respectability, an elder of First Comber Presbyterian Church, and with a youthful intelligence, found Peter a much easier proposition to sell to his business and professional friends. So again, I hoped that this further retreat of the intense, bearded radical from the foreground, might widen confidence, encourage Peter McLachlan and enable him to counter 'bad feedback' with good 'feed-forward'.

Unfortunately, this did not happen, and we began gradually to suffer almost continuously from the kind of 'palace politics' which I had hoped we could avoid as a nonviolent movement based on trust. An article on a difficult issue meant that I was leading from behind McLachlan's back; the expression of concern at the continuing disappearance of our resources without adequate return flow, meant that I was trying to get rid of him. Moreover, the removal of my forceful presence from the Executive did not transform that body into a tangibly democratic committee in other than form. Members of it complained to me that they could not get information on 'what was going on'. This echoed the wider feeling that the Peace People were drifting, and that the new chairman was primarily interested in the funding of projects and little else.

I refused to become a focus for this unease. The last thing I wanted to see develop was a Seventies version of 'McKeown's mafia', partly out of distaste for such a thing, and partly to avoid the creation of a 'personality clash' issue as an excuse for not getting on with the work. Even this was impossible: as I tried to keep out of the way, I was seen as more aloof than ever; when I protested that all the talk of 'bad feedback' was contrary to my own experience of our members, I was told that they were afraid to speak to me, that I intimidated them intellectually. I kept even further out of the way, and even tried making the paper into a more jolly, sociable production. But the social halitosis, apparently, was unabated.

I had to get out of the Peace People anyway, for the sake of my family, for we were deeply in debt, and all of this pettiness would have accelerated my total withdrawal had it not been for the rate at which the prison issue was becoming critical. Whether it caused the most extreme bout of 'bad feedback' or even the outright collapse of the Peace People, somebody had to warn that if the prison crisis was not resolved before it brought death to the streets, then everything the Peace People had helped to achieve would be reversed, with the much more despairing prospect that no new peace movement could possibly enjoy such success. And I still had, as chairman of the Company, the specific responsibility to ensure that our funds were disbursed in the way that we had agreed, and that was worthy of the inspiration which had produced the donations in the first place: to do otherwise would have been to have accepted large monies under false pretences.

No-one expressed the deepening division better than Jim Galway, who felt it acutely. Time and again, he would say that my mind and drive were vital to the movement, but that I must try not to be autocratic, and to make sure that Peter was seen to be the 'leader'.

It was more than a personality clash: it actually expressed a basic Northern Ireland problem: for what Jim was saying, in addition to its face value, was that the people from whom he sprang would not listen to what I thought, wrote and said, vital though he considered it to be, but that they might take it from Peter McLachlan. Jim knew the extent of this bigotry, for he had clashed directly with it when he sought to challenge the Paisleyism in the ranks of his own church by inviting Mairead Corrigan to address the church youth, and suffered an angry reaction, including some ostracisation, even from members of the church session, where a majority, let it be recorded, supported him in the end. I accepted Jim's argument, and would have been only too delighted to promote Peter McLachlan in a vigorous articulation of Peace People policy.

I decided that since the Peace People seemed unable to live with me and unable to live without me, that I should organise my separation from the movement in as orderly a manner as possible, and during the remaining months, try to ensure that its decline was halted, and that the emergency law issue was addressed in as encouraging a manner as such a difficulty might allow. I thought often, and ruefully, during that period of Karl-Friedrich von Weizsäcker, and his utter rejection of my notion of leadership rotation. Max Magee, too, shortly before he left, had said that within six months the founders might have to step back in.

Despite the decline in internal morale and external credibility, I kept hoping that someone, or even a few together, would emerge from within the Executive to reverse the rot, or that the needs of the faltering membership would draw forth the required leadership; or that a genuine realisation of the increasing danger posed from within the prisons might galvanise them. One corner of reassurance was that Steve McBride, as deputy editor of the paper, had proven himself able to produce editions in my absence, and would guard its independence.

The British Prime Minister, James Callaghan, had not called an October general election, as had been widely predicted, so that Roy Mason stayed in office and the H-Block situation, now sending its baleful aroma into the wider community, just got steadily worse. Even yet, it is hard for me to distinguish which was the more depressing: the conviction that in spite of the most hopeful period since the early Sixties we were heading inexorably back towards a more deeply poisoned polarisation; or the realisation that the Peace People, in whom I had invested so much of myself, were coming apart in a most unpleasant manner; or the sense that I had put in hock my family's future, to say nothing of current comfort and safety, for what might turn out to be a miserable disgrace to the whole cause of nonviolence;

or the paralysis induced by the dilemma that if I did nothing, the thing would die, while if I acted, I might kill it. Every way I looked at the situation, within the Peace People and in the wider politic, I found it depressing: yet I had to be careful not to express such a depression, or warn too heavily of worse violence to come, for fear that I might demoralise people and help that very situation to be realised.

In early June 1979, I prepared to go to New York for a meeting of Peace People Inc, USA. I looked forward to the trip, despite a leaden feeling that the hopes of a year earlier were as ashes. I recalled the confidence with which I had encouraged Frank Sutton, International Vice-President of the Ford Foundation, to support us: now I would have to give him a much more negative picture. Before I left, I spoke to Peter McLachlan. He had been visiting our groups in the Derry and Strabane areas, as well as projects which showed little or no sign of paying back loans, and in a few cases, likely to founder. He too was depressed, and agreed with me that the H-Block issue was poisoning away below the media surface in the community.

When our colleagues in the States asked me to report on the situation, I explained that people were becoming demoralised, that the H-Block issue was approaching a critical phase, and would be ready-made for Irish America where support for the Provisionals could recover dramatically from the reverses of the previous two years. I said that we would need more help than ever.

I was stunned to be interrupted by one of them, who said, "Here, wait a minute, we're getting mixed signals, I was talking to Peter on the phone and he tells me things are going well, he has just come back from Derry and the projects are most encouraging." I observed that Peter's spirits must have risen since I had spoken to him on his return from Derry, and that he was very depressed then; but that regardless of any subjective feeling, the general situation was deteriorating, Peace People morale was declining, and the H-Block issue could wipe out all the progress we had made.

I added that if it got much worse, the only alternative might be to go back to old-fashioned nonviolent tactics like non-co-operation with the Emergency Provisions Act, if only to inhibit violence and prevent a return to the downward spiral, with little possibility of a similar peace movement re-emerging to break it.

At this point, I was interrupted even more angrily, and almost lectured by one of those present, who said that he was about to hang out his neck for money for us, and who did we think we were putting his credibility on the line for non-co-operation tactics?

I told him that we would do in our situation whatever we thought was right in the interests of peace in Northern Ireland. Another member, even more influential in Washington political circles, said that her only interest was in the kind of nonviolence Betty and Mairead had started, the whole approach of community development, and giving people their self-respect.

It was overwhelmingly obvious that these good people did not want to hear about anything so uncomfortable as tackling the H-Block issue. I did not bother to point out that the entire philosophy being attributed to Betty and Mairead as the Peace People's distinctive contribution to nonviolence, had flowed from the same brain and the same tongue which was now telling them that the H-Block issue, as symbol of the Emergency Provisions Act, could, and probably would, set all that at naught.

It was also clear that they desperately wanted to believe Peter McLachlan's 'good news', and were horrified that I proposed to give my sombre assessment to the Ford Foundation and others. They leaned on me most heavily not to endanger our contacts there by doing so. I did however give Frank Sutton my gloomy report. To have done otherwise would have seemed to me to be dishonest, like continuing to accept money under pretences that had become false.

The distance and isolation of New York clarified my mind considerably. If distant supporters could be so hostile, the depth of hostility among those vocal in opposition at home could become devastating. I realised with shame—for my own misjudgements were as much to blame as anything—that the Peace People would be utterly useless in their present condition to handle an issue now as menacing as the prison crisis. I also decided that with the projects department costing nearly as much to run as there were resources left to manage, and with return flow never more than a trickle, that it would have to be wound up unless there was a dramatic improvement in the operation of the Company's policy. And finally, that the Peace People's own internal budget would have to be radically pruned, for money was flowing away with little to show for it.

When I got back from New York, the administrator, Pat Johnston, an active member who gave up her own job to succeed Ann Campbell, expressed her grave anxiety that the organisation was just dribbling money away, and that a great deal of staff time and telephone usage was for organisations other than the Peace People. Then I discovered that the Executive sub-committee which had been charged with preparing an improved version of the previous year's submission to Westminster on the emergency law, had failed to come up with the goods in time for the July renewal of the Emergency Provisions Act; and that a two-page letter, which was actually a long way back from the previous year's stance, had been prepared by Peter McLachlan and a young, well-connected lawyer called James Cunningham. Signals were clearly mixed on both sides of the Atlantic.

Since the Peace People would be asking for a further substantial subvention from the Company that month for its running costs, I asked to see its minutes to get some idea of what programming and budgeting it had agreed. The minutes revealed an inconsequential series of meetings, in which decisions were rarely taken, and on the handful of occasions when they were, were almost never followed through.

Fund-raising had been mentioned vaguely but the result was insubstantial. There emerged no sense whatever that the Executive was responsible for a programme of work, in which each item had to be costed, and on the basis of which Mairead and I had spent time lobbying American foundations and to which we had attached our bona fides. It was clear that the majority of members not only did not shoulder their responsibilities, but that they did not even know that they were theirs to bear. They were under some strange impression that 'important matters like that were the business of the Company and Trust', as one of them later put it.

I advised Peter McLachlan that the financial situation was such that he and I should prepare to take three months' notice, that other economies would have to be made, and that the Executive would have to be made aware of the realities. He felt that it would be difficult to get this through to the Executive. I offered, as chairman of the Company which would have to consider honourably whether the Peace People were as worthy as any other applicant to its funds for support, to outline that position to them. I hoped that by conducting this piece of business surgery with his consent and prior knowledge, there would be no danger of misinterpretation as McKeown seeking to get rid of McLachlan.

In the event, the Executive took it very well indeed, acknowledging the 'bad news' as a shock, but grateful for the information, and ready to rally round. But within days, I was hearing that there had been 'bad feedback' from the groups, that Ciaran McKeown had shattered morale in the Executive and was obviously determined to remove Peter McLachlan. It looked as if palace politics would outlast the palace.

I was no longer concerned about negative reactions: I had gone over the figures prepared by our accountant, read back over all the project decisions, made an estimate of what we might reasonably, and with great effort, expect to recover, and what we would have to write off. The picture was clear: the practical side of the Peace People's affairs would have to be put in order by October, or the Assembly would be mandating an organisation headed for bankruptcy, while its sense of purpose was also hopelessly adrift.

Turning from the internal problem, I felt that the only hope on the H-block front would be for Betty, Mairead and myself to shoulder it independently. The Peace People could not help being identified with us, but we were not on the Executive and it would not be too difficult for Peter McLachlan to distance the organisation as such if we were to propose a campaign of symbolic non-co-operation to get the issue raised before violent confrontation became inevitable.

In spite of the previous eighteen months, there was still enough of that instinctive relationship between the original trio for us to review the present crises, both within the Peace People and in the wider community. From the earlier high point of about 100 groups, with over 100,000 signed Declarations, the organisation had maintained something in the order of sixty groups for about two years, and had then begun to decline visibly. In the spring of 1979, the reality was probably about thirty groups, with regular membership of about 500. The imprecision of these estimates is a direct result of a deliberate policy not to have 'card-carrying' membership: while the word 'group', although defined in the Peace People constitution, was often used by no more than a couple of people adopting the name of an entire district!

The drop in numbers was not in itself excessively depressing: much more debilitating was the evident loss in enthusiasm, a sense of being leaderless, and the growth of a sour cliquishness.

We agreed that the organisation could be not very effective on the prison issue, but that it would benefit if we were successful—and could not be much more damaged than it already was if we failed.

Betty was extremely enthusiastic, and offered to chain herself to the railings at Westminster, suffragette-style. I argued that this was rather melodramatic, and was the sort of gesture that would only be appropriate as a last resort. What I had in mind was to prepare ourselves for a very modest form of non co-operation, engaged in only after we had thoroughly prepared the ground, so that people would at least *understand* why we were doing it, however much they disagreed. We would send a detailed case on the counter-productivity of special powers to Westminster, emphasising yet again that trial by emergency procedures was not 'due process' as hitherto understood in the long and often honourable history of British jurisprudence.

We would try to provoke consideration of the issue at the level of the Law Lords and in key places in Europe and the United States. Then, if as anticipated, the process of confrontation persisted, the first non-co-operation might be a friendly refusal to co-operate with a soldier operating a spot-check under the authority of the Emergency Provisions Act. From there, without violence or crowd-scenes, the protest would be on the quasi-judicial conveyor belt, non-co-operating continuing all the way to jail if necessary.

Only at some point near the end of that process might chaining oneself to the railings at Westminster be appropriate: to do it in advance would create drama, but inhibit seriously thoughtful consideration of the very complex and emotive issue.

We agreed this strategy, and I presented it to a meeting of the Peace People, representative of the groups, chaired by Peter McLachlan. I suggested that it might be better if the Peace People stayed at some distance from the tactic, so as to avoid internal division, and so that we would have friends who could correct the distortions that would inevitably appear; and I appealed to those who might disagree with us, not to allow it to destroy friendship: if the Peace People were to stand for anything, it should be the ability to accommodate in friendship genuinely divergent conscientious positions.

The meeting was oddly divided. There were some who felt that the Peace People should go exactly the same way, in line with Assembly policy; others disagreed with it but respected the sincerity with which the strategy was proposed. It was a very distressed meeting, for people were troubled both in conscience and in concern for the Peace People image, as well as for our safety. I was moved by some who approached me afterwards, hugged me, wished me well, and said they would pray for us—even though they disagreed, and thought the government 'should not give in to the prisoners'—which we were not proposing!

I wrote a careful article for *Peace by Peace* introducing the strategy, emphasising the peaceful intent to inhibit otherwise inevitable violence, but signalling the determination of the Peace People founders, including the two Nobel prizewinners, to confront the problem.

Betty Williams came in, agitated, as I was laying the paper out for the printers; apparently she was going off to spend the weekend with Mrs. Christabel Bielenberg in Carlow. She had become very friendly with Mrs. Bielenberg, descendant of an English newspaper family, married to a German, Peter Bielenberg, who had been detained in Hitler's Germany, and had settled in the Irish Republic. Christabel had been helpful with German contacts, and Betty had been our principal representative in Germany, along with Peter McLachlan, who speaks German, and had known Mrs. Bielenberg for years.

Uncharacteristically, Betty seemed unable to come out with whatever was on her mind, and which had taken her out of her way to come into the Peace House to see me. Gradually it came out: she had been thinking about the prison protest, she thought maybe we shouldn't, she knew the situation, she knew it was getting worse, but "there must be some more moderate way of dealing with it".

"There must be some more moderate way of dealing with it": the words echo through my head even yet—for this was not Betty Williams speaking, not the leader pleading for support to go chaining herself to railings at Westminster. I do not know whose phrase it was, but it was not Betty Williams's, for Betty has been spared the boredom of having a moderate bone in her body.

I said to her, "Look, Betty, this is what we agreed," and showed her the typeset story. She glanced at it and without reading it, said, "No, there must be some more moderate way of dealing with it."

"Like what?" I asked.

"I haven't thought of it yet, but there must be some way," she said, and hurriedly left.

I screwed up the front page and threw it in the bin.

Whatever Betty said or did now, even if she changed her mind after the weekend, even if she resumed insistence on the railings tactic, I knew that the 'trio' was now as useless as the Peace People organisation in the face of the looming crisis. Worse, some Peace People and a few others now knew that 'Betty, Mairead and Ciaran' had been preparing to embark on direct involvement on the prison issue: now, when it became known that Betty favoured some 'more moderate way', no-one would ask what 'moderate way' she was talking about, but would merely seize on the phrase to excoriate any action Mairead or I took, and would splash a 'split' story. Any chance of getting the calm, painstaking consideration which the issue demanded, was already wrecked in advance. Our ability to do anything about the H-Block issue before the poison hit the streets, was destroyed; yet, so strongly did I feel about this that I regarded failure to do something about it, by those with any chance of doing it, as a kind of 'murder by omission'.

It was far worse than the Nobel let-down, for lives were much more obviously about to be lost, and the longer-term prospects horribly darkened. I considered whether to proceed on my own. Mairead, who was preparing to embark on a college degree course, would have gone along with me, but I was not too happy with that: the action required that degree of conscious motivation that dictated that one should do it no matter what anyone else did.

On the other hand, if I did it alone, there would be almost no chance in the circumstances of having the issue properly discussed: the media, with some assistance from within the ranks of the Peace

People, would present the action as the 'pacifist fanatic' heading towards his predictable nemesis, to the relief of a few Peace People and quite a few others as well. I could not care less about the media in most cases, but in this instance, there had to be some hope that the purpose of the entire exercise would wriggle through the net of distortions.

Marianne was also opposed to my going ahead: she felt that my judgment was unduly influenced by what had happened to the Peace People after so much unremitting effort and hope, and that I was suffering from exhaustion. She was right in this, in that a few weeks later, I was confined to bed in continuous pain with a frozen shoulder and exhibiting other symptoms of exhaustion: but it was not the pace which was threatening my health, but the internal turmoil, the acute sense of the failure of the Peace People competing with the acute awareness of what was on the horizon to destroy the peace. However egotistical it may be or sound, I felt a sense of personal failure in that my own misjudgments had contributed to this situation, and that that failure was going to cost lives within a very short time. Yet even in this personal agonising, I fought shy of anything that smacked of fanatical lonerism.

I dithered in the hope of some break, like a general election that would remove Roy Mason as Secretary of State, and perhaps also precipitate a change in the leadership in the RUC. I publicly advocated the appointment of Jack (now Sir John) Hermon whom I knew to be concerned that Castlereagh interrogation procedures were damaging police acceptability and endangering the lives of vulnerable men in uniform on the streets.

Mairead and I had met Airey Neave, and had been impressed by his thoughtfulness. He appreciated the reasoning behind our position on the prison issue, but felt that Mr. Mason was unable to do anything else at the time. I did not press him towards any position or statement which might reduce his flexibility in office. What surprised me most was his quite enthusiastic response to our general approach to the creation of consensus, and opposition to constitutional engineering 'from the top down'. We discussed our policy in some detail, emphasising its fundamentally parliamentary nature, its tangible quality of consent to law and other institutions, its strong sense of local involvement and veto. Mr. Neave expressed real interest in this, even the opposition to the party-political structure: he said that involvement in politics today was not the honourable thing it had been when he first went into parliament twenty-five years earlier—politics was now almost a dirty word.

I liked him, and was shocked when he was blown up at Westminster a few weeks later. I think also that he might have been a much better Secretary of State than his predilection for militarism suggested.

If Labour were returned, we could reasonably anticipate a change from Roy Mason, which had to be an improvement. Until his death, we had expected Airey Neave, should the Conservatives win. Now, listening to the tone of Margaret Thatcher as she expressed determination to deal with those responsible for Neave's death, I felt that a change to the Tories might be more worrying. Suddenly the Callaghan government was toppled before the Prime Minister could choose his own time, and Margaret Thatcher was Prime Minister.

Humphrey Atkins was appointed Secretary of State for Northern Ireland, and gave an immediate impression of biding his time, unwilling to be bound by anything that had gone before. Mrs. Thatcher went into 10 Downing Street with the prayer of St. Francis of Assisi on her lips; and this, combined with the fact that she would have to come to terms with reality once in office, allowed hope that the single-minded militarism which she displayed before the election might not be expressed in action, once in power. We have learned otherwise since.

The change of government gave me a subjective excuse for abandoning the non-co-operation strategy until the new Secretary of State enunciated his policies. I now felt the exhaustion that others could see in my face, and prepared to hand over *Peace by Peace* to Steve McBride. Steve is a man of astute political judgement; being from a Unionist background, he was often more angry than many Catholics at what he perceived as old-fashioned Unionist bigotry and anti-Catholicism. He was fully in support of the thrust of the original Peace People approach; with him as editor, I felt I could retire and not wake up a few editions later to find the paper slithering away from its commitment to nonviolence and Peace People policy.

I decided to clear up all outstanding paperwork and then, in place of the Achill seminar, to go down there with Steve and produce a book on *The Best of Peace by Peace* which might serve as a popular illustrated history of the Peace People, three years on. I had also been looking forward to a chat with Michael O'Malley, the postmaster at Keel in Achill, who had given John Healy of the *Irish Times* an image of the Peace People a couple of years earlier, which I was beginning to feel was more apt than any other description I had heard.

Michael keeps bees. He observed that it is impossible to get two swarms of bees into the same hive, unless you put in a partition of newspaper, and introduce the bees on either side. Bees cannot tolerate newspaper in the hive, so they destroy it frenetically by eating it away. By the time they have eaten their way in and out of the paper, the swarms are thoroughly mixed without even noticing it; the newspaper, of course, has disappeared.

Michael felt that the Peace People were the newspaper between two swarms of northern bees, and that we would have to be 'eaten alive' for people of the two traditions to mix . . .

By the time I got to Achill at the beginning of July, the pain in my shoulder had become like a toothache in my whole body, and I had to confine myself largely to bed for a couple of days. Even pints of Guinness in the singing pubs could do little more than make it tolerable and I finally visited the island doctor, whose main advice was to take it easy and have a good time. I took his advice, decided to make no decision of any kind until I felt a lot better, and returned to Belfast a few weeks later in a much healthier state.

I got back to hear that Betty Williams was seriously considering standing for chairmanship of the Peace People, or as co-chairman with Peter McLachlan, who was also proposing to stand again. There was also a lot of talk that 'we should get back to being a women's movement', and make things 'simple' again; and, of course, that Ciaran McKeown was plotting to get rid of Peter McLachlan. The administrator, Pat Johnston, who would shortly be leaving to have a baby in December, was in a most despondent mood about the very survival of the organisation.

Much of this talk would have been nauseating, were it not also comical. I put it down to silly season holiday gossip, of the kind with which all journalists are familiar.

Blattering on

Suddenly the IRA murdered twenty-two people in one day: Lord Mountbatten and three of his party on a boat off the Sligo coast; and near Warrenpoint, about forty miles from Belfast, eighteen soldiers in a double bomb ambush designed to kill those coming to the rescue of the first batch of victims.

It was exactly the kind of clinical militarism which the nihilistic anger of the prison issue was bound to produce, and which would receive lusty support in Irish America, once the initial shock passed off. It was also predictable that the Provisionals would seek to upstage the INLA in their murder stunt of killing Airey Neave in the very Palace of Westminster, by killing a VIP: killing Mountbatten was an attack on the British establishment at several levels, including Royalty.

The IRA had calculated their ploy to perfection. They had the incentive of making it difficult, if not impossible, for the government to concede anything on the prison issue, which was the last area of IRA support, the vehicle to carry the violence into a new generation without the generation skip which had historically marked Ireland's cyclical violence. Provisional Sinn Fein leader Ruairi O'Bradaigh made this very point, appropriately enough in an oration in Belfast's Milltown Cemetery, when he boasted that the struggle had been passed to a new generation.

Had the government been seen to be enlightened and humanitarian in its approach to the prison situation, which so incensed the prisoners' relatives, it would have knocked the bottom out of the reviving support for the IRA, and made their continued militarism, in favour of a declaration of British intent to withdraw, a negligible affair.

The Provos, whom government propaganda had sought to paint as low-grade guerillas and criminal scum, had worked out their position with a colder logic than most. And with Margaret Thatcher in office, they had nothing to worry about, for she could be relied upon to make herself very visible as their personal opponent, which was precisely in line with their needs in terms of community support and 'us versus the Brits' ground rule for war and propaganda alike.

Within the Peace People, instead of a sombre realisation that we had been absolutely right, the opposite effect was created and encouraged by Betty Williams. She was suddenly active, giving interviews, attacking and condemning the Provisionals, and was now surrounded by those who wanted nothing to do with the H-Block issue. The simple-minded myth that the Provos alone were the source of all our woes was aroused behind an hysterical effort to renew the character of August 1976, to make things 'simple'.

Genuinely horrified people were momentarily carried away by this, and flocked briefly to Warrenpoint, and then to Sligo where Peter McLachlan laid a wreath on the waves. 'An end to violence first, then we'll talk about justice', was the dominant theme which I personally regarded as a code-phrase, virtually, for the Paisleyite slogan of 'peace through victory'.

Peter McLachlan identified visibly with this upsurge, even going so far, some time later, as to help draft a statement which some of these people handed out downtown as tracts to passers-by, calling for an end to violence before there could be justice. At the same time, he remained on the record in support of agreed Peace People policy.

He was also serious about standing again as chairman, and content with the idea of working in tandem with Betty Williams. Knowing Betty Williams's opinion of Peter McLachlan, I found their mutual willingness in this matter both puzzling and comical. Since Betty was unlikely to want to attend, let alone chair, meetings, the only explanation was a need to be visibly associated with the Peace People; while Peter McLachlan would be reassured by this direct association with one of the founders.

Mairead was about to go to Argentina for a week to support Adolfo Perez Esquivel, then under 'controlled liberty', after which she would settle down to her studies for a B.A. degree in history, philosophy and politics. The two of us discussed this Peter-Betty, 'women's movement', 'peace before justice', 'keep it simple' development. With the prison issue and the external violence now looming larger, and the Peace People not only powerless to do anything about serious issues but drifting towards both financial and visionary bankruptcy, we decided that we would, if necessary, stand again for the Executive, to prevent any further backsliding, and try to restore some sense of reality and purpose.

I advised Peter McLachlan bluntly that unless money started to flow back into the funds, the project department would have to be wound up, and I offered to recover outstanding monies if he felt unable to do so. I also told him that I would resolutely oppose his becoming chairman of the Executive again, and also oppose the election of any prominent personality as chairman.

There followed weeks of campaigning on behalf of Peter McLachlan, largely based on the assumption that I wanted him out of the Peace People. In fact, I saw the keeping-in of Peter McLachlan as important to the Peace People, for he was the symbol of those who found the prison issue difficult to confront, even though he was still officially supporting Peace People policy on it.

The October Assembly revealed the extent of this campaign. Not only was a consciousness of 'personality clash' well established, but the 'peace first' lobby was vocal. It did not succeed, however, in reversing Peace People policy on prisons and emergency law. Betty Williams took little part in the proceedings, and flew to the States immediately afterwards for one of her tours. Peter McLachlan topped the proportional representation poll in elections to the Executive, with Betty, Mairead and myself coming in behind him: but his surplus did not transfer in any serious way to people supporting him, so that no policy decision, other than support for him in his apparent plight, was implied by the vote. In short, it summed up the Jim Galway approach: we need Ciaran to run the show, we need Peter to appear to.

The Assembly confirmed the commitment to confront the problems arising from the emergency law, as well as all the other main thrusts of Peace People policy.

The first meeting of the new Executive was the start of a long series of tortuous wrangles, beginning with the issue of chairmanship. Mairead and I ruled ourselves out, saying also that we would oppose the election of any prominent person, and that we wanted a low-profile chairman, with each member of the Executive bearing his or her full share of responsibility.

Peter McLachlan said he would stand only if he had wholehearted support around the table: Mairead and I made it very plain that he would not have that. I favoured Jimmy McIlwaine, a shop steward in the Belfast Sirocco engineering works, whose workforce was predominantly loyalist. Jimmy had been one of the key organisers of the 1974 UWC strike which brought down the Sunningdale experiment; thereafter Jimmy, a stout Evangelical Christian, had felt that the politicians had betrayed the workers' action, and he began to question the whole basis of his 'loyalty'. He even went so far as to fight for Catholics to be given union cards to work in Sirocco, which was a very brave stand to take. He was nervous about the alienation potential of our stand on the H-Block issue, and I felt that his would be the truly authentic moderating influence, for he would sense acutely the tussle between conscience and what his fellow-workers would lay on him daily.

A number of members felt that Peter McLachlan should continue if Mairead was unwilling to go forward. Towards the end of a very long evening, during which the functions and role of chairmanship were also debated, the acting chairman said a decision would have to be taken, and that Peter McLachlan seemed to have more people in favour than any other suggested name.

At this point, Mairead said that in that case, she would allow her name to go forward. This offer, had it been made at the beginning of the evening, would undoubtedly have led to Mairead's election: but now, with so many loyalties painfully exposed, it caused consternation. I intervened to say that if Peter McLachlan who had earlier said he was unwilling to stand without whole-hearted support, was now willing to accept the position without that support, he should be deemed to be elected. In great relief, the new Executive adopted this proposal, when Peter McLachlan indicated that he was thus willing.

So we got down to devising a work programme, budgeting every item on it. I allowed myself to hope again, in spite of the previous months, for the long weeks of meetings which followed were the very stuff of growth, with no decision going through until every member understood its priority, the finance related to it, and the authority by which the work would be carried out. After my aloof isolation for so long, it was very pleasant to note deepening relationships, particularly with some who had come on to the Executive prepared to do battle with the 'dictator', but who found that my much-reported forcefulness was forcefulness in outlining detailed information on any proposition, and how it might fit in an overall programme. After all the wobbles, I began to hope that the Peace People were stabilising, and maturing.

The process was interrupted dramatically in late October by a development in the prison issue. Relatives of the prisoners had been trying to arouse public support along lines that seemed distinct from the Provos' propaganda line. I already knew from anguished pleas from some such relatives, that while they did not want to betray their sons, brothers or husbands in prison, they desperately wanted them off the hideous dirt strike, and thought that the approach identified with me might resolve the position, while Mrs. Thatcher would never give in to the prisoners themselves. There was just a chance that this might be possible.

The Provos were uncertain over the H-Block issue. The prisoners themselves wanted the issue to be a top priority, and in the tradition of Irish Republicanism, prisons come second only to graveyards as holy ground. Moreover, the first 'blanketman', Kieran Nugent, had recently been released and others would be emerging who would not let the outside activists forget the men inside.

But some Provos were afraid that if the stakes were raised too high on the issue, the government might concede something, be seen to be enlightened and compassionate, and thus damage Provo propaganda. Especially in Irish America, the British must, for the Provos, appear as relentlessly cruel, intransigent oppressors, and anything less than that damaged the support needed from Irish America for the military campaign for British withdrawal. It was hard for them to decide between a view that Mrs. Thatcher would prove helpfully vengeful, and a fear that the wily British Foreign Office might persuade her to a more subtle stance.

Now, with both emerging prisoners and prisoners' relatives pressing independently, the Provos supported a public meeting on the issue, involving a wider group, with the possibility that this might 'muddy the waters' and inhibit the clear lines of 'us and the Brits', in which alone they felt really comfortable.

The Peace People found themselves invited by prisoners' relatives to attend the meeting in the Green Briar, a restaurant and dance hall in Andersonstown, in West Belfast. We debated this at some length, and decided to attend, to present our position, and make an assessment of what was afoot: we would then decide afterwards where we would or could co-operate. It was agreed that I would present the Peace People case, but that as many Executive members as possible should go along.

Six members attended the all-day Sunday meeting. It was packed, and I noted the presence not only of many women, obviously prisoners' relatives, but of some quiet and watchful gentlemen along the walls: the IRA was obviously present and their disposition indicated that the meeting was going to be 'orderly'. Also present was Michael Farrell of People's Democracy, and other fringe groups were represented.

After some opening statements, including a passionate plea from Kieran Nugent, the man who had started the 'blanket' protest in September 1976, warning that some of the men could not take much more and might go on hunger-strike, the chairperson asked for a list of those who wished to speak in the next part of the meeting. I sent up my name. Peter McLachlan went home at the end of the first part and did not return.

I outlined the Peace People case. We did not accept the claim the prisoners were making for 'political status', and I explained why. We also opposed the government claim that they were criminals convicted by due process. We recognised that they had not been arrested, held, questioned, tried and convicted under normal process of law and we would not dignify their convictions with the phrase 'due process'. We also recognised that the acts of violence for which the convictions had been obtained, were acts arising out of a constitutional emergency, and our purpose was to dismantle the apparatus of emergency and to build a reconciled, nonviolent society. Therefore, if the relatives were contemplating a nonviolent campaign, we would be very open to it. On the other hand, if the relatives' campaign was conducted parallel to a violent campaign, we could not co-operate, for we would not be associated in any way with a violent campaign: violent and nonviolent tactics could not be mixed, and moreover, a violent campaign would make a nonviolent campaign nearly impossible.

This was received in remarkably respectful silence, and quite strong applause broke out as I returned to my seat, where our Executive members were looking very pleased indeed. But just before I could push into my seat, a man jumped up in the middle of the hall, and began to shout: "Ciaran McKeown has one hell of a cheek coming in here, he's an informer, there's a lot of men on the blanket in Long Kesh because of him, he should be thrown out of here!"

His hysteria was infectious and some women around him were screaming similar abuse. Much of the middle of the hall was suddenly on its feet with a lot of arm waving and gesticulating and shouting: the hard men along the walls were on the alert. I turned back towards the platform where the chairperson was banging the table and shouting, "There will be order, there will be order." I raised my hand to reply as I went back up.

There was now a highly charged atmosphere, and I struggled to keep my voice low-key as I started again: "Madam Chairman, the last speaker has raised a most important point, and I think it is important that we understand each other very clearly if there is the slightest chance of co-operation. On this question of informing, yes, we have asked people and we have continued to ask people to inform, and we have deliberately used the word inform, on the whereabouts of arms and explosives; but we have not asked people to inform on people, for we do not want to add to the numbers of people in jail. But equally we want to see no more people shot dead or blown to bits. We want to see all those now in jail released eventually into a nonviolent society. We would even question the whole basis of prisons. But even more do we question killing. That is our position and we have no wish to hide it.

"There are some Peace People who do not approve of us bothering about those they see as murderers. On the other hand we wish to see just laws, and we will campaign everywhere we can, with all our access in Europe and in the United States to help bring about justice. But we can only do that nonviolently: you will simply have to respect our nonviolence, or there can be no co-operation."

This was heard in deep silence. I then walked back to my place a second time, and again to respectful applause with no further hysterical reactions. Freda Lyness, one of the Peace People Executive members present, who comes from a strongly Loyalist background in the Rathcoole area, north of Belfast, and who was therefore, by Belfast law, on enemy territory, was elated, and later described herself as more proud than ever of the Peace People.

Next morning, the *Irish News* had a brief account of my participation in the debate. A *Belfast Telegraph* reporter rang me up, following this report, since the *Telegraph* had had no-one present at the meeting. After a couple of cursory questions, this reporter went on to ask me:

"Mr. McKeown, do you not condemn the Provisional IRA?'

"I do not condemn anybody," I answered.

"Are you telling me that you do not condemn the Provisional IRA?" he repeated.

"I do not go in for condemning people," I replied again.

When he repeated the question again, I told him that I would not have words put in my mouth and added, "I am not in the business of condemning people, that is for God. I am in the business of peacemaking."

That evening the *Belfast Telegraph* inflicted serious damage on the Peace People with a story headlined "McKeown pledges support for H-Block men". The whole gross distortion made no attempt to put our position on the issue, indicated that I was ready to throw the resources of the Peace People, including international support, behind the Provisional IRA's 'dirty protestors' in the Maze, and that I refused to condemn the Provisional IRA. Before we could do anything about this, quite a number of people wrote or phoned to resign, including one group.

The Peace People Executive held its routine meeting on the Tuesday evening. One or two who had not been at the Green Briar had been half inclined to believe that there might be something in the *Telegraph* report, and Jimmy McIlwaine had been getting it hot and heavy from his workmates. But the presence of those who had attended at the Green Briar was more than enough to substantiate my verbatim report, with favourable comment for my handling of it, as well as rage at the *Telegraph*'s conduct. In less than half an hour's discussion on the matter, we decided that Peter McLachlan and I would approach the editor of the *Belfast Telegraph* first thing in the morning, and seek satisfaction, and that if we did not get it, we were to instruct our lawyers to take appropriate action.

The *Belfast Telegraph* interview was like a re-run of the NUJ experience. The editor, flanked by his news editor, opened the proceedings by saying that he would be standing over the story, for the reporter had his notes on the interview. I said that I was perfectly happy with that, since I had a precise memory of both the meeting and the interview. Peter McLachlan then stunned me by telling the editor, in what I suppose he imagined was supportive statement, that "My Executive grilled Mr. McKeown for three hours on this last night and we are satisfied that the *Telegraph* must print a retraction, or my instructions are to see our lawyers."

In the few seconds before the reporter came in, I realised that any legal proceedings were already out of the question, since I had not been 'grilled for three hours', which would shatter Peter McLachlan's credibility in a witness-box; whereas any lawyer for the *Telegraph* would have a field day with the phrase, for here was the Peace People chairman indicating that I might be the sort of person who has to be 'grilled for three hours' before the truth could be established.

It did not take three minutes to establish that the reporter had written his own story regardless of the truth. But he was very honest in this situation, for which I was grateful. He produced his notes, and was able to read his questions to me accurately: when it came to the answers, he had little or nothing; but when I repeated to him exactly what I had said in reply in each case, he acknowledged in each case that that was what I had said.

The *Telegraph* editor made no further reference to standing over his reporter's story, and allowed that there must have been some 'misunderstanding'. He offered us prominent space in the letters section to answer. After a short haggle over what page and on what day, I conceded: after McLachlan's remark, we had no legal lever left, though the editor did not know that.

We got good space for a letter jointly signed by Peter McLachlan and myself. But the damage had been done, duly attributed to me.

It was a mark of the Executive's growing maturity that it settled back immediately to completing its programme and budget. But there were three more direct clashes between myself and Peter McLachlan. All three concerned salaries. The Administrator, Pat Johnston, would be leaving in December to have her baby, and her place would have to be filled. The Welfare Officer would also be going, leaving another place to be filled. The Executive had already decided to get the budget within £20,000 if possible, but certainly no more than £25,000, and we were already close to that.

Peter McLachlan proposed that a particular member of the Executive be appointed as Welfare Officer. I proposed that we should not add to the staff, but promote the Welfare Officer's assistant, as the outgoing man had recommended. The assistant, Pat Hale, had gained considerable experience of prisoners' families and it would have been foolish as well as unjust to pass her over. Moreover the volume of 'resettlement' cases (part of the old 'escape route') had declined considerably, and there was no need for two staff on this job: so we would be holding the experienced person, and saving a few thousand pounds. This was overwhelmingly agreed by the Executive, to the annoyance of the member proposed for the job.

When the Adminstrator's job came up, exactly the same pattern was repeated. Peter McLachlan proposed the same member of the Executive for the post. I suggested that the office secretary, Ann McCann, who had been the first paid secretary employed by us, should be asked if she wanted to be considered, that she was exceptionally suited to the task if she wanted it, and that it would be wrong to pass her over; and again, that we should not recruit an extra secretary, since two were now enough for the Peace People's needs. Ann McCann was indeed willing, and said bluntly that she might well have resigned if the rumour that had reached her of an Executive member being appointed over her, had gone through. Again, the Executive overwhelmingly agreed to promote Ann McCann, who has done an efficient job ever since; and also agreed that no secretary would be needed to restore staff numbers.

The Executive member whom Peter McLachlan had twice proposed now resigned, saying that she had come on the Executive hoping to be able to give herself full-time to the movement, but could only do that on salary: and she added that she could not go along with the movement's being dominated by Ciaran McKeown.

During the course of these salary arguments, noting that the Executive now had almost completed its task, and that the tricky business of the almost redundant projects department was one of the few outstanding features, I announced that I would no longer be accepting a salary from the Ford resource and was putting myself on three months' notice. The programme was such that it no longer justified any 'executive' level salaries. What made my action the more embarrassing was the knowledge that when the Executive and Company came to examine Peter McLachlan's job, they could hardly avoid the logical conclusion that it was absurd to spend some £10,000 to manage a resource of some £10,000. Both the Trust and Company, which were independent entities, open to the applications of all, had already agreed, in the light of the Peace People plight, and noting that the survival of the Peace People was vital to their own ability to fund others, that the budgetary requirements of the Peace People would be their first priority for the time being.

When the Executive had completed its task in late November, only one item remained to be decided: Peter McLachlan's job description and salary, if any. The members were rightly pleased with themselves, for the progress made over six months meant that for the first time, the Peace People had a mature, responsible and informed Executive. To general embarrassment, Peter McLachlan now announced that he would have to consider his future position with the movement, that he was still very unhappy, and knew that many members of the movement were very unhappy about the 'two possible ways forward'. The phrase 'two possible ways forward' had recently taken over from 'bad feedback', but had the same function.

It is a matter of documented fact that the Peace People approach had always been comprehensive; it provided for the aspirations of all, from those who wished to concentrate on low-level reconciliation work of a largely social nature to those who felt impelled to grapple with painful issues at the heart of the conflict, as well as for those, such as Mairead and myself who wished to engage in both. Peter McLachlan's 'two ways' rhetoric sought to force a choice between these two levels, the one being characterised as 'sharing', the other as 'confrontation'. It would be several months before we would discover the reasons for this divisive tactic, but in the meantime, it added steadily and perniciously to confusion of purpose and loyalty among our members, even as the Executive was laying out an agreed programme.

After he had gone on for some time, I said that this 'two ways forward' speech that Peter had been making regularly was coming back to us from our groups as if they were the people making it, and that it was meant to suggest that people must choose between McKeown and McLachlan: but there was now only *one* way forward, namely the budgeted programme agreed by the Executive. To put the matter beyond all doubt, I gave my word that I would not deviate one iota from the Executive's policy, and that if I ever found that I could not conscientiously agree, I would resign.

This was gratefully received by the Executive, and Jim Galway, anxious as ever on Peter's behalf, turned to Peter and said: "Well, Peter, that should set your mind at rest, surely you can accept the position now?"

But to Jim Galway's ire, Peter McLachlan said he would have to "consider his position". None of us was quite sure what position he was talking about, especially since it was far from clear that there was any continuing job for him.

But two things were agreed: firstly that Peter McLachlan would present the agreed programme to the following week's meeting of representatives of Peace People groups; and secondly, that the

Company would be asked if there was enough money to cover his salary, as well as the rest of the Peace People programme. In the light of such information, his job description or otherwise would be defined.

The irritation felt by his stalling to "consider his position" was nothing to the aggravation felt when, rather than present the agreed programme so painstakingly prepared over the seven foregoing weeks, he diverted the representatives' meeting with the 'two ways forward' routine. The meeting turned into an inconsequential affair, with a lot of mouthing about the paper and about imaginary positions on the H-Block issue, and almost nothing about the forward programme of work.

On the following Friday, December 14, the day before the Peace People Company meeting which would have to approve the Executive's budget allocation, and Peter McLachlan's salary position, Jim Galway, the Executive's treasurer, and chairman of the Trust, came to see me very worried. He had spent much of the week going backwards and forwards over the accounts, and talking to our accountant, as well as asking staff how much work was being done for organisations other than the Peace People.

He told me he agreed with my judgement that there was simply no way that we could afford to keep Peter McLachlan on as Projects Manager. But he went on: "I know you don't want any compromise, and that we must face up to the facts. But if we let Peter go immediately, a great number of our members will not believe anything other than that Ciaran McKeown got rid of him. So I am asking you for the sake of the movement to agree to a compromise—that we agree to keep Peter on until the end of the financial year, which is only four months beyond the protective notice."

I had already written to both Peter McLachlan and Steve McBride, advising them that in the light of the current finances, of which they were aware, decisions which could lead to their redundancy, would have to be considered, and that I would be asking the Company to ratify three months' protective notice.

Rather than pay out to save face, I suggested to Jim that the position of Projects Manager be wound up, but that Peter McLachlan be retained to the end of the year, to recover some of the monies, and generally assist the Peace People back towards being a volunteer movement. Jim accepted this compromise of his compromise and undertook to propose it on the following morning. Jim also wanted to propose that Peter be asked to negotiate a charge against the various other organisations which he serviced, using our secretaries and telephones. I suggested that we write that off as goodwill to other organisations. But he had estimated that as much as 50 per cent, and certainly no lower than 20 per cent of our administrative resources were actually being used for outside work, and he did not see why the Peace People should bear the thousands of pounds this represented.

Mairead came in, and Jim briefed her on the proposals he would make the following morning to the Company. Mairead's reaction was that at least no-one would accuse Jim Galway of trying to get rid of Peter McLachlan. I suggested that we should call Peter McLachlan in and advise him of these proposals, since it would be embarrassing for him, if it came out of the blue at the meeting.

He appeared to accept the position as outlined by Jim Galway, and I once again allowed myself to hope that at last we were making progress, that the Peace People, however bruised, maybe all the more mature for being bruised, were on the verge of democratic maturity and financial modesty, with their integrity intact.

The Company met on Saturday December 15 at 10.00 a.m. It was a sombre enough occasion, for we sensed that it was the end of an era, though the beginning, I hoped, of a period of more realistic and rooted growth. The preliminaries over, I was about to introduce the item on the Executive's budget; Jim Galway, almost seventy-seven years of age, a florid colour, was studying his papers, and was about to make his proposal when Betty Williams suddenly arrived at the meeting, apologising for being late. Betty frequently missed meetings, and we had not expected her, since she had been in London the previous day.

She said: "I don't know if you've come to this yet, but I'd better give you this information anyway. I had a telephone call last night from [here she mentioned the name of a German financier whose name had been mooted as a possible supporter in the past] and he says that the money is there for Peter McLachlan's salary, whatever his role."

Jim Galway leaned back in his chair and looked at me; Peter McLachlan sat silently looking down at his papers; Betty Williams looked around smiling.

"Well, Mr. Chairman," Jim Galway said to me, "that's that; if Peter's salary is covered, that was the only outstanding item, then we can pass the budget as it stands."

There was great relief for the majority present, for they were not going to have to take the decision that was staring them in the face.

Unfortunately, I felt obliged to query it. I pointed out that in the minutes of our business over the previous two years, there had been mention of a German trust, and yet not a mark was there to show for it. I also said that I found it highly unsatisfactory to take major decisions on the basis of telephone information to one director from a person whom we did not even officially know.

But the budget was passed, with the addition that the Executive be informed that finance was available for Peter McLachlan's salary, whatever his role. I said that I was far from happy with the decision, that I did not see how we could stand over it in auditing terms, and that I would like a written report on the table at the next meeting, from Peter McLachlan, on the state of the long-reported German trust, and written confirmation of the offer conveyed by telephone. Peter, who had been sent by us to Germany on a number of occasions, had talked about the German trust on a few occasions and he and Betty had mentioned figures varying from 100,000 marks to £100,000. But no money ever appeared.

Peter told us that he was not up to date on developments, but that he understood that Mrs. Christabel Bielenberg, whose contacts were much involved, would be the person to vet projects to which the money could be applied, that the Germans were keen that anything they did would help the German image abroad, and that they would favour social and education projects: in fact, they were required by German law to fulfil these conditions.

I said I saw no reason why we could not work with or through Christabel Bielenberg, provided we had the documents on what projects we were proposing, that the Germans had the same documents, and that all concerned knew exactly where we stood, in black and white. I added that the Germans would hardly expect us to do our business with them on the basis of random telephone calls.

The meeting broke up with members quite pleased, and exchanging Christmas pleasantries. I was profoundly uneasy about the quality of Betty Williams's information: she paid little attention to the minutiae of business proceedings, knew little or nothing of the previous week's work, yet had somehow been alerted to come in urgently to this meeting with this information about Peter McLachlan's salary 'whatever his role'.

Later when Peter McLachlan submitted his draft Company minutes to me before they would be sent out, Betty Williams's intervention was missing and I inserted it. He came back and asked me if I would mind deleting the phrase 'whatever his role' as it might be "embarrassing". I was not quite sure whom it might embarrass; but I deleted it. I kept copies of both versions.

That night there was a pre-Christmas party in the Peace House, and quite a jolly evening going on while I was in my office working on the paper, which had to be prepared early: I was due in Antwerp the following week for a meeting of the Nonviolent Alternatives

Committee, instituted at Dom Helder Camara's initiative. I had two extraordinary visits.

The first was from Jim Galway. He began by saying that he was worried about my leaving the movement to look for work, and said that he felt it would die without me, and that somehow it must be kept alive. He voiced some criticisms, said he thought I was inclined to be autocratic and too impatient on things like the H-Block; that my mind could see farther ahead than others and that I couldn't wait for them to catch up; on the other hand, he allowed that it must have taken quite an effort for me to put up with all the long arguments of the last few months, and he was satisfied that I was genuinely doing my best to accept the democratic wishes of the majority. Then he said: "Now, I don't want you to say no immediately, but discuss it with Marianne if you could stay on with the movement for the time being, and I want to lend you £5,000."

I had been grinning wryly at him as he recounted my failings: now I was surprised and touched and embarrassed, and was starting to reply, when he said, "You can pay me back eventually when things are easier with you. In any case, I have made enquiries with my solicitor, and if I die before you can pay it back, you can pay it to my son."

I was now deeply touched for it was so obvious that Jim Galway had been considering this offer for some time. I thanked him sincerely, told him I would discuss it with Marianne, but that it was unlikely that we could accept for we had already borrowed heavily and that the only way I could get out of debt was to look shortly for work and not have any relief in that pursuit.

He asked me not to reject it out of hand, and repeated that he was making the offer, not so much out of consideration for me, but for the sake of the movement which he felt would die without me.

Shortly after he left, I went downstairs, for Marianne was due at the party. Not long after that, Betty Williams arrived in, and wanted to speak to me urgently for five minutes. We went back up to my office.

I sat in my chair while Betty paced up and down in a way that reminded me of her 'more moderate way' manner six months earlier. Whatever was on her mind was going to have difficulty coming out. She asked me to forgive her, without specifying for what. I said I needed forgiveness aplenty without worrying about forgiving others. So I suggested that she get on with it or that we return downstairs.

She talked of the relationship between Mairead and herself and myself as the most precious thing in her life, and that she didn't want to do anything to damage it; then she apologised for hurting me and hurting the movement. I grasped immediately that she was talking about that morning's meeting, and told her that the person whose forgiveness she should seek was Peter McLachlan since he had gone home to his wife and children thinking he had a job and a salary, and there was no such money and no such job. I asked her who was going to tell the Executive next week that there had been a mistake and that the thing would have to be reconsidered by the Company?

I also told her that I would be in Antwerp the following Thursday when the Executive was due to receive the Company's report.

"Leave Peter McLachlan to me, I'll sort that out in my own way," she said. Then she added, "I want you to know that I always defend you to Christabel Bielenberg." It was news to me that I was under any attack from Mrs. Bielenberg with whom I had had little contact over the previous eighteen months, and who was not a member of the Peace People in Northern Ireland.

"Am I forgiven?" she asked.

"It's not really up to me, but you're forgiven, even for the next time," I laughed, and she returned to the party in the best of spirits.

The German connection, and the conditions attaching to its funds, if any, were beginning to exercise my mind.

I went to Antwerp on Tuesday feeling exhausted and uneasy most of the time. The Executive was so much on my mind that I rang Mairead late on Thursday night, and discovered that the Executive had passed the whole package without being given the slightest indication that Betty's information might be remotely doubtful.

It was Christmas time. The Executive felt it was in charge of its budgeted programme and that it knew where it was going for the first time. It had instructed Peter McLachlan to present the package to the January meeting with no 'two ways forward' deviations, and was impatient to get moving with the new-look Peace People. If I opened the can of worms over the 'money for Peter McLachlan's salary, whatever his role', it might wreck the new-found confidence, and be interpreted in any case as relentless determination on my part to ditch him. On the other hand, if they proceeded, only to find that they had been misled, they would be left feeling twice as stupid and angry.

Moreover, if I did reopen the issue, I would have to be prepared to stay around to bandage the pieces at a time when I was running around trying to get work. The *Sunday Independent* editor, Michael Hand, had offered me a weekly column, and asked other editors to consider giving me other work: but he came under immediate pressure from journalists for even giving me one column.

I decided, rather than having another direct confrontation, to concentrate on getting sufficient funds back from what we were owed to make good the likely shortfall. From then on, the Executive would not be bamboozled by figures or jargon, and would be truculent to know what was being done, by whom, for how much, and by what authority. I also determined to be most particular about the German report.

End Point

Mairead came to see us a couple of days after Christmas. She was struggling to deal with Descartes's 'Cogito ergo sum' and I tried cheerfully to make her sceptical about the seventeenth-century verbiage of the redoubtable René, and to help her realise that she was already familiar, under different terms, with the ideas in Descartes's *Meditations*. But Mairead was distracted, and quite immune to laughter, or to the good cheer of the season.

It was not until she was leaving that she turned at the door and said that her sister Anne had tried to commit suicide on Christmas Day.

Anne and Jackie Maguire had gone with their surviving child Mark to New Zealand, in the Spring of 1977, to make a new start, eight months after the August tragedy. They were already expecting another baby and Joanne was born in July. In spite of preoccupation with the new baby, Anne did not settle, and they returned home within a year. She still did not make steady progress. At times she seemed to be getting better, then would suffer sudden and devastating depressions.

At one point in 1978, when Marianne had been very worried about her fluctuations, she agreed to go with Marianne for a second opinion: this was that she was genuinely suicidal, suffering from psychotic depression and that she needed immediate, radical treatment, and would need subsequent monitoring and treatment, possibly for the rest of her life. She did improve markedly under such treatment for a while in 1978, so much so that she finally abandoned her out-patient visits on the grounds that she was far too well to go and sit among patients much sicker than herself, and who depressed her.

Throughout 1979, her health fluctuated greatly; in June she gave birth to Marie-Louise, and again for a while it seemed as if the new baby might be a healing source of preoccupation. But Anne Maguire was seriously ill: at times she imagined that she saw her dead children playing in the garden. When she visited us shortly before Christmas 1979, Marianne, whose perception at times borders on the psychic, felt that she had gone behind a wall in her mind, and that she might never see her again.

I took it upon myself to consult both the psychiatrist who had recommended and the one who had carried out the treatment which had produced the improvement in 1978. Their prognosis was identical: Anne Maguire would definitely commit suicide unless she received radical treatment to relieve her depression. This was already the second week in January 1980. I reported this to Mairead and we agreed to visit Anne after the January 12 Peace People meeting, to try and persuade her to resume the treatment.

That January 12 meeting of peace group representatives was a most painful affair. Peter McLachlan, to the chagrin of Executive members who realised what was happening, embarked on the 'two ways forward' routine, and did not present the Executive's work programme. When exasperated members did try to get the programme discussed, he sat quiet while group members strayed off this way and that.

When he was faced with the simple position that there was now only *one* way forward, that agreed by the Executive, he moved discussion to whether it was to be presented in an 'abrasive' way or a 'caring' way, and diverted attention to *Peace by Peace*. Executive members resolved to sort the matter out once and for all at the next meeting.

Mairead and I went up to the Maguires': Jackie opened the door. There had always been a sad look about his eyes, ever since I had known him in the wake of their tragedy: now he looked utterly worn out and dejected. He called listlessly up the stairs to Anne that Mairead and Ciaran were here. Anne started to come slowly down the stairs, also wretched looking: her legs had never properly healed and she had the added worry that she would end up in a wheelchair. It was no time for visitors, and I left almost immediately.

Marianne and I, who now had had enough experience of delivering our children in hospitals, had decided to have our sixth at home. No-one had had a planned home delivery in our area since 1972, and there was a little flutter of excitement among the medical people about it. Our doctor was most co-operative and we received instructions on what was required and desirable. The standard of hygiene and consistency of warmth in kitchen, bathroom and bedroom were the basics. So I began to springclean them the following weekend.

By coincidence, I was up on stepladders at a bedroom window in mid-afternoon on Monday, January 21, as I had been on August 10, 1976, when I had been telephoned about the deaths of the Maguire children: now, on this miserably wet winter day, I received a call from Peter McLachlan to tell me that Anne Maguire had committed suicide.

Nothing in my life, which has known its share of murders and suicides and atrocities, has shocked me as much as Anne Maguire's death. I could see her wistful, injured form, dragging herself sadly about.

I recalled that day in our house when Marianne was convinced that she had closed everybody out of her mind, with a sad, but almost serene determination that no-one was going to disturb. I could not bring myself to believe that, nor could I therefore perceive it so accurately as Marianne. I had clung to the hope that with radical medical treatment and the mobilisation of every other possible support, that Anne's life might be preserved against the odds, and that she might slowly return among the living living, instead of walking with the living dead. In the week before she died, she had seemed to be improving, and had told Mairead that she would come into the Peace Office to do a bit of work, to take herself 'out of herself'. She did indeed come into Fredheim on the morning of January 21: but what a morning she picked—it was the darkest and most depressing day of the winter, and there was almost no-one there. Mairead was at college, and even I, who haunted the place, morning, noon and night, was at home springcleaning.

Anne went home at lunch time to start peeling potatoes and get the dinner ready for Mark and Jackie coming home. Shortly afterwards, she made sure that she put herself finally beyond the reach of all medicine. It was an act of courage, coming from her injured depths: the missing children playing in her garden now belonged to a more real world than the world of almost unremitting suffering and loss in which she had tried for so long to endure.

I could not escape the feeling that her death was like an accusation to the peace movement which had been catalysed by her own initial tragedy, that we had not demonstrated and acted with such intense and irresistible love that the silent wounded in our midst might be healed. Surely now, from this vivid grief, a healing energy would flow, this time to heal the peace movement itself.

There followed, instead, three weeks of sustained anguish, resulting in an irreconcilable division.

That evening, I went over to the Corrigans' to find a family which had known more of sudden tragedy than most could bear, stunned, yet thoughtful of others in their grief. Mrs. Corrigan received tearful visitors and relatives, repeating over and over that God is good, God must have His reasons. Mr. Corrigan sat in a corner, broken and moist with grief. Mairead and the other sisters and relatives went back and forth to the kitchen, providing tea and snacks for everyone and anyone who came in.

The media, while respectful, had begun to make enquiries. I told Mairead I would try to fend them off, and tell them simply that Anne had died of a broken heart and that the family wished to be left in peace. I went over to Jackie Maguire's sister's house, where the children were playing with their cousin Mark, children aware that something big and unusual had happened in the grown-ups' world. I had just returned home when Mairead phoned and asked me to come back over.

Betty Williams had arrived in the Corrigans' home and had been asserting that the Provos had killed Anne. Feeling that Betty was very upset, Mairead had gone to the kitchen to get her some tea, when she met a man whom she did not know, in the hall: it was a reporter from UPI International news agency, who had arrived with Betty. Mairead had asked Betty to take the reporter away, saying that the family wanted to be left alone. Betty had departed angrily.

Mairead was still very calm and in complete control of herself. She asked me if I would go and see Betty and calm her down. I told her that there was no point, but that I would try to direct the media to the Peace House, and to ensure that everything was handled with dignity.

In the following morning's papers Betty Williams, was quoted as saying "My wee Anne is dead—we tried so hard to help her". The last thing any of us wanted was any attempt, as was quickly being mooted, to re-launch something like the August 1976 response. I spoke to Peter McLachlan, told him that the families wanted to be left alone and that I would divert the media to the Peace House. I also shook hands with him, and expressed the hope that perhaps now we might all pull together.

A telegram arrived from Cardinal Ó Fiaich, consoling Mairead and her relatives, and expressing the belief that Anne was now happily reunited with her children. This was a great comfort to this devout, orthodox family, that the leader of Ireland's Roman Catholics was making clear that no traditional stigma was attaching to this suicide.

Mairead was now demonstrating the remarkable strength of her personality, and had already decided that her degree course and peace work were entirely secondary to the duty of looking after Anne's children. Over the following twenty-two months, she tried to carry both the leadership of the Peace People and the full responsibilities of housewife and surrogate mother. Finally, she and Jackie Maguire were married in September 1981, and I saw laughter and happiness in Jackie Maguire's face for the first time since I had met him after August 1976.

By the time I was standing at Anne's graveside, I was still stunned by the finality of Anne's act. I thought of her growing up when things were peaceful in West Belfast, falling in love, getting married, beginning to rear a family as the Troubles broke out; then she and Jackie, who had had nothing to do with the Troubles, had had their lives devastated by those Troubles. Half of one young innocent family was thus sent to a cold grave in Belfast's forbidding Milltown cemetery, where, so often, I had stood in the biting wind over various interments. My own relatives, refugees into Belfast from nineteenth century social and political upheavals, were somewhere about under this poor land on the edge of the Bog Meadows, distantly dead. Soon enough, Anne and Joanne and John and Andrew would also be forgotten, with all that suffering. Someday, I too, if I stayed in Belfast, might be interred here, my little life someone else's distant past.

As I walked away from the grave, I became aware of Mrs. Christabel Bielenberg asking me to meet her that afternoon. She would be in the Peace Office, and would see me for half an hour or so to talk about the German trust. It took me several moments to adjust to this arrangement of a business meeting, and then I told her that I simply did not know what I would be doing for the rest of the day, that I had a lot to do, and did not know how much I might be needed otherwise.

She said something about seeing that I was quite upset, and that she would come in in the morning and see me then.

I had also been putting off journalists who had arrived to do retrospective interviews on the Peace People, including some whose approach was to discover what effect Anne's death might have: I wanted to be in a very clear and calm state of mind for that.

The night before the funeral a number of the Peace People veterans had gathered in my house, in a kind of overflow from Corrigans, and Mairead had come over for a while. It was a tender little meeting among a group of people who had been through a lot together. There was some feeling of apprehension that there might be a vulgar attempt to 'bring back August 1976'. We tried to feel our way through this latest tragedy, hoping that out of its pain, a new spirit might heal the Peace People.

I met Mrs. Bielenberg on the morning after Anne Maguire's funeral. She is a formidable lady, obviously used to getting her own way. She had known Peter McLachlan long before the Peace People days, and was staying with Betty Williams. I knew that she was overcoming her distaste for me to deal directly with the matter of the German trust. That she considered me a 'dictator', I took rather as a compliment from one forceful person to another: the only difference being that I felt that those being advised on a decision should have the fullest information possible, whereas Christabel felt that there were things that the 'little people', as she called our members, would not understand.

She began by being extremely solicitous about my health, my financial position and my job prospects. I told her that I was fine, and that my financial situation would be overcome when I was able to go into full-time employment; but added that I would not be free to do that until I was satisfied that my responsibilities, especially my financial responsibilities as chairman of the Peace People Company were fully and honourably discharged—and that one of the things about which I was most unhappy was the status of the proposed German trust.

I told her that it was entirely unsatisfactory for decisions to be taken on the basis of unsubstantiated phone calls from a putative German trustee to a director who was not fully informed. She asked me what I meant, and I recounted to her the Betty Williams intervention at the December meeting—yet here we were six weeks later, and we still did not have the slightest indication whether this trust existed, or whether the finance would be forthcoming. "Oh, I know nothing of any such telephone call," Christabel said.

She impressed upon me that the Germans were putting their confidence in her and that her assent would be required before money could be forwarded for any project. She indicated that only projects which might have some enhancement of the German image abroad could be considered, and that only projects of a broadly social welfare or educational nature would be eligible.

I said that was acceptable, provided that any project forwarded for support in the name of the Peace People, was fully documented by the Peace People, and that all parties—herself, the Germans and the Peace People—knew exactly what was being proposed: which was *not* the case with Betty Williams's information on Peter McLachlan's salary, whatever his role; and that we could not have our staffing policies decided in Germany by anybody, let alone by people whose authority was unknown to us.

Christabel turned the conversation back to her concern for me. She felt that I was born for the intellectual life, the university life, and that I would never be truly happy except in the academic situation. She approved heartily of my proposed 'Achill University of Peace'— "But you would have to go and live there, dear boy," she added most emphatically.

I told her that if all else were equal in this world, I could think of nothing that would make me happier than to spend much of my time in Achill Island, but that that was a pipe dream, for the time being.

I returned to the German problem and told her that I had insisted that Peter lay before the Company at its next meeting a full written report, which we still had not had after six weeks, and on the basis of which we would have to review our position. We would then be able to respond to any proposed trust.

We parted after this conversation, which lasted nearly an hour and a half, on what I imagined were reasonably respectful terms. Having stayed an extra night, she was in a hurry to get home to Carlow, a long drive of perhaps four hours. She popped in to say goodbye to Peter. Three hours later, they were still talking.

The following week saw a vigorous campaign by Betty Williams and Peter McLachlan. At meeting after meeting, puzzled groups were roused to anger over the 'two ways forward'. Betty presented herself as the hurt and much manipulated founder of the Peace People, and said that Mairead was blind in her loyalty to me; much as Betty admired me, it was time to 'give the movement back to the people'. She also attacked reported remarks of mine about the Nobel Prize. Peter McLachlan allowed that there had been continued difficulty in the Executive over the two ways forward; and that I should be treated with great sympathy, that I was a man of exceptional gifts who had been very deeply upset by Anne Maguire's death, and was 'in need of pastoral care'!

Peter called a 'few concerned people' to his home, to talk to them intimately about his sensitive problem in handling me in my present shocked condition, and asked his puzzled guests if there might be some way they could help me, perhaps encourage me with the peace university project. The most important of the 'wee meetings' as they became known, was more or less stopped in its tracks by the very straightforward suggestion of one of those present, that he had been talking to me and that I seemed quite normal, and should I not be present if my future was being discussed?

There was one comical, embarrassing meeting which arose from this frenetic campaigning. A couple of those who had been present at such consultations thought that perhaps they should have a discreet meeting with me to find out how I was and if there was any way they could help. They persuaded Jim Galway to invite me out to his house to discuss how 'things were going'. I arrived to find three of my colleagues. There was a delicate moment or two as they looked from one to the other, as if one of them would have to open up on some sensitive question. They started to ask me about my state of health, and about Marianne and about my job prospects.

I was touched by their concern. I had already rejected Jim Galway's offer of £5,000 and I suspected that they were about to come up with a similar proposition which I would equally reject, but it was touching nevertheless.

I started to turn the conversation towards our work, when one of them explained that they had been concerned about me, and that that was why they had called this meeting. I told them with obvious energy that I was in fine form, and they seemed to accept that. Next day, one of them explained to me about the 'wee meetings', and said he did not know what was going on but that two things were very obvious: the purpose of these meetings was to secure my removal one way or another from the movement, and to close or change the paper. I told him not to worry, that Betty Williams would be going to the States in a couple of weeks and that Peter McLachlan's politicking would fall flat on its face as ever.

But I was now convinced that, for some reason connected with the German trust, my removal and the emasculation of the paper were the top priorities for Betty Williams and Peter McLachlan, and that it had little to do with the 'two ways forward'. The thing also went deeper than Betty's soreness over the Nobel Prize reference which I made to a *Sunday Times* reporter.

In the week after Anne Maguire's death, this man had asked me directly whether I thought the Nobel Prize had helped or hindered our work. I told him that while the prize might have helped us, our handling of it was the worst single mistake that we had made, in my view: it had happened exactly at the time when we had been trying to get people to come to terms with the disillusionment that inevitably followed the high expectations of our launching period; and that it had damaged our credibility greatly within Northern Ireland, especially when it was learned that Betty and Mairead would be keeping the money.

Our members were in troubled disarray, and members of the Executive, so recently heartened, were puzzled and distressed. The 'two ways forward' mythology, once Betty Williams put the full force of her personality behind it, had become an effective divide-and-rule manoeuvre.

I came to the conclusion that if I were to work for thirty hours a day for months, we would end barely holding together on a half-lie, while the serious work remained neglected, the H-Block crisis worsened, and my own career remained in doubt.

In the first week in February, each member of the Executive received a letter from Mr. Bob Rodwell, a freelance journalist who had been a member of the Peace People Executive a couple of years earlier, and who was vehemently opposed to our involvement in the prison issue, to the ethos of nonviolence, as well as any suggestion that we should be actively concerned about Third World issues. His letter, as well as invoking his personal views at some length, called for my resignation for the good of the Peace People.

While I would not have taken any more notice of Mr. Rodwell's views than the majority of Peace People did, his letter was taken to speak for one of the meetings addressed by Betty Williams.

With Alan Senior, then writing for *Peace by Peace*, I rang Mr. Rodwell to correct him factually on a couple of points, including his assertion that people could not sell the paper because of its contents. My rejection of this, endorsed by Alan Senior, from our own experience, made no difference.

Any hope that the Executive might be able to ignore the latest round of lobbying and get on with its work, was disappearing fast. The last straw for me, was a proposal from some members, that rallies be held in the wake of Anne Maguire's death on a peace-before-justice theme.

I made up my mind to present the Executive with a clear choice between two ways forward: either I would stay, unpaid, and concentrate on sorting out the mess in which our projects department floundered, put our financial house in order, sort out the German funds, if any, hand the paper over completely to Steve McBride, and make sure that every group and every member knew exactly the work proposed by the Executive; or I would happily resign and look after my family and career. The only condition was that I would not work a day longer on the same Executive as Betty Williams or Peter McLachlan.

Mairead urged me not to do this. We had quite a heated argument about it. She said we should give it another try, that no matter what Betty said at meetings, she would always support me face-to-face. She outlined Peter McLachlan's qualities and the fact that without Betty's support, he was too weak to do anything. She argued that the whole thing would split and kill the movement.

I argued that the Peace People had been dying on their feet for months, and were being split constantly; and that if the movement were killed by my action, at least it would clear the way for others to try something else. I disparaged her suggestion of any 'man-to-man' meetings. Finally she said that if I went ahead, she would support me. I told her to make up her own mind regardless of what happened to me, and that she should consider staying on even if my departure was the outcome.

The Split

The February 7 meeting of the Peace People Executive began at about 8 p.m. with long-serving member Eddie McCotter in the chair. Almost at once, I asked that the agenda be suspended, since not everyone around the table would be a member of the Executive at the end of the meeting: either I would still be a member, and Betty Williams and Peter McLachlan would not; or they would, and I would not.

Betty Williams at once declared her love of the movement, and said that she did not want anything to happen to it, and there was no need for any split, that she was resigning and she got up to leave. I asked her to stay, since we could not allow her absence to inhibit discussion of things concerning her, and added that it was not fair to leave Peter McLachlan to bear the burden of explanation.

She left, despite pleas from others. To this day, reports appear, as they did from the first week, in spite of our statements to the contrary, that Betty Williams resigned in protest over the removal of Peter McLachlan from the Peace People Executive: the fact is that she resigned before the substantial discussion began.

I then gave at some length the reasons that I would no longer have confidence in either of them. Members were in varying degrees dismayed and angry that their own months of work seemed a secondary matter. A few then reported on 'wee meetings' they had been called to, to the chagrin of those who had not been so summoned.

But all of us were surprised when, after the question of the German money arose, Peter McLachlan announced that he had had a report from Christabel Bielenberg. He retired to his office to fetch it, while members seethed that a person who was not even in the Northern Ireland Peace People might indirectly be telling the Executive what to do.

The indignation exploded when Mrs. Bielenberg's letter revealed that the proposed German trust had about £2,000 available, none of which the Peace People could necessarily call upon, since it could be applied only to projects approved by Mrs. Bielenberg: yet the Executive had increased its budget provision, on the basis of this presumed resource, to cover the salary and secretarial expenses of Peter McLachlan, by some £10,000. The letter, moreover, dated January 29 and addressed to the Company chairman, that is, myself, had arrived shortly thereafter: this was the first we had heard of it, and it was far from being the full report requested.

Mairead said that she could not go on papering over the cracks, that it was like living a lie. In response to reports from an East Belfast meeting, suggesting that Betty had decided to keep her half of the Nobel money *after* Mairead, a single girl who needed the money, had decided to keep hers, Mairead outlined the events leading to the Nobel cash decision.

Jim Galway bridled at what he called my autocratic stance, and accused me of dictating to the Executive. Usually, I would let the charge pass; but on this occasion reminded the Executive that I had one voice and one vote, and that the only dictation was from German money in the hands of people we scarcely knew.

Some members did say, effectively for the first time, that it was about time that the Executive took responsibility for its own decisions, and that we had been too happy for too long to let Ciaran McKeown take the stick for any unpopular aspect of policies agreed by Assembly after Assembly.

The turning point for several was quite simply that Peter McLachlan failed to answer the case made. He made muted points about being concerned about different ways forward, and needing time to consider his position; his invocation of Christabel Bielenberg's name, reporting her worry about the future of the movement after a conversation with me, merely alienated members. When he recounted Mrs. Bielenberg's opinion that I was in need of pastoral care, this evoked both mirth and contempt.

Everyone present understood that the dream of the Peace People as a cohesive force was over for the time being, and that friendships were going to be strained to snapping point: so the anger and deep frustration was held in check by a sense of responsibility to do what was right for what so recently had been such a force for good in the land.

Three propositions were put to the meeting: that Peter McLachlan be asked to leave the Executive; that our projects department be examined to decide if there was a job there which he might retain, or if the German funds would justify such a job, in either case this role to be separated from the Executive's work; and that no-one divulge anything of the meeting until the next meeting could decide how to present the outcome, and whether a project management job might be described.

The proposal to make the meeting entirely confidential was accepted by everyone, including Peter McLachlan. Members cast about for ways of blunting the starkness of the proposal that he be asked to leave. One idea was that all four known personalities should quit the Executive, leaving the unsplit remainder to get on with it, and thus avoiding the circus that would erupt around the high-profile figures. Both propositions were put, with seven in favour of Peter McLachlan leaving on his own, four in favour of all the 'personalities' retiring.

A curious confusion arose with Jim Galway: Jim was hard of hearing, and he was not clear whether Peter McLachlan had indicated that he was willing to stay on as projects manager, should such a job exist. Peter McLachlan, after some initial confusion, indicated that he would be prepared to consider this, just as the vote was being called: but Jim thought that he was not and tendered his resignation.

As he was leaving, I said to him, "Jim, wait, I think you are mistaken about Peter, he is willing to stay on if separate project work is possible."

"Ah, Ciaran," Jim replied, "there is no chance of getting the German money now." I was deeply surprised at his answer, and made no further attempt to dissuade him.

It was all over at about 2 a.m. and Peter McLachlan and Betty Williams were off the Executive. But far from feeling that I had 'won', I felt closer to defeat than at any time. I had prevailed over Betty Williams's vociferous opposition to persuade her and others to appoint Peter McLachlan, just as I had prevailed over himself and others in October 1976 to ignore media split stories and bigotry, to stay in and get on with the work: now I was agent of his removal.

If there was an external 'victory', there was an internal humiliation. Far from its getting easier with time to accommodate this feeling, I have gradually come to the conclusion that I was, in some subconscious way, dodging the responsibility of leadership that was mine: my fine theory of rotating leadership was a self-deceptive way of passing the buck.

The other humiliating realisation was that I had put both Betty Williams and Peter McLachlan in positions in which they could hardly have behaved other than they did. I now see, as I did not at the time, that I was a much more intimidating presence to them than I imagined. My forcefulness must have come over as dictation: the charge of 'dictator' so frequently made had a psychological validity that I did not fully recognise; and this put people under a stress, with consequences for their behaviour.

I do not say, however, that it made it impossible for them to approach the Peace People straightforwardly, or even get to Mrs. Bielenberg to do it, and say: 'Look, you're finished as a peace movement with any influence to get things done on issues like the prisons: but if you drop all your controversial and political aspects, and confine yourselves to social and educational projects, we can raise large German funds for that purpose." My presence prevented that from happening, but I can never know if my absence would not merely have resulted in the purpose of the Peace People being emasculated, without our members even realising what was going on.

For months before this climax, the Peace People had been plagued by harebrained flyers in the newspapers, of the 'inspired leak' variety. While work proceeded in a buoyant atmosphere of relief the day after the meeting, we waited for the media to erupt with some destructive invention attributed perhaps to 'concerned members'. To our astonishment nothing appeared. As Friday, then Saturday passed without a word being breathed, we began to hope that that we might get through this crisis without a media circus.

Betty Williams rang me on Saturday to say that she was going South to stay incommunicado until Wednesday when she would be going to the United States. She said that if the media caught up with her, she would simply say that she wanted peace to be with her family. She wished Mairead and myself all her love and support for the future of the movement.

Then, on Sunday afternoon, I was telephoned by the Manchester news desk of the *Daily Mail*. A long report from the freelance journalist Bob Rodwell, was read over to me. It was the story which, substantially, was used throughout the world over the following days, and is the standard version for the 'Peace People Split' when papers refer back to the organisation in such stories as Betty Williams's departure from Northern Ireland, or her remarriage, or the 'where are they now' pieces.

It proclaimed the split between the two Nobel prizewinners, after trouble had come to a head over the support given by Mr. McKeown to the Provisional IRA dirty protestors; this had led to the dismissal of Mr. Peter McLachlan; Betty Williams had resigned 'in protest over Mr. McLachlan's removal', as had the movement's treasurer, Jim Galway.

The quotations in the report attributed to Peter McLachlan corresponded with the version he gave in interviews that evening and the following day. He said: "Many people are unhappy about the movement's high-profile political activity. The attitude towards politicians had often been critical, and the attitude to the Church on one occasion very critical. This style of approach has gradually alienated people from the movement. It is at the heart of the internal conflicts."

Peter McLachlan genuinely surprised me by giving interviews at all. The next time I heard his voice was on BBC radio, allowing that "The H-Block issue was one of several which had caused division and aroused concern."

As far as the world was concerned, those two wonderful women Betty Williams and Mairead Corrigan had been split by the support for Provisional IRA prisoners from "the Svengali figure who manipulates the movement behind the backs of Betty and Mairead," to use the *Sunday Times* description.

Vague references to finance, never *once* accurate, to my knowledge, were tossed in to reinforce the destructive effect of the ensuing coverage. I could not resist a wry smile when the *Belfast Telegraph* editorialised—after noting that the clash was over 'personalities' and 'attitudes to the H-Block controversy'—that 'there is an admirable integrity about an organisation which decides to divide on principle, rather than survive on compromise'.

The Peace People Press Officer, Joe Johnston, rang round as many Executive members as he could, to get approval for a minimal statement that would still respect the Executive's confidentiality on the German money and other issues which were the real reason for its decisions: it simply recorded that Betty Williams had resigned *before* Peter McLachlan had been asked to leave, and that both were on the record supporting Peace People policy on the H-Block issue and had not declared any deviation from that, nor was this or any other such policy or personality reason behind the proposal to ask both to leave, as Betty Williams would have been asked, had she not resigned first. Against the deluge of distortion, this statement had all the visibility of a tadpole in a tidal wave.

The Executive held an emergency meeting. With remarkable maturity, it decided to waste no energy fighting the misrepresentations. In general, it decided that we would proceed doggedly with our work: if the work was worthy, it would shine by its own light; if it were not, there was no point in getting involved in a public dog-fight.

It also decided that there could be no question of Peter McLachlan's being associated in any way with the Peace People, after his statements to the media. At the same time, it was felt that we should not allow his breach of confidentiality to cause us to do the same, and that we would ask our members to trust us in keeping it confidential, rather than go over the whole nasty business again in semi-public.

On Wednesday, February 13, the recently appointed new Chief Constable of the RUC, Jack Hermon, made his first public statement in his new post. It was an excellent address, in which he expressed the hope that the RUC could become a force winning the support of all, a force in which a policeman could one day again walk down a street, among neighbours, without a flak jacket.

It was exactly the kind of policy change we had been hoping for, and I, as the agreed spokesperson on justice issues, issued a statement welcoming it, and gave a radio interview in response. We were going to get on with this kind of work and put the 'split' behind us.

Minutes after I came off the radio interview, I was telephoned by the same station, about a statement allegedly issued by Betty Williams before departing to the United States. The statement which had been left with her house companion for transmission, had all the hallmarks of a professional job, drafted by someone other than Betty Williams. It included the untruth that she had resigned in protest over the removal of Peter McLachlan, and denied my reported comment on her good wishes to myself and Mairead.

The media had begun to speculate that there would be an 'alternative peace movement' led by Betty Williams and Peter McLachlan, so the story kept boiling. We remained determined to silence. Yet on the very day that the Company was to meet to consider the terms under which Peter McLachlan's relationship with us might formally be severed, I was again phoned by news desks, quoting a freelance journalist, that the topic for the Company's meeting was *my* resignation, and that Peter McLachlan was to be 're-instated'. I simply refused to comment.

The *Belfast Telegraph*'s front-page headline was 'McKeown silent on quit claims'. A freelance journalist had also advised the media that there would be a press conference that evening on 'McKeown's resignation': so while the Company of which I was Chairman debated for hours the precise terms of Peter McLachlan's dissociation from us, Steve McBride had to stand downstairs telling newspeople that there was no press conference. Angry reporters directed much of their ire at the Peace People, urging us to 'get our act together'; a few reserved their abuse for the freelance journalist. In spite of all this, further sketchy stories appeared, all reiterating the same gross misrepresentations. Our own members were in great distress, the more so because we remained silent on the background to the crisis.

A request reached the Executive to hold a special meeting of the Assembly, which was due to meet in any case in just over six weeks' time. We discovered that some of those purported to have signed the request had not even been consulted, while others had signed, not knowing what the purpose of meeting was to be. The request was ruled out of order, but the genuine people involved were advised that there would be a representative meeting in two weeks' time, with an Assembly a month later, so that the ruling made no material difference.

The Executive finally decided, still without disclosing the substantial reasons for the February 7 decisions, to challenge the relentless distortions. We circulated a press release to news desks, naming a name. The release was not used, but the distortions stopped. The person sued for libel. The Executive's solicitor advised that however justified members might feel, it would be wiser to settle out of court, with an agreed form of apology circulated in the same manner to news desks, and with a few hundred pounds for the litigant. The Executive agreed to this advice, despite opposition from both myself and Mairead.

The March meeting in Newry of group representatives was a highly charged event. Betty Williams made a short appearance in which she professed her love for "those two wonderful people, Mairead and Ciaran", said that she was leaving the movement now and wanted to be left in peace. She rejected appeals from this wonderful person to stay, and not to leave Peter McLachlan once again to bear the burden of explanation. The meeting gave overwhelming support to the Executive, on a proposal to that effect from Jim Galway. And the programme of work that had been agreed three months earlier was at last presented to the members.

The internal healing that began in Newry, deepened remarkably at the April Assembly, held in Benburb. The anguish of the foregoing months had eased, an almost tangible spirit of renewal was present, and the Saturday night social event was a happy, uncomplicated affair. Then, just as the closing session on Sunday afternoon prepared to put its resolve into concrete terms, Mrs. Christabel Bielenberg, who had arrived from Carlow, rose to speak from a long script which she also distributed to the media.

It was an astonishing speech. The central theme was that all her life since the days of Hitler, she had opposed dictators, and that that was what she was doing now, the dictator in question being Ciaran McKeown. But while the Peace People became more and more incensed at her attacks on me, in the presence of Marianne and all six of our children, I was much more interested in what Christabel was revealing in her anger.

It emerged that the controversial issues raised in *Peace by Peace* were the stumbling block to the establishment of the German trust, which could not in any way be associated with controversy in another country. Christabel explained that they had been hopeful in June 1979 that Ciaran McKeown was leaving, so that the paper would then be less 'unsatisfactory' to the would-be German sponsors. As for Betty Williams's telephone information from a German financier, Christabel now told the Peace People that it was herself who had given Betty this information (that there would be money for Peter McLachlan's salary whatever his role). As indignation was rising around me, I found myself admiring Christabel's guts in coming to state her case, even if she seemed blind to its irony: the only shortcoming, in a way, was the absence of any explanation on how £2,000 could guarantee £10,000, and why the Peace People had not been informed earlier about these German-based plans for their future.

The Peace People shifted and seethed thoughout the long and revealing address. But they received her politely enough. Immediately afterwards, Mairead Corrigan got up and, without directly attacking the previous speaker, said that it was about time that the Peace People answered back when Ciaran McKeown was being attacked as a dictator.

When she declared that Marianne and I had given more than anyone to this movement, and that all we got for our pains was abuse, the Assembly rose to its feet in tribute.

The next day, the coverage in the *Irish Times* of the Peace People's recovery Assembly focussed on Mrs. Bielenberg's comparisons with Hitler. But with Mairead now chairman, the media coverage gradually became more sympathetic, even if it was less. I set about recovering outstanding loans. In some substantial cases, the money was returned without undue difficulty, and occasionally even with a note of thanks. In many, there was simply a nil response, in some, outright hostility, since they had understood, letter of contract notwithstanding, that they would not have to repay. I made a few more enemies, but rather more than £25,000 was recovered, with a larger amount written off.

In June, we circulated *Time for a Change*, a booklet on the (Temporary) Emergency Provisions Act. I did an hour-long phone-in on local BBC radio on its contents, and we hoped that it might affect the government's approach to the renewal of the Act, even as the H-Block situation deteriorated. It was an excellent booklet, based on a splendid body of research carried out by Yale postgraduate student Tom Foley, who was working with us as a volunteer. Tom later produced an even more telling legal document on such law for the Yale *Law Journal*. The quality of the material, and the complexity of the issue did not prevent the phone-in from being a fairly continuous stream of bigotry, laced with suggestions that we were communists. When I came out of the studio, I remarked to the BBC senior radio producer, "Here I am doing a phone-in on emergency law, trying to get some normality back here, and with every word I'm making it harder for myself to get a normal job." He looked at me as if I was daft to even think of getting a normal job: "Sure, Ciaran, you'll never work in journalism here again."

I was grateful for his straightness. He suggested that I try the public relations branch of the media, which could use my unique experience. But my 'unique experience' was, predictably enough, even more frightening to the PR wing of journalism.

I was surprised that this also applied in Dublin, where my former colleague, Michael Keane, now in an executive position with the Irish Press Group, also told me that I would "never work in mainstream journalism again". I got the same response at RTE, if a little less bluntly. The best version was a kind of Catch-22: I would be accepted as an objective journalist again when I had written enough objective articles for long enough. But I could hardly get started since I was outside the pale.

I wish I could say that my informal exclusion from journalism arose from the profession's acute regard for standards of precision and objectivity, which might bar anyone known to have strong views of any sort. I could not say that with conviction, but perhaps the fact that I was a 'controversial' public figure was sufficient: in mitigation I would argue that I am controversial because of an uncompromising commitment to the force of truth, which is not, presumably, unconnected with journalism's code of ethics. The happiest light in which I can respond to the exclusion is to presume that the editors and directors of the various organs know that they would never know the day when I might quit the pack again for conscientious reasons. I cannot be relied on to 'play the game'; in Reaganese, I am not a 'team player', in the sense required. If I lived in Eastern Europe, I suppose I would be called a dissident, and Westerners would campaign for my freedom to work.

The Peace People settled down steadily to a modest programme of work, which won quiet respect for the sheer fact of persistence. As the situation in the prisons worsened dramatically in 1980, there were voices raised in support of our 'emergency status' solution, notably those of Bishop Edward Daly and the distinguished surgeon John Robb.

I found that people who had resisted thought about the issue now conceded that it was the most serious threat to developing reconciliation. The only group with whom I sensed any alienation over it was the Irish Council of Churches, whose approach of supporting the government in 'not giving in' was largely based on the need not to offend people who had suffered from terrorism: I felt that their lightweight contributions on the topic, and its low level of priority on their agenda bespoke a closeness to the Unionist tribal position rather than a commitment to the Gospel. Still, it made a change to be out of step with Protestant prelates rather than Catholic ones!

The area in which, ironically, I detected most convergence with our views was with the Chief Constable Sir John Hermon and the British Army Commander in Northern Ireland, Sir Richard Lawson. Both reiterated the desirability of scaling down the military profile and returning to normal policing; and I know that they were actively considering recommendations to remove parts of the Emergency Provisions Act, as a move in the same process. However, the personalised confrontation between Mrs. Thatcher and the Provisional IRA was becoming more shrill.

While she reiterated her 'crime is a crime is a crime' statement, the prisoners continued to smear the walls with excrement, and the stalemate deepened in its quality of malevolence. The Peace People lobby to get the issue defused and resolved before it burst into murder on the streets, fell on mostly deaf ears. The public was continuing to enjoy the decline in violence, and did not want to think about something so hideous as the prison issue was becoming.

At times, I must confess, I had the feeling that some of the protagonists in the dispute somehow wanted renewed confrontation for its own sake: people can become hooked on violence as surely as on drugs, and on all of the attendant drama. Such people, and they are not few, would be bored by a solution to our endemic crises.

When there is no dynamic vision to inspire a community to creative enterprises of all sorts, then the alternatives are stagnation or violent disintegration. And in 1980, the lull was tangibly a prelude to violence.

Our ability to campaign on this ground severely compromised, the Peace People nevertheless persisted in efforts to draw the poison, and with renewed attempts at dialogue at the trickier ends of the conflict. The October Assembly 1980, the last time I guided it through its agenda, also marked the organisation's demise as an agency with significant impact in the community. It was, in some ways, one of the best Peace People meetings of all.

While the British government could not get the politicians to talk, and the paramilitary organisations slanged each other through the hate-sheets, the Peace People Assembly staged an open dialogue session in the Europa Hotel in central Belfast, with representatives of both political parties and paramilitary organisations on the same platform.

The Assembly finished on a very familiar note, with the *Belfast Telegraph* producing a vintage flyer on its front page: 'Peace People in cash crisis', 'Headquarters may go', etc. The 'authority' for this damaging gem was a piece of idle speculation at the microphone by a former Executive member on what might happen if we ever ran out of cash. I saw it coming when the reporter and a Press Association colleague buttonholed the person who made the fatuous remarks, and I took the trouble to explain to both reporters the exact position, that the Peace People had enough resources for their work, and that there was no question of selling the headquarters.

The fact that the best informed member of the Peace People, the chairman of the Company which funded the Peace People, took these reporters through the audited accounts, was not allowed to interfere with the chance of running a cheap Saturday afternoon flyer, which went all over the world within twenty-four hours.

When I made representations to both the paper and the agency, both issued retractions, but naturally, on nothing like the scale of the original. Our friends, near and far, were yet again left doubting our competence or our credibility.

It was sometimes suggested among us that the relentless misrepresentation which we endured might have been some kind of conspiracy, following our involvement on such as the prison issue. I reject such theories. Much of the distortion was the result of our own openness, and the playing of the 'leak' game by anonymous insiders, so that the sloppiness was often at both ends of a story.

Moreover, the ideas and activities we advocated did not fit the conventional left-wing, right-wing categories: they required reflection, and daily newspaper deadlines and needs do not cater for thoughtfulness.

The issues, debates, and participants at the October 1980 Assembly represented a remarkable event at a time of impending polarisation. It fascinated and inspired visitors: it was of no interest to local media. Perhaps, like so many, the media were war weary after ten years, and could not summon the thoughtfulness to consider that there might be some way to avoid what was on the horizon.

If people at home were unable to summon the effort to address our problems with sufficient energy, the same could not be said that year of others half a world away, in Los Angeles.

In July, another little bombshell had dropped among us. There had been rumours for two years, after Betty Williams had returned from one of her U.S. trips saying, 'they want to make a movie about me!' It seemed at the time half-serious, that a movie about the Peace People, centred on Betty, was already the subject of negotiation. Certainly, one Hollywood company had already respected our request that no movie be considered.

Now, out of the blue, I received a phone call from a woman acting on behalf of an American production company, and liaising with the

William Morris agency (in turn acting for 20th Century Fox), wanting to negotiate with me on a movie about the Peace People.

I told her that she was wasting her time, but she and a colleague arrived at my house, exuding professional determination. She outlined the proposition, acknowledging the very good reasons which we might have for resisting, and offering contracts to Jackie Maguire, Mairead Corrigan and myself, under which we would be very well paid for doing nothing other than allowing our names and activities to be the subject of the movie. I was offered an extra inducement as 'script consultant' since they knew that I 'was the guy who really ran the show'.

I was struck throughout this presentation by the absence of any offer of contract to Betty Williams, whose name featured centrally on the proposed contracts, and queried this omission. She told me that 'was a separate matter'. I told the lady that we wanted no movie made.

I added that we had heard long ago about Betty's negotiations over a movie, and that it was a bit late in the day to be coming to us for the facts.

When she raised the thousands of dollars for doing nothing, I told her that our lives were invested in our efforts, and that while we needed money like anybody else, money was not the issue: we wanted no movie to be made.

She said she appreciated the difficulties we had had with Betty Williams and gave an assurance that Betty Williams would have no say whatever in the script.

But the real punch came when she said: "Look Mr. McKeown, this movie is going to be made. Now the studio is prepared to put up twenty million dollars for a serious version, hiring the best scriptwriter they can get, and making sure you guys are fully consulted. This is a serious business and we think there is going to be a market soon for a peace-issue movie. But the bottom line is that if we can't get the co-operation to do the job properly, we are going ahead with a low-budget six million dollar movie, and we can fictionalise and dramatise with what is on the public record."

This was strong stuff. I had visions of the balloon going up all over again, and appealed to her that a movie would just blow the bottom out of everything we were trying to do. Her response was to offer a facility fee to the Peace People, and also that crowd scenes might be filmed in Belfast.

I heard myself saying, "How can you be so sure that Betty Williams can have no say in the script?" She gave a convincing series of reasons, and then added, "I can call Betty right now and you can clear it yourself."

I had the horrible feeling that I was being sucked into a web of negotiation over something I wanted nothing to do with, and an equally horrible feeling that if I kept out of it, the Peace People would be suffocated without trace by a cheap movie. From the days when Betty had been uttering what sounded like fantasy about thousands of dollars, and 'Jane Fonda playing me', to this lady sitting in my home urging me to phone the Morris agency lawyers in New York, was absurdity on top of nightmare.

I spoke to the lawyers who were well briefed, enthusiastic, plausibly genuine—and impatient because the project had already been held up for some considerable time.

My threat to sue if they made any movie without our consent, was cheerfully and politely derided by reference to the resources available to the movie people to contest any law suits.

I said that I would have to have lawyers look at the contracts, and in the meantime, would want at least one clause, reserving all rights on the story of the Peace People, included, regardless of what movie they might wish to peg around Betty Williams personally. They accepted this readily enough.

Some days later, Tom Foley, coming once again to the vital assistance of the Peace People, got a Yale friend in a Los Angeles law firm to take our case as 'a public interest case' which would therefore cost us nothing. By that time, we knew that an initiation budget in the order of a quarter of a million dollars was available—simply to start the project up: it would be written off, if the project failed to get off the ground. After Tom and his friend had done their work, we heard no more, which is just as well, for we would have been operating 'out of our league'.

In December 1980, I tidied up the remainder of my responsibilities as chairman of the Peace People Company, and retired from all but membership. Like myself, the organisation has had to come to terms with a sense of failure as shattering as the early promise was invigorating. It persists, its facilities and resources intact, with such efforts as it can, in a circumstance of uncertain stalemate. Now and again, it sparks into life, as when a Norwegian volunteer, Eleanor Brenna, along with Sheena Flynn, Paul Smyth and Martin O'Brien, revived the youth section.

Eleanor's work has continued to bear fruit as the 'youth' have become young adults, taking a leading role in the current Peace People activities.

Like Eleanor and Tom Foley, other overseas volunteers have provided fresh energy among a group that was exhausted with its internal and external struggles. At the time of writing, an American,

Bob Gordon, is, with some of the younger members, busily establishing a Peace People farm project. It will not, of itself, bring 'peace' to Northern Ireland: but it is, like many ideas and activities, part of the creative residue of an effort whose 'failure' is not like that of armies which leave corpses on battlefields, and scars on lives.

If I mention these welcome overseas volunteers for their particular initiatives, it is not for a moment to obscure the regular meetings and activities of those peace workers who have persisted, both in the Peace People and like organisations, with their efforts for a more civilised future.

They are a leavening influence who represent the hope of renewed drives in the future, and the inspiring example of persistence in unfavourable circumstances. In the period of my 'retirement' to start a new career, and put my life in order, I see from time to time my neighbours Mina Caskey and Catherine Hanna doing their door-to-door sales of *Peace by Peace*. They inspire me to work harder, to work for a day when I can once again put all my energies into the passion for peace, and I cannot but imagine that they leave something of that feeling among all whose doors they so regularly approach.

Epilogue

During the three years and several attempts to produce this book, there have been changes in the lives and circumstances portrayed, which might be footnoted here.

The H-Block hunger strike of October 1980 by seven republicans ended when the acting leader of the non-striking prisoners accepted an arrangement offered by the Northern Ireland Office. Christmas 1980 and New Year 1981 were briefly hopeful as that leader, Bobby Sands, persuaded his fellows to begin co-operating with the new deal. It broke down, and Sands then took the lead in a new hunger strike.

He died in May 1981 and will therefore be remembered forever in the folklore of Irish revolutionary mythology. During the two months of his final protest, he was elected Member of the Westminster Parliament for the constituency of Fermanagh and South Tyrone. Thus began the emergence of Provisional Sinn Fein as a serious ballot-box political organisation which has now, in the shape of its president, Gerry Adams, taken Gerry Fitt's old seat in West Belfast.

The Sands election was an example of Irish people opposed to the IRA voting for an IRA man in a mixture of compassion to save his life, and the Irish Nationalist instinct to support one of their own against the belligerence of the British Prime Minister, Mrs. Thatcher, who made herself a highly personal adversary of the prisoners.

The hunger strike led to the deaths of ten prisoners and of sixty-seven people outside in directly associated violence. It polarised the community deeply, suggesting that many more lives will be lost over the years as a result—unless the lessons are learned, and exceptional efforts are made at last to resolve the original conflicts.

Initiatives by Humphrey Atkins and then by James Prior, who has tried another Stormont Assembly, have all but failed, thus further damaging belief in the parliamentary process.

I stand by my long belief: democratic consensus can only be built painfully slowly across the ground in Northern Ireland, giving real power and finance to units small enough not to contain any sizeable minority community of either tradition; and when that foundation has been thoroughly developed, centralised parliamentary structures can be agreed in an entirely different climate.

By the same inexorable logic, all efforts to solve the problem through the agencies of the British and Irish governments, or some wider international influence, will fail; and in their very failure, they will deepen cynicism and prolong the predisposition to maintain armed organisations enjoying cultural tolerance, however illegal or otherwise discouraged. As someone remarked in a discussion of the potential helpfulness of the EEC in solving the old Irish question— "you do not solve a problem by making it bigger!"

The orthodoxies still make peace-like noises but have yet to move decisively towards that nonviolence which alone, I believe, can begin to heal the death culture. Certainly, there are many encouraging efforts at ecumenism, and it remains the underlying truth that the majority of Northern Irish people are not only friendly, and desirous of a decent and peaceful life, but genuinely religious people. For that very reason, they would be more likely than most to respond to leadership from the orthodoxies in the direction of nonviolence. Having seen the failure of parliaments, armies, police and peace movements to create 'the promised land' on earth, they will scarcely trust any initiative that does not tune in credibly with orthodox authority.

Moreover, it is, again in my opinion, only the passionate commitment which nonviolence releases that can inspire the generosity of spirit our situation demands. No clever solution, no cobbled-up structure at the top, no amount of financial or other inducement will set the Northern Irish on the road to creative stability, without that vision.

Northern Ireland's unemployment is now an endemic 20 per cent: we are the most advanced post-industrial society in the world. Artistic and cultural activities are enjoying exceptional vitality.

Mairead and Jackie Maguire have had another boy and are enjoying the peace of a rural home south of Belfast.

Betty Williams is now Betty Perkins and has, I hope, found happiness in her new life. None of the disappointments outlined in this book, can extinguish the spark between us which once worked so well for good.

Peter McLachlan was employed by a welfare society immediately after leaving the Peace People.

I signed on the dole in December 1980, an interesting experience not only for me, but, it seemed, others in the same queue. The man who took a great deal of work off my shoulders and made Peace People publications look so well, Gerry O'Reilly, offered to train me as a typesetter. I am now a self-employed typesetter.

My life has also been enriched by involvement as honorary secretary of Belfast's Lyric Players Theatre, especially during this period of promise with so many new writers.

But most of all, as may have been obvious between the lines, I have the riches of Marianne, and our seven children, Marianne, Rachel, Susan, Simon, Ruth, Leah and Hannah, growing up around us, giving us so much to be grateful for, and so much to look forward to in the generations ahead.

The process of setting down this record has been, for me, another part of the peace pilgrimage, an exploration in solitude of a relationship in community. The narrative will have revealed, I hope, my own egotisms as much as anyone's, the impatience and sharpness of tongue that must often have unwittingly wounded. Deeper still, the connection between naïveté, arrogance, and self-deception, lurking subtly in the flawed human psyche, has been, for me, one of the discoveries of this pilgrimage, a source of personal violence, self-destructive and damaging to relationships.

Yet deeper still is that desire to celebrate the inexpressible miracle of this life, my own, those with whom I am most immdiately in love, all the dead and living and unborn, everything that moves or is still. I am more at peace than ever, able to relish the mysterious wonder of our existence, in everything from the existential quality of a garbage can to the awesome explosions of the sun which sustains life so abundantly on this planet, threatened only by humankind's ignorance and distorted relationships. This peace, even in the most frightening era of human experience, is not that of seeking a tranquil sunset, but a restlessly dynamic vitality, moving constantly between stillness and intense activity. It is truly a passion.

Index